THE TRUTH ABOUT VARIABLE ANNUITIES

Debunking The Myths

John P. Huggard, J.D., CFP, ChFC, CLU
HUGGARD OBIOL & BLAKE, P.L.L.C.
Attorneys At Law
Raleigh, North Carolina 27605

This publication is designed to provide accurate and authoritative information in regard to the subject matter covered. It is sold with the understanding that the author and publisher are not engaged in rendering legal, accounting or other professional service. If legal advice or other expert assistance is required, the services of a competent professional person should be sought-From a declaration of principles jointly adopted by a committee of the American Bar Association and a committee of publishers.

First Edition ver. 1

Printed in the United States

Huggard, John P.
          The Truth About Variable Annuities / by John P. Huggard - 1st ed.
           368 pages
          Includes index.
          ISBN 978-0-9792478-0

Reader Inquiry Branch   Book orders
Parker-Thompson Publishing   (919) 832-2687
124 St. Mary's Street
Raleigh, NC 27605
(919) 832-9650

RESEARCH PROJECT DISCLAIMER

This book is the result of a research project conducted by the author over the last ten years. Statements and information in this book were compiled from sources that the author considers to be reliable or are expressions of the author's opinion. As an ongoing research project, this book is not intended to be complete, and therefore the author cannot guarantee its complete accuracy. This book is an ongoing research project designed to examine the myths and misconceptions surrounding variable annuities and mutual funds. The examples and data included are designed to provide useful information regarding the subject matter covered. This book is sold with the understanding that the author and the publisher are not engaged in rendering legal, financial or other professional services. Because laws vary from state to state, readers should not rely upon this or any other publication for financial or tax guidance but should do their own homework and make their own decisions. This book is not to be considered a solicitation or orders for financial products. Annuities are long-term investment vehicles designed for retirement purposes. Variable annuities are subject to market fluctuation, investment risk and possible loss of principal. Variable annuities are not insured or guaranteed by the FDIC. IRAs and qualified plans already have the tax-deferral found in annuities. For an additional cost, variable annuities can provide other enhanced benefits, including death benefit protection and the ability to receive a lifetime income. All guarantees made by variable annuity issuers are based solely on the financial strength of the issuing company. Annuities may impose tax penalties and contingent deferred sales charges for early withdrawal. The purchase of any investment, whether a mutual fund or variable annuity, should only be made after consultation with financial and tax professionals. The advice contained in this book (including any supplements) was not intended or written to be used, and it cannot be used by any taxpayer, for the purpose of avoiding any IRS penalties that may be imposed on the taxpayer. The advice contained in this book (including any supplements) was written for continuing education training only. This book is intended for use by professionals practicing in the areas of finance law, insurance and accounting. This book is not and should not be made available for public use. A reader requiring legal or other expert advice should seek the services of a competent attorney, CPA, financial planner or other professional. Comments, criticisms and suggestions for improving this book are welcome. The author can be reached at (919) 832-9650 or hoblawfirm@aol.com.

ABOUT THE AUTHOR

John Huggard is the senior member in the Raleigh law firm of Huggard, Obiol and Blake, P.L.L.C. He limits his practice to consultation in the areas of estate planning and financial litigation. John is a retired college professor. For thirty-two years, he taught introductory and advanced courses in law and personal finance at North Carolina State University. John was named an Alumni Distinguished Professor in 1994 and was a member of the university's Academy of Outstanding Teachers. John is a Board Certified Specialist in Estate Planning and Probate Law and a Certified Financial Planner (CFP). John has also earned the ChFC and CLU designations. He is the author of *THE ADMINISTRATION OF DECEDENTS' ESTATES IN NORTH CAROLINA* (Michie Pub. Co.), *THE NORTH CAROLINA ESTATE SETTLEMENT PRACTICE GUIDE* (West Pub. Co.), *LIVING TRUST, LIVING HELL: WHY YOU SHOULD AVOID LIVING TRUSTS* (Parker-Thompson Pub.) and *INVESTING WITH VARIABLE ANNUITIES - FIFTY REASONS WHY VARIABLE ANNUITIES MAY BE BETTER LONG-TERM INVESTMENTS THAN MUTUAL FUNDS* (Parker-Thompson Pub.) . Additionally, John has had many of his articles published in *Financial Planning, On Wall Street* and other similar financial magazines. John has been extensively interviewed or quoted in *The Wall Street Journal, Smart Money, USA Today, Variable Product Specialist* and other financial publications. John regularly lectures to professional groups on topics dealing with probate issues, investment taxation and financial planning. John received his undergraduate degree (Phi Beta Kappa) and law degree from the University of North Carolina at Chapel Hill and his master's degree from Duke University. John joined the U.S. Marine Corps in 1964 and served as a platoon sergeant in Viet Nam. He received a direct commission and served in the Navy Reserve JAG Corps for 30 years before retiring as a captain in 2005. John's hobbies include flying, competitive target shooting, motorcycling and deep ocean diving.

DEDICATION

This book is dedicated to those true financial professionals who help their clients understand the truth about their investments rather than repeating unfounded myths.

ACKNOWLEDGMENTS

This book is the result of ten years of research. It would not have been possible to summarize this research in a readable format without the assistance and support of my colleagues at the university and the numerous CPAs, attorneys and financial professionals who provided me with data and constructive criticism over the years.

Special thanks go to my friend and assistant, Donna R. Buck Spiers who reworked and corrected the original manuscript and each subsequent edition. To the extent that this edition has any clarity or cohesiveness is owed entirely to Donna's suggestions and corrections.

Readers are encouraged to contact the author with suggestions on how to clarify or improve on the contents of this book.

John P. Huggard
HUGGARD OBIOL & BLAKE, P.L.L.C.
Raleigh, North Carolina
(919) 832-9650

TABLE OF CONTENTS

"That which has always been accepted by everyone, everywhere, is most certain to be false."
– Paul Valery

– CHAPTER 1 –
GENERAL OVERVIEW

§101. INTRODUCTION

For thirty-two years I taught law and finance courses at a major university. During my teaching career I had the opportunity to witness first-hand the mistakes the investing public made with their investments. I many cases, investment decisions were made on the faulty and skewed information that abounds in the investment world. Although these mistakes dealt with a broad range of investments, most related to mutual funds and variable annuities. The inaccurate information relied on by variable annuity and mutual fund investors could, in most cases, be traced back to the media. This includes newspapers, magazines and financial talk shows broadcast on television and radio. For reasons that will be discussed in Chapter 7 below, the media have over the years, without any attempt being made to verify their reports, disseminated false *negative* information about variable annuities while generating false *positive* information about mutual funds. This defective reporting has resulted in several myths that, when taken as a whole, seem to warn investors to avoid investing in variable annuities in favor of mutual funds. Because accurate information about variable annuities and mutual funds is not available to the investing public, investors are unable to make valid comparisons of these two investments. This book was written with the goal of providing correct information about variable annuities so that financial professionals can help their clients make informed decisions when considering an investment in a variable annuity or mutual fund. During my teaching career I was able to isolate sixteen myths dealing with variable annuities and mutual funds. In studying these myths I have found that *none* of them are true. By providing correct information about variable annuities to my clients and students they have been able to make better investment decisions. I hope this book will do the same for the investing public.

I have written several articles and reports over the years in an effort to help the investing public understand the truth about variable annuities. Several years ago I wrote a book titled *Investing With Variable Annuities: Fifty Reasons Whey Variable Annuities May Be Better Long-Term Investments Than Mutual Funds*.[1] Many other lawyers, CPAs and financial professionals have also written similar articles, reports and books addressing the advantages of variable annuities. As a result, the pendulum of negative variable annuity press is beginning to swing the other way. In fact, for the past several years the sale of variable annuities has increased dramatically. Today, it is not unusual for annual variable annuity sales to exceed $150 billion a year.[2] Each month I see more and more articles casting variable annuities an a positive light. Many of these articles are designed to educate the public about the many benefits available to

---

[1] This book is updated annually and is available by contacting Parker-Thompson Publishing at 919-832-2687.

[2] See footnotes to Chapter 5.

them through variable annuity ownership.

When I retired from teaching, several financial executives and practitioners suggested that I write a book that addresses all of the myths surrounding variable annuities and explain why these myths are not true. Because financial professionals must deal with variable annuity myths everyday, a book examining and debunking these myths seemed in order. This book was written in an effort to fill this need.

§102. PURPOSE OF THIS BOOK

This book is not intended to argue that variable annuities are a more superior investment than mutual funds, stocks, etc. Although this may be true for some investors, it is just as common to find that many investors may be better served by purchasing investments other than variable annuities. The primary purpose for writing this book is to encourage financial professionals to supply correct information to their clients so that these clients can make informed decisions as to which financial products will best help them reach their goals.

At the end of most chapters, especially those dealing with a variable annuity myth, is a section that sets out questions financial professionals should ask when recommending the purchase of a variable annuity or mutual fund to their clients. These questions are designed to help investors make financial decisions based on fact rather then myth. Also at the end of many chapters, especially those dealing with a variable annuity myth, is a sources section. This section will list independent sources that can be consulted to attain a better understanding of the material presented in a specific chapter. The author has also heavily footnoted this book with cites to as many articles, reports and books as possible so that financial professionals will have independent sources they can read to verify the information discussed in this book. Hopefully, this will aid financial professionals in helping their clients determine which of several investments choices might be the best one for them. Many chapters will contain one or more review questions that financial professionals can answer to ensure that they understood the information discussed in each chapter before proceeding to new material.

§103. ARE MUTUAL FUNDS AND STOCKS GOOD INVESTMENTS?

Absolutely! The author's investment portfolio contains 45% mutual funds and stocks (the remaining 55% is held in variable annuities). As mentioned earlier, the intent of this book is not to argue that variable annuities are better investments than mutual funds or vice versa. The author hopes that by arming investors with accurate information it will help prevent investors from buying the wrong financial product because their decision (or their financial advisor's decision) was based on myth rather than fact.

A good example of the losses that occur when inaccurate information is relied on occurred a short while ago when the author was assisting a 67 year-old widow with her estate planning. The facts of the case are set out below:

FACTS:

Mrs. Ethel Woods (name changed) was widowed in 1995. Her life savings of $700,000 was held in bank CDs. Several family members and their financial advisors tried to convince Ethel to take her money out of her bank CDs and invest it in some good stocks and mutual funds. Ethel resisted these suggestions until 1998. Ethel invested $200,000 in some mutual funds and did quite well with them. Later in 1998, she added to her mutual fund portfolio so that by early 1998 her life savings were fully invested in the stock market. During 1998, her financial advisor suggested that Ethel buy more aggressive mutual funds which she did. By 1999 Ethel's mutual funds had grown in value to $840,000. Beginning in 2000, Ethel's portfolio value began to drop dramatically and by late 2002 Ethel's life savings had dropped to $530,000. At that point, Ethel sold her mutual funds and put all of her money back into bank CDs. In talking with Ms. Woods it became apparent to the author that variable annuities offering a GMAB rider[3] would have been a better investment than the mutual funds Mrs. Woods purchased. The variable annuity would have paid Mrs. Woods $700,000 in November of 2008. Instead, Mrs. Woods received her mutual fund account value of $530,000. When the author asked Mrs. Woods why she didn't consider a variable annuity with a GMAB rider for her investments in 1998, Mrs. Woods said she was told by her advisor that variable annuities were more expensive to own than mutual funds. By relying on this myth,[4] Mrs. Wood lost $170,000 that would not have been lost with a similar investment in variable annuities. Once Mrs. Woods learned about how variable annuities could have protected her, she realized her "cheaper" mutual turned out to be the most expensive investment she will ever make.

§104. TYPES OF ANNUITIES – MEDIA CONFUSION

There are many different types of annuities. The most common annuities sold today are:

- Fixed annuity – This annuity allows an investor to own a tax-deferred product that pays a set rate of return that is usually added back to the annuity's value. They are often used as substitutes for money market accounts or bank CDs when an investor desires tax deferral. Income earned may be withdrawn.

- Immediate annuity – This annuity pays out a fixed income to the owner for a set period or, more commonly, for life. Amounts not paid out to the owner during his lifetime are usually paid to the owner's survivors as a death benefit until the principal amount invested is fully paid out.

- Income annuity – This annuity requires the payment today in order to provide income for life at some age in the future.

- Index annuity – This annuity is a fixed annuity that instead of paying a fixed rate pegs the rate it pays to an index such as the S&P 500.

- Variable immediate annuity – This annuity is similar to an immediate annuity

---

[3] A GMAB - Guaranteed Minimum Accumulation Benefit.

[4] The author determined that the cost of a variable annuity with a GMAB rider would have been approximately ½% a year more to own and would have protected Mrs. Woods' $700,000 initial investment from any stock market loss.

3

except that the payments can increase or decrease with the stock market's fluctuations because the owner's money is actually invested, at least partially, in the stock market.

- Variable annuity – This annuity, in its simplest form, is nothing more than a financial vehicle that allows an investor to purchase diversified investments[5] without having to pay income taxes on the gains made on these investments as long as they are held. Frequently, variable annuities are referred to as deferred annuities or deferred variable annuities because any income taxes owed on any gain made in the sub-accounts purchased through the variable annuity are deferred until withdrawn in the future. The word variable annuity refer to the fact that a variable annuity can move up or down in value depending on the performance of the stock market and sub-accounts selected by the variable annuity owner. Like any other investment, a variable annuity owner is always free to close out his variable annuity and take the account value at any time.[6]

Example

Betty invested $12,000 a year in a variable annuity for 12 years. Her net return was fairly constant at 7%. At the end of 12 years, she had accumulated $229,688[7] and decided to cash out of her variable annuity to buy a small farm. The growth in her account was $85,687.[8] Betty paid $18,851 in income taxes at 22% on the growth and used the balance of nearly $211,000 to buy her farm.

Tax deferral merely delays income taxes until some future date when withdrawals are taken from the variable annuity. At that time, income taxes will be due. The major benefit of the tax deferral obtained with variable annuities is that a variable annuity owner's investments grow in value to a much larger amount than if they were held in a taxable investment because no income taxes are currently paid on gains. Once investors realize that variable annuities are essentially a way to purchase diversified investments without having to pay current income taxes, they are usually more receptive to learning abut the many other benefits offered by variable annuities. For the remainder of this book, the term variable annuity will be used as a synonym for deferred annuity or deferred variable annuity. (See Chapters 24 and 25 for more on tax deferral).

§105. CHAPTER LAYOUT

This book examines the sixteen most common myths surrounding variable annuities by discussing each myth in a summary chapter followed by another chapter that supplies a more detailed discussion of the myth. This process was selected because there are financial professionals who are aware of many of the myths associated with variable annuities and need nothing more than a brief review of these myths by way of a shortened discussion of why the

---

[6] Surrender penalties and IRS penalties may apply to early withdrawals from a variable annuity. A variable annuity owner who is a long-term investor, need not be concerned about these penalties.

[7] $12,000 per year x 7% x 12 years = $229,688.

[8] $229,688 - $144,000 = $85,687.

myth has no merit. In other cases, financial professionals may not fully understand a myth as well as he or she would like. For these professionals, the detailed chapters following the summary chapters will be more helpful.

§106. WHAT IS BEING COMPARED?

This book compares actively managed, equity-based, non-qualified variable annuities sold by financial professionals with actively managed, equity-based, non-qualified mutual funds sold by financial professionals because there are the most common variable annuities and mutual funds purchased through financial professionals. These variable annuities and mutual funds will be referred to as "typical" variable annuities and mutual funds in this book.[9] (See §303 for the comparison of qualified variable annuities and mutual funds). To compare no-load mutual funds with variable annuities sold by financial professionals or vice versa would not be a valid comparison. If one wants to compare no-load mutual funds with variable annuities, then the variable annuities selected for comparison should also be no-load variable annuities sold directly to the public.

§107. REVIEW QUESTIONS (TRUE OR FALSE)[10]

1. Mutual funds and stocks are poor investments when compared to variable annuities.
2. There are essentially two types of annuities.

§108. CONCLUSION

This book was written solely to provide accurate information about investing in variable annuities. No investment, including variable annuities, is the best investment for everyone. However, an investment that is purchased based on a myth almost always turns out to be the worst investment for the investor buying it. This book encourages financial professionals to provide their clients with correct information about variable annuities or any investment they recommend. Once this is done accurate information can be applied to the client's needs, wants, desires or goals which, in turn, will yield the best investment for the client.

---

[9] The term non-qualified is used to refer to mutual funds and variable annuities not held in a retirement account such as an IRA, Roth IRA, 401(k), 403(b), etc.

[10] Both review questions are false.

– CHAPTER 2 –
VARIABLE ANNUITY BENEFITS

§201. INTRODUCTION

Variable annuities are not the best investment for all investors nor are mutual funds. However, today's variable annuities offer many benefits, that once understood, make them the best investment for a large portion of the investing population.

§202. VARIABLE ANNUITY BENEFITS

The author's first book discussed fifty reason why variable annuities might be a better long-term investment choice than mutual funds.[1] The fifty reasons are set out in the next section in summary fashion because many of these reasons debunk several of the myths associated with variable annuities and will be discussed more fully in this book. For readers who are interested in examining these fifty reasons, the book referenced above is available from the publisher.[2]

§203. THE FIFTY REASONS

The following list sets out fifty reasons why actively managed, equity based, non-qualified variable annuities may be better long-term investments than actively managed, equity based, non-qualified mutual funds as long-term investments: (See §303 below for information concerning the comparison of qualified variable annuities and mutual funds).

1. Non-qualified annuities grow tax-deferred, mutual funds don't.

2. Mutual funds rarely provide the 15% long-term capital gains rate that they claim owners receive. On the other hand, variable annuity payments received in retirement are taxed at 15% when the recipient's tax bracket is 25%.

3. Mutual funds create an income tax trap for individuals purchasing funds late in the year. Variable annuities do not present a similar problem where late year purchases are made.

4. Mutual funds can make annual taxable distributions to fund owners even where the value of their fund has gone down because mutual funds contain "embedded gains." In some cases, the taxation on these embedded gains can run into triple digits. Variable annuities do not present a similar embedded gain problem.

5. Mutual fund ownership along with the annual distributions made by such mutual funds can subject the fund owner to taxation under the alternative minimum tax (AMT) structure. The AMT always results in increased income taxes. Variable annuity ownership cannot trigger the AMT in the same manner as mutual funds

6. Variable annuities are easy to position so that at the owner's death the variable annuity will not be subject to either estate or income taxes. The same tax reduction techniques do not work nearly as well with mutual funds.

7. Mutual fund ownership can result in the loss of tax exemptions. This does not occur

---

[1] *Investing With Variable Annuities – Fifty Reasons Variable Annuities May Be Better Long-Term Investments Than Mutual Funds.* To order contact Parker-Thompson Publishing at 919-832-2687.

[2] See contact information in note 1 above.

where variable annuities are owned.

8. Ownership of mutual funds can result in the loss of income tax deductions. Variable annuity ownership does not create the same tax loss.

9. Mutual fund ownership can cause the owner to lose tax credits. This does not occur where variable annuities are owned.

10. Variable annuities allow for restricted beneficiary designations and allow non-qualified "stretches".

11. Under the current tax climate, it is more likely that capital gains rates and capital gains holding periods will increase than a decrease. If either capital gains rates or their holding period increase, it will raise income taxes for owners of mutual funds. Variable annuities, being tax-deferred, would be unaffected.

12. Beneficiaries of variable annuities usually receive a larger amount by inheriting a variable annuity than a mutual fund even though the mutual fund beneficiaries receive a step-up in basis.

13. The ownership of mutual funds can restrict or eliminate one's ability to own other retirement accounts such as IRAs. Mutual fund ownership can also prevent one from converting a traditional IRA to a Roth IRA. Variable annuities present no such restrictions or limitations.

14. The ownership of mutual funds can, in many cases, cause Social Security to be subject to income taxes. Variable annuity ownership does not present the same problem.

15. When a variable annuity is sold at a loss, the tax treatment of that loss is more beneficial than an equal loss with a mutual fund.

16. The ownership of mutual funds may require the mutual fund owner to pay estimated taxes. Variable annuity ownership does not create the same tax problem.

17. Mutual funds are subject to state and local income taxes in those states that have such taxes. Variable annuities, because they are tax-deferred, are not subject to state and local income taxes while in the accumulation phase.

18. Variable annuities almost always prove to be less expensive to own than equivalent mutual funds. In addition, mutual fund costs tend to go up over time. Variable annuity costs are always fixed at the time the variable annuity is purchased and guaranteed not to go up.

19. The record-keeping requirements for owning mutual funds are significantly more complex than the record-keeping requirements for owning variable annuities.

20. Many states provide either complete or partial statutory protection to variable annuities from the claims of creditors. No state provides protection from creditors for mutual funds.

21. Mutual funds are commonly part of a decedent's estate which makes such funds available to all creditors of the estate. Variable annuities, on the other hand, are almost always non-probate property that do not pass through a decedent's estate and therefore are not subject to the reach of creditors of a decedent.

22. Mutual funds, because they are almost always part of a decedent's estate, are subject to the delays and expenses of probate. Variable annuities, because they pass outside of probate directly to beneficiaries, are not subject to similar delays and costs.

23. Attempting to position mutual funds so they will not pass through probate almost always results in additional taxes, costs or delays.

24. Mutual funds may disqualify the owner from obtaining tuition assistance for a child to attend college. Variable annuities do not present the same problems.

25. Owners of variable annuities can adjust their annuities so that they are not considered assets for Medicaid qualification. Mutual funds, except for principal protected funds, cannot be adjusted in a similar manner.

26. Variable annuities provide basic as well as enhanced death benefits to the beneficiaries of the variable annuity owners. Mutual funds, except for principal protected funds, do not provide any death benefit whatsoever.

27. Variable annuities provide dollar-cost averaging to variable annuity owners at no expense. Mutual funds do not provide this benefit on a cost-free basis to fund owners.

28. Mutual funds do not provide cost-free asset re-balancing whereas variable annuities do.

29. Many variable annuities offer premium bonuses. Mutual funds offer no similar bonuses.

30. Many variable annuities today provide guaranteed protection against loss of principal. Mutual funds, except for a few stable value funds, do not offer this same protection.

31. Many variable annuities today provide a guaranteed rate of return on fixed accounts within variable annuities. Mutual funds do not provide the same benefit.

32. Variable annuities can be used to keep a life insurance owner from having to sell a life insurance policy at a loss. Mutual funds cannot be used for this purpose.

33. Withdrawals can be made from variable annuities and used to purchase things such as retirement homes, yachts, etc., without having to pay income taxes on the withdrawals.

34. The risk of company insolvency rests with the owner of a mutual fund. Variable annuity owners are not exposed to similar insolvency risks.

35. Variable annuities allow the annuity owner to trade funds among different families on a commission-free basis. This is rarely true for owners of mutual funds.

36. A variable annuity owner may exchange his variable annuity for a completely different variable annuity without triggering income taxes. A mutual fund owner cannot move his funds from one mutual fund company to another without triggering an income tax.

37. Variable annuities provide long-term fixed income options. Mutual funds do not.

38. Variable annuity owners receive an income tax deduction under IRC §691 when inheriting a variable annuity. Mutual funds do not receive a similar income tax deduction.

39. If the Untied States tax system is modified to include a flat tax, mutual fund owners will be at a disadvantage while variable annuity owners will reap a tax windfall. The

same will occur with a national sales tax.

40. Variable annuities can provide their owners with a guaranteed stream of income for their entire lifetime. Mutual funds cannot provide the same benefit.

41. The exclusion ratio allows a variable annuity owner to shelter large portions of variable annuity payments from income taxes. Mutual funds do not provide a similar exclusion ratio.

42. Mutual funds are subject to intangibles taxes in those states where intangible taxes are levied. Variable annuities are universally exempt from intangibles taxes.

43. The owner of a variable annuity who selects to dollar-cost average into mutual funds usually receives an interest rate well above the market rate on money awaiting to be invested. Mutual fund owners who seek the benefit of dollar-cost averaging do not receive similar above market rates of interest on money awaiting investment.

44. Variable annuities allow owners to control precisely how much money will be withdrawn from their variable annuity and thus allow the variable annuity owner to control taxes. Mutual fund owners have no similar control. Mutual fund owners are subject to involuntary mutual fund distributions of capital gains and dividends each year whether they want such distributions or not.

45. If other mutual fund owners redeem their shares and leave a fund, this will have the impact of raising the potential tax burden of those mutual fund owners who remain in the fund. This tax trap is referred to as the embedded gain problem. Variable annuities contain no similar tax disadvantage.

46. Many variable annuities waive any surrender penalties when individuals suffer a serious illness, are required to go into a nursing home, lose their job, etc. Mutual funds do not provide a similar benefit where contingent deferred sales charges are imposed on mutual fund owners.

47. Variable annuities, when initially purchased, allow the owner a period of time to revoke his purchase without cost. Mutual funds do not allow this benefit.

48. Some mutual funds dictate when a mutual fund owner may sell his mutual funds or impose a redemption fee when funds are sold. Variable annuities can be sold at any time without restriction. Variable annuities never charge additional redemption fees if one wants to sell their variable annuity.

49. There are costly tax traps associated with the buying and selling of mutual funds. Similar tax traps do not exist for variable annuities.

50. Mutual funds not only require annual taxation when the mutual fund is going up in value, but also impose income taxes when the mutual fund is going down in value. Variable annuities, being tax-deferred, impose no annual income taxes regardless of whether the variable annuity is increasing or decreasing in value.

§204. QUESTIONS TO ASK

- When mutual fund proponents are asked to list advantages that mutual funds provide to long-term investors, they are rarely able to list more than a few. If variable annuities have 50 reasons why they might be better long-term investments than mutual funds, wouldn't it be important to learn something about variable annuities rather than relying on the inaccurate information disseminated by the media?

§205. SOURCES

- Investing With Variable Annuities– Fifty Reasons Variable Annuities May Be Better Long-Term Investments Than Mutual Funds. To order contact Parker-Thompson Publishing at 919-832-2687.

§206. REVIEW QUESTIONS[3]

- There are ___ benefits that variable annuities provide long-term investors that cannot be obtained with mutual funds.

    A. 10

    B. 20

    C. 30

    D. 40

    E. 50

§207. CONCLUSION

The above list demonstrates that there could be many reasons why a long-term investor should consider a variable annuity. Many of the benefits listed actually debunk several variable annuity myths and will be discussed in later chapters.

---

[3] The answer to the review question is 'E'.

– CHAPTER 3 –
EXPLANATION OF COMPARISON DATA

§301. INTRODUCTION

Comparing mutual funds and variable annuities can be a difficult task unless reasonable data and assumptions are used in making such comparisons. This chapter discusses the data and methodology used to compare mutual funds and variable annuities in this book.

§302. WHAT DATA IS BEING COMPARED?

As §106 stated, this book compares actively managed, equity-based, non-qualified variable annuities sold by financial professionals with actively managed, equity-based, non-qualified mutual funds sold by financial professionals because these are the most common variable annuities and mutual funds purchased through financial professionals today. These variable annuities and mutual funds will be referred to as typical variable annuities and mutual funds in this book[1] (See §303 for the comparison of qualified variable annuities and mutual funds). To compare no-load mutual funds with variable annuities sold by financial professionals or vice versa would not be a valid comparison. If one wants to compare no-load mutual funds with variable annuities, then the variable annuities selected for comparison should also be no-load variable annuities sold directly to the public. The author encounters many individuals who like to compare variable annuities to index funds. The problem with this is twofold. First, such a comparison is not an apples-to-apples comparison. Secondly, any conclusion reached based on such a comparison would equally apply to both variable annuities and actively managed, equity based mutual funds. For example, if one compares a typical variable annuity to an index fund, they would correctly conclude that the index fund was less expensive to own. But this same conclusion would have to be reached if an index fund is compared to an actively managed, equity based mutual fund. Index funds may be great investments for some investors, but low cost alone does not necessarily mean they are better investments than typical variable annuities or mutual funds. This can be demonstrated in the following example:

> **Example**
> Jill, who was 60, invested $500,000 in three index funds because they were low cost investments. She needed $25,000 a year in income from her funds. Jill got caught in a bear market that, together with her annual $25,000 withdrawals, has reduced her fund's value to $400,000 in three years. Depending on what the stock market does in the future, Jill could run out of money before she dies. Had Jill purchased a more expensive variable annuity with a lifetime income rider she would be guaranteed to have $25,000 a year for her entire lifetime. Her income could go up with a rising stock market but would be guaranteed never to go down. Her variable annuity would also provide a death benefit in case Jill died

---

[1] The term non-qualified is used to refer to mutual funds and variable annuities not held in a retirement account such as an IRA, Roth IRA, 401(k), 403(b), etc.

prematurely. To get these benefits, Jill does not have to annuitize her variable annuity contract. She always has full access to her account balance.

As the above example demonstrates, the cheaper index fund cannot offer what the more expensive variable annuity can. Like anything else, people get what they pay for.

§303. QUALIFIED VARIABLE ANNUITIES AND MUTUAL FUNDS

It is critical to understand that all of the material in this book can be applied to the comparison of *qualified* variable annuities and mutual funds. When qualified variable annuities and mutual funds are compared all of the tax issues relating to these two investment products become mute because both products are treated identically for tax purposes. Neither has any tax advantage over the other. For example, investors owning *non-qualified* mutual funds may believe that those who inherit their mutual funds will be better off tax-wise because such beneficiaries will receive the tax benefit provided by the step-up in basis which is not available to those who inherit *non-qualified* variable annuities. This common myth becomes completely moot if the mutual funds and variable annuities being compared are *qualified*. The reason for this is that the tax treatment beneficiaries receive when they inherit *qualified* mutual funds or *qualified* variable annuities is *identical* because the step-up in basis rule does *not* apply to *qualified* mutual funds that are inherited. In short, if *qualified* mutual funds and variable annuities are being compared, their tax treatment is identical and therefore only their other characteristics, such as the cost of ownership, should be used when making comparisons of these two products.

§304. ANNUAL OWNERSHIP COSTS OF MUTUAL FUNDS AND VARIABLE ANNUITIES

Both mutual funds and variable annuity companies charge an annual expense that is used to pay their investment managers and other related management expenses. On average, mutual funds have annual expenses of 1.5% (which includes 12b-1 fees) while variable annuities have average annual expenses of 2.2% (which includes 12b-1 fees). This 2.2% figure also *includes* a mortality and expense (M&E) charge which averages 1.3% for the typical variable annuity. Investors should feel free to adjust these percentages to better reflect their actual situation. For example, if an investor wants to compare a mutual fund with an annual expense of 1.4% with a variable annuity with an annual expense of 2.1%, then these actual figures should be used to make comparisons. Annual expenses for mutual funds (technically called annual expense ratios) are generally imposed quarterly on the mutual fund's account value. This book, for simplicity purposes, will levy such expenses only once a year's end. Variable annuity expenses and M&E charges are also generally assessed quarterly against account values. They too will be levied annually in the comparisons made in this book.

14

§305. ANNUAL GROSS RATE OF RETURN

The rate of return is the easiest piece of comparison data to establish. As long as both the variable annuities and mutual funds being compared use identical and reasonable rates of return a valid comparison can be made. Unless stated to the contrary, the examples that compare mutual funds and variable annuities in this book use a 10% gross rate of return. The 10% gross rate of return was selected because it is realistic and reasonable given that the overall market for more than three decades (as measured by the S&P 500) has produced annual returns slightly in excess of this 10% figure.

§306. COMMISSIONS AND LOADS

In addition to annual management expenses averaging 1.5% mutual funds usually charge commissions in one of four ways:

- Up-front commissions of from 2% to 6%. (Commonly called A-share loads).
- Deferred sales charges where no up-front commission is charged but instead, the annual expense of owning the fund is increased by approximately 1%. (Commonly called B-share or back-end loads).
- An additional fee added to the cost of the mutual fund of .75% to 1.50% until the fund is sold. (Commonly called C-share loads).
- An annual money management fee paid to a fee only financial planner to select and manage an investor's mutual fund portfolio (usually holding no-load mutual funds).

There are other commission structures of mutual funds, but the four listed above are the most common. Rather than assume investors pay commissions only in one of the four ways mentioned above, the examples in this book will alter these methods. The method of paying commissions will be specified in the examples. In some cases, commissions or loads may even be ignored to cover those situations where one has obtained their mutual funds by gift or inheritance or in some other manner where a commission or load may not have been paid by the current owner. It is important for investors to use the actual commission or load they are paying, or will pay, for their mutual funds when comparing these funds to variable annuities. Mutual fund commissions are discussed more fully in Chapters 22 and 23. Commissions on variable annuities are paid differently than for mutual funds. As a basic rule, the variable annuity companies pay commissions directly to the professionals who sell their annuities. Variable annuity companies advance commissions based on the assumption that the buyers of their variable annuities will be long-term investors and these advanced commissions can be recouped in the annual ownership fees charged by the variable annuity issuer. For this reason, variable annuity issuers have holding periods. If a variable annuity purchaser buys a variable annuity with a holding period of six years and sells his variable annuity before this period expires, he will be charged a contingent deferred sales charge or CDSC that is designed to help the variable annuity issuer recoup some of the commission it advanced to the financial professional involved when the annuity was purchased. CDSCs usually run for an average of six years and decline 1% a year until they disappear. This book will assume a 7% CDSC that declines 1% a year for seven years unless otherwise noted.

§307. ANNUAL INCOME TAXATION OF MUTUAL FUNDS

Mutual funds are taxed each year based on realized (i.e., actual) gains resulting from the purchase and sale of investments by the mutual fund company. Distributions of realized gains are allocated to fund owners proportionately based on their ownership interest in the fund. For example, a fund holder with $100,000 worth of a mutual fund would get a distribution that is ten times larger than a fund owner who owned only $10,000 worth of the fund. Realized gains are reported to both the IRS and fund holders annually. Fund holders must report these realized gains on their income tax returns and pay taxes on them. Several of the country's leading researchers who have studied the impact of income taxes on mutual fund ownership have put the current average annual income tax loss at 2.0% of a fund's annual gain. Tom Roseen, a senior research analyst with Lipper, Inc., recently authored a detailed study of the reduction in annual mutual fund gains resulting from federal income taxation.[2] This current research demonstrates that federal income taxes, on average, reduce mutual fund gains by 2.0% or more. Joel Dickson, who heads Vanguard's Active Quantitative Equity Group, agrees that the current annual federal income tax loss on gains generated by the typical equity mutual fund is approximately 2.0%, as does Robert Arnott, who is the Chairman of Research Affiliates, L.L.C. and the former editor of *Financial Analysts Journal*. This book uses a 2% tax loss figure in its examples where mutual funds and variable annuities are being compared. Chapters 12-16 discusses more fully the tax liability of mutual fund ownership. Regardless of the tax loss assumed in this book, investors should use their *actual* annual tax loss when comparing a potential mutual fund investment with a potential variable annuity investment. The following example demonstrates the use of a 10% annual rate of return for a mutual fund reduced by 2% for income taxes.

> **Example**
> Paul purchased a mutual fund for $100,000. He held it for ten years. The annualized rate of return was 10%, but this return was reduced to 8% due to the imposition of annual income taxes. Paul's mutual fund would be worth $215,892[3] after ten years. This example ignores any non-tax costs associated with the purchase of the mutual fund (i.e., commissions, etc.).

As mentioned, an investor should always use his actual income tax loss when comparing mutual funds and variable annuities. For example, if an investor owns $100,000 worth of a

---

[2] The most detailed study on mutual fund income taxes is Lipper, Inc.'s "Taxes in the Mutual Fund Industry - 2007 - Assessing the Impact of Taxes on Shareholders' Returns." Tom Roseen was the senior researcher on this project. The annual tax loss referred to in this chapter deals only with *federal* income taxes. State and local income taxes are discussed where appropriate.

[3] $100,000 x 10 years x 8% - $215,892.

mutual fund that distributes 10% of its value resulting in income taxes of $2,000, he should use a 2% annual tax loss figure in any calculations he makes regarding his mutual fund. On the other hand, if he pays $3,000 in income taxes, then he should use a 3% annual tax loss instead.

§308. TAXATION OF MUTUAL FUNDS WHEN SOLD

Not all of a mutual fund's annual growth is paid out in realized gains. Some gains are paper gains or unrealized gains that are not taxed currently. They will be taxed at a later time when these paper gains are realized or the fund is sold. The following simplified example demonstrates how realized and unrealized gains are taxed to mutual fund owners.

Example

Ron invested $100,000 in a mutual fund. A year later, the fund had increased in value by 10% to $110,000. Of this $10,000 gain, only 60%, or $6,000, was realized gain. The other 40%, or $4,000, was unrealized gain and is not subject to current taxation. When Ron reports the $6,000 realized gain on his tax return, he will be able to add this $6,000 to his original $100,000 purchase price of his fund. This process is referred to as making an upward adjustment to cost basis. This prevents a mutual fund owner from paying taxes on a realized gain previously taxed when the mutual fund is later sold. For example, Ron's cost basis after reporting and paying taxes on the $6,000 realized gain he made will now be $106,000. If Ron sells his fund tomorrow for $110,000, he will have to pay taxes only on the remaining profit of $4,000. The $4,000 would represent the unrealized gain that would become a *realized* gain when the fund was sold by Ron. Non-tax costs are ignored in this example.

§309. TAXATION OF VARIABLE ANNUITIES

The major advantage of owning variable annuities is that, unlike mutual funds, variable annuities grow income tax-deferred. Income taxes are paid on the gains earned by the variable annuity at ordinary income tax rates when these gains are withdrawn in the future. In this book, variable annuity gains are reduced by the tax bracket that would be most appropriate for the facts presented.

Example

Alice purchased a variable annuity for $100,000 and held it for ten years. The annuity increased at an annual net rate of return of 7.3%. After ten years, Alice's variable annuity was worth $202,301.[4] Of this amount, $102,301 is profit and if subject to income taxation at 25%, it would reduce the gain to $76,726. This amount combined with the original purchase price of $100,000 would make the variable annuity worth $176,726 on an after-tax basis. For clarity, non-tax costs are ignored in this example.

§310. TRADING COSTS

Both mutual funds and variable annuities have trading costs. These are the costs incurred by mutual fund and variable annuity companies to buy and sell investments. Studies have

---

[4] $100,000 x 10 years at 7.3% = $202,301.

shown that trading costs for mutual funds can reach 1% or more.[5] The trading costs for variable annuities are slightly lower at an average of 0.7%. This minor difference is a result of the slightly greater selling activity of mutual funds. Every quarter (especially in the last quarter of the year) mutual fund companies engage in "window dressing" which involves the massive selling of losing positions in order to reduce potential capital gains taxes for the fund's owners as well as dress up the books with more gaining transactions than losing transactions.[6] The comparisons in this book will use 0.7% as the trading cost for mutual funds and 0.5% for variable annuities. Actual trading costs should not be used when non-hypothetical comparisons are being made.

§311. MISCELLANEOUS MUTUAL FUND AND VARIABLE ANNUITY COSTS

Both mutual funds and variable annuities have some minor costs associated with their ownership. Mutual funds often impose annual administrative costs and miscellaneous fees. Variable annuities impose similar administrative costs and fees. These miscellaneous fees for mutual funds and variable annuities are usually quite small. In many cases these costs are waived or reduced. These minor fees will be ignored in the comparisons made in this book. However, it must be remembered that any miscellaneous costs actually charged in real comparisons must be factored into such comparisons.

§312. USING THE COMPARISON DATA

Unless the facts of an example state otherwise, the comparisons made in this book will assume that the gross annual return for both mutual funds and variable annuities will be 10%. Commissions will be set at 5% for A-share mutual funds and will be reduced for break-points. Annual expense ratios for mutual funds, including 12b-1 fees will be set at 1.5% and trading costs at 0.70%. Annual expenses for variable annuities will be set at 1.0%, mortality and expense fees (M&E) will be set at 1.2% and trading costs at 0.5%. Annual taxes imposed on mutual funds will be set at 2.0% of the fund's net gain. Unrealized gains for mutual funds will be taxed as if 30% of the mutual fund gain at liquidation is unrealized gain that becomes realized at sale. These gains will be taxed at appropriate long-term capital gains rates. As mentioned earlier, variable annuities will be taxed at a rate of 25% subject to adjustment if the facts of an example so dictate.

Example

Ben, who is 50, was interested in buying a mutual fund for $25,000. He planned on holding the fund for ten years. (Sara, Ben's wife wanted him to buy a variable annuity). Ben and Sara pay income taxes at 25%. Ben's commission to buy the fund was 5%, the annual expense ratio was 1.5%, trading costs were 0.7% and income taxes would reduce the fund's 10% rate of return by 2%. Based on this

---

[5] *Better Investing*, July 2001, p. 9 citing a Plexis Group Study.

[6] The turnover for variable annuities is 84% according to *Morningstar Principia*. For mutual funds it is 118. Thus trading costs for variable annuities would be approximately 71.1% that of mutual funds. Trading costs for mutual funds average 1.0% per year. Trading costs for variable annuities would be approximately 71.1% of the average mutual fund trading costs of 1% or 0.7%.

information, the mutual fund Ben was considering would have a net rate of return of 6.064%. This is calculated as follows:

> $25,000 less 5% commission = $23,750. $23,750 + 10% gross return = $26,125 less 2.2% (annual expenses and trading costs) = $25,550.50. $25,550.50 less $23,750 (amount invested) = $1,800.50 gain less 20% (2% of 10%) income tax = $1,440.20 ÷ $23,750 (amount invested) = 6.064% net rate of return.

Example

Sara (Ben's wife), who is 50, was interested in investing $25,000 in a variable annuity. (Her husband Ben [in the last example] thought a mutual fund would be a better investment). Sara and her husband pay income taxes at 25%. Sara planned on holding the annuity for ten years. The annuity charged no commission but had a 7% CDSC that declined 1% a year. The combined annual expense (1.0%) ratio and M&E (1.2%) were 2.2% and trading costs were 0.5%. Based on this information, the variable annuity Sara was considering would have a net rate of return of 7.03%. This is calculated as follows:

> $25,000 + 10% gross return = $27,500 less 2.7% (annual expenses, M&E and trading costs) = $26,758 - $25,000 investment = $1,758 gain ÷ $25,000 = 7.030% net rate of return.

Once a net rate of return is determined it can be used to calculate investment results over time. The results must be reduced for any income taxes due upon the ultimate sale of the investments being compared.

Example

In the previous examples, it was determined that the net rate of return that Ben could get from his mutual fund was 6.064% and that Sara could get a net rate of return of 7.030%. By applying these rates of return to the amounts invested, ending values ten years from now can be determined as follows:

- Ben's Mutual Fund: 6.064% x 10 years x $23,750 = $42,790
- Sara's Variable Annuity: 7.030% x 10 years x $25,000 = $49,317

The ending values determined above must be reduced by any income taxes that would be owned if these two investments were liquidated.

- Ben's Mutual Fund: $42,790 (ending value) - $23,750 (investment) = $19,040 in gain. Assuming 30% of the gain is long-term capital gains or $5,712. At a 15% tax this capital gain would generate a tax of $857. Ben's net (after-tax) mutual fund value after ten years would be $41,933 ($42,790 - $857).

- Sara's Variable Annuity: $49,317 (ending value) - $25,000 (investment) = $24,317 - 25% income tax = $18,238 + $25,000 (investment) = $43,238 net (after-tax) variable annuity value after ten years.

§313. THE 2.0% MUTUAL FUND INCOME TAX LIABILITY – DETAILED EXPLANATION

As mentioned above, the typical, actively managed, equity-based, non-qualified mutual fund loses 2% of its gain every year to federal income taxes. Some readers may assume that if a 2% tax liability is imposed on a mutual fund's gross gain, that 100% of the fund's gain is subject to federal taxation in a given year. This is an inaccurate interpretation. What researchers have found is that *regardless* of a fund's gross gain (e.g., 8%, 9%, 10%, etc.), two percentage points on *average* are lost to the IRS each year. In some cases the loss could be 30% on a fund returning 10%, a tax loss of 20% might be found with a mutual fund returning 9%, and so on. The point the researchers are trying to make is *regardless* of a fund's annual return, the fund will lose on average two percentage points to the IRS. This 2% tax loss is an *annual* tax liability and in no way eliminates the requirement that a fund owner pay income taxes on unrealized gains that become realized when the mutual fund is sold.

§314. ANNUAL MUTUAL FUND INCOME TAXES – THE SOURCE FOR PAYMENT

In the examples used in this book, the annual federal income tax liability of 2% is paid out of the mutual fund. This is rarely done in actual practice. The majority of mutual fund owners usually pay any annual income taxes from sources *other than* the mutual funds themselves. The reason this book assumes that taxes are paid out of the mutual funds that generate the income tax due is that it makes the math needed to do various comparisons much easier. If it were assumed that taxes were paid from other sources, a computer would be needed to make accurate comparisons rather than a calculator. The examples used in this book also assume that all costs and taxes will be made from a variable annuity upon surrender. This will make comparisons easier to understand.

When annual income taxes are paid out of the mutual funds that generate them, the owner has "freed-up" the out-of-pocket taxes he would have paid. The value of these freed-up payments must be accounted for where mutual fund taxes are paid out of the mutual fund. For example, if an investor purchases a mutual fund for $30,000 and holds it for seven years, his net after-tax and after-cost ending value will be $46,741 if annual taxes (including liquidated taxes) are paid from other sources. If the annual taxes (including liquidation taxes) are paid from the mutual funds themselves, the net ending value will be $42,448. However, in this last situation, the fund owner does not have to pay income taxes out of his pocket each year and therefore the amount of these tax payments may be invested elsewhere. If invested at an after-tax return of 8%, these payments will grow to an after-tax value of $4,548 in seven years. If this $4,548 is accounted for, the real ending value of the mutual funds which were reduced every year to pay annual income taxes increases to $46,996 which is almost exactly the ending value of the mutual fund investment where income taxes were paid from other sources. In other words, whether income taxes are paid from a mutual fund or from other sources, the economic effect is nearly identical. (Chapters 24 and 25 expand on this topic).

§315. SKEWING OF COMPARISON DATA

The data selected for the comparison of mutual funds and variable annuities in this book has been skewed in favor of mutual funds in almost all regards. For example:

- An annual tax loss of 2.0% was selected because it is slightly lower than the annual tax loss figure most mutual fund owners currently pay. Taxes in years past were greater than 2%. Mutual fund owners frequently lose more to annual income taxes than the 2% figure used in this book. For one to have a 2% annual tax loss on his mutual funds merely requires the payment of $200 a year in taxes per $10,000 worth of funds returning 10%. Most mutual fund owners pay taxes well in excess of these amounts.

- A 10% annual rate of return was selected because it represents the stock market's long-term rate of return.

- It is assumed that when any variable annuity mentioned in this book is surrendered, it is surrendered all at one time and all income taxes are paid in a lump sum at the owner's highest tax rate. This rarely occurs. When annual withdrawals are taken from a variable annuity instead of in a lump sum, income taxes are greatly reduced.

- The fact that sub-accounts held in variable annuities may perform better than their counterpart mutual funds held outside of variable annuities (see Chapter 32) is ignored in all calculations.

- Gains on the sale of mutual funds will be deemed to contain only 30% unrealized capital gains although this figure can be higher.

- The opportunity cost advantage of variable annuity tax deferral, although a major benefit is ignored in nearly all comparisons made in this book. (See Chapters 24 and 25).

- The commissions and loads on mutual funds used in the many hypothetical examples in this book do not exceed 1% a year. In reality, mutual fund commissions can easily exceed 1%. In *The Great Mutual Fund Trap* by Baer and Gensler (at page 101) the authors found the average annual mutual fund commission to be nearly 1.4% a year.

- State and local income taxes are ignored in the examples in this book although annual state and local income taxes can add as much as 0.5% to the annual cost of owning a mutual fund.

- The typical holding period for mutual funds is three years. This book often assumes holding periods of 15 to 25 years without imposing any additional commission costs or taxes on the fund owner for trading that most likely would occur.

- A Dalbar Study demonstrated that mutual fund investors move in and out of their mutual funds in such a manner that they can lose up to 60% of the fund's potential gain. Market timing with mutual funds is ignored in the comparisons made in this book.

- Rebalancing is commission-free with variable annuities and does not trigger an income tax. Rebalancing with mutual funds is often commission-free but will always generate an income tax where gains are realized. Although rebalancing with mutual funds and variable annuities is common, any tax cost involved with such rebalancing will be ignored for comparisons made in this book.

- All comparisons are made in upward moving markets. In reality the stock market has down years. These down years negatively affect the taxation of mutual funds but not variable annuities.

Financial professionals reading this book should use the material discussed as a basic guide to comparing mutual funds with variable annuities. Once a basic understanding is accomplished, the actual data for a specific client can be used with actual mutual funds or variable annuities being considered by a client. Only by making myth-free comparisons based on a client's actual data can a professional help determine whether a mutual fund or variable annuity is the best investment for their client.

§316. REVIEW QUESTIONS

- What are trading costs?[7]

§317. CONCLUSION

When comparing variable annuities and mutual funds on a hypothetical basis, reasonable and consistent data must be used. By using actual data, financial professionals can determine whether variable annuities or mutual funds are the better long-term investment for their clients. Only when a fair, impartial and myth-free comparison of variable annuities and mutual funds is made, are investors able to make proper long-term investment decisions. It should be remembered that no existing method of determining the net ending value of a mutual fund or variable annuity is flawless. One need only review the website for the SEC and FINRA and examine the "mutual fund" calculators they provide to the public to realize this. Good financial professionals should create a method for obtaining net ending values for mutual funds and variable annuities that they are comfortable with and can fine tune and improve over time. A suggested method for accomplishing this is discussed in Chapter 11.

---

[7] See §310.

– CHAPTER 4 –
FOLLOWING THE SMART MONEY

§401. INTRODUCTION

Let's examine a hypothetical to start this chapter.

Hypothetical

Jack has $50,000 to invest in real estate. He is interested in coastal real estate. He has talked to several real estate brokers who have tried to sell him inner-city real estate. Whenever Jack asked about coastal real estate, all the brokers Jack talked to gave many reasons why he should not buy coastal real estate. All the brokers pushed inner-city real estate. In doing some research, Jack has found that lots of money was being invested along the coast of the state he lives in. Some of this property was being purchased by the same real estate brokers that recommended inter-city property to Jack. He noticed that the amounts were six figures or more in most cases. Based on his research Jack decided to ignore the brokers he was dealing with and invested his money in coastal real estate. He has done very well since making his investment. Jack made his investment decision on facts he uncovered rather than investing his money where others, who had their own best interest at heart, wanted him to invest his money.

§402. INCREASING VARIABLE ANNUITY SALES

The reason for starting this chapter with the above hypothetical was to demonstrate that oftentimes it is not a bad idea to "follow the smart money." This is true with variable annuities. Considering all the negative information the public receives regarding variable annuities, certainly the sale of variable annuities would be down or flat at best. The truth of the matter is that variable annuity sales have been dramatically increasing for the past several years. These sales seem to be increasing at an increasing rate. Many variable annuity issuers have found that the size of the investments made in variable annuities is frequently very close to six figures. Annual sales of variable annuities in just the past few years have averaged more than $150 million.[1]

§403. THE AUTHOR'S EXPERIENCE

As an estate planner, the author deals with wealthy people every day. A review of their assets shows that wealthy individuals frequently invest in variable annuities. It is not unusual to find variable annuities worth *millions* of dollars among the assets of wealthy estate planning clients. Common responses received when these estate planning clients are asked why they own

---

[1] See note 1 in Chapter 5. Net sales (new money sales) have also increased. Some people point out that many sales of variable annuities today are the result of §1035 exchanges or purchasing a new variable annuity with the proceeds from the sale of a previously owned variable annuity. This is true because many investors want to get out of older variable annuities and purchase variable annuities with guaranteed living benefits. It should be pointed out that the purchase of most mutual funds and stocks are funded with the proceeds from the sale of previously owned mutual funds and stocks. It is also important to note that once a variable annuity is sold the proceeds can be used to purchase any financial product, yet such proceeds are commonly used to purchase new variable annuities that offer benefits not available with any other financial products.

variable annuities rather than stocks and mutual funds include:

- "Whenever the surrender period expires on one of my annuities I can exchange it for a different one without incurring income taxes or new sales commissions."

- "My variable annuity guarantees that if I hold my variable annuity for ten years my principal will always be guaranteed if the stock market is down." ("Mutual funds and stocks don't offer such guarantees").

- "Mutual funds can generate income taxes even if the mutual fund has not increased or worse yet has lost value. I'm not going to pay taxes on a losing investment." (Variable annuities generate income taxes only on gain and only when the investor decides what amount and when to withdraw that gain).

- "I've deferred income taxes for years. By doing so I've avoided paying 30% or more in taxes on my investments each year. When I retire I will be able to control my income and keep my tax burden to 15% to 20%." (Mutual funds do not provide tax deferral).

- "My variable annuity will guarantee me a stream of income for the rest of my life and the life of my spouse. That income can go up but it can never go down." (Stocks and mutual funds offer no such guarantees).

- "I have a death benefit that will protect my spouse if I die in a down market." (Stocks and mutual funds do not offer death benefits).

§404. BEN BERNANKE'S VARIABLE ANNUITIES

In the July 26, 2006 issue of *The Wall Street Journal* it was reported that over half of the investments held by the Chairman of the Federal Reserve, were variable annuities.[2]

§405. QUESTIONS TO ASK

- If an average of $150,000 billion[3] has flowed into variable annuities in just the past three years, shouldn't an investor try and learn more about these investments?

- If the Chairman of the Federal Reserve has most of his investable assets in variable annuities, wouldn't it be wise to learn something about these investments?

§406. SOURCES

- "Fed Discloses Bernanke's Financial Assets", *The Wall Street Journal* (Eastern edition), New York, New York. July 26, 2006.

- *National Underwriter (Life and Health)*, June 18, 2007, p. 8 and January 7, 2008, p. 7.

---

[2] These annuities are held in Mr. Bernanke's TIAA-CREF retirement account and were funded when he was a college professor. As an alternative to his annuity account Mr. Bernanke could have opted for a state pension, and chose not to. Mr. Bernanke could sell any portion or all of his variable annuities at any time with out any income tax liability and buy other investments in an IRA, but has chosen not to do so.

[3] Today, $1.5 trillion are invested in variable annuities.

- *National Underwriter (Life and Health)*, June 25, 2007, p. 7 and September 10, 2007, p. 8 and January 7, 2008, p.7.
- *Financial Advisor*, November 2007, p. 170.

§407. REVIEW QUESTIONS

The Chairman of the Federal Reserve has how much of his investable assets invested in variable annuities?[4]

 A. 10%

 B. 20%

 C. 30%

 D. 40%

 E. 50%+

§408. CONCLUSION

The purchase of variable annuities has increased steadily over the past several years. In just the last couple of years, purchases of variable annuities have exceeded $150 billion. Chapter 5 discusses whey variable annuities have increased so dramatically.

---

[4] The answer is 50%+.

– CHAPTER 5 –
WHY VARIABLE ANNUITY SALES ARE SOARING
§501. INTRODUCTION

The prior summary chapter pointed out purchases of variable annuities for the past several years have been dramatically increasing to the point where $150 billion in annual variable annuity sales has become common place. This detailed chapter documents this trend and discusses why variable annuity sales are reaching new highs each year. This chapter also discusses how the media distorts the truth about variable annuities and finishes with a brief overview as to why savvy investors are drawn to variable annuities.

§502. RECORD VARIABLE ANNUITY SALES

For the past seventeen years, the sale of variable annuities has soared to record levels. From 1990 through 2005 the amount invested annually in variable annuities rose from a modest $12 billion to more than $132 billion.[1] In 2006, the sale of variable annuities reached a new record – $157.3 billion.[2] The sale of variable annuities for 2007 is expected to exceed $170 billion.[3] Net flows (i.e., new money) have also been increasing.[4] This reflects the fact that fewer variable annuity sales are the result of tax-free exchanges and more are the result of new investments.[5] Lower commissions, lower fees and the popularity of guaranteed living benefits, especially in volatile markets, are being credited with these record sales.[6] In just the last three years, the investing public has purchased variable annuities at an average rate exceeding $150 billion annually.[7] Currently, there is $1.5 *trillion* invested in these annuities.[8]

The average variable annuity sale is in the range of $97,500.[9] Using this figure, approximately 1.85 million individual variable annuity contracts were purchased in 2007 alone. Although there are no statistics indicating the average number of variable annuity contracts sold each year by financial advisors, it can be safely assumed that of the 1.85 million annuity contracts purchased by investors in 2006, many of them were due to multiple sales by financial professionals. Assuming that financial advisors were responsible for selling ten variable annuity contracts each, this would mean that there were approximately 185,000 financial professionals involved in helping clients invest in variable annuities in 2007.

---

[1] Variable Annuity Research and Data Service (VARDS); National Association for Variable Annuities (NAVA); *National Underwriter* (Life and Health), March 7, 2005, p. 6, March 13, 2006, p. 12 and September 7, 2007, p. 8.

[2] *Investment News*, April 9, 2007, page 8.

[3] See note 1 and 2 above. Also see notes 8 and 9 below.

[4] National Association for Variable Annuities, Reston, Virginia.

[5] IRC §1035.

[6] *Investment News*, April 9, 2007, p. 8 and *National Underwriter* (Life and Health), September 10, 2007, p. 8.

[7] See notes 1, 2, 8 and 9. First quarter sales for 2007 were $40.1 billion and net flows increased. *National Underwriter* (*Life and Health*), June 18, 2007, p. 8 and January 7, 2008, p.7.

[8] National Association for Variable Annuities, Reston, Virginia. *National Underwriter* (Life and Health), June 25, 2007, p. 7, September 10, 2007, p. 8 and January 7, 2008, p.7. Also see *Financial Advisor*, November 2007, p. 170.

[9] *National Underwriter (Life and Health)*, January 7, 2008, p. 19.

§503. THE MEDIA – REPORTING INACCURACY

Today there are some financial journalists who write inaccurate articles about variable annuities primarily as a result of their sloppy or non-existent research. These reporters frequently repeat what others have said in the past or take previously written articles and change them just enough to pass them off as their own work. There are also a few radio and TV commentators who broadcast or televise incorrect information to the public about variable annuities because, unlike true media professionals, they do not want to take the time to verify what they are saying. In reading or listening to such reports and commentary, one would surely believe that the reason that variable annuity sales constantly reach new highs each year is that there are 185,000 financial advisors in the United States who get up each morning with one goal in mind – to rip-off as many of their clients as they can in order to shove as much money in their pockets as possible. A small group of biased reporters and commentators wants the public to believe that there are tens of thousands of dishonest financial advisors preying on the general public because people are so gullible that they will write a check for their entire life savings to some stranger who wants them to invest their money in something that, according to these reporters and commentators, is too complex for them to understand, is very costly and obviously will do these investors no good whatsoever. These same so-called reporters and commentators want the public to believe that none of these financial professionals care that their improper actions will ultimately ruin their reputations, put their livelihoods at risk and expose them to lawsuits that could eventually result in them having to forfeit their professional licenses to state or federal regulators.

§504. THE TRUTH ABOUT FINANCIAL PROFESSIONALS

Contrary to what a handful of hack financial reporters and commentators would like the public to believe, the overwhelming majority of financial advisors are hard-working and ethical.   Government statistics bare this out. The number of disciplinary actions brought by the NASD over the past several years involving unsuitable variable annuity sales averaged less than one-third of one percent a year. This fact clearly demonstrates the great majority of financial professionals who help their clients purchase variable annuities take their mandate to do what is best for their clients quite seriously.[10] Financial advisors, like all honest professionals, get up every morning with a single goal – to help their clients attain financial security. In performing this task, they will often recommend mutual funds, bonds, stocks and, in some cases, variable annuities if these recommendations are in the best interest of their clients. These advisors are aware of the fact that the financial industry provides them with the opportunity to make a good living while enabling them to help their clients reach their financial goals. Most financial advisors have worked too long and hard for their various credentials and licenses, as well as the

---

[10] *National Underwriters, Life & Health*, September 26, 2003, p. 6. This statistic covers the five year period from September of 2000 to September of 2005.

trust of the people they work with, to throw all of this away by taking financial advantage of a client.

As an estate planning attorney, the author has come in contact with many wealthy individuals who have, for many reasons, purchased variable annuities. Contrary to the media's view that these people are financially unsophisticated and will invest in anything presented to them, I have found them to be exceptionally bright, especially when it comes to financial matters. They know exactly what they are doing and, with the assistance of their financial advisors, have used variable annuities as one of the major foundations for securing their financial future. A 2005 Gallup survey found that:[11]

- 62% of all variable annuity owners had some college education or had graduated from college;
- 22% of all annuity owners had completed some post-graduate work or had received advanced college degrees;
- Over 54% of the owners of variable annuities were business owners, corporate officers, professionals or individuals who worked in a supervisory capacity;
- The spouses of variable annuity owners were themselves supervisors, corporate officers, professionals or business owners; and
- The annual household income for a significant number of variable annuity owners exceeded $100,000.

A LIMRA study conducted in 2003 showed that more than 25% of investors with $500,000 or more in investable assets owned variable annuities.[12] It is interesting to note that in a recently filed financial disclosure document, Ben Bernanke, the Chairman of the Federal Reserve, disclosed that approximately half of his total investment assets were held in variable annuity accounts.[13]

§505. BAD APPLES

There is not a single profession practiced in the United States that does not have its share of dishonest individuals. The financial services industry is no different. There will always be a few people with financial training who will use their knowledge to take advantage of other people. Every time this happens it hurts the overwhelming majority of financial advisors who are honest, ethical and hardworking. This same problem is found in all professionals. The media is not exempt from having its share of bad apples. Recently, two senior editorial executives of *The New York Times* resigned because they allowed a reporter to falsify data that he reported in their newspaper.[14] Shortly after that, several editorial staff members of *USA Today* were fired because

---

[11] See www.annuity-insurers.org

[12] Study on annuitization conducted by LIMRA International, (2004). Also see, "Deferred Annuity Owner Study: Characteristics and Attitudes," by Matthew Drinkwater and Robert Chanerda, LIMRA International, (2003).

[13] *USA Today*, §B, p. 1, July 26, 2006.

[14] This refers to the Jayson Blair incident involving the *New York Times*.

they did not monitor one of their reporters who was filing false reports.[15] A reporter for the *New York Post* was recently caught on videotape agreeing not to publish negative stories about a wealthy businessman if the businessman would pay the reporter a large sum of hush money.[16] A popular radio talk show host who has, in the past, argued for stricter drug laws, recently entered a plea bargain with state prosecutors in an effort to settle criminal fraud charges brought against him for violation of Florida's prescription drug laws.[17] Even the viewing of the evening news on the major television networks has been declining over the last few years. Many believe this is a result of the public's perception that television news reporters are biased and untrustworthy.[18] During the last presidential election, one of the national television networks was caught using questionable documents for a story about President Bush's military service without attempting to verify the authenticity of these documents. This ultimately led to the firing of several network employees and forced the retirement of a well known news anchor.[19] There are a handful of reporters and commentators around the country who continue to report negatively on variable annuities even though they have been provided with information showing that their reports and commentaries are deceptive and misleading. They have chosen to ignore the truth so that they can continue to make their false statements in order to generate newspaper sales or increase their listener or viewer base. These media bad apples give honest, hard-working journalists the same black eye that financial advisors suffer when individuals in their profession are dishonest, biased or deceitful. A study conducted by David Michaelson, Ph.D., which examined media coverage of variable annuities found that the media, when reporting on variable annuities, made inaccurate statements 74% of the time.[20] One of the most interesting things about some journalists who write negative articles about variable annuities is that they buy variable annuities for themselves and their families. For example, a well-known *Wall Street Journal* reporter who rarely has anything good to say about variable annuities recently admitted in one of his articles that he had purchased variable annuities for himself and his family.[21] These reporters have picked up on the fact that negative stories about variable annuities will keep people reading their newspaper columns. What they invest in with their own money seems to be a different story.

---

[15] This refers to the Jack Kelly incident involving *USA Today.*

[16] This refers to the J.P. Stern incident involving the *New York Post.*

[17] This refers to the plea bargain of talk show host Rush Limbaugh.

[18] *USA Today*, 9 August 2005 (cover story), see also *USA Today*, August 1, 2005, p. 40.

[19] This reference is to the retirement of Dan Rather of CBS over the questionable documents dealing with President Bush's military service.

[20] "Content Analysis of Recent News Coverage of Annuities," by David Michaelson, June 2003. This study covered the period of 2001-2003.

[21] "Eating His Own Cooking: Our Columnist Details How He Invests His Portfolio," by Jonathan Clements, *The Wall Street Journal*, September 13, 2004, p. D1. At least one other nationally syndicated financial reporter who rarely reports variable annuities in a positive light recently admitted placing his wife's retirement funds in a variable annuity. See *Milwaukee Journal Sentinel* article (online), June 25, 2005 by H. Cruz.

§506. THE GOOD NEWS

Sophisticated investors understand the importance of making well thought out investment decisions. These investors, like the general public, occasionally read negative media articles about variable annuities. However, because of their educational level and financial resources, these investors are able to consult with financial advisors who can provide accurate information on how variable annuities might help them attain financial security. When weighing the advice of their trusted financial professionals against the negative media reports coming from a handful of biased, intellectually lazy reporters and commentators, it becomes obvious that these investors are paying no attention to the reporters and commentators. In short, as between the media and their financial advisors, sophisticated investors believe their advisors. A 2004 LIMRA study showed that 75% of high net worth investors who purchased a variable annuity from a financial advisor purchased additional investments from that same advisor.[22] A recent survey found that a majority of pre-retirees described their relationship with their financial advisors was as strong or stronger than their relationship with either their clergy or their doctors.[23] A *Money* magazine survey released in May of 2006 listed the most admired occupations. The third occupation on the list was that of being a financial advisor. The only occupations listed above that of financial advisor were software engineer and college professor.[24] The job of journalist, needless to say, did not appear on the list. However, a Harris poll conducted in 2005 did determine that, based on prestige, journalists ranked 19 out of the 22 professions the poll examined.[25]

§507. THE BAD NEWS

Today, there is a small segment of the population that is not well-educated in financial matters, nor do they have the financial resources that will allow them to work one-on-one with a financial professional. These individuals are often put in the position of making financial decisions based on inaccurate information they pick up from the media. In many cases they rely on misleading reports generated by a few reporters or commentators who are more interested in creating controversy or selling their own promotional materials than helping the public understand how to invest for their future. A good example of this occurred during a live CNBC interview with the financial commentator Suze Orman where she stated that the only guarantees offered by variable annuities arose only if the variable annuity owner died. This single statement proves just how little Ms. Orman knows about variable annuities. The truth is that every major issuer of variable annuities today offers guarantees that will protect the owners of variable annuities from a declining stock market while allowing these investors to reap the

---

[22] Study on annuitization conducted by LIMRA International, (2004). Also see, "Deferred Annuity Owner Study: Characteristics and Attitudes," by Matthew Drinkwater and Robert Chanerda, LIMRA International, (2003).

[23] Survey by Hartford Financial Service Group, Inc., discussed in *Investment News*, June 27, 2005.

[24] *Money*, May 2006.

[25] Harris Poll, August 2005. Discussed in *Registered Representative*, November 2005, p. 24.

benefits of rising stock prices. Other guarantees protect lifetime streams of income for variable annuity owners. (These "living benefits" are discussed below). Investors relying on inaccurate information disseminated by the Suze Ormans of the financial world are frequently led to invest their money in inappropriate investments because of the biased financial information they must rely on.

The primary reason for the increase in variable annuity sales in the past few years has been attributed to the living benefits offered by variable annuity issuers. These benefits, for the first time, allow long-term investors to fully participate in the upside of the stock market while, in effect, eliminating the downside risk of the stock market.[26] Some annuity issuers are reporting that many of the variable annuities they sell with living benefit riders are for amounts that are well into the six figure range. This would indicate that wealthier investors are purchasing variable annuities that offer the new living benefits. A recent survey conducted by Prince and Associates confirmed this. This study found that millionaires are more than *twenty* times more interested in learning about annuities than mutual funds.[27]

As sad as it is, there is little that can be done to prevent those individuals who lack the financial education or economic resources from having to rely on incompetent media-generated financial advice. What many of these individuals do not understand is that most financial reporters and commentators are unlicensed, unregulated and generally have no financial training or background. Those few reporters or commentators who claim they have any financial training usually prove to be washouts who could not make a living as a financial professional. Relying on their advice would be no different than making important health decisions based on a medical advice column appearing in a local newspaper that was written by someone who flunked out of medical school.

The author has never met a financial reporter or commentator who attained wealth by following their own financial advice. Most journalists exist on meager salaries. Those few television and radio commentators who have attained any wealth have not done so following their own financial advice, but by selling books or cassette tapes to the public. The AARP in their June 2006 issue of the *AARP Bulletin* published an article by an individual who chronicled the mistakes he had made in preparing for his retirement. These mistakes, according to the author, ranged from waiting too late to plan for his retirement and failure to seek advice from a financial planner to losing money by attempting market timing and getting caught in the credit card trap. The most interesting thing about the author is that he wrote a book that gives advice on how to plan for a financially successful retirement.[28]

---

[26] Harris Poll, August 2005. Discussed in *Registered Representative*, November 2005, p. 24.

[27] *Registered Representative*, September 2005, p. 42.

[28] "Don't Do What I Did," by Stan Hinden, *AARP Bulletin*, June 2006, pgs. 24-26.

Ben Stein, a nationally known commentator, economist and lawyer made the same observation in an article he wrote:

> My parents bought [variable annuities] when they first came out and it made them well-to-do. My sister and I still get income from them. I love the fact that financial journalists raise doubts about [variable annuities]. I never in my life met a financial journalist as well off as my economist father and mother, and they did it with variable annuities.[29]

§508. WHY INVESTORS ARE DRAWN TO VARIABLE ANNUITIES

As a finance professor, I meet and work with well-educated investors everyday. When discussing their investments, I often find that these investors not only understand variable annuities, but own them in their own investment portfolios. When asked why they invested in variable annuities, they usually give several reasons, including the following:

Commission-free Investing - Unlike most mutual fund and stock investments, when variable annuities are purchased, no up-front, out-of-pocket commission is charged to the investor. A declining contingent deferred sales charge is imposed if the variable annuity is not held for an agreed holding period that averages six years. Long-term investors are rarely concerned about contingent deferred sales charges (CDSC) because they hold their variable annuities for the agreed holding period, thus avoiding these charges.[30] Purchasers of variable annuities, depending on their needs, can select variable annuities with holding periods ranging from zero to ten years.[31] Typical mutual funds and stocks require investors to pay up-front, out-of-pocket commissions. Knowledgeable long-term investors realize that investing without having to incur commissions will increase their investment gains over time. (This topic is discussed more fully in Chapters 22 and 23).

Low Annual Cost of Investing - The annual cost of owning the typical, actively managed equity based variable annuity, whether in a taxable account or retirement account (i.e., IRA, 401(k), etc.), is less than the annual cost of owning the typical, actively managed equity mutual fund.[32] An actively traded stock portfolio can generate commissions and taxes that can exceed the annual cost of owning the typical equity variable annuity.[33] (This topic is discussed more fully in Chapters 9 and 10).

---

[29] *The American Spectator*, "Off Golden Pond," by Ben Stein, October 2004.

[30] Any commission paid to a financial professional who sells a variable annuity is paid by the annuity company, not the investor. The annuity company recoups the commission they advance from the annual fees it charges the owner each year. As mentioned in notes 29 and 30 above, these costs are usually less than the costs incurred in mutual fund and variable annuity investing.

[31] Variable annuities offering reduced surrender periods often impose slightly higher annual ownership costs.

[32] The average variable annuity has an annual expense of approximately 2.3% a year. An A-share equity mutual fund has an annual expense ratio of 1.5%. In addition, A-share mutual funds, unlike variable annuities, charge mutual fund investors up-front, out-of-pocket commissions. A 5% commission for a mutual fund held for 5 years generates a 1% annual commission cost. Income taxes paid by mutual fund investors will reduce the fund's gain by 20% a year (according to a 2005 Lipper study). For a mutual fund earning 10% a year, income taxes can reduce this amount by 2%. Stopping here, the average A-share equity mutual fund has an annual cost of 4.5% as compared to the 2.3% annual cost of the variable annuity.

[33] If a stock is purchased and sold a year or so later, a 1.5% commission to buy, sell and re-buy a new stock will cost the investor 4.5% of his investment.

Tax-Deferred Investing - Variable annuities grow tax-deferred. This not only simplifies owning variable annuities but eliminates the payment of income taxes that some investments, like mutual funds, generate annually regardless of whether the funds increase or decrease in value. Successful and knowledgeable investors understand the importance of tax-deferral. John D. Rockefeller once said, "The surest way to accumulate wealth is to make sure you never pay taxes on income you don't use." Because variable annuities grow tax-deferred, income taxes are not paid until withdrawals are made from these annuities. Tax conscious investors realize that by avoiding taxes today, their variable annuity will grow to a larger amount than taxable investments and may be subject to lower income taxes after retirement. A LIMRA study conducted in 2003 found that 67% of affluent households cited income tax considerations as the leading reason for contacting financial professionals. (This topic is discussed more fully in Chapters 14, 15, 24 and 25).

No-Cost/Tax-Free Trading - Variable annuity owners may trade among the different fund families in their variable annuity without paying commissions. In addition, these trades do not result in taxable transactions. Changing investments among different mutual fund companies or buying and selling stocks may involve either an additional commission or the triggering of an income tax liability or both. (This topic is discussed more fully in Chapters 22 and 23).

No-Cost Asset Rebalancing - Nearly every variable annuity issuer today will, without cost, automatically rebalance a variable annuity owner's investments on a periodic basis. Even if automatic rebalancing is not provided, variable annuity owners are free to rebalance their investments without cost and without triggering an income tax liability. Cost-free rebalancing is not generally available with mutual funds and stock accounts. Where such rebalancing is accomplished by a mutual fund or stock owner, such changes often result in the imposition of additional commissions or taxes or both. (This topic is discussed more fully in Chapters 22 and 23).

Tax-Efficient Withdrawals at Retirement – Most mutual funds involuntarily force income on their fund owners each year. This creates an income tax liability which in turn produces a nest egg that will be smaller than if variable annuities were owned. The reason for this is that variable annuities grow on a tax-deferred basis. Many people assume that the income tax liability for retirees who own variable annuities will be greater than that for those who own mutual funds. This rarely proves true. Few people are aware of the fact that a retired couple who can keep their gross income at or below $85,000 a year and who have average deductions and personal exemptions will pay federal income taxes on their taxable income at 15% *regardless* of how much of this income comes from variable annuity withdrawals (including all of it!).[34] For such couples, seeking to obtain a *temporary* 15% long-term capital gains rate would not seem to

---

[34] Assume a married couple has a gross income of $73,000 and they take $12,000 from a variable annuity they own every year. Their gross income is $85,000. Normal exemptions and deductions at this level would be $19,705, leaving a taxable income of $65,295. The tax in 2005 on $65,295 is $9,794 or 15% of the couple's taxable income. For 2006 it would be less.

be all that critical.[35] (This topic is discussed more fully in Chapters 12-15).

Death Benefit - Variable annuities, unlike any other investment, provide a death benefit that will refund all net investments made by a variable annuity owner to their survivors when the annuity owner dies if the variable annuity account value reflects a loss. Many variable annuities, for a small fee, will provide a death benefit that increases at a stated rate (e.g., 5% - 7%) each year. By exchanging variable annuities at the end of a surrender period, a new death benefit equal to the annuity's current value can be obtained without cost.[36] Mutual fund and stock investments offer no such protection to an investor's family. (This topic is discussed more fully in Chapter 37).

Principal Protection and Guaranteed Lifetime Income - A recent *Barron's* lead article pointed out that wealthy clients were, "...more interested in preserving their wealth than making huge gains."[37] This may be one reason for the increased popularity of variable annuities among sophisticated investors. Today, 85% of variable annuity issuers provide one or more living benefit riders with their annuities. These riders are designed to protect long-term investors from losing their principal while allowing them to participate in the potential upward movement of the stock market. In addition, these riders may also guarantee a stream of income for the life for the annuity owner. This stream of income can increase with a rising stock market but cannot decrease in a declining stock market. Most of these modern lifetime income riders do not require the variable annuity owner to annuitize their annuity to obtain these benefits. Access to the annuity remains with the owner. In addition, these new annuities also provide a substantial death benefit for the surviving spouse. Neither mutual funds nor stocks provide similar benefits. The total annual cost of owning a variable annuity that provides income for life, a death benefit and principal protection or guaranteed income for life is actually less than the annual cost of owning an average, actively managed equity mutual fund that fully exposes the investor to all loses resulting from a declining stock market.[38] (This topic is discussed more fully in Chapter 33).

Better Performance - The annual cost of owning the typical mutual fund can be as much as 2% more than the annual cost of owning a similar variable annuity. For this reason, it is not surprising that the annual performance of variable annuities is better than that of mutual funds and stocks. (This topic is discussed more fully in Chapter 32).

---

[35] 2003 Annuity Study by LIMRA.

[36] Assume a variable annuity owner is 51 and plans to hold his annuity until he retires at 65. If he purchases a variable annuity for $100,000 and ten years later it is worth $400,000, he can exchange it tax-free (via IRC §1035) and cost-free for a variable annuity with a four year surrender period. After such an exchange, the owner's new death benefit will be $400,000. His ten year holding period will not have changed.

[37] *Barron's*, 24 April 2006.

[38] The annual expense ratio for a typical stock mutual fund is 1.5%. The annualized commission cost for such a fund is approximately 1.0%. Federal income taxes reduce mutual fund gains by 2.0%. These three costs alone amount to 4.5%. The annual cost of a variable annuity is 2.4% on average. If 0.6% is added for a living benefit rider, the cost rises to 3.0%. All guarantees are based on the credit worthiness and financial solvency of the issuing company.

Tax-Efficient Wealth Transfer at Death - Variable annuity investors have learned from their tax advisors that variable annuities can be transferred at death in a very tax-efficient manner. As a tax attorney, I often point out to my clients who own variable annuities that with some very basic tax planning, variable annuities can avoid both estate taxes as well as any income taxes that might be owed by the beneficiaries who inherit them. Such a result often saves significantly more in estate and income taxes than can be saved by relying on the step-up in basis so often touted as a benefit by those who sell stocks and mutual funds. (This topic is discussed more fully in Chapters 18-20).

§509. QUESTIONS TO ASK

- With all the advantages offered by variable annuities, shouldn't I want to know more about what variable annuities might do for my clients?

§510. REVIEW QUESTIONS

Can you discuss two reasons why variable annuity sales are soaring?

§511. CONCLUSION

What I have found in dealing with both financial advisors and investors is that:

(1) Financial advisors understand the important role that variable annuities can play in helping their clients reach their financial goals and they do an excellent job of explaining the many benefits that variable annuities can provide to their clients;

(2) Educated and financially successful investors do not make important investment decisions based on the biased opinions of unqualified reporters and commentators. They seek out qualified and trusted financial advisors when making decisions that will impact their financial future;

(3) The reporters and commentators that disseminate inaccurate and biased information regarding variable annuities are not being listened to today and will not be listened to tomorrow. Everyday these reporters erode what little trust and credibility is left between them and the public. One absolute that never varies is that the truth will always prevail; and

(4) As long as there are financial advisors who strive to help their clients reach their financial goals and as long as investors take the time to examine the unique features and benefits variable annuities offer, the sale of variable annuities will continue to set new records.

– CHAPTER 6 –
HOW MYTHS START

§601. INTRODUCTION

All myths are based in ignorance. When this ignorance is reinforced by some authority figure supporting the myth, the myth will grow in acceptance. Once a large enough number of people believe a myth, it then becomes treated as fact. All myths eventually succumb to factual examination. This chapter discusses how myths arise to the level of fact and more specifically how the many myths surrounding variable annuities have come to be accepted as fact.

§602. A SHORT PRE-TEST

Before going into the material for this chapter, readers are encouraged to take the following short pre-test. There are five true-false questions set out below. Place a "T" next to those statements that are true and an "F" next to those statements that are false. Later in this chapter this test (and its answers) will be discussed more fully.

TRUE-FALSE QUESTIONS

_____ 1. Both the capitol of Texas and the capitol of Nevada lie east of Los Angeles, California.

_____ 2. The first Model-T Fords to roll off the assembly line were painted one color – black.

_____ 3. The predominant language spoken in Mexico City, Rio de Janeiro and Havana is Spanish.

_____ 4. Charles Lindbergh was the first person to fly non-stop across the Atlantic Ocean.

_____ 5. One of the major benefits of incorporation is that the personal assets of the incorporators are not available if the corporation is sued.

§603. IGNORANCE – THE DRIVING FORCE BEHIND ALL MYTHS

The term ignorance as used in this chapter is not intended nor used in a negative context. The term is used to mean that one does not have personal knowledge of a specific fact. Everybody is ignorant about many things. We all tend to know our particular jobs and those things that are important to us. For example, an airline pilot knows the proper speed needed to land a plane safely because it's his job to know this. The pilot is most likely also aware that sport utility vehicles (SUVs) use more gas than small four cylinder cars. The pilot knows this information because it can impact him financially when he is in the market for a new car. If a pilot is asked what the specific gravity of lead is or what the average surface temperature of the sun is, he probably would not know. Ignorance of these facts should be expected because neither the specific gravity of lead nor the sun's average surface temperature are important to pilots in their job or in their daily living. If a pilot ever needed to know the specific gravity of lead or the sun's average surface temperature, he would defer to scientific sources that could supply this information. In short he would rely on authoritative experts or sources he could trust to supply this information.

§604. RELIANCE ON OTHERS

As mentioned above, whenever one lacks personal knowledge of something it is common to rely on persons or sources that they trust and believe are authoritative. When many people rely on such authoritative people or sources and these people have provided false information, the mere number of people who believe the myth will almost always elevate this false information to the status of truth.

§605. FACTUAL EXAMINATION – THE MYTH DESTROYER

People accept as fact information that is provided by authoritative sources especially when this information is subject to constant factual examination. Because scientists are constantly monitoring the sun's average temperature, there is little chance that incorrect data about this subject would be widely disseminated. Because of the constant factual examination regarding the sun's temperature, people accept the fact that the sun's average surface temperature is 10,000 degrees Fahrenheit and the specific gravity of lead is 11.35.

Defective information or data not subject to constant factual examination usually is a fertile breeding ground for myths. Sadly there are many examples where a myth has become so widely believed that they are accepted as fact by everyone. Again, one reason for this is the myth was most likely reinforced by authority figures who merely report the myth themselves or have some ulterior motive for keeping the myth alive. Another reason that myths survive for long periods of time is no one is willing to challenge or attempt to debunk these myths. As soon as factual examination is applied to a myth, the myth is destroyed and the truth prevails.

History provides many examples of this phenomenon. Only a few hundred years ago everybody on the planet believed that the earth was flat and that the earth was the center of the solar system. These myths were reinforced by scientists, professors, clergy and others. Only when Magellan and Galileo factually examined these myths did the world learn the truth – the earth is not flat and the sun is the center of the solar system.

§606. THE TOOTH FAIRY MYTH

At one time, every adult in the U.S. believed in the tooth fairy when they were children. Today, all adults know that the tooth fairy is a myth. Why did they believe the myth when they were younger? The reason for this is their ignorance was reinforced by authority figures (parents) who were trusted. Our parents told us that the tooth fairy was real and we did not have the ability (or desire) to factually examine this story to see if it were true. However, at some point we all started to question the validity of the tooth fairy story. We gathered information from other sources (i.e., older siblings and friends) which allowed us to begin questioning this myth. What happened in most cases is that the authority figures we trusted to provide accurate information to us (our parents) ultimately admitted there was no factual basis to the existence of the tooth fairy – it was all a myth. Myths concerning Santa Clause, the Easter Bunny and others came about in the same manner – ignorance coupled with reinforcement by an authority figure. In many cases the authority figure knows the truth but will reinforce a myth because to do so benefits the authority figure. Parents know there is no Santa Clause, but will perpetrate the myth for several reasons – least of which is making their kids believe that Santa will not come to visit them unless they are good and do what the parents say.

§607. YOUR JOB AS A FINANCIAL PROFESSIONAL

As a financial professional you should be able to rely on others when you need to know the specific gravity of lead or the average temperature of the sun. However, you make a living selling financial products. Many people entrust their financial well-being to you. At a minimum you can not rely on magazines, financial gurus seen on TV or heard on the radio, and others without *personally* conducting a factual examination of what is being said about the financial products you sell. In short, financial professionals need to be a Magellan or Galileo and help their clients understand the truth.

§608. THE BASIS OF VARIABLE ANNUITY MYTHS

Nearly every myth related to variable annuities is based on their inaccurate comparison to mutual funds. For example, the following five myths regarding variable annuities are commonly believed by the investing public (and many financial advisors):

- Variable annuities have annual costs that are greater than mutual funds.
- Variable annuities are less liquid than mutual funds.
- The commissions paid to buy a variable annuity are greater for variable annuities than mutual funds.
- Because the annual income taxation of mutual funds is limited to 15%, these funds are more tax efficient investments than are variable annuities because variable annuity gains are subject to higher ordinary income tax rates.
- If an investor dies with a mutual fund, his beneficiaries will receive more than had he died with a variable annuity because mutual fund beneficiaries receive a step-up in basis and variable annuity beneficiaries do not.

Notice that each of the myths set out above must be compared to mutual funds in order to give some credence to the myth. For this reason, in this book, whenever a variable annuity myth traces its basis to a comparison with a mutual fund, both investments will be compared in an effort to determine to what degree the variable annuity myth is factual.

Let's go back to the five true-false questions set out in §602 above. All of the answers are false. Most people will answer true to as many as three of the questions. The point is that much of what we think we know is wrong. Any question that was answered as true occurred due to a lack of knowledge about the subject coupled with some reinforcement by a parent, teacher, the media or some other authoritative source. The reinforcement leads to reliance and if a factual examination is not conducted by someone, the false statement (i.e., myth) will be treated as the truth. The reasons each of these five questions are false are set out below:

1. Carson City, the capital of Nevada lies *west* of Los Angeles.

2. The first Model-T Fords were green with an orange strip. Later, Henry Ford started painting his cars black to save money.

3. Rio de Janeiro is located in Brazil. Portuguese is the native language of Brazil, not Spanish.

4. Charles Lindbergh was the first person to fly *solo* non-stop over the Atlantic Ocean. Prior to his flight, blimps carried dozens of passengers over the Atlantic on non-stop flights.

5. Incorporators of corporations do not receive any protection regarding their personal assets. *Shareholders* who are not corporate officers do receive this protection.

§609. VARIABLE ANNUITY MYTHS

As pointed out above, many people rely on authorities to supply correct information to them on many subjects. Frequently, people relying on others assume that the information being provided has been subjected to factual examination. Where variable annuities are concerned, this is usually not the case. When the public wants to know something about a variable annuity they rely on financial magazines, financial commentators, newspaper reporters, etc. The problem with this is that an examination of the facts is rarely attempted by any of these "authorities". This often results in a myth cloaking itself as fact. An additional problem, discussed in Chapter 7, is that once a myth about variable annuities reaches the public, there are many people and financial entities that benefit from these myths. In many cases, they know that the myth is untrue and in other cases they do not want to know the truth because this will impact them negatively. Perpetuating the myth serves their best interest.

A simple example might help. A widely held myth about variable annuities is that their annual cost of ownership is more than for a similar mutual fund. The public believes this and the media and others reinforce it by stating this myth as if it were fact. The myth that mutual funds are less expensive to own each year than are variable annuities is perpetrated by the media and others by telling the public that mutual funds only cost 1.5% a year to own. The public is also told that the annual cost of owning the typical variable annuity is 2.3%. The myth is now set – 2.3% is greater than 1.5%. This statement is so often cited and so often repeated (though rarely subjected to factual examination) that the public, media and some financial professionals accept the myth as fact. The media and others with a bias against variable annuities never mention that the 1.5% figure they quote for the annual cost of owning a mutual fund is only the annual expense ratio or the money that is taken from the fund each year to pay fund managers.[1] What the public is not told is that, in addition to this 1.5% fee, mutual fund owners pay (or have

---

[1] This figure also includes a 12b-1 fee. This fee is discussed in Chapter 10 below.

taken from their mutual fund return) commissions, income taxes, trading costs, etc. These other costs will typically total 4%. When added to the 1.5% annual expense ratio, the typical mutual fund can have a *true* annual ownership cost in excess of 5%. Several books have been written documenting that the total annual cost of owning the typical mutual fund exceeds 5% a year.[2]

Although all of the research done on the cost of mutual funds clearly shows the typical mutual fund will have an annual cost of nearly *twice* that of a similar variable annuity, the media continues to perpetuate the cost myth by repeating it without verifying their facts although this would be easy to do. Others (who know the truth) perpetrate the cost myth because it is in their best interest to do this. Chapter 7 discusses come of the people and entities that have a bias against variable annuities.

The purpose of this book is to factually examine the various variable annuity myths to show why they are exactly that–unsupported myths.

§610. QUESTIONS TO ASK

- If my clients rely on me as a financial professional to provide accurate information about financial products, don't I have the obligation to give them correct information rather than repeating unverified data?

§611. CONCLUSION

Myths arise whenever an individual does not have factual information and relies on someone else to provide such information. If the person being relied on does not verify the information he provides or does not want the person relying on him to know the truth, a myth is either created or strengthened. Our clients rely on us to provide accurate information about potential investments.

---

[2] These books are cited in the notes to Chapter 10 below.

– CHAPTER 7 –
WHO DISLIKES VARIABLE ANNUITIES AND WHY

§701. INTRODUCTION

Many people and financial entities have reasons to perpetrate inaccuracies about variable annuities. By reinforcing the myths that have grown up around variable annuities, these people are usually able to protect an interest that is important to them. This chapter discusses those people or entities who dislike variable annuities and examines the ulterior motives they have for helping maintain variable annuity myths.

§702. ANTI-VARIABLE ANNUITY BIAS AND CONFLICTING INTERESTS

There are many individuals or entities who want the myths surrounding variable annuities to continue for as long as possible. Some of these individuals or entitled actually know the truth about variable annuities but do everything possible to keep the truth from getting to the public. Almost always there is some ulterior motive associated with these attempts to suppress the truth.

Several centuries ago, the church had good reason for wanting the general population to believe that he earth was the center of the solar system. Any contrary view could possibly raise questions about religious tenants and might weaken the power the church had over the general population. By the time Galileo discovered that the sun was at the center of the solar system, many scholars within religious circles knew that Galileo was correct. However, they had an ulterior motive for suppressing the truth. For this reason the myth that the earth was the center of our solar system persisted for many decades.

§703. THE GENERAL MEDIA

The media is responsible for perpetrating many of the myths associated with variable annuities. The primary reason for this is that very few media members do any personal research concerning variable annuities. They are famous for cutting and pasting together negative reports about variable annuities that were written by others and then passing them off as their own work. In the media, truth has taken a backseat to meeting a deadline or coming up with a controversial (but false) story. A study conducted by David Michaelson, Ph.D., which examined media coverage of variable annuities found that the media, when reporting on variable annuities, made inaccurate statements 74% of the time.[1]

§704. STOCKBROKERS

Stockbrokers get paid by commissions. If a client buys and holds an investment, the stockbroker will make no money. Most stockbrokers have learned that when stocks and mutual funds are sold to their clients that these clients will start trading their investments with some

---

[1] "Content Analysis of Recent News Coverage of Annuities," by David Michaelson, June 2003. This study covered the period of 2001-2003. At least one other nationally syndicated financial reporter who rarely reports variable annuities in a positive light recently admitted placing his wife's retirement funds in a variable annuity.

regularity. When a variable annuity is sold to clients they typically hold on to them for several years primarily to avoid having to pay surrender penalties. Many brokerage firms severely limit the ability of a stockbroker to liquidate a client's variable annuity if there might be a surrender charge imposed on the client at the time of sale. Variable annuity owners are free to trade among all of the investments offered by their variable annuity on a *no-commission* basis. Because variable annuities are buy-and-hold investments usually purchased by long-term investors they do not generate as much commission as stocks and mutual funds which are more frequently traded. The additional benefit of commission-free trading, although a boon for variable annuity owners, does nothing to increase the income earned by stockbrokers.

It is important to understand that not all stockbrokers are driven by how much commission they can earn. There are many stockbrokers today that are more concerned with what is in the best interest of their clients than how much they will earn in a given year and do recommend variable annuities when it is in their clients' best interest. The good news is that the number of such stockbrokers has grown annually for the past several years.

§705. UNLICENSED FINANCIAL ADVISORS

Anyone can call themselves a financial advisor. All they have to do is pay a fee to state or federal regulators and follow the rules promulgated by these regulators. It is no exaggeration that on Monday an individual can be working at Jiffy Lube and on Tuesday be a Registered Investment Advisor. What the public does not know is that variable annuities can only be sold by individuals who have passed a Series 6 or Series 7 exam given by the Financial Industry Regulatory Authority (FINRA). In addition to passing one of these two rigorous exams, an individual must also be a life insurance agent properly licensed with the insurance department for the state in which he lives. Such an individual must also meet the licensing requirements of each variable annuity issuer he represents. Financial advisors who do not (or cannot) meet these strict licensing requirements can't sell variable annuities. If someone can't sell a variable annuity, it can be easily understood why they would want their clients to believe all the myths about variable annuities.

§706. BANKS

Banks, up until recently, were not big fans of variable annuities. Variable annuities competed with their in-house CDs and other financial products. There are still many banks that continue to spread myths about variable annuities in an effort to direct money that their customers have into the bank's CDs, proprietary mutual funds, etc. The good news is that every *major* bank in the U.S. has taken a long, hard look at variable annuities (especially those with living benefit riders) and are making the sale of these products a priority.

§707. CERTIFIED PUBLIC ACCOUNTANTS (CPAs)

Many CPAs frequently repeat myths about variable annuities out of self interest. A client with significant mutual fund and stock holding will have to deal every year with capital gains distributions, qualifying and non-qualifying dividends, wash sales, etc. This almost always results in having to hire a CPA to prepare their tax return.

Variable annuities require no tax reporting until they are sold. When a variable annuity is sold, the gain is put on one line of the tax return. Until then, variable annuities and their gains are ignored for tax reporting purposes. If a client has his investments in variable annuities, his tax picture is greatly simplified and the need to hire a CPA to do their tax return becomes a rare event. The good news is that many CPA firms have started to learn about variable annuities and are actually helping their clients obtain these investments. These CPAs are concerned with what's in the best interest of their clients rather than worrying about the number of tax returns they will prepare each year.

§708. ATTORNEYS

Attorneys who do probate and estate settlement work do not like variable annuities because these annuities are non-probate property and do not generate probate fees when the annuity owner dies. Assume Mike owns a one million dollar house jointly with his wife and a one million dollar mutual fund portfolio in his name alone. If Mike dies and leaves everything to his wife, she will get the house immediately because it is non-probate property. The one million dollar mutual fund portfolio must go through probate. This could easily generate $50,000 to $100,000 in probate fees to the attorney handling the estate. If Mike had his investments in a variable annuity portfolio, both his house and variable annuities would immediately pass to his wife at his death and neither asset would generate a probate fee. Probate attorneys who stand to lose hundreds of thousands of dollars when their clients die owning variable annuities can begin to see why maintaining all the myths about variable annuities would be in their self interest.

§709. STATE REGULATORS AND BUREAUCRATS

State regulators and bureaucrats know less about variable annuities than anyone. They can't tell one variable annuity from another. Most state regulators who attack variable annuities do so because it gives them high visibility in the media which is needed for their number one goal in life – election to a higher office.

It is interesting to note that certain state bureaucrats (i.e., attorneys-general) complain about annuities without ever mentioning that no annuity can be sold in any state without the approval of another state regulator (i.e., the Insurance Commissioner). If Insurance Commissioners did what they were elected to do, unsuitable annuities could not be sold.

§710. MUTUAL FUND COMPANIES

Obviously, mutual fund companies have a high stake in perpetuating variable annuity myths because they are competing for America's investment dollars. The one variable annuity myth that the mutual fund industry spends a fortune each year to reinforce is that variable annuities cost more to own each year than do mutual funds. This is not true as Chapters 9 and 10 discuss in detail. However, this does not keep the mutual fund industry and their trade organizations from trying to convince the public that their products have an annual cost that is less than that of variable annuities. The mutual fund industry is not beyond "cooking the books" or falsifying data to make their point. The problem with this is they often get caught when they attempt this charade. An example of this appears in the article titled "The Road Less Expensive."[66]

§711. POPULAR FINANCIAL MAGAZINES

Financial magazines like *Money, Smart Money, Kiplinger's Personal Finance* and other similar magazines receive the bulk of their advertising revenue from brokerage firms and mutual fund companies. It is in their best interest to run stories that will keep their readers buying and selling stocks and mutual funds. Every month financial magazines have lead articles with titles similar to these:

"Ten Stocks to Own this Year"

"Eight Mutual Funds No One Should Own"

"Should You Dump These Stocks Now?"

"Mutual Funds That Will Make You Rich"

Very rarely will one ever see an article in these magazines about variable annuities. On those rare cases where variable annuities are mentioned, it is usually in a negative light. If investors knew the truth about variable annuities they would invest less in mutual funds and stocks which would most certainly cause more than a few financial magazines to go out of business.

If a company published a magazine called *American Autos* and received most of its ad revenues from Ford, Chevy, Buick and other American made autos, common sense would dictate that stories about Toyotas and Hondas would be rare. When such stories appeared, they would most likely not be flattering to foreign car manufacturers.

§712. CONCLUSION

Many people and entities out of ignorance, laziness or the intent to deceive, perpetrate myths about variable annuities. A true financial professional will always want to know the truth about the financial products that are available to his clients.

---

[2] *Forbes*, September 18, 2006, p. 152.

– CHAPTER 8 –
VARIABLE ANNUITY MYTHS

§801. INTRODUCTION

Over the years, the author has isolated sixteen myths surrounding variable annuities. The sections that follow set out each of these myths and briefly states what the truth is concerning these myths. Chapters 9 through 37 discuss each of these myths in detail.

§802. MYTH #1: THE TOTAL ANNUAL COST OF OWING THE TYPICAL VARIABLE ANNUITY IS MORE THAN OWNING A SIMILAR MUTUAL FUND

Myth #1 is not true. The truth is that the typical mutual fund will have an annual cost that is nearly double that of the typical variable annuity. (See Chapters 9 and 10).

§803. MYTH #2: ANNUAL CAPITAL GAINS TAXES ON MUTUAL FUND DISTRIBUTIONS ARE CAPPED AT A MAXIMUM OF 15% UNDER CURRENT TAX LAW

Myth #2 is not true. The truth is that capital gains taxes are not capped on annual mutual fund distributions. Many mutual fund investors pay well in excess of 15% each year on their mutual fund distributions (See Chapters 12 and 13).

§804. MYTH #3: PAYING ORDINARY INCOME TAXES UPON THE LIQUIDATION OF VARIABLE ANNUITIES MAKES THEM LESS ATTRACTIVE INVESTMENTS THAN MUTUAL FUNDS THAT RECEIVE CAPITAL GAINS TREATMENT UPON LIQUIDATION.

Myth #3 is not true. The truth is that ordinary income taxes paid on the sale of a tax-deferred variable annuity will often provide a larger net value than that received by mutual fund owners who are taxed on the sale of their mutual funds at long-term capital gains rates (See Chapters 14 and 15).

§805. MYTH #4: THE LIQUIDITY, FLEXIBILITY AND CONTROL ONE HAS WITH VARIABLE ANNUITIES IS LESS THAN THAT AVAILABLE WITH SIMILAR INVESTMENTS SUCH AS MUTUAL FUNDS AND STOCKS

Myth #4 is not true. The truth is that the liquidity of a variable annuity is no different than any other investment. The *cost* of liquidating a variable annuity can often be less than other investments. The control and flexibility one receives with a variable annuity is greater than with stocks or mutual funds. (See Chapters 16 and 17)

§806. MYTH #5: THE STEP-UP IN BASIS IS A BENEFIT MUTUAL FUNDS PROVIDE THAT VARIABLE ANNUITIES DO NOT. BECAUSE OF THIS, VARIABLE ANNUITIES MAKE POOR WEALTH TRANSFER VEHICLES

Myth #5 is not true. The truth is that for several reasons, the after-tax inheritance of a variable annuity can be larger than the inheritance of a mutual fund that receives a step-up in basis. (See Chapters 18 and 19).

§807. MYTH #6: BECAUSE OF SURRENDER FEES AND IRS PENALTIES, THE BREAK-EVEN POINT WITH VARIABLE ANNUITIES IS NEARLY 20 YEARS WHEN COMPARED TO A SIMILAR MUTUAL FUND INVESTMENT.

Myth #6 is not true. The truth is that when all costs, fees and taxes are included, the break-even period between a mutual fund and variable annuity is closer to six or seven years. (See Chapter 21).

§808. MYTH #7: THE COMMISSIONS PAID BY AN INVESTOR TO OWN A VARIABLE ANNUITY ARE HIGHER THAN FOR OTHER INVESTMENTS. THE SELLERS OF VARIABLE ANNUITIES MAKE MORE IN COMMISSIONS THAN THEY MAKE SELLING OTHER FINANCIAL PRODUCTS.

Myth #7 is not true. The truth is that the commissions paid to own a variable annuity or earned for selling a variable annuity are rarely any greater than the commissions paid or earned when mutual funds and stocks are purchased. (See Chapters 22 and 23).

§809. MYTH #8: THE TAX DEFERRAL BENEFIT RECEIVED BY VARIABLE ANNUITY OWNERS IS NOT REALLY A MAJOR BENEFIT.

Myth #8 is not true. The truth is that once the opportunity cost of an investment offering tax deferral is compared to one that does not, the advantage of tax deferral becomes an obvious benefit. (See Chapters 24 and 25).

§810. MYTH #9: BECAUSE VARIABLE ANNUITIES ARE TAX-DEFERRED THEY SHOULD NOT BE PUT IN IRAS OR OTHER QUALIFIED PLANS.

Myth #9 is not true. The truth is that unless an investor is considering *only* the benefit of tax deferral, there are many reasons why variable annuities should be placed in qualified accounts or funded with qualified money. (See Chapters 26 and 27).

§811. MYTH #10: THE U.S. TAX CODE FAVORS OTHER INVESTMENTS MORE THAN VARIABLE ANNUITIES.

Myth #10 is not true. The truth is that many tax provisions within the IRS code favor variable annuity owners much more than stock and mutual fund owners (See Chapters 28 and 29).

§812. MYTH #11: VARIABLE ANNUITIES ARE NOT SUITABLE INVESTMENTS FOR SENIOR INVESTORS.

Myth #11 is not true. The truth is that today's variable annuities offer protections and guarantees senior investors need. Modern variable annuities often turn out to be the best possible investments for senior investors. (See Chapters 30 and 31).

§813. MYTH #12: VARIABLE ANNUITIES, OVER THE LONG-TERM, DO NOT PERFORM AS WELL AS STOCKS AND MUTUAL FUNDS.

Myth #12 is not true. The truth is that the performance of variable annuities and mutual funds is nearly identical. Where there is a difference, it is to the advantage of the variable annuity. (See chapter 32).

§814. MYTH #13: VARIABLE ANNUITIES ARE JUST AS RISKY AS OTHER INVESTMENTS AND ARE REALLY NOTHING MORE THAN TAX-DEFERRED MUTUAL FUNDS.

Myth #13 is not true. The truth is that variable annuities offer riders that can protect principal and/or protect a set stream of income for life. Stocks and mutual funds can do neither. (See Chapter 33).

§815. MYTH #14: THE ONLY WAY YOU CAN GET YOUR MONEY OUT OF A VARIABLE ANNUITY IS IN A STREAM OF LIFETIME PAYMENTS.

Myth #14 is not true. The truth is that no issuer of variable annuities mandates annuitization. Annuitization is optional with the variable annuity owner. (See Chapter 35).

§816. MYTH #15: THE INVESTMENT SELECTION PROVIDED BY VARIABLE ANNUITIES IS NOT AS GOOD AS THAT PROVIDED BY SIMILAR INVESTMENTS.

Myth #15 is not true. The truth is that the investment selection offered by variable annuities is as good or better than the investment choices provided by many mutual fund companies. (See chapter 36).

§817. MYTH #16: OVER TIME MOST INVESTMENTS, INCLUDING VARIABLE ANNUITIES, GO UP IN VALUE AND THEREFORE THE DEATH BENEFIT PROVIDED BY VARIABLE ANNUITIES IS OF LITTLE VALUE.

Myth #16 is not true. The truth is that the death benefit provided with a variable annuity can increase with the value of the variable annuity thus offering a real benefit that stocks and mutual funds do not offer. (See Chapter 37).

§818. CONCLUSION

There are 16 myths concerning variable annuities. When examined, these myths prove to be unsupportable. True financial professionals should review these myths and determine what the truth is. By doing so, they will be in a position to help their clients make investments based on fact rather than myth.

– CHAPTER 9 –
THE COST MYTH – SUMMARY DISCUSSION
§901. INTRODUCTION

The most prevalent myth concerning variable annuities and mutual funds is that mutual funds are less expensive to own than variable annuities. This is not true. When all of the annually reoccurring costs of owning mutual funds and variable annuities are combined with their respective income tax liability, it is the variable annuity that usually turns out to be the less expensive financial product to own.

§902. THE COST MYTH

The myth that mutual funds are less expensive to own than variable annuities continues to be accepted as fact primarily because the media has been trained to tell the public that the *only* cost associated with mutual fund ownership is the annual expense ratio (including 12b-1 fees) which averages around 1.5%. This figure is frequently compared to the average annual cost of owning a variable annuity which is approximately 2.7%. This 2.7% cost figure includes trading costs, mortality and expense (M&E) fees, money management fees and 12b-1 fees. In short, this 2.7% figure is an all-in annual cost. The problem with such comparisons is that mutual funds have three other annual ownership costs that are not included in the 1.5% cost figure so often quoted to the public. These costs are up-front, out-of-pocket commissions,[1] trading costs and an annual income tax liability.[2] These three costs, when combined, usually total 3.7%. When this 3.7% is added to the annual expense ratio of 1.5%, the total annual cost of owning a typical mutual fund increases to 5.2% which is nearly twice the annual cost of the typical variable annuity. Variable annuities do not impose up-front, out-of-pocket commission and grow tax-deferred. Because of this, there is no need to adjust the 2.7% average annual cost of the variable annuity like there is with the mutual fund.[3]

Even when the mutual fund and variable annuity are sold and liquidation taxes are factored in, the net value of the variable annuity is frequently greater than the net value of an equivalent mutual fund. Chapter 10 discusses several examples that demonstrate this point.

§903. A COST ANALOGY

What would you say if you read the following report in the auto section of your local newspaper that was written by a reporter who claimed he was an expert on autos?

---

[1] B-share mutual funds do not impose up-front, out-of-pocket commissions. Their commission structure is similar to that of the typical variable annuity. See Chapter 10 below.

[2] Both variable annuities and mutual funds have trading costs. Trading costs for mutual funds tend to be slightly higher than for equivalent variable annuities. See Chapter 10 below.

[3] Commissions paid to those who sell variable annuities are almost always paid by the annuity issuer. The annuity issuer increases the cost of their variable annuity and/or impose contingent deferred sales charges to recoup these advanced commissions. Variable annuities do come in an A-share format where an up-front, out-of-pocket commission is paid. However, these variable annuities are rarely purchased by the public. See Chapter 10 below.

Nearly everyone should own an automobile. I think Fords are a better buy than Chevrolets because of their lower annual ownership costs. When insurance, taxes, tolls, parking, fuel, oil, maintenance and other costs are taken into consideration it will cost the typical Chevrolet owner $10,000 to operate his automobile for a year. The only annual cost of owning a Ford is the gas you put in it. This fuel cost is about $2,000 a year which is significantly less than the $10,000 one will spend to own a Chevrolet each year.

Most people reading such a report would spot the inappropriate cost comparison. What the reporter did was compare *one* annual cost of owning the Ford (gas cost) with the *total* annual cost of owning the Chevrolet.

Although the above analogy is laughable, it is exactly what financial reporters do today. They compare *one* cost of owning a mutual fund with the *total* cost of owning a variable annuity. The sad thing about this situation is that the public believes such reports. This is a good example of a myth taking hold because the public knows little about financial products and therefore they rely on so-called financial experts or authorities who publish defective reports that are rarely subjected to factual examination.

§904. CONCLUSION

When *all* of the costs of owning a mutual fund and variable annuity are considered, the variable annuity will usually prove to be the less expensive financial product to own on an annual basis. Chapter 10 discusses the cost myth in detail.

– CHAPTER 10 –
THE COST MYTH – IN DETAIL

§1001. INTRODUCTION

Members of the investing public have been led to believe that the typical mutual funds they buy from their financial professionals are less expensive to own on an annual basis than equivalent variable annuities. This is rarely the case. The annual cost of owning the typical mutual fund, whether in a qualified or non-qualified account, is usually greater than that of a typical variable annuity. This finding is not new. Several separate studies dealing with the annual cost of owning mutual funds and similar separate studies dealing with the annual cost of owning variable annuities have reached the same conclusion. The primary reason the investing public believes that mutual funds are less expensive to own than variable annuities is because of the common practice used in the financial industry of comparing one or two of the costs of owning a mutual fund with all of the costs of owning a variable annuity. Inaccurate information concerning the actual costs associated with mutual fund and variable annuity ownership, when relied on by the public, can result in investors making incorrect investment decisions. This book provides sources, data and the methodology that will assist financial professionals to understand the true annual cost of owning a mutual fund or variable annuity.

§1002. PUBLIC'S LACK OF AWARENESS

Mutual fund investors are generally unaware of the true cost of owning their mutual funds. A study conducted by the SEC and the Office of the Comptroller of the Currency found that 81% of investors could not hazard a guess as to amount their mutual funds charged them.[1] The public has been led to believe that the *total* annual cost of owning an average, actively managed equity mutual fund, whether in a taxable or tax-deferred account is approximately 1.5%.[2] In fact, the true annual cost of owning a typical mutual fund, ignoring income taxes, is more than *double* this figure. Several detailed studies that have focused on the annual expense of mutual fund ownership have reached this same conclusion. These studies were conducted by mutual fund CEOs[3], university scholars[4], former senior U.S. Treasury officials[5] and others.[6] All of these studies confirm that the annual cost of owning the average actively managed equity

---

[1] "Your Funds May Be Making You Rich...But You're Also Getting Robbed." *Money*, Feb. 1997, p. 62-74.

[2] Morningstar has calculated the annual expense ratio of the average mutual fund and found it to be 1.67%. See *Investment News* article "Fund Fees Baffle MBA Students" by David Hoffman, April 24, 2006. The Investment Company Institute, a mutual fund advocacy organization, places this average at 1.53%. *Boomer Market Advisor*, August 2006, p. 24.

[3] *Common Sense on Mutual Funds: New Imperatives for the Intelligent Investor*; John Bogle; Wiley & Sons (1999).

[4] *Your Money, Your Choice...Mutual Funds - Take Control Now and Build Wealth Wisely*, Professor Charles Jones (North Carolina State University), Prentice Hall, 2003. Also see "Portfolio Transaction Costs at U.S. Equity Funds," by Prof. Edward Oneal, *et al.*, Wake Forest University.

[5] *The Great Mutual Fund Trap*, Gary Gensler (Former Undersecretary of the U.S. Treasury 1999-2001) and Gregory Baer (Former Assistant Secretary for Financial Institutions for the U.S. Treasury) Broadway Books, New York, 2002.

[6] *The Trouble With Mutual Funds*; Richard Rutner. Elton-Wolf Pub. (2002). "Deciphering Funds' Hidden Costs," John Hechinger, *The Wall Street Journal*, March 17, 2004, p.D1.

mutual fund is not the 1.5% the public has been led to believe, but a figure much closer to 3.1%. This figure does not include federal income taxes that are paid each year by those who own mutual funds in taxable accounts. When federal income taxes are factored in each year, the annual cost of owning an average, actively managed equity mutual fund can easily exceed 5%. The annual cost of owning the average, actively managed variable annuity is approximately 2.2%. This figure has been calculated by insurance experts[7], independent research organizations[8], government regulatory agencies[9] and other groups.[10] This 2.2% figure applies to *average* variable annuities. For an *equity* based variable annuity this figure is closer to 2.5%.[11] The components of this 2.5% cost figure are discussed in the sections that follow. In addition, trading costs will increase this figure to approximately 3.0%. In short, what all of the mutual fund and variable annuity studies mentioned above show, when taken together, is that the average, actively managed domestic equity mutual fund held in a taxable account will have an annual cost of ownership that *exceeds* that of a similar variable annuity *before* taking federal income taxes into consideration. When annual income taxes are added, the annual cost of owning a typical mutual fund is usually twice that of a similar variable annuity. Many investors make incorrect investment decisions because they have relied on inaccurate information concerning the true cost of owning mutual funds and variable annuities. This inaccurate information comes primarily from two sources – a few misinformed advisors and members of the media who, without conducting any research or verification, repeat unsubstantiated and incorrect cost data that others have previously reported in the same manner.

§1003. THE ANALYSIS

As mentioned in Chapter 3, this book limits its analysis to the typical actively managed, equity based, taxable mutual funds and variable annuities because they are the most commonly purchased mutual funds and variable annuities. Mutual funds and variable annuities that are designed to short the stock market, leveraged mutual funds and similar atypical mutual funds and variable annuities are excluded because they are rarely purchased by the general public. The data used in this book is intended only to reflect average figures solely for the purpose of helping readers determine how to calculate the annual cost of owning both actively managed, taxable, equity based mutual funds and variable annuities. None of the data used is intended to represent inflexible, absolute figures. For example, this book may compare a 0.7% annual mutual fund trading cost to a 0.6% variable annuity annual trading cost merely to show how such

---

[7] *The New Life Insurance Investment Advisor* by Ben Baldwin, CLU, ChFC, CFP, page 354.

[8] The VARDS report, a product of Finetre Corporation, an independent research organization, recently determined that the annual cost of owning a variable annuity was 2.34%. This figure included 0.3% for miscellaneous fees.

[9] Joint SEC/NASD Report on variable insurance products (June 9, 2004, page 6). This report states the average annual expense of owning a variable annuity ranges from 1.3% to 2.2%. The higher figure is used by the author.

[10] National Association for Variable Annuities Fact Book 2003, p. 37. Also see Baer and Gensler, p. 282.

[11] *NAVA Outlook*, Nov/Dec 2005, page 6, citing *Morningstar* data.

costs must be factored into the calculation of the total annual cost of owning a mutual fund or variable annuity. If the reader is comparing an *actual* a mutual fund with a trading cost of 0.5% and a variable annuity with an actual trading cost of 0.6%, then the *actual* trading cost figures should be used in any comparison. The figures provided by the author should be used as general guidelines.

§1004. A COST ANALOGY

The following hypothetical illustrates, by analogy, how a few advisors and members of the media mislead the investing public:

Hypothetical:
Dan Slick owns an auto dealership. He sells only fully equipped Porsche sports cars and Ford sedans. Needing a new car, the local high school coach went to Dan Slick's auto dealership and asked Slick for assistance in buying an automobile. The coach told Slick that he was on a limited budget and that his wife stayed at home with their three small children. Slick took the coach over to one of the Fords in the showroom and showed him that the total sticker price for the Ford was $25,000. Slick then took the coach over to one of the Porsche sports cars on the showroom floor. Slick moved his finger half way down on the new car sticker and stopped at the word engine. He moved his finger to the right which showed the price for the Porsche engine to be $20,000. Based on this, Slick convinced the coach to purchase the Porsche sports car based on the fact that the Porsche was cheaper to own than the Ford sedan.

Anyone reading this hypothetical, after laughing, would conclude that Slick was dishonest and a discredit to his profession. If Slick were an honest auto dealer, he would have compared the *total* cost of the Porsche sports car with the *total* cost of the Ford sedan. In doing so he would have helped his client select the best automobile based on the client's needs and finances.

Although the above hypothetical seems rather silly, it perfectly mirrors what a small number of advisors and members of the media do today when comparing the cost of owning mutual funds and variable annuities. It is important to understand that advisors or members of the media will rarely *intentionally* mislead the public regarding the cost of owning mutual funds and variable annuities. Misleading information is usually the result of an advisor or member of the media failing to thoroughly examine or research their data before disseminating it. Sad to say, there are a few cases where advisors and members of the media are fully aware of all of the costs associated with mutual fund and variable annuity ownership and choose to intentionally mislead the public by reporting false data.

§1005. MISINFORMED ADVISORS

Misinformed advisors can include financial advisors, lawyers, CPAs and others. It is not uncommon to find these advisors repeating inaccurate and unverified information regarding the costs involved in owning mutual funds and variable annuities. When information regarding the total cost of owning mutual funds and variable annuities is incorrectly disseminated by misinformed advisors, the investing public can be led into making costly investment decisions. In addition, when advisors provide inaccurate investment information to clients they can expose themselves to potential litigation. For example, a few years ago the author received such a case from another securities attorney for review. The case involved a gentleman who went to a brokerage firm and told a stockbroker there that he wanted to purchase the same variable annuity that his sister owned because she was happy with her annuity's performance, tax deferral and other features. The stockbroker advised against such a purchase and suggested a mutual fund instead. When asked why the mutual fund was recommended over the variable annuity, the stockbroker stated that the variable annuity was too expensive to own. To make his point, the stockbroker showed his new client that the annual cost of owning the variable annuity, according to its prospectus, was 2.6%. The stockbroker stated that the annual expense ratio for the mutual fund he was selling was only 1.5%. Based on this information the client invested a significant amount in the mutual fund. What the stockbroker did was exactly what Dan Slick, the dishonest auto dealer did – he based his recommendation on a comparison of the *total* annual cost of owning the variable annuity (2.6%) with the annual expense ratio of the mutual fund (1.5%). The problem with this is that a mutual fund's annual expense ratio, which includes 12b-1 fees, accounts for only two of five major components that make up the *total* annual cost of owning a mutual fund.[12] Later the client discovered that the true *total* annual cost of owning the mutual fund he bought was not 1.5% he was quoted but was actually 5.6%. The client promptly called his lawyer. What the stockbroker did, whether intentionally or not, was to deceive his client. This material misstatement of fact exposed both the stockbroker and his employer to potential litigation. Such a financial advisor should not be in the investment business. Similar advice often comes from attorneys and CPAs who, instead of taking the time to ensure that they provide complete and accurate information to their clients concerning investment costs, simply repeat incorrect information spread by others.

§1006. MEMBERS OF THE MEDIA

The great majority of reporters and commentators who cover financial matters are diligent in their efforts to report financial information as accurately as possible. As competent professionals, they take the time to verify their data before reporting it.[13] However, as with any profession, there are a handful of financial reporters and commentators who use data and information for their reports which is incomplete or inaccurate. Like some advisors, they too copy or repeat unsubstantiated data others have reported in the past without verifying its

---

[12] The annual expense ratio is made up of money management fees and 12b-1 fees.

[13] Good examples of such reporting include, "Deciphering Funds' Hidden Costs." *The Wall Street Journal* by John Hechinger. March 17, 2004, page D1 and "Monthly Mutual Funds Review – Fundamentals: Adding Up The Cost of Your Fund – Whether It's A Load, 12b-1 Fees or Expense Ratio, Fees Can Eat Into Returns." *The Wall Street Journal*. By Theo Francis. November 4, 2002.

accuracy. Such reports regularly appear in newspapers and magazines. They are also reported via radio and television. For example, newspaper reports similar to the following appear with some regularity:

When considering an investment in a mutual fund or variable annuity one must keep an eye on costs. The typical stock mutual fund has an annual expense ratio of 1.6% while the annual cost of owning a similar variable annuity can be as much as 2.6%.

The impression left with investors who read such articles is that mutual funds are cheaper to buy and own on an annual basis than are variable annuities. The statement made in the hypothetical newspaper article set out above did exactly what Dan Slick, the dishonest auto dealer did. The reporter compared *all* of the annual costs of owning a variable annuity with *some* of the annual costs of owning a mutual fund. Such reporters are, either negligently or intentionally deceiving the investing public. Inaccurate reporting of this nature usually occurs when a reporter is taking a short cut by repeating something someone else previously reported without bothering to verify or substantiate the prior report. Inaccurate reporting of this nature is becoming a common-place problem. Within the past few years, editors for two of the largest newspapers in the country were forced to resign when it was discovered that their reporters were publishing articles containing unverified and inaccurate information.[14] Recently, a major television network fired one of their top news executives for allowing a news report that was based on unverifiable documentation. Their news anchor was obviously embarrassed by the event and recently announced his retirement.[15]

§1007. THE ANNUAL COST OF MUTUAL FUND OWNERSHIP

As mentioned, a small number of advisors and members of the media cite a mutual fund's annual expense ratio as if it were the *only* cost of owning a mutual fund. Doing so is deceptive. Other costs, such as commissions, taxes and trading costs must be added to the annual expense ratio in order to accurately reflect a mutual fund's *total* annual cost of ownership. For example, a study recently conducted by three university finance professors found that commonly reported annual expense ratios for domestic stock mutual funds nearly *double* when annual trading costs and commissions are taken into consideration.[16] When former SEC attorney, now law professor, Mercer Bullard was asked to comment on this research he stated, "This study demonstrates conclusively what consumer groups have argued for years – fund expense ratios are misleading."[17]

There are many annual costs associated with the ownership of mutual funds. The six

---

[14] The newspapers involved were *The New York Times* (Jayson Blair incident) and *USA Today* (Jack Kelley incident).

[15] Dan Rather of CBS reported a story about President Bush based on unverified documents that led to the firing of several executives of CBS.

[16] This study was commissioned by Zero Alpha Group (www.zeroalphagroup.com) and was reported in *Research*, April 2004, p. 18.

[17] *Id.*

most common costs are:

- Fees paid to the fund's investment managers.
- 12b-1 fees paid to the fund company to cover advertising and marketing expenses.
- Up-front or deferred sales charges paid to those who sell the mutual fund.
- Trading costs incurred by the mutual fund company for buying and selling stock.
- Annual income taxes.
- Miscellaneous costs.

One of the problems with determining mutual fund costs is the fact that many of these costs are taken out of the mutual fund's gain each year by the mutual fund company. The only two expenses that a mutual fund owner will actually pay out of his pocket are up-front A-share mutual fund commissions and annual income taxes owed on the mutual fund. Even this last cost is not actually paid separately, but is included in the total tax liability paid by the fund owner annually to the IRS on *all* of his income. For this reason, it is not surprising that 92% of mutual fund investors admit that they have no idea of what their mutual funds cost each year to own.[18] Even MBA students have trouble figuring out mutual fund costs.[19]

All six of the costs listed above must be considered when attempting to determine the total annual cost of owning a mutual fund. Each of these six costs is discussed fully in the sections that follow.

§1008. THE MUTUAL FUND'S ANNUAL EXPENSE RATIO

As stated above, the most common mutual fund cost is what the mutual fund industry refers to as the fund's annual expense ratio. This expense ratio contains only two of the six costs set out above. The Securities Exchange Commission (SEC) requires that fees paid to those who manage mutual funds be included in the annual expense ratio together with any 12b-1 fees charged by the mutual fund company. 12b-1 fees are charged to mutual fund owners each year to enable mutual fund companies to market and advertise their funds to potential buyers. 12b-1 fees are sometimes used to pay additional annual compensation to the financial professionals who sell a company's mutual funds to compensate them for providing continuing service to fund purchasers. The average annual expense ratio for domestic equity mutual funds sold has been computed by several industry groups, government regulators, scholars and researchers. A summary of these results appears in Table #1 below:

---

[18] See note 164 below.

[19] See note 60 above

TABLE #1: AVERAGE A-SHARE
MUTUAL FUND ANNUAL EXPENSE RATIOS

SOURCE	ANNUAL EXPENSE RATIO
Baer and Gensler[20]	1.61%
Investment Co. Institute[21]	1.52%
Prof. Charles Jones[22]	1.50%
Rutner Data[23]	1.60%
Morningstar[24]	1.60%
Securities Exchange Commission[25]	1.56%

As mentioned above, the major problem with reported annual expense ratios is that they are often cited as if they constitute the *only* annual expense a buyer incurs to own a mutual fund. This is not true. To cite a fund's annual expense ratio as if it were the only cost of mutual fund ownership would be no different than a real estate broker telling a potential home buyer that the only cost of owning a house was the interest charged on the loan obtained to buy the house. Home buyers realize that taxes, insurance and principal re-payments must also be factored in when trying to determine the total annual cost of owning a home. When these costs are included, the real annual cost of owing a home will be significantly higher than just the interest owed on the money borrowed to buy the home. The same is true of owning mutual funds. The cost of such ownership is not just the annual expense ratio but also includes annual income taxes, commissions and trading costs. The real cost of owning a mutual fund can be three or four times the annual expense ratio that is so often quoted to mutual fund purchasers. It is important for the investing public to have access to accurate information regarding all of the annual costs associated with owning a mutual fund. The average expense ratio for the A-share mutual fund is approximately 1.3%. Typical 12b-1 fees for A-share mutual funds are 0.25%. This yields an average annual expense ratio of 1.55% which is used in this book. This figure also reflects the findings set out in Table #1 above. The following sections discuss the additional costs of owning mutual funds not included in a fund's annual expense ratio.

§1009. MUTUAL FUND LOADS AND COMMISSIONS

The cost of owning a mutual fund frequently overlooks sales loads, charges or commissions. John Bogle, in his book, *Bogle on Mutual Funds*, found that "with the exception of *Consumer Reports*, the press ignores the impact of sales loads on [mutual fund] returns.

---

[20] Baer and Gensler, p. 102.

[21] The president of the Investment Company Institute, a mutual fund trade organization, provided this annual expense ratio to the House Committee on Commerce on September 29, 1998.

[22] Jones, p. 32. See also *The Wall Street Journal*, April 7, 2003, p. R33.

[23] *The Trouble with Mutual Funds*. Richard Rutner. Elton-Wolf Pub. (2002), page 58.

[24] *NAVA Outlook*, Nov/Dec 2005, p.6. See note 130 below.

[25] "Funds Should Reveal After-Tax Returns, SEC Says." Dan Culloton (Morningstar) 2000. www.morningstar.com.

As a result, the returns on funds that carry loads are overstated."[26] The plain truth is that financial professionals who sell actively managed mutual funds receive fees, commissions or sales loads for their services (Because all of these terms are essentially synonymous, the term commission will be used in this report). Mutual fund commissions are varied. The most common commissions imposed on mutual fund purchases are A-share, B-share and C-share commissions. A complete coverage of the differences between these commission structures and others cannot be accomplished in a short book and no such attempt will be made here. The basic characteristics of the major types of mutual fund commissions are briefly discussed here so that potential mutual fund purchasers can properly account for these commissions when trying to determine the *total* annual cost of purchasing a mutual fund.

The A-share mutual fund commission is an up-front commission that, for the typical mutual fund investor, runs between 4% and 5½% depending on the amount invested in the fund.[27] Break points or commission discounts are available for purchases of mutual funds in larger amounts. This commission is imposed on the full value of the mutual fund purchase and is paid out of the pocket of the purchaser. For example, a 4% commission on a $30,000 mutual fund purchase would result in $28,800 being invested in the mutual fund and $1,200 being paid as an up-front, out-of-pocket commission to the financial professional selling the fund. As a general rule, when an A-share mutual fund is sold by the owner, no further commissions are imposed.[28] Additionally, sales and purchases taking place within the same fund family do not result in new commissions although an income tax liability may result from such transactions if they occur in a taxable account. In addition to charging an up-front, out-of-pocket commission, A-share mutual funds charge annual ownership fees. The annual ownership fee charged for owning a mutual fund is expressed in terms of a percent of a mutual fund's year-end net value and is referred to as an annual expense ratio. As mentioned earlier, the annual expense ratio for an A-share mutual fund will usually range from 1.5% to 1.6%, including 12b-1 fees.[29]

The B-share commission does not require a mutual fund purchaser to pay an up-front commission out of his pocket. For example, if $30,000 is invested in a B-share mutual fund, the purchaser's entire $30,000 is invested in his mutual fund unreduced by any commission. When a B-share mutual fund is sold by a financial professional, the mutual fund company will prepay or advance to that professional a commission as compensation for selling the mutual fund. This commission typically ranges from 4% to 5½% on average.[30] When a B-share commission is chosen by a mutual fund purchaser, the annual expense ratio for the fund's A-shares is usually

---

[26] *Bogle on Mutual Funds.* John Bogle. Irwin Pub. (1994), page 161.

[27] Technically, this cost can be as little as zero or as large as 8½%.

[28] Income taxes may be imposed if the funds are held in taxable accounts.

[29] Mutual fund companies deduct costs quarterly. For ease of math, they will be deducted annually in this report.

[30] See note 84 above. This assumes an up-front commission is requested in lieu of a trailing commission.

increased by approximately 0.80% so that the mutual fund company can, over time, recoup the commission it advanced to the financial professional who sold the fund.[31] Most of this increase is in 12b-1 fees. As mentioned above, the typical annual expense ratio for an A-share equity mutual fund will be in the range of 1.5% to 1.6%. Thus the annual expense ratio for a B-share mutual fund will be approximately 0.80% more or in the range of 2.3% to 2.4%. In addition to paying an increased annual expense ratio, B-share mutual funds impose what is technically referred to as contingent deferred sales charges (CDSC).[32] With a CDSC, if a B-share mutual fund is redeemed (i.e., sold) by the owner within a certain period of time, usually about six years, the fund owner will be required to reimburse the mutual fund company for some or all of the commission the company advanced at the time the fund was purchased. CDSCs are designed so they decline over a period of time. For example, if a B-share mutual fund with a six-year CDSC is sold by its owner within the first year of ownership, the mutual fund company would keep 6% of the fund's purchase price which would be deducted from the sales proceeds. If the same fund is sold in the second year of ownership, there would be a 5% CDSC based on the fund's purchase price that would be deducted from the sale proceeds, and so on. If the B-share mutual fund is held for the requisite time period of six years the CDSC disappears and no sales charge is imposed when the fund is sold by the owner after that point. In short, CDSCs are imposed to help offset the initial commission advanced by the mutual fund company to the financial professional who sells the mutual fund if the owner of the fund sells the fund involved before the expiration of the holding period reflected in the CDSC. Briefly stated, the combination of an increased annual expense ratio and a CDSC is designed to ensure that the mutual fund company recoups the commission it advances to the financial professionals who sell their mutual funds. If a fund owner holds his fund for several years the CSDC will disappear while the increased annual expense ratio will help the fund company recoup any advanced commissions it paid out. If a mutual fund owner sells his fund early on, the mutual fund company will not receive much in the way of an increased annual expense ratio but will recoup advanced commissions via their CDSC. In summary, the money received by a mutual fund company from increasing its annual expense ratio will ensure that between the two they recover any commissions they advance to those who sell their mutual funds. The approximate 0.80% increase in the annual expense ratio for a B-share mutual fund purchase mentioned above is usually temporary. When the CDSC holding period expires (or after an eight year period) the annual expense ratio of a B-share mutual fund is usually reduced from the higher B- share level to the normal (and lower) A-share annual expense ratio for the

---

[31] Jones, p 75. There are a few mutual funds that charge a fixed back-end load of 5% of the contract's purchase price or account value. These back-end loads do not decline like the CDSC imposed by B-share mutual funds.

[32] CDSCs should not be confused with a rarely used commission structure called a back-end load. With a back-end load, a flat commission equal to an A-share commission is charged on the original investment amount when the fund is *sold*. This commission does *not* decline over time.

mutual fund. For example, Judy invested $30,000 in a B-share mutual fund. The fund had a six-year holding or surrender period. The fund's annual expense ratio for its A-share fund is 1.55%. Because this is a B-share fund purchase, it will be assumed that the annual expense ratio will be increased for the first six years of ownership by 0.80% to 2.35%. After six years, if the fund is still owned, the 2.35% annual expense ratio for the B-share mutual fund will drop to the A-share level of 1.55%. For the reasons stated above, this book will use an annual expense ratio of 2.35% for B-share mutual funds. This figure includes 12b-1 fees.

C-share mutual funds have annual expense ratios that are approximately 0.8% higher than the A-share class for the same mutual fund.[33] Most of this increase is in 12b-1 fees. When a C-share mutual fund is first purchased, the selling professional typically receives a 1% commission from the issuing mutual fund company. For each year, after the first, the selling professional will receive an additional 1% annual commission. Such commissions are called trailing commissions. When the mutual fund is sold by the fund owner, trailing commissions stop. Unlike B-share mutual funds, which convert to A-shares after a period of time, C-share mutual funds never convert to a less expensive share class. A few C-share mutual funds also impose a small up-front, out-of-pocket commission of approximately 1%. Nearly all C-share mutual funds impose a contingent deferred sales charge (CDSC) for the initial year or year and a half of the fund's ownership. This book will use an annual expense ratio for C-share mutual funds of 2.35%.

§1010. ANNUALIZATION OF MUTUAL FUND COMMISSIONS

For the purpose of approximating the total *annual* cost of a mutual fund purchase, any *out-of-pocket* commission paid by a fund purchaser must be factored in to the fund's total cost on an *annualized* basis. For example, if a mutual fund charges a 5% commission it would not be fair or accurate to treat this entire 5% as a cost of ownership in the first year. This commission should be spread over the entire period of time the mutual fund is going to be held. For A-share mutual funds, this calculation is easy. An investor need only divide his A-share commission by the number of years he believes he will hold the mutual fund. For example, an A-share commission of 5% for a fund that will be held for five years will result in an *annualized* commission of 1%. Mutual fund purchasers must be realistic in estimating how long they plan to hold their mutual fund purchases. They should review how long they have held previous mutual fund purchases when trying to determine how long they might hold a new mutual fund purchase. Many mutual fund purchasers are overly optimistic. Statistics show that the *average* period of time that a mutual fund is held is about three years.[34] The average A-share mutual fund commission is 4.1%.[35] This would indicate an average annualized A-share commission of slightly more than

---

[33] C-share mutual funds will have annual expense ratios in the range of 2.35%.

[34] Baer and Gensler, p. 101.

[35] *Id.*

1.36%.[36] This book will assume a more conservative 1% annualized commission rate for the mutual funds discussed herein. Financial advisors who charge fees to manage mutual funds for clients usually charge 1% for their services each year rather than accept commissions. Where such advisors are discussed this 1% figure will be used.

For B- and C-share mutual funds, the purchaser is *not* charged a commission that is paid *out of his pocket* at the time of purchase. For this reason, the buyer of a B- or C-share mutual fund should reflect their annualized commission cost as zero. (Remember, a few C-share mutual funds do charge a small up-front, out-of-pocket commission). As mentioned above, the annual expense ratio for B- and C-share mutual funds is increased in order to recoup the commission advanced by the mutual fund company to compensate the financial professionals who sell their mutual funds. For example, if a mutual fund would normally have a 1.55% A-share annual expense ratio but a B- or C-share commission is chosen, the increased annual expense ratio of approximately 2.35% should be included as part of the calculation to determine the total annual ownership cost of the mutual fund. This latter figure is used in the comparisons made in this book.

§1011. MUTUAL FUND TRADING COSTS

Mutual funds are in the business of trying to make a profit for their investors by buying and selling stock. Like all buyers and sellers of stock, mutual fund companies must pay brokerage commissions to the stock brokerage firms with whom they do business. These trading costs are ultimately paid by the owners of the mutual fund. Currently, the SEC does not require that a mutual fund company's trading costs be disclosed to fund investors. However, Congress may change this rule in the near future. An investor can only find information about the trading costs incurred by his mutual fund company (and passed on to him) by contacting the SEC or obtaining a *supplemental* prospectus for his mutual fund.[37] Trading costs have not changed significantly in the past ten years.[38] The annual trading costs for the typical actively managed stock mutual fund has been determined by many researchers. A summary of these findings appears in Table #2 below:

---

[36] Although this report annualizes A- share commissions so they are spread over a mutual fund's holding period, it should be remembered that A- share commissions reduce any mutual fund investment by the amount of the commission as of the date of purchase. This front-end loading of an A- share mutual fund has the effect of reducing its overall gain vis-a-vis spreading out the commission over the assumed holding period.

[37] Mutual fund companies do not generally like to provide supplemental prospectuses [technically called a Statement of Additional Information (SAI)]. No one should invest in a mutual fund without reading this material as it pertains to costs of mutual fund ownership.

[38] Finding by the Plexus Group. See *Better Investing*, July 2001, page 29. "Mutual Fund Matters," by Amy Crane, www.geocities.com.

TABLE #2: MUTUAL FUND TRADING COSTS

SOURCE	TRADING COST
Lipper Analytical[39]	0.41%
Baer and Gensler Study[40]	½% to 1%
Bogle Research[41]	0.70%
Rutner Data[42]	0.70%
Chambers-Edeley-Kadlec Study[43]	.59% - .78%
Prof. Charles Jones[44]	1.4% - 1.6%
Plexus Group[45]	1%

The table above indicates that trading costs for mutual funds can easily approach 1%. The comparisons in this book will use a much more conservative trading cost figure of 0.7%.

§1012. ANNUAL MUTUAL FUND INCOME TAXES

One of the most frequently overlooked expenses of mutual fund ownership is the annual income tax that must be paid each year to the IRS by mutual fund owners. The *total* cost of *any* investment must always include that investment's annual income tax liability. The SEC has determined that "taxes can be the most significant cost of investing in mutual funds."[46] An investor who owns and rents out warehouses must include as a cost of ownership the annual property and income taxes he must pay on his warehouses activities. One who owns a trucking company must include, in addition to property taxes, annual road use and income taxes as a cost of operation. So too must a mutual fund investor take into consideration, as part of the cost of owning his fund, the income taxes he must pay each year for owning his funds.

Mutual funds, unlike any other investment, can generate annual income taxes even if the fund owner does not initiate any activity in his mutual fund. Worse yet, even if the mutual fund's value is unchanged or has gone down in value in a given year, the fund can still generate an annual income tax liability. During the 2000-2002 bear market the investing public became painfully aware of this detrimental tax feature that is unique to mutual funds. During this three-year period, mutual fund investors were saddled with sizeable losses while at the same time having to pay income taxes on the funds generating these losses.

Over the past several years, many scholars, government regulators and research groups have determined the average annual income tax liability (i.e., gain lost to income taxes) arising

---

[39] "Deciphering Funds' Hidden Costs." *The Wall Street Journal* by John Hechinger. March 17, 2004, page D1.

[40] Baer and Gensler, p. 104.

[41] *Kiplinger's Retirement Report*. January 2002, page 1 and www.Windsorwealth.com/Mutual Fund Pros and Cons.

[42] *The Trouble With Mutual Funds* by Richard Rutner. 2002 Elton-Wolf Pub.

[43] *Mutual Fund Trading Costs*. Wharton School (University of PA). By Chamber, Edelen and Kadlec (1999).

[44] Jones, p. 126.

[45] *Better Investing*. July 2001, page 29.

[46] Paul Royce, Director of the SEC's Investment Management Division. SEC.gov/news/mfaftert/htm. January 19, 2001.

from mutual fund ownership. Table #3 summarizes these findings:

TABLE #3: AVERAGE ANNUAL INCOME TAX LIABILITY FOR EQUITY BASED MUTUAL FUNDS (GAIN LOST TO FEDERAL INCOME TAXES)

SOURCE	ANNUAL INCOME TAX LIABILITY
Securities Exchange Commission[47]	2.50%
The Wall Street Journal[48]	2.60%
Baer and Gensler[49]	2.50%
Vanguard Research[50]	2.50%
Industry Publications[51]	2.50%
Baldwin Data[52]	2.50%
Jones Data[53]	2.50%
Morningstar[54]	2.65%

A common shortcoming of the studies set out in Table #3 above is that they were calculated based on marginal income tax rates and long-term capital gains rates that were in effect over the past several years. The problem with this is that both marginal income tax rates and long-term capital gains rates have declined over the past few years. To obtain a more accurate estimate of the annual income tax loss incurred by equity mutual fund owners, these tax reductions must be taken into consideration.

From 1998 through 2005, the average marginal tax rate was 27.28%.[55] For 2006 and 2007, the average marginal tax rate was 24.33%.[56] This would indicate that marginal tax rates have dropped, on average, 10.8% over the past nine years.[57] From 1998 through 2005, the average long-term capital gains tax rate was 18.34%.[58] For 2006 and 2007 this rate was 15%. This indicates that long-term capital gains tax rates have dropped, on average, 18.2% in the past nine years.[59] The difference in average marginal tax rates and long-term capital gains rates over

---

[47] www.sec.gov (KPMG-Peat Marwick Study). Quote from *Investors Business Daily* regarding a statement by Arthur Levitt, former SEC Chairman pointing out that the annual income tax liability of mutual funds, although averaging 2.5%, could be as high as 5.6%. March 27, 2001, p. 131.

[48] August 25, 2002, p. R-1.

[49] Baer and Gensler, p. 108.

[50] Joel Dickson Study done for the Vanguard Group. Also see Jones, p. 134.

[51] For example: *On Wall Street*, May 2002, p. 86, *Senior Market Advisor*, Sept. 2001, p. 88 and *Better Investing*, July 2001, p. 5.

[52] "Life Insurance in Retirement Planning." Ben Baldwin. *Retirement Planning.* December 2002, pages 5-8.

[53] Jones, p. 134.

[54] *Better Investing.* July 2001, page 25.

[55] 29.92% (1998-2000); 29.56% (2001); 25.93% (2002); 24.33% (2003-2005). 218.24 ÷ 8 = 27.28%.

[56] 35% + 33% + 25% + 15% + 10% = 146 ÷ 6 = 24.33%.

[57] 27.28% - 10.8% = 24.33%.

[58] 20% (1998-2002); 20% (1/1/03 - 5/6/03); 15% (5/7/03 - 12/31/03); 15% (2004-2005). 146.726 ÷ 8 = 18.34%.

[59] 18.34% reduced by 18.2% = 15%.

the past nine year period has been 14.5%.[60] If this difference is used to reduce the historical consensus average annual income tax loss of 2.5% incurred by equity mutual fund owners, this 2.5% tax loss figure drops to 2.14%.[61]

Several of the country's leading researchers who have studied the impact of income taxes on mutual fund ownership put the current average annual income tax loss at 2.0% of a fund's annual gain. Tom Roseen, a senior research analyst with Lipper, Inc., recently authored a detailed study of the reduction in annual mutual fund gains resulting from federal income taxation.[62] His current research demonstrates that federal income taxes, on average, reduce mutual fund gains by 2.0% or more.[63] Joel Dickson, who heads Vanguard's Active Quantitative Equity Group, agrees that the current annual federal income tax loss on gains generated by the typical equity mutual fund is approximately 2.0%, as does Robert Arnott, who is the Chairman of Research Affiliates, L.L.C. and the past editor of *Financial Analysts Journal*.[64]

A quick and easy way to determine how much of one's mutual fund gain is lost to federal income taxes for a given year is to divide the fund's gain (in dollars) into the amount sent to the IRS for taxes generated by the mutual fund's distribution. (This later data can be obtained from 1099s and tax returns for the year in question).

Example

Donna owns a mutual fund. Last year the fund increased in value by 10% from $26,000 to $28,600 for a gain of $2,600. The fund's distribution required Donna to pay $730 in long- and short-term capital gains taxes. From this data Donna was able to determine that the percentage of her mutual fund gain that was lost to federal income taxes was 2.8%.[65] (This calculation should be done for more than one year so the results can be averaged. Doing so provides a better estimate of the annual income tax burden a mutual fund owner will incur).

A recent article in *The Wall Street Journal* discussed an actual case similar to the above hypothetical example involving Donna. In the *Journal* article, the owner of $30,000 worth of Fidelity's Magellan mutual fund was required to pay $900 to the IRS based on the fund's recent distribution. Even if this fund had increased by 10% year-to-date (which it didn't), the fund's owner incurred a 30% federal income tax liability. In other words, this 30% tax would equate to a 3% federal income tax loss on the owner's fund gain *if* it returned 10%.[66]

There are other ways to estimate the annual income tax liability of owning a mutual fund. For example, *Investors Business Daily (IBD)* reports the five-year total, *after-tax* returns

---

[60] 18.2% + 10.8% = 29% ÷ 2 = 14.5%.

[61] 2.5% reduced by 14.5% = 2.1375%.

[62] "Taxes In The Mutual Fund Industry – 2006 – Assessing The Impact of Taxes on Shareholders' Returns"

[63] "Taxes In The Mutual Fund Industry – 2006 – Assessing The Impact of Taxes on Shareholders' Returns"

[64] Telephone interviews with Joel Dickson and Robert Arnott by the author in May of 2006.

[65] $730 ÷ $2,600 = 28%. A 28% tax loss on a 10% annual return equates to a 2.8% tax loss on the 10% gain.

[66] "Magellan Investors Are Biting The Tax Bullet," by Jennifer Levitz. *The Wall Street Journal*. May 10, 2006, page C1.

for mutual funds each week in its Monday edition. *USA Today* reports the five-year total, *pre-tax* returns for mutual funds on the first Monday of each month. By comparing these reports, investors can easily estimate the average, annual federal income tax liability one incurs by owning a specific fund. For example, *Investors Business Daily* recently reported that the five-year total, *after-tax* gain for Janus Small Cap Value (A-share) Mutual Fund was 39%.[67] On the same day, *USA Today* reported the five-year total, *pre-tax* return for this fund to be 52%.[68] On an *annual* basis, the pre-tax return for this fund was 10.4% and the after-tax return was 7.8%. This would indicate that, over a five year period, income taxes reduced this fund's gross annual return by 25%. In calculating such a fund's after-tax return, this 25% income tax loss would have to be considered. This data would suggest that the owner of Janus Small Cap Value Fund, over the last five years, lost 2.6% of his 10.4% annual gain to federal income taxes. The annual income tax liability for specific mutual funds can also be obtained from web sites such as www.personalfund.com.

The discussion set out above relating to income tax losses resulting from mutual fund ownership includes only *federal* income taxes. State and local taxes are ignored even though 43 states and several municipalities impose an income tax on mutual fund gains. If an investor lives in a state or city that imposes an income tax on mutual funds, these taxes will increase the annual income tax cost of owning a mutual fund to a larger amount than was determined above. This book ignores annual state or municipal income taxes that might be imposed on mutual fund owners.

Mutual fund investors who are subject to the alternative minimum tax (AMT) pay an effective income tax rate of 21.5% rather than the 15% long-term capital gains tax rates available to those who are not subject to the AMT.[69] In short, the AMT will increase the effective annual income tax burden of owning a mutual fund to a figure greater than that which was determined above.

It should be remembered that the income tax liability incurred by mutual fund owners over the last five years was somewhat mitigated by tax-loss carry forwards that mutual fund companies stockpiled during the last bear market. However, these tax-loss carry forwards have all but disappeared. This has resulted in higher annual income tax burdens for those who own mutual funds.

 Mutual fund distributions can result in forcing a taxpayer to phase out or reduce certain exemptions, deductions and credits. For example, if a $20,000 mutual fund distribution results in the loss of $4,800 in exemptions, deductions or credits and this in turn increases a taxpayer's

---

[67] *Investor Business Daily*, August 7, 2006, p. A11.

[68] *U.S.A. Today*, August 7, 2006, p. 7B.

[69] "Special Tax Cost Investors Tax Breaks, Report Shows" by David Cay Jolinson, *New York Times*, May 10, 2006.

income taxes by $1,200, the effective income tax burden generated by the mutual fund will be 6.0% ($1,200 ÷ $20,000) higher than the tax liability that the mutual fund would normally generate.

It should be remembered that under current tax law, long-term capital gains rates are scheduled to increase to 20% after December 31, 2010. The Democrats have indicated they will raise this rate to a higher amount if they win the 2008 elections. This book uses a 2.0% average annual income tax loss for equity mutual funds because this figure is a consensus figure currently used by experts and is lower than the long-term capital gains rate was in the past.

§1013. MISCELLANEOUS MUTUAL FUND COSTS

Mutual fund companies sometimes impose miscellaneous expenses like administration, maintenance and redemption fees. These fees can range from twenty to forty dollars a year and up. These miscellaneous costs are usually disclosed in the prospectus and can increase the annual cost of owning a mutual fund. Mutual fund purchasers should determine whether the mutual fund they are considering for purchase imposes any of these miscellaneous costs. This book assumes *none* of these expenses or costs exist for any mutual fund examples discussed.

§1014. SUMMARY OF ANNUAL MUTUAL FUND OWNERSHIP COSTS

From the sources discussed above it can be determined that the total annual cost of owning the average, actively managed, taxable, equity mutual fund is *conservatively*, in the range of 5.25%. The costs that comprise this figure are:

- Annual expense and 12b-1 fees   1.55%
- Commissions/fees   1.00%
- Trading costs   0.70%
- Owner's annual income tax liability   2.00%
- Total   5.25%

Similar B- and C-share mutual funds will have total annual ownership costs that are in the same range as the A-share mutual fund.[70]

It is interesting to note that the SEC on its website (www.sec.gov) where they discuss their mutual fund cost calculator, indicate that the annual costs associated with mutual fund ownership is 4.2% *before* commissions. Their cost calculator annualizes commissions. Therefore, if a 5% commission is annualized for five years, that 1% average figure would have to be added to the other costs of 4.2%. This would yield a *total* annual ownership cost of 5.2% for the typical mutual fund. This is the same figure experts have calculated for the annual ownership cost of a typical mutual fund.

§1015. THE ANNUAL COST OF VARIABLE ANNUITY OWNERSHIP

Like mutual funds, the total annual cost of owning a variable annuity is made up of

---

[70] See note 135 below. With B- and C-share mutual funds the up-front, out-of-pocket commission cost is zero, but the annual expense ratio increases by an amount that is just about equal to the commission cost that is saved.

several fees, charges, etc. Commonly, these expenses are combined into one or two expense figures to comprise an annual ownership figure for a variable annuity.

The six major components of the total annual cost of owning a variable annuity are:

•Fees paid to the variable annuity's investment managers.

•12b-1 and administrative fees.

•Contingent Deferred Sales Charges.

•Mortality and expense fees (M&E).

•Trading costs incurred by the variable annuity issuer for buying and selling investments.

•Miscellaneous expenses.

Because all of the annual costs of owning a variable annuity are taken from a variable annuity owner's account each year by the issuers of the variable annuity, it is often difficult for a variable annuity owner to fully understand what he or she is paying each year to own their annuity. For this reason, it is important for variable annuity investors to understand *all* of the annual costs associated with owning their annuities. Each of these costs is discussed below.

§1016. INVESTMENT MANAGEMENT FEES

Just like mutual funds, variable annuity companies hire investment managers to invest assets in mutual fund-like investments held in their variable annuities. These investments are technically called sub-accounts. The annual cost that variable annuity owners pay for the services of the investment managers hired by variable annuity companies to manage their sub-accounts is approximately 1.0% for the average, domestic equity based variable annuity according to *Morningstar*.[71] This figure is often 50 to 60 basis points (0.5% to 0.6%) less than similar investment management fees charged by similar mutual fund companies.[72] The reason for this difference is that many of the administrative tasks carried out by variable annuity issuers can be accomplished at a cost that is lower than can be obtained by mutual fund companies. The 1.0% variable annuity investment management cost discussed above is increased to 1.15% in the comparisons conducted in this book. This larger management fee reflects the slightly higher cost associated with equity based variable annuities.

§1017. MORTALITY AND OTHER FEES

Variable annuity issuers impose a charge to cover the cost of providing a death benefit to the purchasers of their variable annuities. This expense is commonly referred to as a mortality cost or M&E fee and averages 1.2% a year for an average equity variable annuity. Approximately 0.20% of this 1.2% charge pays for providing a death benefit made available by most variable

---

[71] *NAVA Outlook*, Nov/Dec 2005, p. 6.

[72] Morningstar has recently calculated the annual expense ratio of the average mutual fund to be 1.67%. Similar fees charged to a variable annuity owner is usually about 1%. See *Investment News* article "Fund Fees Baffle MBA Students" by David Hoffman, April 24, 2006.

annuity issuers. The remainder covers profits and other expenses. When the owner of a variable annuity dies, his beneficiaries are guaranteed to receive 100% of all net investments made in the variable annuity or the account value, whichever is higher. For example, assume an investor purchased a variable annuity for $100,000 in 2000 and watched it drop in value to $60,000 by late 2002 and then died shortly thereafter. Because of the variable annuity's insurance benefit, the investor's beneficiaries would receive $100,000 from the variable annuity company. Had the investor's variable annuity been worth $150,000 at the time of death, his beneficiaries would have received this larger amount. Mutual fund companies do not charge for or provide similar insurance protection. Beneficiaries of mutual funds receive only the actual account value of the mutual fund when the owner dies. This figure can be larger or smaller than the total net amount invested in the mutual fund. In addition to M&E expenses, variable annuities charge administrative and distribution fees that typically amount to 0.15%.[73] The total charges to cover mortality expenses (1.2%) together with administrative and distribution costs (0.15%) amount to 1.35%.[74] This is the figure that will be used in the comparisons made in this book.

§1018. VARIABLE ANNUITY COMMISSIONS

The overwhelming majority of variable annuity companies do *not* charge an up-front, out-of-pocket commission when an investor purchases one of their annuities. When a variable annuity is initially purchased, the issuing company will pre-pay or advance to the financial professional selling the variable annuity a commission typically ranging from 5% to 6½% of the variable annuity's selling price. Much like B-share mutual funds, variable annuities usually include in their total annual cost of ownership an amount that will, over time, help the variable annuity company recoup the commissions they advance to the sellers of their annuities. In addition to including the cost of advanced commissions in its annual expense charge, variable annuity companies also impose contingent deferred sales charges (CDSC). This is a charge imposed on the variable annuity owner if he or she sells their variable annuity within a certain period of time after its initial purchase. This period, called a holding or surrender period, is usually three to ten years with the average being six to seven years. Over this period, the CDSC usually decreases by a stated amount each year until it disappears. For example, Jim purchased a variable annuity for $30,000. He was not charged an up-front, out-of-pocket commission for this purchase. However, Jim's annual cost of owning his variable annuity *includes* an amount designed to offset the commission advanced by the variable annuity company to the financial professional who sold Jim his annuity. Jim's variable annuity also has a six-year holding period during which he will be charged a CDSC, or early surrender fee, if he sells his variable annuity before the six-year surrender period expires. Assuming Jim sells his variable annuity in the

---

[73] *NAVA Outlook*, Nov/Dec 2005, p. 6.
[74] *NAVA Outlook*, Nov/Dec 2005, p. 6.

first year of ownership, he will pay a 6% CDSC based on his initial investment to the issuing company when it is surrendered. If the sale occurs in the second year, the CDSC will be 5%, and so on. If Jim holds his variable annuity for more than six years, the CDSC is reduced to zero. CDSCs for complete surrenders are usually imposed on the initial amount invested although some variable annuity issuers impose their surrender charges on the ending account value. For partial withdrawals, the surrender fee is usually imposed on the amount withdrawn. An investor contemplating a variable annuity purchase may want to ask about how CDSC's are imposed. If a variable annuity owner holds his annuity long enough for the CDSC to disappear, the annual cost of owning the variable annuity will allow the annuity company to recoup the commission they advanced to the financial professional who sold their annuity. If a variable annuity owner sells his variable annuity early on, the variable annuity company will not receive much in the way of annual expense charges, but will recoup advanced commissions via their CDSC. In short, the money received by a variable annuity company from annual expenses and imposition of a CDSC will ensure that, between the two, the variable annuity company will recover the commissions it advances to the financial professionals who sell their annuities. This commission structure is very similar to that of the B-share mutual fund discussed above. It is important to remember that variable annuity purchasers do not have to pay an up-front, out-of-pocket commission to the financial professional who helps them purchase their variable annuity. This cost is *included* in the annual expenses charged to own a variable annuity. These expenses were outlined earlier in this report. For this reason, the up-front, out-of-pocket commission for purchasing a variable annuity, like that of a B-share or C-share mutual fund is zero. Instead, the annual expense of owning the variable annuity (just as with the mutual fund) is increased by the issuing company so as to allow it to recover the cost of advancing a commission to the sellers of its variable annuities. The variable annuity commission structure is different from the B-share mutual fund commission structure in three respects. First, annual withdrawals of 10%-15% of a variable annuity's value are generally allowed without being subject to surrender (CDSC) fees. Mutual funds do not offer this benefit. Second, once the holding period for a variable annuity expires, the annual ownership expense is not always reduced like the annual expense ratio of a B-share mutual fund although some variable annuity issuers do reduce the annual expense after the holding period expires. Finally, all CDSCs are voided at a variable annuity owner's death. At the death of a B-share mutual fund owner, CDSC still apply and are charged to beneficiaries of the fund when it is sold.

§1019. VARIABLE ANNUITY TRADING COSTS

Trading costs are the commissions paid by variable annuity money managers to buy and sell investments. Few in-depth, detailed studies specifically dealing with the trading costs of variable annuities have been done. However, trading costs incurred by variable annuity sub-account managers can be obtained by reviewing current data regarding mutual fund turnover ratios. A mutual fund's turnover ratio is a good measure of how frequently the mutual fund company turns over its entire portfolio. Variable annuity sub-account managers buy investments for their sub-accounts in essentially the same manner as mutual fund managers buy investments for their mutual funds. Even if the improper use of "soft money" by mutual fund companies is ignored, there is no data available that would suggest that the commissions paid by large institutional buyers like variable annuity and mutual fund companies would differ. In fact, common sense would dictate that competition by brokerage firms for institutional business would result in both relatively low and essentially identical commission rate structures. What does differ is the *amount* of trading mutual fund companies do in comparison with that of variable annuity companies. There is substantial data evidencing that variable annuity sub-account managers trade *less* than mutual fund managers. The average turnover ratio for equity mutual funds is 118.[75] The average turnover for the typical variable annuity is 84.[76] This indicates that the turnover for variable annuities is 28.8% less than the turnover for mutual funds and would therefore indicate that the average trading cost for variable annuities would be 28.8% less than that of mutual funds. Table #2 above demonstrated that mutual funds have trading costs that range from 0.41% to 1.6% or approximately 1% on average. Based on this data, it can be determined that the trading costs for the average variable annuity would be 28.8% less than this 1%, or approximately 0.712%. One reason for the higher trading costs for mutual funds is the fact that mutual fund companies engage in year-end selling called "window dressing". This selling activity is designed to sell off losing positions to offset the capital gains distributions that must be sent to mutual fund owners for tax purposes. Because variable annuities do not have year-end capital gain distributions that they must attempt to offset by selling losing investments, their selling activity is slightly less than it is for mutual funds on an annual basis. Variable annuity issuers, like mutual fund companies, report trading cost separately in a supplemental prospectus that is also called a statement of additional information or SAI. This cost must be added to the other costs of a variable annuity in order to obtain a total annual ownership cost. Earlier it was stated that the trading costs for mutual funds would be set at 0.7% for the comparisons made in this book. This will result in trading costs for variable annuities to be set at 0.5%, which is approximately 28.8% less than 0.7%.

§1020. MISCELLANEOUS EXPENSES

Variable annuity companies, like mutual fund companies, sometimes impose miscellaneous expenses and fees. For example, some variable annuity companies charge

---

[75] The average stock mutual fund has a turnover ratio of 118. *The Educated Investor* (Winter 2001), page 2 (118%); William Harding (Morningstar) bankrate.com 2002 (130%); Special Report by Stan Luxenberg (118%) wealth.bloomberg.com. *As Turnover Skyrockets, Investor's Costs Take Off* by Amy Crane citing a 118.6% turnover ratio. Bogle Financial Markets Research Center (118%). A turnover ratio of 118 indicates a mutual fund is turning over its entire portfolio in ten month cycles.

[76] *Morningstar Principia*, Research provided by Annette Larson of Morningstar.

anywhere from twenty to forty dollars as an annual maintenance or contract fee. As a general rule, this fee is not normally charged on larger variable annuity purchases. Even with smaller variable annuity purchases, such fees are minimal. A $20 contract fee charged on a $20,000 variable annuity purchase amounts to an additional annual cost of 0.1%. Whenever a variable annuity is purchased, this fee, and others, should be factored in as a part of the total annual cost of owning the variable annuity. It should be remembered that mutual fund companies also impose similar administrative fees. As was done for mutual funds, this book will assume no such miscellaneous fees exist for any variable annuities discussed in this book.

§1021. SUMMARY OF ANNUAL VARIABLE ANNUITY OWNERSHIP COSTS

From the information discussed above it can be determined that the total annual cost of owning the average, actively managed, domestic equity based variable annuity can reach 3.00%. The costs that comprise this figure are:

- Investment management and 12b-1 fees   1.15%
- Mortality and expense (M&E) fees   1.20%
- Administrative/distribution fees   0.15%
- Trading costs   <u>0.50%</u>
- Total   3.00%

When comparing variable annuities and mutual funds, an investor must ensure that all annual costs imposed to own either of these investments are included in any cost comparison analysis conducted for these two investments. The next section summarizes all of the cost data discussed earlier.

§1022. TOTAL ANNUAL MUTUAL FUND AND VARIABLE ANNUITY COSTS

The cost data discussed in prior sections is summarized in Table #4 below:

TABLE #4: TOTAL *ANNUAL* COST OF OWNING A
NON-QUALIFIED, EQUITY BASED MUTUAL FUND AND VARIABLE ANNUITY

COST FACTOR	A-SHARE MUTUAL FUND	B-SHARE MUTUAL FUND	C-SHARE MUTUAL FUND	VARIABLE ANNUITY
Money Mgmt. & 12b-1 Fees[77]	1.55%	2.35%	2.35%	1.15%
Mortality and Other Fees[78]	0	0	0	1.35%
Out-of-Pocket Commissions[79]	1.00%	-0-	-0-	-0-
Income Taxes Paid By Owner[80]	2.00%	2.00%	2.00%	-0-
Trading Costs[81]	0.70%	0.70%	0.70%	0.50%
Misc. Expenses[82]	0.00%	0.00%	0.00%	0.00%
TOTAL	5.25%	5.05%	5.05%	3.00%

Table #4 appears to show the total annual cost of an A-share mutual fund to be greater than for a B- or C-share mutual fund. It should be remembered that for *estimation* purposes only, the A-share mutual fund shows an annual commission of 1%. In reality, A-share mutual fund commissions are deducted in full at the time of purchase and are not imposed annually. For this reason, the A-share mutual fund, after it is purchased, would have an approximate annual cost of about 1% *less* than a B- or C-share mutual fund. However, it should be remembered that the amount actually invested for the purchaser of an A-share mutual fund will be less than the amount invested if a B- or C-share mutual fund is purchased. All of the calculations in this book that deal with A-share mutual funds impose any commissions at time of sale and do *not* include them later as annual expenses. This reflects what actually occurs when one buys a mutual fund.

---

[77] The annual expense ratio for the A- share fund was set at 1.55% which reflects a typical annual expense ratio for A-share domestic stock mutual funds. 0.80% basis points was added to the annual expense ratio for the B-share and 0.80% to the C-share. The C-share mutual fund has a one-year CDSC. The B-share fund has a six-year CDSC holding period. The variable annuity's annual expense (M&E and other expenses) was set at 2.5% which is the average figure for equity based variable annuities.

[78] The M&E expenses for a typical variable annuity, according to NAVA, is 1.35%. This figure includes administrative fees of 0.15%.

[79] According to Baer and Gensler (p. 101) the average A-share commission is 4.1% and the average holding period for such funds is three years. This results in an annualized commission of 1.37% per year. Table #4 uses a more conservative 1% annualized commission. Commissions would include fees charged by fee-only planners.

[80] Variable annuities, due to their tax deferral, do not produce an *annual* income tax liability. It is assumed, for the purpose of Table #4, that the mutual fund gain averages 10% (the historical market average) and 2.0 percentage points of this 10% is lost to income taxes as was determined in this study. This will result in a 2.0% reduction of an average mutual fund portfolio's value. The textual material following Table #4 should be reviewed to determine the best way to calculate the tax loss a mutual fund owner might incur in a given year. This report has income taxes paid out of mutual fund gains. This is done to simplify comparisons. In reality this rarely occurs. Mutual fund owners usually pay income taxes from other sources. It is important to note that neither the actual income tax liability nor the net gain of the fund are changed by assuming that income taxes are paid out of mutual fund gains.

[81] Trading costs for all funds was set at a below average figure of 0.70%. Variable annuities have trading costs that are approximately 70% that of mutual funds. 70% of 0.7% = 0.5%.

[82] None of the investments are assumed to incur any miscellaneous costs. Variable annuities purchased for amounts under $25,000 may carry a twenty to forty dollar annual maintenance fee. Mutual funds have similar account maintenance and redemption fees.

It is also important to note that Table #4 only reflects the approximate *annualized* costs for owning mutual funds and variable annuities. There is one major *non-annual* cost associated with owning mutual funds and variable annuities – the income tax liability owed on these two investments when they are liquidated. The final liquidation tax owed on a variable annuity will almost always be larger than for a mutual fund. The reason for this is that variable annuities grow tax-deferred while mutual fund ownership usually requires the payment of income taxes annually on the distributions made by the mutual fund company as long as the fund is owned. All untaxed gain in a variable annuity is taxed at ordinary income tax rates. Unrealized capital gains that have built up in a mutual fund over the time are taxed at long-term capital gains rates when the fund is sold. Because income taxes are paid on mutual fund distributions each year, the unrealized capital gains that become realized at the time of sale usually account for a small portion of the fund's ending value when sold. In this report it will be assumed that unrealized capital gains in mutual funds will constitute only a conservative 30% of the fund's gain when sold and will be taxed at the long-term capital gains tax rate of 15%. A comparison of the annual costs of owning mutual funds and variable annuities must also consider the income tax cost of liquidating these two investments. By doing so, an investor can more accurately determine which investment will generate the largest *net* return when liquidated. The material in the next section discusses this issue.

§1023. A COMPLETE COMPARISON OF THE TOTAL COSTS OF MUTUAL FUND AND VARIABLE ANNUITY OWNERSHIP

Investors considering a possible investment in either a mutual fund or variable annuity should compare the *total* annual costs of owning both products and their tax liability at liquidation before deciding which investment will net them more. The following hypothetical demonstrates how an investor might calculate and compare the total cost of owning either a mutual fund or variable annuity.

Hypothetical #2:
Sara, who is married and fifty-five years old, recently inherited $30,000 and wants to invest it for her retirement in ten years. Sara and her husband will be in a 20% average tax bracket in retirement. Sara's brother suggested that she consider a mutual fund for her $30,000 investment. Because Sara was not an experienced investor, she sought the assistance of a financial professional to help her invest her $30,000. Sara's financial professional suggested Sara consider a variable annuity. Sara was concerned with this advice because she had recently read a newspaper article that claimed variable annuities were more expensive to own than mutual funds. The mutual fund Sara was considering was available in a A-, B- and C-share commission format. The same fund was also available as a sub-account in the variable annuity Sara's financial advisor recommended. Sara's financial planner obtained a prospectus for both the mutual fund and variable annuity Sara was considering. The cost for owning either investment was in the average range

for mutual funds and variable annuities. The findings made by Sara and her advisor are set out in Table #5 below:

TABLE #5: ANNUAL COST OF OWNING AN AVERAGE NON-QUALIFIED, EQUITY BASED MUTUAL FUND AND VARIABLE ANNUITY

COST FACTOR	A-SHARE MUTUAL FUND	B-SHARE MUTUAL FUND	C-SHARE MUTUAL FUND	VARIABLE ANNUITY
Annual Expense[83]	1.55%	2.35%	2.35%	2.50%
Commission[84]	0.50%	-0-	-0-	-0-
Income Taxes[85]	2.00%	2.00%	2.00%	-0-
Trading Costs[86]	0.70%	0.70%	0.70%	0.50%
Misc. Expenses[87]	-0-	-0-	-0-	-0-
TOTAL	4.75%	5.05%	5.05%	3.00%

The 4.75% total cost figure for the A-share mutual fund reflects an approximate *annual* cost for owning such a fund. The 5% commission is *annualized* over ten years to yield an average annual commission of 0.50%. It should be remembered, as mentioned earlier, actual comparisons will impose the 5% commission at the time of the fund's purchase and *not* include it as a separate expense each year.

As can be determined from Table #5 above, the *annual* cost of owning a mutual fund, whether an A-, B- or C-share, is more than that of owning a variable annuity. Other research has reached the same conclusion.[88] As mentioned above, the major difference between the *annual* cost of owning a mutual fund and the annual cost of owning a variable annuity is the annual income tax liability mutual fund owners must pay while owning their mutual funds. Three important points need to be understood at this point concerning the *annual* income tax liability of mutual fund ownership:

- If any of the mutual funds listed in Table #5 were held in a retirement (IRA, etc.) account, the mutual fund would lose two of its major benefits. All of the fund's gain would be taxed at ordinary income tax rates and the mutual fund would lose the benefit of the step-up in basis rule. The variable annuity loses none of its benefits if it is held in a retirement account.

---

[83] See note 135 above.

[84] A commission of 5.0% annuitized over a ten year period is assumed.

[85] See note 138 above.

[86] See note 139 above.

[87] See note 140 above.

Vanguard's John Bogle determined that even a no-load mutual fund could cost 5.2% a year to own. "The Pros and Cons of Mutual Funds." www.windsorwealth.com/mfprosandcons. Another study by Kyle Alkins, CLU, ChFC in the January 2004 issue of the Journal of Financial Service Professionals, page 33, mirrored Bogle's results.

- Although variable annuities, due to tax deferral, do not have an *annual* income tax liability, they eventually must pay taxes when liquidated. As mentioned above, it would be unfair (and deceptive) to compare the cost of owning a mutual fund with the cost of owning a variable annuity without factoring in the income taxes that will *ultimately* have to be paid on the gain made in the variable annuity. The comparison of any two investments should only be made, as is done below, on a *net* basis after factoring in *all* the costs and *all* the income taxes generated by the investments.

- When *all* of the costs and *all* income taxes associated with purchasing and liquidating a mutual fund and variable annuity are factored in, the variable annuity will usually net more for the investor than a mutual fund in the great majority of cases. This is especially true where the variable annuity is going to be held for seven years or more. The reason for this is due to a combination of the lower investment management costs and the tax deferral benefit provided by the variable annuity. This point is demonstrated below where Sara's potential *net* return on a $30,000 investment in a variable annuity is compared with her potential *net* return on a $30,000 investment made in the various share classes of a similar mutual fund.

If Sara reviews Table #5 above and compares *all* of the costs and *all* of the income taxes she will pay to buy and eventually sell either the variable annuity or the mutual fund she is considering, she will learn that the annuity will provide the largest net gain. The following calculations taken from Table #5 demonstrate this:

Calculation A (A-Share Mutual Fund):
Assuming Sara can obtain a 10% rate of return on her mutual fund, her net rate of return after deducting her annual costs and income taxes will be 6.02%.[89] A mutual fund returning 6.02% for ten years on an A-share mutual fund investment of $30,000 will grow to $51,136.[90] Assuming unrealized capital gains are 30% of the gain and are taxed at 15%, this will reduce the $51,136 value by $951 to $50,185.[91] This example assumes, unrealistically, that the same mutual fund will be held for ten years and no trading will take place. By making this assumption, a single 5% commission is spread over ten years. This will artificially increase the mutual fund's net ending value. It is also important to realize the 15% long-term capital gains rates may be higher after December 31, 2010 or earlier if the Democrats take over the administration.

Calculation B (B-Share Mutual Fund):
Assuming Sara can obtain a 10% rate of return on her mutual fund, her net rate of return after deducting her annual costs and income taxes will be 5.316%.[92] A

---

[89] $30,000 - 5% = $28,500 + 10% = $31,350 - 2.25% = $30,644 - $28,500 = $2,144 - 20% tax = $1,715 ÷ $28,500 = 6.02% net rate of return.

[90] 6.02% x 10 years x $28,500 = $51,136.

[91] $51,136 - $30,000 = $21,136 x 0.30 x 0.15 = $951. $51,136 - $951 = $50,185.

[92] $30,000 + 10% = $33,000 - 3.05% = $31,993 - $30,000 = $1,993. $1,993 less 20% tax = $1,595 ÷ $30,000 = 5.316% net rate of return

mutual fund returning 5.316% for ten years on an investment of $30,000 will grow to $50,358.[93] Assuming the expense ratio is adjusted downward after the end of the sixth year because it is a B-share fund, the actual ending value will be $51,717.[94] Assuming unrealized capital gains are 30% of the gain and are taxed at 15%, this will reduce the $51,717 value by $977 to $50,739.[95] It is important to realize the 15% long-term capital gains rates may be higher after December 31, 2010 or earlier if the Democrats take over the administration.

Calculation C (C-Share Mutual Fund):

Assuming Sara can obtain a 10% rate of return on her mutual fund, her net rate of return after deducting her annual costs and income taxes will be 5.32%.[96] A mutual fund returning 5.32% for ten years on an investment of $30,000 will grow to $50,358.[97] Assuming unrealized capital gains are 30% of the gain and are taxed at 15%, this will reduce the $50,358 value by $916 to $49,442.[98] It is important to realize the 15% long-term capital gains rates may be higher after December 31, 2010 or earlier if the Democrats take over the administration.

Calculation D (Variable Annuity):

Assuming Sara can obtain a 10% rate of return on her variable annuity, her net rate of return after deducting her annual costs will be 6.70%.[99] A variable annuity returning 6.70% for ten years on an investment of $30,000 will grow to $57,381.[100] Of this figure, $27,381 is gain. At an average tax rate of 20% this gain will be reduced to $21,905.[101] This would make the variable annuity worth $51,905[102] after *all* of the costs and *all* federal income taxes are factored in. [It is important to realize that for Sara and her husband to pay taxes at an average income tax rate of 20%, their *taxable* income in retirement would have to be close to $140,000. In reality, married couples in retirement are usually in much lower average tax brackets. A lower average tax bracket would have the effect of *increasing* Sara's net variable annuity investment gain.]

As the above calculations demonstrate, when *all* the costs of owning a mutual fund and variable annuity, including all federal income taxes, are taken into consideration, the variable annuity will frequently provide the greater net gain due to its tax-deferral and lower investment expenses. It is important to note that the above calculations assume a ten-year bull market. If one or two of these years are changed to down years, which would be more realistic, the tax cost of owning any of the mutual funds could increase. The reason for this is that mutual

---

[93] 5.316% x 10 years x $30,000 = $50,358.

[94] 5.316% x 6 years x $30,000 = $40,934. $40,934 + 10% = $45,027 - 2.25% = $44,015 - $40,934 = $3,081 - 20% tax = $2,464 ÷ $40,934 = 6.02%. 6.02% x 4 years x $40,934 = $51,717.

[95] $51,717 - $30,000 = $51,717 x 0.30% x 0.15% = $977. $51,717 - $977 = $50,739.

[96] $30,000 + 10% = $33,000 - 3.05% = $31,993 - $30,000 = $1,994 - 20% tax = $1,595 ÷ $30,000 = 5.32%.

[97] 5.32% x 10 years x $30,000 = $50,358.

[98] $50,358 - $30,000 = $20,358 x 0.30 x 0.15 = $916. $50,358 - $916 = $49,442.

[99] $30,000 + 10% = $33,000 less 2.85% = $32,060 - $30,000 = $2,060 ÷ $30,000 = 6.865%.

[100] 6.865% x 10 years x $30,000 = $58,274.

[101] $27,381 - 20% tax = $21,905.

[102] $21,905 + $30,000 = $51,905.

funds frequently generate an annual income tax liability even when the value of these funds are declining.

§1024. CAVEAT TO INVESTORS

Although detailed studies concerning the various components of mutual fund and variable annuity costs have been conducted by academic experts, *The Wall Street Journal*, financial research organizations, the Securities Exchange Commission and other entities that clearly demonstrate that the average actively managed stock mutual fund is actually *more* expensive to own than an equivalent variable annuity, there will continue to exist, as there has been in the past, a few uninformed individuals and members of the media who will continue to tell investors just the opposite. The easiest way for investors to protect themselves from being exposed to inaccurate advice or faulty information is to make sure that *all* of the costs and income taxes imposed for owning a mutual fund and variable annuity are included in any comparison of these two investment vehicles. Additionally, investors should be skeptical of anyone who attempts to make any comparison of a mutual fund and variable annuity that:

- Compares actively managed variable annuities sold by financial professionals with passive index mutual funds sold directly to the public by the issuing fund company;

- Compares a mutual fund that has no options, riders or other benefits with a variable annuity that provides options and other benefits to an investor who wants and is willing to pay an additional fee for these options and benefits.

- Attempts to treat as an actual cost of owning a variable annuity a *potential* cost that can be completely avoided by a purchaser.

Each of these topics is discussed in the sections that follow.

§1025. INACCURATE COMPARISONS

In years past, a few uninformed advisors and members of the media have compared the costs of owning actively managed variable annuities sold by financial professionals with *passively* managed index funds *not* sold by financial professionals. Such comparisons are similar to comparing apples to oranges and are misleading. For example, it is not difficult to find media reports that compare variable annuities that have average annual ownership expenses of 2.3% with index funds that have annual expense ratios much lower than 2.3%.[103] The problem with such comparisons is that these two investments provide entirely different benefits to their purchasers. For example, variable annuities sold by financial professionals come with the benefit of ongoing advice and assistance by the selling professional. The less expensive index fund provides no such advice or assistance.[104] Frequently, such comparisons of variable annuities

---

[103] The Vanguard S&P 500 Index Fund is an example of such a fund.

[104] The Investment Company Institute recently determined that over 67% of fund investors want professional assistance with their fund purchases.

and index funds are made intentionally in an attempt to indicate that *all* mutual funds are less expensive to own than *all* variable annuities. This is not the case and investors must be wary of anyone who would engage in such deceptive comparisons. If one is going to compare a no-load passively managed mutual fund, like an index fund to a variable annuity, then a no-load variable annuity or index annuity should be used in the comparison. Investors must ensure that whenever a comparison of any two investments is made, the investments being compared are similar in what they provide. If not, an improper and costly investment decision may result.

§1026. INCOMPLETE COMPARISONS

Another way in which mutual funds are improperly compared with variable annuities occurs when a basic mutual fund is compared with a variable annuity that provides additional benefits the annuity purchaser has elected to buy that are not available with the mutual fund. If an auto dealer compared the price of his basic sedan, without options, to a competitor's more expensive sedan that had several options desired by the buyer, most people would spot such a price comparison as deceptive. However, it is not uncommon for the cost of owning a basic mutual fund to be compared to a more expensive variable annuity without any disclosure being made that the variable annuity includes fees to pay for benefits that the mutual fund does not offer. For example, many variable annuities, in addition to offering a death benefit, offer an option that will guarantee the investor will get back 100% of his investment as a *living* benefit after a certain period of time even if the stock market has declined in value over this period. This important option protects the annuity investor against loss of his principal. It would be unfair to compare such a variable annuity to a slightly less expensive mutual fund that offers no similar protection.

§1027. FACTORING IN AVOIDABLE EXPENSES

Some advisors and members of the media like to include *potential* surrender fees and IRS penalties that are charged when a variable annuity owner surrenders his annuity early or makes withdrawals from their variable annuity before age 59½ as an *actual* cost of owning a variable annuity. To do so is misleading. Avoidable fees and penalties are not part of the cost of owning either a mutual fund or variable annuity. It is interesting to note that whenever the cost of owning a B-share mutual fund is discussed, any early surrender penalty that may potentially be charged is never treated as a cost. However, when variable annuities are discussed, every effort is made to treat early surrender charges as a cost of owning the variable annuity. Nearly all workers today fund retirement accounts such as 401(k)s, 403(b)s, IRAs, etc. Each of these retirement accounts may impose potential early surrender fees or IRS penalties for withdrawals made prior to age 59½. Whenever the cost of funding a 401(k), IRA or other retirement account is discussed, the cost of owning these accounts never includes any potential early surrender fees or IRS penalties. The reason for this is that it is assumed that people who buy B-share mutual funds or contribute to their retirement accounts will hold them long enough to avoid any surrender fees or penalties.

Variable annuities should be compared on the same basis. It must be assumed that people who buy variable annuities with *potential* early surrender fees or IRS penalties plan to hold their investment long enough to keep from having to pay these fees and penalties. In addition, the likelihood that a variable annuity investor will be faced with paying surrender fees or IRS penalties can be significantly reduced. For example, variable annuity investors can buy annuities with short surrender periods, or none at all. Nearly all variable annuities allow withdrawals of 10% to 15% of the annuity's value without any surrender penalty. B-share mutual funds, which are similar to variable annuities, do not offer a similar withdrawal benefit. Many variable annuity companies allow complete liquidation of an annuity without penalty when the owner becomes disabled or unemployed, needs nursing home assistance or becomes terminally ill. Mutual fund companies do not offer a similar benefit. Additionally, there are numerous ways to avoid the 10% IRS penalty for pre-age 59½ withdrawals from a variable annuity. It is important to note that there are several potential costs associated with mutual fund ownership that are *more* likely to occur than are the surrender charges and IRS penalties associated with owning a variable annuity.[105] For example, rebalancing or re-allocation among different mutual fund families in a portfolio held in a taxable account, which is commonly done, almost always results in triggering additional commission costs or income taxes. Variable annuities do not charge for re-balancing or reallocation and when these investment tools are used by variable annuity owners they do not result in additional commission costs nor do they trigger income taxes. If an investor moves from one mutual fund family to another in a taxable mutual fund account, even if additional commission or surrender penalties are ignored, such transactions will still result in the imposition of income taxes. A variable annuity owner can move from one variable annuity company to another on the same facts via IRC §1035 without incurring any income taxes. Only if a potential cost, such as a surrender charge or IRS penalty is actually incurred, should it be included as a cost of owning a mutual fund or variable annuity.

§1028. RELATED ISSUES

If investors are not sure of the costs associated with variable annuity and mutual fund ownership they can reach incorrect conclusions that could prove costly. One area where this occurs deals with the reporting of performance data.

Mutual fund companies report net performance based on the difference between gross returns and the fund's annual expenses, 12b-1 fees and trading costs. For example, if a fund has a gross return of 10% and annual expenses, 12b-1 fees and trading costs totaling 2.2%, the net return is reported as 7.8%. Variable annuity companies report net performance in a similar

---

[105] Mutual funds can increase probate costs and Social Security taxes for owners and, in some cases, disqualify mutual fund owners from Medicaid benefits or college tuition assistance. These collateral costs are rarely incurred by variable annuity owners. If mutual fund proponents want to include the avoidable costs related to surrender fees and IRS penalties, then these potentially avoidable costs of owning mutual funds should be factored in to any comparison of these two investments.

fashion. For example, a 10% gross rate of return is reduced by annual expenses, 12b-1 fees, trading costs and other administrative fees. Assuming these costs are 2.8%, the net return to the investor is 7.2%. Investors can often be fooled into thinking that the mutual fund's net performance at a 7.8% is better than the variable annuity's net performance of 7.2%. However, the mutual fund company's method of reporting net returns can be misleading because the net return for the mutual fund is not a true net return. It does not reflect each mutual fund investor's annual tax liability or commission costs. In defense of the mutual fund companies, it is only fair to point out that they do not have access to these two pieces of data and therefore cannot be expected to take them into consideration when reporting their "net" returns. However, investors must take these two additional costs into consideration. It should be remembered that these two costs will differ among mutual fund investors. If the 7.8% "net" return reported by the mutual fund company is reduced by income taxes and annualized commissions that total 3%, the *true* net rate of return for the hypothetical mutual fund discussed is 4.8% not 7.8%.

Because variable annuity investors do not incur up-front, out-of-pocket commissions or pay annual income taxes, the net return of 7.2% in the hypothetical case would remain unchanged. Thus, the true annual performance of the hypothetical mutual fund discussed above is not 7.8% but 4.8% while the variable annuity's true net rate of return is 7.2%. Investors must be aware of how performance is reported for mutual funds and variable annuities if they hope to make correct investment decisions.

§1029. QUESTIONS TO ASK

- If I'm going to recommend an investment to a client do I not have the obligation to inform the client of all of the costs associated with the recommended investment?
- If I inform a client of all of the costs of owning one investment and only some of the costs of owning another, am I serving my client as a good financial professional?
- By not providing complete information do I expose myself to legal liability?

§1030. SOURCES

- *The Great Mutual Fund Trap* (Baer and Gensler)
- *Your Money, Your Choice ... Mutual Funds: Take Control Now and Build Wealth Wisely* by Professor Charles P. Jones
- See all magazines and journal articles cited in the footnotes to this chapter.

§1031. CONCLUSION

A few years ago, Arthur Levitt, the former Chairman of the SEC stated that 92% of mutual fund investors had no idea what their mutual funds cost.[106] Most mutual fund investors

---

[106] Arthur Levitt, the former SEC Chairman puts this figure at 92%. See *Mutual Fund Matters* by Amy Crane, June 2001, www.geocities.com/amycrane

are generally unaware of the true cost of owning their mutual funds. Studies have found that MBA students cannot figure out the costs associated with mutual fund ownership.[107] The purpose of this report was to provide data and sources that will allow investors to accurately determine the true cost involved in purchasing a variable annuity or a mutual fund. The key to a proper comparison of these two investment vehicles is twofold. First, *all* of the costs and taxes associated with owning a variable annuity and mutual fund must be considered rather than comparing *all* of the costs and taxes of owing a variable annuity with *some* of the costs and taxes of owning a mutual fund. Second, any mutual fund and variable annuity compared should be similar as to their nature, who they are purchased from and what options or additional benefits they provide. When these two steps are followed, investors will learn that the total annual cost of owning an average actively managed variable annuity purchased from a financial professional will often be *less* than owning an equivalent mutual fund purchased under similar circumstances. This fact will usually result in the variable annuity yielding a larger net return to long-term investors than a similar mutual fund investment.

---

[107] See note 60 above.

–CHAPTER 11–
THE NET ENDING VALUE ACID TEST

§1101. INTRODUCTION

No one would buy a new car by comparing only the cost of the tires on the cars they were considering. No one would buy a new home based solely on the cost of the faucets that would be installed in the house. In both cases, car or home buyers would want to know what the *total* cost of the car or house would be prior to actually committing to either of these two major purchases. The author has questioned for years why large investments in variable annuities and mutual funds are made by comparing *only* money manger fees, or only surrender fees, etc. The only rational way to compare two investments where risk is the same, is to determine which of the competing investments will *net* the largest value to the investor over the same period of time after *all* costs, taxes fees and other factors have been considered.

§1102. HOW TO CONDUCT A NET-TO-NET COMPARISON OF TWO INVESTMENTS

Because this book deals with variable annuities and mutual funds, the explanation of how a net ending value is determined will be limited to these two investments. Net ending value refers to the net value obtained by an investor at the end of an investment period after all fees, costs, taxes and other factors are considered.

§1103. INFORMATION NEEDED FOR COMPARISONS

In order to compare a variable annuity to a mutual fund on a net-to-net (i.e., net ending value) basis one needs certain information. For a variable annuity one needs:

- Amount invested
- Investment or holding period
- Gross rate of return
- Investment management fees and 12b-1 fees
- Mortality and expense (M&E) fee
- Administrative fees
- Trading costs
- Income tax liability at liquidation

For a mutual fund one needs:

- Amount invested
- Investment or holding period
- Gross rate of return
- Annual expense ratio with 12b-1 fees
- Commission or similar fees
- Trading costs
- Annual income tax liability

- Income tax liability at liquidation

All of this information is discussed in Chapters 9 and 10. The data used in the comparisons made in this book are discussed in §312. All of the information mentioned above can be obtained from websites like www.personalfund.com or from mutual fund and variable annuity issuers.

§1104. CALCULATION OF NET ENDING VALUES

There are many ways to obtain the net ending value of mutual funds and variable annuities. The charts that appear on the next two pages demonstrate how this can be done.

SAMPLE NON-QUALIFIED A-SHARE MUTUAL FUND/VARIABLE ANNUITY
NET-TO-NET WORKSHEET (53 Year-Old Investor)

NO.	DESCRIPTION	MF	VA	MF	VA
1.	Holding Period (Same for MF/VA)	7 years	7 years		
2.	Amount Invested (Lump or Periodic - same for MF/VA)	$25,000 (lump sum)	$25,000 (lump sum)		
3.	Gross Return (Same for MF/VA)	10.0%	10.0%		
4.	Annual Exp. Ratio/12b-1 Fee/M&E	1.5%	2.2%		
5.	Gross Commissions or fee (Zero for VA) A-Share	5.0%	-0-		
6.	Trading Costs	0.7%	0.5%		
7.	Annual Taxes (% of Gain)	2.0%	-0-		
8.	Net Return (3 less 4, 5, 6, and 7)	6.064%[1]	7.03%[2]		
9.	Gross Value at End of Holding Period (1 x 2 x 8)	$35,862	$40,223		
10.	Gross gain (9-2)	$10,862	$15,223		
11.	Surrender Charges	-0-	-0-		
12.	10% IRS Penalty on Gain (Line 10) (If <59½ for Vas but not MF)	-0-	-0-		
13.	Unrealized Capital Gains 30% of Line 10 (None for VA)	$3,258[3]			
14.	Taxes on unrealized Capital Gains (15% of Line 13 for MF)	$489			
15.	Taxes on VA Gain (25% of Line 10)		$3,806[4]		
16.	Net Value at End of Holding Period (Line 9 less 11, 12, 14, 15)	$35,373	$36,417		

---

[1] $25,000 - 5% + 10% - 2.2% (1.5% + 0.7%) = $25,550 - $23,750 = $1,800 x .8 = $1,440 ÷ $23,750 = 6.064%.

[2] $25,000 + 10% - 2.7% (2.2% + 0.5%) = $26,758 - $25,000 = $1,758 ÷ $25,000 = 7.03%.

[3] May be higher or lower than 30%.

[4] A client's average tax rate may be higher or lower than 20%.

SAMPLE NON-QUALIFIED B-SHARE MUTUAL FUND/VARIABLE ANNUITY
NET-TO-NET WORKSHEET (53 Year-Old Investor)

NO.	DESCRIPTION	MF	VA	MF	VA
1.	Holding Period (Same for MF/VA)	4 years	4 years		
2.	Amount Invested (Lump or Periodic - same for MF/VA)	$50,000 (lump sum)	$50,000 (lump sum)		
3.	Gross Return (Same for MF/VA)	11.0%	11.0%		
4.	Annual Exp. Ratio/12b-1 Fee/M&E	2.3%	2.2%		
5.	Gross Commissions or fee (Zero for VA) A-Share	-0- (B-Share)	-0-		
6.	Trading Costs	0.7%	0.5%		
7.	Annual Taxes	.1818	-0-		
8.	Net Return (3 less 4, 5, 6, and 7)	6.28%[5]	8.00%[6]		
9.	Gross Value at End of Holding Period (1 x 2 x 8)	$63,793	$68,032		
10.	Gross gain (9-2)	$13,793	$18,032		
11.	Surrender Charges (1% of $50,000)	$500	$578[7]		
12.	10% IRS Penalty on Gain (Line 10) (If <59½ for Vas but not MF)	-0-	$1,803		
13.	Unrealized Capital Gains 30% of Line 10 - Line 11 (None for VA)	$4,138[8]			
14.	Taxes on unrealized Capital Gains (15% of Line 13 for MF)	$620			
15.	Taxes on VA Gain (25% of Line 10 - Line 11)		$4,508[9]		
16.	Net Value at End of Holding Period (Line 9 less 11, 12, 14, 15)	$62,673	$61,143		

[5] $50,000 + 11% = $55,500 - 3% (2.3% + 0.7%) = $53,835 - $50,000 = $3,835 - 18.18% (2% of 11%) = $3,138 ÷ $50,000 = 6.28%.

[6] $50,000 + 11% = $55,500 - 2.7% (2.2% + 0.5%) = $54,002 - $50,000 = $4,002 ÷ $50,000 = 8.00%.

[7] One year surrender charge of 1% of 85% of $68,032 (15% of withdrawals are surrender-fee free).

[8] May be higher or lower than 30%.

[9] A client's average tax rate may be higher or lower than 25%.

§1105. NET-TO-NET CALCULATIONS

With the information discussed above and a calculator, a very exacting net-ending value can be obtained for both mutual funds and variable annuities. The following examples are set out below to demonstrate how this can be done.

Example

Mary, who is 52 is considering a mutual fund purchase of $30,000 for 8 years. The fund is assumed to yield a gross annual return of 10 %. The fund charges a 5% commission. Mary's annual income tax liability will be 2.0% and the fund considered charges a 1½ % management fee and has a trading cost of 0.7%. Eight years from now Mary's mutual fund's *net* value would be $44,941. This assumes the same mutual fund is held for eight years. Mary is also considering a variable annuity purchase of $30,000. She assumes the annuity will gross 10% annually. She will buy her variable annuity from a financial professional. Mary's tax rate when the variable annuity is sold will be 25%. Her annual expenses are 2.2% and trading costs are 0.5%. Eight years from now Mary's variable annuity would have an after-tax value of $46,246. This assumes the variable annuity is liquidated all at one time. The variable annuity will yield $1,304 more than the mutual fund over eight years on a *net* basis.

The net-ending values of the mutual fund and variable annuity were obtained by conducting a simple net-to-net analysis using a financial calculator. This analysis appears on the pages below.

NET CALCULATIONS FOR LUMP SUM OR ANNUAL
INVESTMENTS IN QUALIFIED OR NON-QUALIFIED ACCOUNTS*

I. **DETERMINING THE NET ENDING VALUE OF A MUTUAL FUND AND VARIABLE ANNUITY INVESTMENT HELD IN A TAXABLE ACCOUNT**

   A. MUTUAL FUND NET ENDING VALUE

   1. To determine the net ending value of a mutual fund, three inputs are required:
      a. Net annual rate of return.
      b. Net amount invested.
      c. Length of investment.

   B. A MUTUAL FUND'S NET ANNUAL RATE OF RETURN IS CALCULATED BY:

   1. Reducing the gross amount invested by any up-front commission. ($30,000 - $1,500 = $28,500)

   2. The result in step B.1. is increased by the gross rate of return. ($28,500 + 10% = $31,350)

   3. The result in step B.2. is reduced by the annual expense ratio (1.5%) and trading costs (0.7%). ($31,350 - 2.2% = $30,660)

   4. The result in step B.3. is reduced by the after-commission amount determined in Step 1 to yield the pre-tax return. ($30,660 - $28,500 = $2,160)

   5. The result in step B.4. is reduced by the 20% annual income tax liability (2% of the 10% return) to yield the net (after-tax) annual gain on the mutual fund. ($2,160 - 20% = $1,728)

   6. The net annual gain of the mutual fund is divided by the net amount invested (See step B.1.) to yield the net annual rate of return for the mutual fund. ($1,728 ÷ $28,500 = 6.064%)

   C. CALCULATING A MUTUAL FUND'S NET ENDING VALUE

   1. The net annual rate of return (See step B.6.) is multiplied by the amount invested less commissions (See step B.1.) which is then multiplied by the number of years the investment will be held. (6.064% x $28,500 x 8 years = $45,645)

   2. The result obtained in C.1. is the ending value of the mutual fund investment before any reduction for income taxes on unrealized capital gains due on sale ($45,645).

---

* For annual investments, multiply the net annual rate of return for the mutual fund or variable annuity involved (See B.6. or E.3.) by the amount of the periodic payment for the number of years the investment will be held to yield the net value (use PMT not PV button on your calculator). The mutual fund periodic payment must also be reduced for any commissions charged. Step I.B.5 is omitted for qualified investments.

3. Some reduction in the result determined in C.2. must take place to account for taxes due on capital gains realized upon sale. The gain on the sale of an average mutual fund will usually contain approximately 30% long-term capital gains. This gain should be reduced by the long-term capital gains rate expected to be in effect at the time of sale (15% should be used for conservative estimates). ($45,645 - $30,000 = $15,645 x 30% = $4,694 x 15% = $704)

4. The ending value determined in step C.1. ($45,645) must be reduced by income taxes due on sale ($704 - See step C.3.) to yield the mutual fund's net ending value of $44,941. [See notes on mutual fund holding periods, etc.].

   [NOTE: In tax-deferred accounts (IRAs, etc.) steps B.5. and C.3. are omitted.]

D. VARIABLE ANNUITY NET ENDING VALUE

   1. To determine the net ending value of a variable annuity, three inputs are required:
      a. Net annual rate of return.
      b. Initial amount invested.
      c. Length of investment.

E. A VARIABLE ANNUITY'S NET ANNUAL RATE OF RETURN IS CALCULATED BY:

   1. Increase the initial amount invested by the gross rate of return. ($30,000 + 10% - $33,000)

   2. The result in step E.1. is reduced by annual expenses (2.2%) and trading costs (0.5%). ($33,000 less 2.7% = $32,109)

   3. The result in step E.2. is reduced by the amount invested (See step E.1.) to yield the annual gain. This figure is divided by the full amount invested (See step E.1.) to yield the annual net rate of return for the variable annuity (annual income taxes are not imposed with tax-deferred variable annuities). ($32,109 - $30,000 = $2,109 ÷ $30,000 = 7.03%)

F. CALCULATING THE VARIABLE ANNUITY'S NET ENDING RATE OF RETURN

   1. The net annual rate of return of 7.03% (See step E.3.) is multiplied by the amount invested ($30,000 - See step E.1.) which is then multiplied by the number of years the investment will be held (8). (7.03% x $30,000 x 8 years = $51,661)

   2. The result obtained in step F.1. is the net ending value of the variable annuity before income taxes.

   3. Any gain in the variable annuity must be reduced by the average tax bracket of the annuity owner (usually 15% to 25%). ($51,661 - $30,000 = $21,661 less 25% of the gain = $16,246)

   4. The after-tax value of the variable annuity ($16,246, See step F.3) must be added to the original investment ($30,000) to yield the variable annuity's net-ending value of $46,246. [See adjustment notes dealing with surrender fees, the 10% IRS penalty and taxation of lump sums].

PROBLEM

Mary has $30,000 to invest for eight years. She is now 52 and plans to retire at age 60. She is considering an A-share mutual fund and a variable annuity. The mutual fund charges a 5% commission, has an annual expense ratio of 1.5% and trading costs of 0.7%. Taxes are expected to reduce the gross rate of return by 2%. The variable annuity has an annual expense ratio of 2.2% and trading costs of 0.5%. The variable annuity has a 7% CDSC that declines 1% a year for seven years. Both investments are expected to return 10% a year. Mary will be in a 25% tax bracket at age 60.

QUESTION

Which investment will net more to Mary over eight years, the mutual fund or variable annuity?

SOLUTION

Mutual Fund: $30,000 less a 5% commission = $28,500 (amount invested), $28,500 increased by 10% (gross rate of return) = $31,350 less 2.2% (1.5% annual expense ratio and 0.7% trading costs) = $30,660 less $28,500 = $2,160 pre-tax gain less 20% tax (2% of 10%) = $1,728 ÷ $28,500 = 6.064% net annual rate of return. 6.064% (net annual rate of return) x $28,500 (amount invested after commissions x 8 years = $45,645. Of the $45,645 ending value, $15,645 is gain. Of this gain, 30% or $4,694 is long-term capital gains subject to a 15% tax of $704. This results in a net ending value of $44,941 for the mutual fund.

Variable Annuity: $30,000 (amount invested) increased by 10% (gross rate of return) = $33,000 less 2.7% (2.2% annual expense ratio and 0.5% trading costs) = $32,109 less $30,000 (amount invested) = $2,109 annual gain ÷ $30,000 = 7.03% annual rate of return. 7.03% x $30,000 x 8 years = $51,661 less $30,000 (amount invested) = $21,661 gain reduced by 25% in taxes = $16,246 plus $30,000 (amount invested) = $46,246 net ending value for the variable annuity.

SUMMATION

The variable annuity will produce $1,304 more in gain than the mutual fund on a net basis. (This ignores the fact that the mutual fund portfolio may be changed over time resulting in additional taxes or costs. This also assumes the variable annuity will be sold at one time and all taxes incurred in a single day).

ADJUSTMENTS TO THE NET-TO-NET ANALYSIS

Mutual Fund Holding Periods

The basic net-to-net analysis is designed to compare investments with holding periods that fall in a standard or average range. Mutual funds are typically held for three years. A net-to-net analysis going out for more than six or seven years will artificially increase the mutual fund's net ending value because it spreads a single commission over an unrealistically long holding period. For example, if a 5% commission is charged to buy a mutual fund that will be held for five years, the net-to-net analysis will spread the 5% commission over five years. However, if the net-to-net analysis will cover 15 years, the original 5% commission will be spread over 15 years. This greatly reduces the true impact of the fund's commission if the same fund is not actually held for the full 15 years.

Example

Bill is going to invest $30,000 for 15 years. His initial commission is 5%. The assumed rate of return is 10%, the annual expense ratio is 1.5%, trading costs are 7.70% and the average annual income tax is 2.0%. Based on these facts, Bill's net ending value will be $67,171.[10]

The problem with the above example is that it is unlikely that an investor would buy and hold a mutual fund for 15 years. To correct for this, the initial commission in Step B.1. should be changed to zero and the annual expense ratio and trading costs should be increased by the actual annualized commission. This method of adjustment is referred to as the cost adjustment method. For example, if the initial commission is 5% and the fund will be traded in five-year cycles over 15 years, the annual expense ratio and trading costs for this 15 year period should be increased by 1% (i.e., from 2.2% to 3.2%). An annual fee of 1% charged by a fee-only planner would be treated in the same manner. Another and more accurate way to correct for normal mutual fund holding periods is to conduct a standard net-to-net analysis for the fund's actual holding period. The fund's net ending value can then be reinvested for the next holding period, and so on. This method of adjustment is referred to as the reinvestment method. Whenever an investor is going to sell a mutual fund and repurchase a new one in less than five year cycles, the cost adjustment or reinvestment method discussed above should be used. The results of these two methods of adjustment for the hypothetical case involving Mary are set out below:

---

[10] $30,000 - 5% = $28,500 + 10% = $31,350 - 2.2% = $30,660 - $28,500 = $2,160 - 20% (2% of 10%) = $1,728 ÷ $28,500 = 6.064%. 6.064% x $28,500 x 15 years = $68,923. $68,923 - $30,000 = $38,923 in gain x .30 = $11,677 x .15 = $1,752. $38,923 - $1,752 = $37,171. $37,171 + $30,000 = $67,171.

METHOD USED	NET ENDING VALUE
15-year hold	$67,171
Cost Adjustment	$61,734[11]
Reinvestment	$61,589[12]

Income Tax Liability At Liquidation (For Non-Qualified Accounts)

The basic net-to-net analysis, as its last step, reduces any gain in the mutual fund or variable annuity by all income taxes due. These taxes are paid in a lump sum. On net ending amounts up to $100,000, this adjustment for income taxes will provide fairly accurate comparison information. For large net ending values, paying all taxes in a lump sum is not only unrealistic, but artificially reduces net ending value of the variable annuity. For example, a variable annuity with a $40,000 gain in its net ending value may create an average income tax liability of 25%. However, if the gain in the net ending value is $250,000, and all income taxes are paid at once, the tax liability could approach 35%. In light of the fact that investors are unlikely to take 100% of their investment at one time and unnecessarily expose themselves to an increased income tax liability, a reasonable adjustment should be considered. For example, if the net ending value of a variable is $900,000 and $250,000 is gain, it would be more reasonable (and accurate) to assume an investor might withdraw a portion of this amount each year and pay income taxes only on this withdrawal. This will more accurately reflect the tax liability on net ending values. The same assumption would have to be made for a mutual fund because mutual fund owners do not withdraw all of their mutual fund gains and pay taxes on these gains all at one time.

Variable Annuity Surrender Charges

Variable annuities have surrender charges. If a net-to-net analysis is done comparing a mutual fund and variable annuity and the variable annuity is not held for its entire required holding period, the appropriate surrender charge should be factored in.

> **Example**
> Jack, who is 60, purchased a variable annuity seven years ago for $35,000. It had a seven year holding period. At the end of the holding period the variable annuity was worth $70,000. Jack exchanged his variable annuity (via IRC §1035)

---

[11] It is assumed that the annual commission will be 1% for each of the 15 years involved. $30,000 + 10% = $33,000 - 3.2% = $31,911 - $30,000 = $1,911 - 20% = $1,529 ÷ $30,000 = 5.1%. 5.1% x 15 years x $30,000 = $63,229 less 15% of 30% of the gain of $33,229 ($63,229 - $30,000) or $1,495 = $61,734.

[12] $30,000 - 5% = $28,500 + 10% = $31,350 - 2.2% = $30,660 - $28,500 = $2,160 - 20% tax = $1,728 ÷ $28,500 = 6.064% x 5 years x $28,500 = $38,625 less 15% capital gain tax on 30% of gain = $38,237 - 5% = $36,325 + 10% = $39,957 - 2.2% = $39,078 - $36,325 = $2,753 - 20% tax = $2,203 ÷ $36,325 = 6.064% x 5 years x $36,325 = $48,758. $48,758 less 15% capital gains tax on 30% of gain = $48,302 - 5% = $45,887 + 10% = $50,475 - 2.2%. $49,365 - $45,887 = $3,478 - 20% tax = $2,782 ÷ $45,887 = 6.063% x 5 years x $45,887 = $61,589.

for a new variable annuity with a new seven years holding period. Four years later the $70,000 invested in the second variable annuity grew to $100,000 and Jack surrendered the variable annuity. The second variable annuity had a seven year surrender period. Jack decided to liquidate his variable annuity. Jack must reduce his initial $70,000 investment by any surrender fee charged by the second variable annuity issuer. Assuming the surrender fee was 3% of $70,000, Jack must reduce his net ending value by $2,100. (Income taxes at liquidation must be deducted also).

The procedure discussed above would also apply to 10% early withdrawal penalties imposed by the IRS on variable annuity owners who are under 59½ when withdrawals are made. Surrender fees for making withdrawals of more than the standard 10%-15% must also be factored in to any net-to-net analysis. B-share mutual funds have surrender fees also and would require similar adjustments. For qualified accounts, both mutual funds and variable annuities must also be adjusted for any pre-59½ withdrawals.

Taxes Paid from the Mutual Fund Investment

In the example discussed above, the annual federal income tax liability of 2% is paid out of the mutual fund. This is rarely done in actual practice. The majority of mutual fund owners usually pay any annual income taxes from sources *other than* the mutual funds that generate these taxes. The reason this example assumes that taxes are paid out of the mutual funds that generate the income taxes is that is makes the math needed to do various comparisons much easier. If it were assumed that taxes were paid from other sources, a computer would be needed to make accurate comparisons rather than a calculator. When annual income taxes are paid out of the mutual funds that generate them, the owner has "freed-up" the out-of-pocket taxes he would have paid. The value of these freed-up payments must be factored into any comparison between where mutual fund taxes are paid out of the mutual fund or paid from separate sources. For example, if an investor purchases a mutual fund for $30,000 and holds it for seven years, his net, after-tax and after-cost ending value will be $46,741 if annual taxes (including liquidation taxes) are paid from other sources. If the annual taxes (including liquidation taxes) are paid from the mutual funds themselves, the net ending value will be $42,448. However, in this last situation, the fund owner does not have to pay income taxes out of his pocket each year and therefore these payments may be invested elsewhere. If invested at an after-tax return of 8%, these payments will grow to an after-tax value of $4,548 in seven years. If this $4,548 is accounted for, the real ending value of the mutual funds which were reduced each year to pay annual income taxes increases to $46,996 which is almost exactly the ending value of the mutual fund investment where income taxes were paid from other sources.

The example below is similar to the hypothetical involving Mary that was discussed above. The net-to-net analysis for the hypothetical case involving Kim appears on the pages following the example.

Example

Kim is 50 and has $50,000 to invest for her retirement at age 60. One financial advisor recommended a mutual fund and another recommended a variable annuity with a GMAB living benefit. If the mutual fund is purchased there will be a 3.5% commission. The fund's annual expense ratio and 12b-1 fees are 1.6% and trading costs are 0.7%. In Kim's tax bracket, she will lose two percentage points of her fund's annual gain to the IRS. When the fund is sold, Kim will only have to pay 15% on unrealized capital gains which are assumed to be 30% of her gain at liquidation. If the variable annuity is purchased, the living benefit rider will cost 0.5%. In addition, the annual ownership and M&E costs (2.1%) and trading costs (0.5%) will add another 2.6% bringing the annual cost of owning the variable annuity to 3.1%. When the variable annuity is sold, Kim will have to pay 22.5% tax on the gain. Kim expects an 10% annual rate of return on any investment she makes. The variable annuity will *net* Kim $84,606. The mutual fund will *net* Kim $84,583. The variable annuity has a higher net ending value while, at the same time, offering both a death and living benefit.

NET-TO-NET CALCULATIONS FOR LUMP SUM OR ANNUAL INVESTMENTS IN QUALIFIED OR NON-QUALIFIED ACCOUNTS*

I. **DETERMINING THE NET ENDING VALUE OF A MUTUAL FUND AND VARIABLE ANNUITY INVESTMENT HELD IN A TAXABLE ACCOUNT**

A. MUTUAL FUND NET ENDING VALUE

   1. To determine the net ending value of a mutual fund, three inputs are required:
      a. Net annual rate of return.
      b. Net amount invested.
      c. Length of investment.

B. A MUTUAL FUND'S NET ANNUAL RATE OF RETURN IS CALCULATED BY:

   1. Reducing the gross amount invested by any up-front commission. ($50,000 - $1,750 = $48,250)

   2. The result in step B.1. is increased by the gross rate of return. ($48,250 + 10% = $53,075)

   3. The result in step B.2. is reduced by the annual expense ratio (1.6%) and trading costs (0.7%). ($53,075 - 2.3% = $51,854)

   4. The result in step B.3. is reduced by the after-commission amount determined in Step 1 to yield the pre-tax return. ($51,854 - $48,250 = $3,604)

   5. The result in step B.4. is reduced by the 20% annual income tax liability (2% ÷ 10% return) to yield the net (after-tax) annual gain on the mutual fund. ($3,604 - 20% tax = $2,883)

   6. The net annual gain of the mutual fund is divided by the net amount invested (See step B.1.) to yield the net annual rate of return for the mutual fund. ($2,883 ÷ $48,250 = 5.976%)

C. CALCULATING A MUTUAL FUND'S NET ENDING VALUE

   1. The net annual rate of return (See step B.6.) is multiplied by the amount invested less commissions (See step B.1.) which is then multiplied by the number of years the investment will be held. (5.976% x $48,250 x 10 years = $86,213)

   2. The result obtained in C.1. is the ending value of the mutual fund investment before any reduction for income taxes on unrealized capital gains due on sale ($86,213).

---

* For annual payments, multiply the net annual rate of return for the mutual fund or variable annuity involved (See B.6. or E.3.) by the amount of the periodic payment for the number of years the investment will be held to yield the net value (use PMT not PV button on your calculator). The mutual fund periodic payment must also be reduced for any commissions charged. Step I.B.5 is omitted for qualified investments

97

3. Some reduction in the result determined in C.2. must take place to account for taxes due on capital gains realized upon sale. The gain on the sale of an average mutual fund will usually contain approximately 30% long-term capital gains. This gain should be reduced by the long-term capital gains rate expected to be in effect at the time of sale (15% should be used for conservative estimates). ($86,213 - $50,000 = $36,213 x 30% = $10,863 x 15% = $1,630)

4. The ending value determined in step C.1. ($86,213) must be reduced by income taxes due on sale ($1,630 - See step C.3.) to yield the mutual fund's net ending value of $84,583.

[NOTE: In tax-deferred accounts (IRAs, etc.) steps B.5. and C.3. are omitted.]

D. VARIABLE ANNUITY NET ENDING VALUE

1. To determine the net ending value of a variable annuity, three inputs are required:
    a. Net annual rate of return.
    b. Initial amount invested.
    c. Length of investment.

E. A VARIABLE ANNUITY'S NET ANNUAL RATE OF RETURN IS CALCULATED BY:

1. Increase the initial amount invested by the gross rate of return. ($50,000 + 10% - $55,000)

2. The result in step E.1. is reduced by annual expenses (2.1%), trading costs (0.5%) and living benefit rider (0.6%). ($55,000 less 3.1% = $53,295)

3. The result in step E.2. is reduced by the amount invested (See step E.1.) to yield the annual gain. This figure is divided by the full amount invested (See step E.1.) to yield the annual net rate of return for the variable annuity (annual income taxes are not imposed with tax-deferred variable annuities). ($55,295 - $50,000 = $3,295 ÷ $50,000 = 6.59%)

F. CALCULATING THE VARIABLE ANNUITY'S NET ENDING RATE OF RETURN

1. The net annual rate of return of 6.59% (See step E.3.) is multiplied by the amount invested ($50,000 - See step E.1.) which is then multiplied by the number of years the investment will be held (10). (6.59% x $50,000 x 10 years = $94,653)

2. The result obtained in step F.1. is the net ending value of the variable annuity before income taxes.

3. Any gain in the variable annuity must be reduced by the annuity owner's income tax liability. ($94,653 - $50,000 = $44,653 less 22.5% = $34,606)

4. The after-tax figure determined in Step F.3. ($34,606) is added back to the original investment ($50,000) to yield the variable annuity's net ending value ($84,606).

SUMMATION

The variable annuity with a living benefit will produce more in gain than the mutual fund on a net basis. (This ignores the fact that the mutual fund portfolio may be changed over time resulting in additional taxes or costs. This also assumes the variable annuity will be sold at one time and all taxes incurred are paid in a single day). The adjustments to the net-to-net analysis discussed after the hypothetical case involving Mary (discussed above) would apply to Kim also.

§1106. USING THE SEC'S MUTUAL FUND COST CALCULATOR

The SEC has a mutual fund cost calculator that can be found at www.sec.gov. To obtain the approximate net ending value for a typical mutual fund, five pieces of information are needed:

(1) The length of time the mutual fund will be held (e.g., 7 years);

(2) The amount of the initial investment (e.g., $20,000);

(3) The assumed average annual rate of return (e.g., 10%);

(4) The up-front, out-of-pocket commission (sales charge) to be paid for the mutual fund (e.g., 4%, 5%, etc.);[13]

(5) Total *annual* taxes and expenses of owning the mutual fund.[14]

By entering these five pieces of information into the SEC cost calculator, an ending value for a mutual fund can be obtained. The SEC cost calculator does not reduce this figure for liquidation taxes. However, this figure is usually quite small. A good general rule of thumb is that when a typical mutual fund is sold, only 30% of its gain is subject to taxation and that gain would currently be subject to the 15% long-term capital gains rate. This reduction results in a net-ending value for the mutual fund. The SEC cost calculator ignores state income taxes which is appropriate because they differ among states. However, they should be considered when mutual funds are sold in states that have an income tax.

The net ending value of an equity based variable annuity can be obtained by using the same cost calculator except there would be no entry made for income taxes or commissions because variable annuities are tax deferred and purchasers of variable annuities do not pay any up-front, out-of-pocket commissions to purchase variable annuities. The annual cost of owning the variable annuity would have to include a figure for the variable annuity's M&E charge (e.g., 1.3%, 1.4%, etc.). The SEC cost calculator does *not* account for liquidation income taxes for variable annuities and therefore a variable annuity's value must be reduced for income taxes. This is a simple calculation. Whatever gain has been earned by the variable annuity over its holding period must be reduced by the investor's ordinary income tax rate.

The hypothetical example involving Mary that was discussed earlier in this chapter is repeated below. The information from this hypothetical has been run through the SEC's cost calculator.

---

[13] B-share mutual funds have no up-front, out-of-pocket commissions so this figure would be entered as 'O'.

[14] These costs would include annual income taxes, trading costs which average 0.7%, *annual* income taxes which average 20% of the annual gain (See Item 3) and the fund's annual expense ratio and 12b-1 fees which average 1.5%. All of these figures can be obtained from www.personalfund.com.

Example

Mary, who is 52 is considering a mutual fund purchase of $30,000 for 8 years. The funds are assumed to yield a gross annual return of 10 %. The fund charges a 5% commission. Mary's annual income tax liability will be 2.0% and the funds considered charge a 1½ % management and 12b-1 fees and have trading costs of 0.7%. This assumes the same mutual fund is held for eight years. Mary is also considering a variable annuity purchase of $30,000. She assumes the annuity will gross 10% annually. She will buy her variable annuity from a financial professional. Her annual expenses are 2.2% and trading costs are 0.5%. Her income tax rate will be 25% when she sells her variable annuity. Eight years from now Mary's variable annuity would have a value of $51,661. After reducing her gain of $21,661 by 25%, her after-tax (net-ending) value according to the SEC's cost calculator would be $46,246. This assumes the variable annuity is liquidated all at one time. The net-ending value of the mutual fund would be $42,742 (after taxes on unrealized capital gains). The variable annuity will yield $3,504 more than the mutual fund over eight years on a *net* basis according to the SEC's cost calculator.

The results obtained by using the SEC's cost calculator shows the variable annuity will produce a larger net result than the mutual fund. The amount of the difference is more than $3,500. When the net-to-net analysis was conducted on these facts earlier in this chapter the difference between the variable annuity's net ending value and the mutual fund's net ending value was just over $1,300. The reason for this is that the SEC's cost calculator is not as accurate as the computer designed net-to-net analysis that was used earlier. The difference between the net-ending value of the mutual fund and variable annuity would be $1,304 not the $3,504 figure obtained by using the SEC's cost calculator.

§1107. CONCLUSION

The whole point of this chapter is to encourage advisors to recommend variable annuities and mutual funds like any other major purchase – by comparing *all* costs, fees, taxes, etc., to obtain the net ending value for their clients. To select an investment in any other manner will most likely lead to defective investment decisions.

– CHAPTER 12 –

THE ANNUAL 15% CAPITAL GAINS TAX MYTH – SUMMARY DISCUSSION

§1201. INTRODUCTION

Many investors believe that their annual taxation on the mutual funds they own is capped at the 15% long-term capital gains rate. This myth is not true.

§1202. MUTUAL FUNDS AS PASS-THROUGH ENTITIES

Certain entities do not receive deductions for their losses and do pay income taxes on their gains. Three such entities are:

- Partnerships
- Sub-chapter 'S' Corporations
- Mutual Fund Companies

These entities are referred to by the IRS as pass-through entities. Gains and losses pass through to the owners of the entity. The *nature* of the gain or loss (e.g., long-term, short-term, tax-free, etc.) in the hands of the pass-through entity are also passed to the owners of the entity. When a mutual fund makes a profit on an investment, that profit is passed proportionately to the fund's owners. If the profit was a short-term capital gain, it must be treated as a short-term capital gain when received by the mutual fund owner.

§1203. MUTUAL FUND DISTRIBUTIONS

The easiest way to understand the concept of pass through entities, such as mutual fund companies, is with an example.

Example

Dr. Jones purchased a mutual fund three years ago. Dr. Jones currently pays taxes to the IRS at 33%. This is his current marginal tax bracket for ordinary income. Dr. Jones just received a mutual fund distribution notice. The mutual fund distribution was for $20,000. Half of this amount was for long-term capital gains and qualifying dividends and the other half was for short-term capital gains and non-qualifying dividends. Dr. Jones will pay 15% on half of his mutual fund distribution and 33% on the other half. This yields a 24% average tax on the mutual fund distribution. The fact that Dr. Jones has owned his mutual fund for more than a year is immaterial.

§1204. CONCLUSION

Regardless of any myth to the contrary, annual mutual fund distributions received my mutual fund owners are not taxed at 15%. There are many factors that result in mutual fund distributions being taxed at rates well above 15%. Chapter 13 discusses these factors in detail.

– CHAPTER 13 –
THE ANNUAL 15% CAPITAL GAINS TAX MYTH – DETAILED DISCUSSION
§1301. INTRODUCTION

Many mutual fund owners believe that the annual income taxes they pay each year on their funds is capped at the current 15% long-term capital gains tax rate. This myth is not true. There is no cap on the income tax liability a mutual fund owner must pay. This chapter discusses this myth.

§1302. QUALIFIED ACCOUNTS

This book, as mentioned earlier, compares non-qualified variable annuities and mutual funds. When qualified accounts are involved, the income tax liability of both mutual funds and variable annuities, in all regards, is identical and can be ignored for comparison purposes.

§1303. MUTUAL FUND OWNERSHIP DOES NOT GUARANTEE ANNUAL TAXATION WILL BE LIMITED TO THE 15% CAPITAL GAINS RATE

Many actively managed mutual fund investors have been led to believe that long-term ownership of these funds results in an annual income tax liability which is capped at the maximum capital gains tax rate of 15%, while withdrawals from variable annuities are subject to significantly higher ordinary income tax rates. Mutual fund proponents argue that the difference between a capital gains rate of 15% and an ordinary income tax rate of more than 15% makes long-term investing in mutual funds more attractive than similar investments made in variable annuities. This argument is a commonly held myth among mutual fund investors. The assumption that holding appreciating mutual funds for more than a year will result in an annual income tax liability of no more than the current maximum 15% capital gains tax rate is not accurate. The actual tax paid by long-term mutual fund investors each year can be significantly higher. The reason for this is that mutual fund companies must, on an annual basis, distribute realized gains generated from their investment activity to the funds' owners. These distributions are usually made late in the year and are reported to the IRS and fund owners on IRS Form 1099-DIV. Individual mutual fund owners use these tax forms to report mutual fund gains on their income tax returns. The *nature* of the annual income tax liability that long-term mutual fund owners incur is exclusively a function of how long their mutual fund *company* holds its underlying investments and has nothing to do with how long a mutual fund *owner* holds his or her fund. The frequency with which a mutual fund company buys and sells its investments is referred to as its turnover. It is a mutual fund company's turnover that determines the nature and therefore the rate at which an investor will pay income taxes on the realized gains reported by his mutual fund company each year. A turnover ratio of 100 means that, on average, a mutual fund company sells and replaces its entire portfolio once a year. A turnover ratio of less than 100 means that a mutual fund company, on average, takes more than a year to completely turnover its entire portfolio. Thus, a mutual fund company with a turnover ratio of 50 would, on average, completely turn over its portfolio every two years. A mutual fund company with a turnover ratio of more than 100 means the company, on average, takes less than a year to turn over its entire portfolio. Therefore, a mutual fund company with a turnover ratio of 200 would completely sell its portfolio and replace it with new investments, on average, every six months. By dividing a mutual fund's turnover ratio into 1,200 one can determine, on average, how many *months* investments are held by the mutual fund company. For example, a mutual fund with the current average turnover ratio of 118 holds its investments for approximately ten months. As a general rule, the higher a fund's turnover ratio the higher the potential ordinary income tax burden for the owner. A simple way for a mutual fund investor to estimate his or her tax liability on a mutual fund distribution is to compare the tax liability on taxable income before and after including a potential mutual fund distribution. The following example illustrates how this can be done.

Example #1:

Paul and Sue are young professionals who each have taxable incomes of $70,000. In early January of 2008, they determined that they would owe federal income taxes for 2007 of $28,193 on their combined taxable income of $140,000 for the year. This would result in an average income tax liability of 20.14%.[1] Shortly thereafter, Paul and Sue each received a $15,000 distribution from their mutual fund investments. Half of each distribution was long-term capital gains and dividends (taxed at 15%) while the other half was short-term capital gains (taxed at ordinary income tax rates). When these distributions were added to Paul and Sue's taxable income for the year, their taxes rose by $6,450 to $34,643.[2] Based on their higher joint taxable incomes of $170,000, their average income tax liability would actually increase slightly to 20.39%.[3] This 20.39% tax liability represents the average tax for *all* of Paul and Sue's taxable income including their mutual fund distributions. Both Paul and Sue were disappointed that they did not receive the 15% tax treatment they were told they would get as mutual fund owners.

Another shorthand method of approximating the annual income tax liability for a mutual fund distribution is to multiply the long-term capital gains and qualifying dividend portion of the distribution by 15% and the short-term capital gains and non-qualifying dividend's portion of the distribution by the owner's approximate tax bracket. For example, if Judy receives a $10,000 mutual fund distribution which is half long-term capital gains and qualifying dividends and half short-term capital gains and non-qualifying dividends, her annual income tax liability, if she is in a 28% marginal tax bracket, will be 21½% rather than 15%.[4] Once mutual fund investors realize

---

[1] $28,193 ÷ $140,000 = 20.13%.

[2] $15,000 x 15% = $2,250 + $15,000 x 28% = $4,200. $2,250 + $4,200 = $6,450 + $28,193 (Note 1) = $34,643.

[3] $34,643 ÷ $170,000 = 20.39%.

[4] 15% x $5,000 = $750 + 28% x $5,000 = $1,400. $750 + $1,400 = $2,150 ÷ $10,000 = 21.5%.

that the annual income tax burden they pay for owning their funds is not 15%, but what could easily exceed 20%, a more accurate comparison can be made between investing in mutual funds and variable annuities.

The confusion regarding taxation of mutual funds arises because the 15% tax rate *only* applies to long-term capital gains and qualifying dividends distributed yearly and unrealized capital gains and qualifying dividends when a mutual fund is sold if the fund has been held for more than one year. The current 15% tax rate does *not* apply to short-term capital gains distributed annually, non-qualifying dividends or unrealized short-term capital gains if a fund is sold within a year of its purchase. To add to the confusion, these rules change after December 31, 2010 when the 15% capital gains tax rate is scheduled to increase to 20%. Dividends will be subject to ordinary income tax rates of up to 35% starting on the same date. The likelihood that the 15% capital gains rate will be extended becomes more remote as the federal deficit increases. The Democrats have indicated that they intend to raise this tax rate if they prevail in the 2008 elections.

§1304. THE TRUE ANNUAL MUTUAL FUND INCOME TAX LIABILITY

Several of the country's leading researchers who have studied the impact of income taxes on mutual fund ownership put the current average annual income tax loss at 2.0% of an equity fund's annual gain. Tom Roseen, a senior research analyst with Lipper, Inc., recently authored a detailed study of the reduction in annual mutual fund gains resulting from income taxation. His research demonstrated that, over the past ten years, income taxes on average reduced mutual fund gains by as much as 2.5%.[5] Because of recent changes in our income tax laws this figure is, in his opinion, more in the range of 2.0% to 2.15%.[6] Joel Dickson, who heads Vanguard's Active Quantitative Equity Group, agrees that the current annual income tax loss on gains generated by the typical equity mutual fund is approximately 2.0%, as does Robert Arnott, who is the Chairman of Research Affiliates, L.L.C. and the past editor of *Financial Analysts Journal*.[7] The annual income tax liability for specific mutual funds can also be obtained from web sites such as www.personalfund.com. This book will use 2.0% as the average annual income tax loss incurred by equity mutual funds because it is the consensus figure used by many experts.

The tax liability discussed above refers only to the mutual fund's *annual* income tax. The seller of a mutual fund is also obligated to pay income taxes on the unrealized gains that are realized on sale. These gains average about 30% for the typical mutual fund when it is sold. Mutual fund owners need to understand that their annual income tax liability can be significantly larger than the 15% capital gains tax rate they think they are receiving.

---

[5] "Taxes In The Mutual Fund Industry – 2006 – Assessing The Impact Of Taxes On Shareholders' Returns"

[6] Telephone interview with Tom Roseen by the author in May of 2006.

[7] Telephone interviews with Joel Dickson and Robert Arnott by the author in May of 2006.

§1305. STATE INCOME TAXES

The discussion set out above relating to income tax losses resulting from mutual fund ownership includes only *federal* income taxes. State and local taxes are ignored even though 43 states and several municipalities impose an income tax on mutual fund gains. If an investor lives in a state or city that imposes an income tax on mutual funds, these taxes will increase the annual income tax cost of owning a mutual fund to a larger amount than was determined above. This report ignores annual state or municipal income taxes that might be imposed on mutual fund owners.

§1306. THE ALTERNATIVE MINIMUM TAX (AMT)

Mutual fund investors who are subject to the alternative minimum tax (AMT) pay an effective income tax rate of 21.5% rather than the 15% long-term capital gains tax rates available to those who are not subject to the AMT.[8] In short, the AMT will increase the effective annual income tax burden of owning a mutual fund to a figure greater than that which was determined above.

§1307. MUTUAL FUND LOSS CARRY-OVERS

It should be remembered that the income tax liability incurred by mutual fund owners over the last five years was somewhat mitigated by loss carry-overs that mutual fund companies stockpiled during the last bear market. However, these loss carry-overs have all but disappeared. This has resulted in higher annual income tax burdens for those who own mutual funds.

§1308. HIDDEN INCOME TAX LIABILITY

Mutual fund distributions can result in forcing a taxpayer to phase-out or reduce certain exemptions, deductions and credits. For example, if a $20,000 mutual fund distribution results in the loss of $4,800 in exemptions, deductions or credits and this in turn increases a taxpayer's income taxes by $1,200, the effective income tax burden generated by the mutual fund will be 6% ($1,200 ÷ $20,000) higher than the tax liability that the mutual fund would normally generate. On these facts, if a mutual fund generates an annual tax of 17%, the additional $1,200 tax loss will increase this tax liability to 23%.

§1309. THE IMPACT OF ANNUAL MUTUAL FUND INCOME TAXES

The larger than expected income tax liability borne by mutual fund owners can have a dramatic impact on a fund's long-term performance. For example, assume two investors, Ann and Bill are forty years old. Ann invests $100,000 in mutual funds returning 10% and Bill invests the same amount in similar investments within a variable annuity that also returns 10%. The negative impact of Ann's income tax burden can be seen when the total value of these two hypothetical portfolios is computed over a twenty-five year investment period. If Ann's annual tax liability is set at 2%, which is on the low end of the annual mutual fund tax loss determined

---

[8] "Special Tax Cost Investors Tax Breaks, Report Shows" by David Cay Jolinson, *New York Times*, May 10, 2006.

by the experts mentioned above, Ann's 10% rate of return will be reduced to an after-tax return of 8%. Based on this assumption, Ann's mutual fund portfolio will be worth $684,848 in twenty-five years.[9] Bill's variable annuity portfolio, because of tax deferral, will grow to $1,083,471 during the same period of time.[10] Even if Bill's actual 32.18% average, federal income tax liability for 2007 is imposed on the gain of $983,471, the after-tax value of the variable annuity will be $767,050.[11] In short, the variable annuity investment produced an after-tax return of $82,202 more than the mutual fund investment.[12] It is important to note that income taxes on the mutual fund's unrealized capital gains that became realized when the fund's were sold have been ignored. The above calculation ignores the fact that over twenty-five years, trading in the mutual fund would most likely have occurred. This could result in higher income taxes.

§1310. NON-TAX COSTS CONSIDERED

When proponents of mutual funds are faced with such results they usually argue that variable annuities are more expensive to own than mutual funds and this increased cost lowers returns and thereby reduces the income tax advantage that annuities have over mutual funds. The problem with this argument is that it rarely proves to be the case. The annual cost of owning the average variable annuity is 2.2%.[13] This figure includes a mortality and expense (M&E) cost, administrative fees as well as the fees paid to investment managers. Annual trading costs for variable annuities average 0.5%, bringing the total annual cost of owning the average variable annuity to 2.7%.[14] The annual cost of owning the average actively managed mutual fund, *exclusive* of any annual income tax loss, is approximately 3.2%. The major components of this 3.2% annual mutual fund cost figure are annual expenses for investment management (including 12b-1 fees), commissions and trading costs that average 0.7%,[15] bringing the total non-tax annual cost of owning a mutual fund to 3.2%.[16] With annual taxes included, the annual cost of owning a mutual fund can exceed 5% or nearly *double* the annual cost of owing a variable annuity. When all the costs of owning a mutual fund and variable annuity are factored into a comparison of these two investments, the variable annuity will usually provide a larger *net* return. For example, if Ann's $100,000 investment in the example discussed above is recalculated to take into consideration *all* of the costs of ownership, her mutual fund will have an after-cost, after-tax

---

[9] 8.0% x $100,000 x 25 years = $684,848.

[10] 10% x $100,000 x 25 years = $1,083,671.

[11] $983,471 - $349,700 = $633,771 x .35 = $221,819.85 + $94,601 = $316,420.85 ÷ $983,471 = 32.18% average tax. 32.18% of $983,471 = $316,421. $983,471 - $316,421 = $667, 050 + $100,000 = $767,050.

[12] $767,050 - $684,848 = $82,202.

[13] *The Great Mutual Fund Trap* by Baer and Gensler, p. 282.

[14] M&E fee of 1.3% + investment management and administrative fees of 0.9% + trading costs of 0.5% = 2.7%.

[15] Plexis Group puts the trading costs of mutual funds at 1%. See *Better Investing*, July 2001, p.29.

[16] Annual expense ratio (1.25%) + 12b-1 fees (0.25%) + commissions (1.0%) + trading costs (0.70%) = 3.2%. Studies show that annual mutual fund commission actually exceed 1.35%. See *The Great Mutual Fund Trap* by Baer and Gensler, p. 101. A more conservative 1% commission figure is used in this report.

value of $410,242 in twenty-five years.[17] Bill's variable annuity would have an after-cost value of $546,560.[18] In the highly unlikely event that Bill would elect to cash out of his variable annuity in a single day and pay an average income tax rate of 28.77598% on his gain, his annuity would have an after-cost, after-tax value of $418,038[19] which is still $7,796 more than Ann received with her mutual fund investment.[20] The above calculation ignores the fact that over twenty-five years, trading in the mutual fund would most likely have occurred. This could result in higher income taxes. The same results occur for smaller investments for shorter periods of time. A ten year investment of $25,000 in a mutual fund that has an after tax return of 8% will grow to $53,973. A variable annuity investment of $25,000 for ten years that grows at 10% will grow to $64,844. If the variable annuity's gain of $39,844 is taxed at 25%, the after-tax value of the variable annuity will be $54,883 or $860 more than the mutual fund yielded (termination taxes on the mutual fund were ignored).

§1311. MUTUAL FUND TAXATION IN FLAT AND DOWN MARKETS

One of the most misunderstood tax aspects of mutual funds is the fact that these funds can generate income taxes when they show no gain and, worse yet, can actually generate income taxes when they *lose* value. This negative tax feature is a primary reason why the annual income tax liability mutual fund owners pay, over time, exceeds the 15% long-term capital gains tax rate.

Pretend you live in a country that taxes gains from businesses at a maximum of 15% a year. If a business shows no gain or loss, they must send in the same amount of tax that they paid when their business last showed a gain. Under such a tax regimen it would be pure stupidity to state that income taxes were capped at 15%. If a businessman had a gain of $10,000 in a given year, his tax would be $1,500. If in the next year the businessman broke even he would still have to send $1,500 to the tax collectors. In the next year if the businessman lost $5,500, his tax liability would still be $1,500. After three years of business the businessman would have had a net profit of $4,500 before taxes and zero after taxes. In other words, his income tax would be 100% over three years or 33 1/3% per year not 15%.

The analogy in the previous section is exactly what mutual fund owners face today.

---

[17] It is assumed Ann purchased an A-share mutual fund charging a 2½% commission, having a 0.7% trading cost and an annual expense ratio of 1.5%, annual taxes are assumed to be 2% of gain. The fund is assumed to grow at an average of 10% a year. $100,000 - $2,500 = $97,500 + 10% = $107,250 - 2.2% = $104,891 - $97,500 = $7,391 x 0.8 = $5,913 ÷ $97,500 = 6.064%. 6.064% on $97,500 for 25 years = $424,861 - $14,619 realized gain on sale (30% of $324,861 = $97,458 x 15% = $14,619). $424,861 - $14,619 = $410,242.

[18] It is assumed Bill's variable annuity has an annual expense ratio of 2.2% and trading costs of 0.5%. The variable annuity is assumed to grow at a 10% average rate of return. $100,000 + 10% = $110,000 - 2.7% = $107,030 - $100,000 = $7,030 ÷ $100,000 = 7.03%. 7.03% x $100,000 for 25 years = $546,560.

[19] $446,560 gain is subject to income taxes of $128,502 ÷ $446,560 = 28.77598. $546,560 - $100,000 = $446,560 less 28.77598% tax = $318,038 + $100,000 = $418,038.

[20] $418,038 - $410,242 = $7,796.

Example

In year one, Mary bought a mutual fund that went up in value by $15,000. $10,000 was a distributed gain requiring Mary to pay $1,500 in income taxes. In the second year Mary's mutual fund did not move a cent but she had distributions requiring her to send $1,500 to the IRS. In the third year Mary's mutual fund lost $7,000. Mary had to send $1,500 to the IRS because she received a taxable distribution. Today, after three years, Mary's fund has a paper gain of $8,000 but the taxes she sent to the IRS totaled $4,500. This is a total tax burden of 56.25% over three years or an annualized rate of 18.75%.

Example

On January 1, 2007, Jack purchased three mutual funds. By the end of the year his first fund was up $20,000. The fund made a $10,000 distribution requiring Jack to pay $1,500 to the IRS. Jack's second fund was flat for the year, but made a distribution requiring Jack to send $1,500 to the IRS. The third fund was down $15,500 and also required a $1,500 tax to be paid to the IRS on his distribution. Jack's gain in his three mutual funds is $4,500 ($20,000 - $15,500) but Jack's tax obligation to the IRS is also $4,500. The tax liability amounts to a 100% tax and wipes out all of Jack's net gains for the year. Had three variable annuities been purchased on the same facts, Jack would be going into his second year of investing with a $4,500 net gain due to the advantage of tax deferral.

What the above example point out is that even where mutual funds are taxed at 15% annually on their gains, paying income taxes in a flat year or a year where a loss is taken will increase the 15% tax rate paid in any year there was a gain.

§1312. LOW TURNOVER MUTUAL FUNDS

Mutual fund proponents claim that the negative annual income tax impact of owning actively managed mutual funds can be eliminated by purchasing funds with lower turnovers so that a larger portion of a mutual fund's gains can be taxed upon liquidation at the more favorable long-term capital gains rate. This method of purchasing mutual funds is rarely used by those who buy actively managed mutual funds for several reasons. Among them are: a) most mutual fund purchasers have little or no understanding of what turnover is or what its tax implications are; b) most buyers of mutual funds pick their funds based on potential return and not the fund's turnover; c) brokers and financial advisors usually recommend mutual funds to clients based on potential performance of the fund and not the fund's turnover; d) mutual funds cannot completely control their turnover. For example, a fund with a favorable turnover can have this turnover increased dramatically if redemptions by fund holders increase. This forces the fund to sell shares that may generate short-term capital gains; and e) funds with a low turnover still generate some short-term capital gains each year which are taxed to fund owners as ordinary income.

Another problem with buying funds with low turnover so more gain can be taxed at 15% upon sale of the funds is that such a sale must occur before December 31, 2010. Any mutual funds held beyond this date, according to the current income tax laws, will be taxed at an increased rate of 20%. Selling mutual funds before December 31, 2010 may not solve the tax problem facing mutual fund investors. Although the sale of mutual funds prior to December 31, 2010 will result in the sale proceeds being taxed at 15%, the after-tax proceeds from such a sale will need to be reinvested. Capital gains rates on any reinvested proceeds will be subject to the increased 20% tax rate. Additionally, commissions may have to be paid to sell and repurchase replacement funds. Any gain resulting from dividends will be taxed at ordinary income tax rates.

Advisors must ensure that clients understand that long-term ownership of mutual funds will not guarantee an annual income tax liability of 15%. Annual mutual fund taxation can be well in excess of 15%. As mentioned above, the actual annual income tax liability for owning mutual funds has been determined by several researchers to be significantly higher than 15%. Once the investing public realizes that they might be paying annual income taxes on their mutual fund distributions at significantly higher tax rates than the 15% they believe they will receive, the advantage of deferring all taxes by buying variable annuities may become an attractive alternative.

§1313. QUESTIONS TO ASK

- Do my clients understand that their income tax liability is not capped at 15% while they hold their mutual funds?
- Do my clients understand that the 15% capital gains tax liability they hear so much about will most likely increase in the next few years?

§1314. SOURCES

- *The Great Mutual Fund Trap* (Baer and Gensler)
- *Your Money, Your Choice ... Mutual Funds: Take Control Now and Build Wealth Wisely* by Professor Charles P. Jones

§1315. CONCLUSION

The 15% long-term capital gains rate many investors associate with mutual fund investing does *not* apply to *annual* taxation of mutual funds. A mutual fund owner can pay much more than 15% on his annual mutual fund distributions. Current tax law will increase the current 15% long-term capital gains rate to 20% after December 31, 2010. The job of a good financial professional is to help his clients understand the true tax burden they face when buying any investment.

– CHAPTER 14 –
THE CAPITAL GAINS/ORDINARY INCOME TAX MYTH –
SUMMARY DISCUSSION

§1401. INTRODUCTION

The last chapter set out many reasons why mutual fund owners are unlikely to receive 15% long-term capital gains treatment on their annual mutual fund distributions during their accumulation phase. This summary chapter and the more detailed chapter that follows examines the income tax liability of mutual funds and variable annuities when they are liquidated.

§1402. THE CAPITAL GAINS/ORDINARY INCOME TAX MYTH

Many investors believe that because mutual funds are subject to taxation upon liquidation at the current long-term capital gains rate of 15% that they are better off with these mutual funds than those who own variable annuities because all of the gain in a variable annuity is subject to ordinary income taxation at liquidation. Upon examination, this myth rarely proves accurate for several reasons.

§1403. WHY ORDINARY INCOME TAX TREATMENT MAY BE BETTER THAN CAPITAL GAINS TAX TREATMENT

Chapter 15 will discuss several reasons why the ordinary income tax liability imposed on variable annuity gain might produce a better net investment result than an equivalent mutual fund might produce although taxed at lower capital gains rates. A few of these reasons include the following:

- Mutual funds, in addition to paying income taxes at liquidation must also pay annual taxes each year whether their fund goes up in value, remains unchanged or go down in value. As pointed out in the last chapter these taxes can easily exceed the current 15% long-term capital gains rate.

- Liquidation income taxes are only one cost of owning a variable annuity. To the extent these taxes might be greater than long-term capital gains rates, the lower costs of owning a variable annuity will frequently offset these higher taxes.

- Variable annuities grow tax-deferred and therefore grow to a larger amount than a similar mutual fund that has higher annual costs of ownership and annual taxes. The variable annuity's larger net ending value, which is a result of tax deferral, will frequently offset any higher income taxes that might be due when variable annuities are sold.

- Variable annuity owners can use the income tax savings provision of IRC §1035 while mutual funds cannot.

- Changing mutual fund investments can generate income taxes. Changing variable annuity investments do not generate income tax liability.

Each of these points is discussed below in Chapter 15.

§1404. CONCLUSION

An investor would be making a major error to believe that variable annuities are less attractive than mutual funds as investments because at liquidation the former is taxed at ordinary income rates and the latter at long-term capital gains rates.

– CHAPTER 15 –
THE CAPITAL GAINS/ORDINARY INCOME
TAX MYTH – DETAILED DISCUSSION

§1501. INTRODUCTION

When variable annuities are liquidated (i.e., surrendered or sold) the gain in the variable annuity is subject to ordinary income taxation. When mutual funds are liquidated or sold any untaxed gain receives long-term capital gains treatment. This difference in tax treatment is often cited as a reason for not purchasing variable annuities. However, this capital gains/ordinary income tax myth can be misleading.

§1502. VARIABLE ANNUITIES AND MUTUAL FUNDS – COMPARING LIQUIDATION TAXES

The ordinary income taxation of gains at upon the liquidation (i.e., surrender) of a variable annuity may produce better net results than mutual funds that are taxed at the current 15% long-term capital gains rate when they are sold. At first blush it would seem that taxation at the 15% long-term capital gains rate would always be better than taxation at ordinary income tax rates of 15% or more. However, upon closer examination this simple observation does not hold up in most cases dealing with the liquidation of variable annuities and mutual funds. As was pointed out in the last chapter there are many reasons that produce this result. The three primary reasons are:

- Mutual funds, in addition to paying income taxes at liquidation must also pay annual taxes each year whether their fund goes up in value, remains unchanged or go down in value. As pointed out in the last chapter these taxes can easily exceed the current 15% long-term capital gains rate.

- Liquidation income taxes are only one cost of owning a variable annuity. To the extent these taxes might be greater than long-term capital gains rates, the lower costs of owning a variable annuity will frequently offset these higher taxes.

- Variable annuities grow tax-deferred and therefore grow to a larger amount than a similar mutual fund that has higher annual costs of ownership and annual taxes. The variable annuity's larger net ending value, which is a result of tax deferral, will frequently offset any higher income taxes that might be due when variable annuities are sold.

§1503. ANNUAL INCOME TAXATION OF MUTUAL FUNDS VS. THE VARIABLE ANNUITY'S DEFERRAL OF INCOME TAXES

Which produces a larger net return, a mutual fund that is taxed every year and still has a liquidation income tax at 15% or a variable annuity that defers all income taxes until liquidation at which point all of the variable annuity's gain is taxed at ordinary income? Many people would be surprised to learn that the variable annuity will often produce the larger net gain.

Example

Fred purchased a mutual fund for $25,000. Its gross return for a ten year period was 10% a year. This 10% was reduced to 8% due to annual taxes (See Chapters 9, 10, 12 and 13). Ignoring commissions and other costs, Fred's mutual fund will be worth $53,973 in ten years. Had Fred purchased a variable annuity returning 10% a year, his variable annuity would grow, tax-deferred, to $64,844. Of this $64,844, $39,844 is gain and, if subjected to an ordinary income tax of 25%, would yield a net (after-tax) value of $54,883. This figure is larger than the mutual fund's net ending value of $53,973 *before* reducing this value by the 15% long-term capital gains rate due on realized capital gains when the fund is sold.

What the above example shows is that the tax deferral provided by variable annuities coupled with a mutual funds constant annual taxation can result in the after-tax value of the variable annuity being greater than the mutual fund. This is true even though the mutual fund received long-term capital gains treatment at liquidation while *all* of the gain in the variable annuity is exposed to ordinary income taxes.

§1504. OTHER COSTS

Liquidation taxes are only one cost of owning a variable annuity or mutual fund. As Chapters 9-13 pointed out there are many other non-tax costs associated with variable annuity ownership. As Chapter 11 pointed out, no one should make any major purchase of anything by looking at only one cost of that product. To do so is not very smart.

Example

Judy wanted to buy a new car. She boiled her decision down to a Ford and Chevrolet sedan. Both cars had the same options and were nearly identical. Judy asked each of the salesman involved what the cost of the moon roof was in each car. For the Ford, the cost was $790. For the Chevrolet it was $985. Based on this *one* cost Judy purchased the Ford. A few days later she found out the *total* cost of Chevrolet was $24,500. She paid $29,800 for the Ford.

In the above example, Judy made a major purchase based on *one* cost of the two cars she was comparing instead of comparing the *total* cost of both cars. Had *total* costs been compared, Judy would have saved over $5,000.

The example involving Judy is no different than an investor only considering liquidation taxes when comparing a mutual fund and variable annuity. Both of these products have several non-tax costs that must be considered. Much like the automobile example set out above, investors should factor in *all* of the costs of owning a mutual fund and variable annuity including liquidation costs. Only then can a correct decision be made as to which of these two financial products will produce the largest net return at liquidation.

Example

Mark, how is 53, wants to invest $25,000 in a mutual fund or variable annuity for seven years. He assumes both will return 10% a year. The mutual fund and variable annuity have the typical cost of ownership associated with them as was discussed in §312 above. After seven years the mutual fund investment would be worth $35,862 before any liquidation taxes are paid. The variable annuity would have a value at the end of seven years of $40,223 before liquidation taxes. If the $15,223 in variable annuity gains is taxed at 25%, the *after-cost, after-tax* value of the variable annuity will be $36,418 which is more than the mutual fund's *pre-liquidation tax* value of $35,862.

What the last example demonstrates is that when *all* the costs of owning a mutual fund and variable annuity are considered, the variable annuity will frequently yield a larger net return even though the investor's ordinary income taxes will be higher at liquidation than the current 15% long-term capital gains rate. The reason for this result is a combination of the variable annuity's tax-deferred growth and the variable annuity's lower cost of ownership which together offset any difference in liquidation taxes between the mutual fund and variable annuity.

§1505. NET-TO-NET COMPARISONS

Chapter 11 discussed in detail how to calculate net ending values for a mutual fund and variable annuity based on their respective costs and potential tax liability during ownership and at liquidation. Net-to-net comparisons are the only way to properly determine which of two investments will produce the largest net return to an investor.

§1506. MARGINAL TAX RATES (MTR) – A COSTLY TRAP

The author has been a tax attorney for over three decades. Over this time the author has witnessed many people (and businesses) making costly financial decisions based on their misunderstanding of marginal tax rates. Many people believe that they pay taxes to the IRS based on their highest marginal tax rate multiplied by their gross income. In other words, many people believe that if they make $80,000 a year and are in a 25% marginal tax bracket that their tax liability is $20,000. This is a myth. The truth is that income taxes are paid at blended tax rates that consider *all* marginal tax brackets (not just the highest one) and this blended tax rate is then applied to a taxpayer's *taxable* income. For example, an $80,000 gross income, after exemptions and deductions, might yield a taxable income of $64,000. Although this $64,000 falls within a 25% marginal tax bracket, it would be subject to a blended tax rate of 13.82% not 25% and would generate an income tax liability of $8,848 not $20,000. This is a big difference.

As a tax attorney, the author has heard many stories where people have turned down pay raises or bonuses because they would move the potential recipient into a higher marginal tax bracket. This is plain stupidity. The truth is there is no way one can be worse off economically by increasing their earned income no matter what tax bracket this new income might place them in.

§1507. LOOKING AT ONE MARGINAL TAX BRACKET – A FAULTY CHOICE

In Chapter 11, it was pointed out that making a financial decision on just *one* cost rather than the *total* cost of owning an investment could result in faulty investment choices. The same thing occurs when one concentrates on only the last or marginal tax they will pay rather than trying to determine what their total tax liability will be if they make an investment choice. Outside of investing, no one would make an economic decision based on the *last* cost associated with something they wanted to purchase. The following two examples demonstrates this.

Example #1

Betty wants to purchase a new sports car. She is very concerned with fuel costs. One sports car she is considering has a 15 gallon gas tank. Gas costs $3.00 a gallon. An identical sports car has the same size gas tank but requires a quart of special additive be added to the car every time the gas tank is filled. A quart of gas cost 75¢ ($3.00 ÷ 4), however a quart of the special additive costs $1.50. Which of the following statements is true?:

- It costs twice as much to fill the gas tank on the second sports car as it does the first.

- The cost to fill the gas tank on the first sports car is $45.00 ($3.00 x 15) and $45.75 ($3.00 x 14¾ + $1.50) to fill the gas tank of the second car.

Technically both of the statements made about fuel costs are correct. However, if Betty relies on the first statement she is merely looking at the cost of the *last* quart of fuel put in both sports cars. She might be led to believe incorrectly that the *total* cost of fueling the second sports car is really twice that of the first. The second statement looks at the *total* cost of fueling both sports cars. Based on this data, Betty would know that the total cost of fully fueling both sports cars would vary by only 75¢. Based on this Betty would most likely look at other aspects of these two sports cars in deciding which to buy. Certainly, fuel costs would be a non-issue.

Example #2

Jack recently purchased a hotel for $15 million. He wants to completely refurbish it. Which of the following methods would be the best for Jack to select one of two companies to do the refurbishing work:

- Ask each company what the cost of the last item of work they will do will cost (i.e., carpeting the hotel); or

- Ask each company what the *total* cost of doing *all* of the refurbishing work will be?

As a businessman, Jack would be foolish to select a company to refurbish his hotel based on the last (or marginal) cost incurred – installing carpet. If Jack did this, one company could have a carpet cost that is lower than the other company by a few thousand dollars but will charge a million dollars more for the entire project. This is why Jack would want to select a refurbishing company based on *total* costs rather than marginal costs.

§1508. TEST QUESTION

Let's check our understanding of marginal tax rates with a question:

Example

Mike and Mary are 61, married and retired. Their gross retirement income is $76,400. Their exemptions and deductions are $17,650. Their taxable income is

116

$58,750. At this level of taxable income, Mike and Mary are in a 15% marginal tax bracket. Mike recently withdrew $5,000 from a non-qualified annuity he had. The entire withdrawal is subject to ordinary income taxation and puts Mike and his wife in a 25% tax bracket for 2007. What amount of Mike and Mary's income is subject to a 25% tax?

    a. $79,000

    b. $74,000

    c. $61,350

    d. $5,000

    e. $50

Many people looking at this problem would assume that because the $5,000 variable annuity withdrawal pushed Mike and his wife into a 25% tax bracket, 25% of the $5,000 withdrawal or $1,250 would go to the IRS. The truth of the matter is the only portion of the $5,000 variable annuity withdrawal that is subject to a 25% marginal tax is that portion that actually *exceeds* the 25% marginal tax rate. In Mike's case the variable annuity withdrawal exceeded the 25% marginal tax rate by only $50.[1] Mike will pay 25% on $50 where he used to pay 15%. This is a difference of five dollars. There is a big difference between $1,250 and $5.

§1509. MARGINAL TAX RATES VS. BLENDED TAX RATES

It is critical for investors to understand that income taxes are not imposed on a taxpayer's marginal tax rate. They are imposed on a taxpayer's average or blended tax rate. In other words, if a taxpayer is in a 25% marginal tax bracket he does not pay taxes at 25%. His taxes will be based on a blend of *all* of the marginal tax brackets up to and including 25%. This results in some of his taxable income being taxed at 10%, some at 15% and some at 25%. Blended tax rates for many taxpayers are often eight to ten percentage points less than the taxpayer's highest marginal tax rate. The following table provided by the IRS makes this point:

2007 TAX RATES (Married Filing Jointly)

ORDINARY TAXABLE INCOME	MARGINAL TAX BRACKET	BLENDED TAX RATE
$0 - $15,650	10%	0 - 10%
$15,650 - $63,700	15%	10% - 13.8%
$63,700 - $128,500	25%	13.8% - 19.4%
$128,500 - $195,850	28%	19.4% - 22.4%
$195,850 - $349,700	33%	22.4% - 27%
OVER $349,700	35%	27% - <35%

---

[1] $0 - $15,650 @ 10%; $15,650 - $63,700 @ 15%; $63,750 - $63,700 = $50 @ 25%.

Let's use this table to determine the difference between a taxpayer's highest marginal tax rate and his blended or average tax rate.

Example

Bill and Martha earned $160,000 in gross income in 2007. Their exemptions and deductions reduce this figure to $130,000 in taxable income. Their highest marginal tax bracket is 28%. They will *not* pay 28% on either $160,000 or $130,000. Their tax liability will be blended as follows:

$$0 - \$15,650 \times 10\% = \$1,565.00$$
$$\$15,650 - \$63,700 \times 15\% = \$7,207.50$$
$$\$63,700 - \$128,500 \times 25\% = \$16,200.00$$
$$\$128,500 - \$130,000 \times 28\% = \underline{\$420.00}$$
$$\$25,392.50$$

This blended tax rate yields an income tax of $25,392.50. This is 19.53% of Bill and Martha's taxable income not 28%. The difference between Bill and Martha's highest marginal tax bracket and their blended tax bracket rate of 19.53% is 8.47 percentage points.

§1510. ORDINARY INCOME TAX RATES CAN BE AS LOW AS 15% FOR HIGH INCOME TAXPAYERS

Many people do not realize that the ordinary income tax liability they pay to the IRS each year may not exceed the current 15% long-term capital gains rate even where their income is relatively high. This fact is particularly important for retired people as the following example points out:

Example

Bob and Linda, both 61, are retired. The pension income is $89,680. They withdraw $6,000 from a variable annuity each year for vacations. Their gross income is $95,680 and all of it is ordinary income. Their exemptions and deductions reduce their gross income to a taxable income of $71,525. Although Bob and Linda are in a 25% marginal tax bracket at their gross *and* taxable income level, their tax liability to the IRS is only $10,729 which is 15% of their taxable income.

The above example demonstrates that a retired couple owning variable annuities can have an income in excess of $95,000 and pay an ordinary income tax rate of 15% which is the current long-term capital gains rate.

What if Bob and Linda, in the last example, had owned a mutual fund instead of variable annuity? The following problems would have had to be of some concern to them:

- The long-term capital gains rate today is 15% but over the last 20 years it has been much higher. Bob and Linda may have paid long-term capital gains rates that were in excess of 15% over the years.

- There is no cap on the annual income tax liability while mutual funds are owned. This could have resulted in increased taxes for Bob and Linda.

118

- Bob and Linda's investment portfolio for retirement will be smaller with a mutual funds because they do not grow tax-deferred like variable annuities.

- The capital gains rate is most likely to rise in the near future to a rate above 15%.

- Bob and Linda would have had income forced on them. The nature of such income could not be controlled.

- Bob and Linda may have had to pay income taxes on their mutual fund even though the fund lost money.

The above example raises an interesting question. Why would someone own an investment (i.e., mutual fund) that requires annual taxation at both ordinary income rates and long-term capital gains rates, forces income on the investors, has unstable tax rates when a variable annuity poses none of these problems and will most likely be taxed at 15% anyway?

§1511. HOW MARGINAL TAX RATES ARE USED TO CONFUSE INVESTORS

Let's start with a question. Bill and Sue have a taxable income of $63,700 for 2007. All of this income comes from consulting that Bill does. They are at the very top of the 15% marginal tax bracket. If they withdraw $4,000 from a variable annuity late in the year it will put them in a 25% tax bracket. At what rate will the variable annuity withdrawals be taxed? Many investors can be convinced that the $4,000 will be subject to the 25% marginal tax bracket. People who have a bias against variable annuities would make this argument. However, what they are doing is assigning specific marginal tax rate to specific sources of ordinary income. Often this is done based on an assumption that income that comes in later in the year is taxed at rates that are higher than for income that comes in earlier in the year. It is interesting to note that people with a bias against variable annuities treat variable annuity withdrawals are always treated as the income that comes in last. This tax treatment is defective because income taxes are *never* assessed in this manner. As mentioned above, the way the IRS would impose taxes in this case would be to take the *total* of all ordinary income ($67,700) and apply a blended tax rate to this figure. For 2007 a taxable income of $67,700 will generate an income tax of $9,772.50 which is an average tax rate of 14.44% for all of Bill and Sue's income.

It is inappropriate to assign specific marginal tax rates to sources of ordinary income whenever the author sees someone doing this he poses the following question:

If Bill and Sue receive taxable income of $4,000 from a variable annuity withdrawal on January 3 and received $63,700 in taxable income later in the year, wouldn't the variable annuity income be subject to the 10% marginal tax rate?

Those people who have a bias against variable annuities or don't understand how our tax system works will be quick to point out that assigning a 10% marginal tax rate to the variable annuity would be wrong.

Another way to understand this issue is to pretend that the $67,700 mentioned in the above example came entirely from a variable annuity withdrawal. The tax on $67,700 that comes entirely from a variable annuity withdrawal will be taxed at exactly $9,772.50 which is a tax rate of 14.44%. This is true even though the $67,700 places the taxpayers in a 25% marginal tax bracket.

§1512. THE TAX DEFERRAL ISSUE

Many investors make incorrect decisions because they believe a 15% capital gains tax rate is much better than say an ordinary income tax rate of 25% or more. This belief can be costly. The only time such a statement would be correct would be where two investments grew tax-deferred and had the exact same annual cost of ownership. This is not the case with mutual funds and variable annuities. Mutual funds generally are taxed annually each year whether they go up, down or remain unchanged while variable annuities grow tax-deferred. In addition, as was pointed out earlier, the annual cost of owning a typical mutual fund is greater than that of owning the typical variable annuity. Because of these variations is it critical that taxes, which constitute only one cost of owning a mutual fund or variable annuity, be combined with other costs to determine the net ending value of any investments being compared. The example in §1504 pointed out that a variable annuity subject to ordinary income taxes of 25% could produce a larger net gain for an investor than he could obtain with a similar mutual fund investment taxed at both long-term capital gains rates and ordinary income tax rates. The reason this occurred was a combination of the variable annuity's tax-deferred growth and the mutual fund's higher annual cost of ownership.

§1513. IGNORING PREVIOUSLY PAID INCOME TAXES – A COSTLY ERROR

The author has talked with clients who have determined that their taxes would be lower with a mutual fund portfolio than a similar a variable annuity. The following table was recently presented to the author by a husband and wife who are retired and are tax clients of a local CPA.

2007 TAXES

	VA Ownership	MF Ownership
Wages	$80,900	$80,900
MF Short-term Capital Gain	-0-	$2,000
MF Long-term Capital Gain	-0-	$4,000
VA Withdrawal	+$6,000	-0-
Adj. Gross Income	$86,900	$86,900
Item Deduction	-$12,050	-$12,050
Exemptions	-$6,800	-$6,800
Taxable Income	$68,050	$68,050
Tax Due	$9,866	$9,466
Tax Percentage	14.50%	13.90%

The clients used this chart to show is that for the same withdrawal in retirement ($6,000) this couple would pay $400 less each year in income taxes because they owned mutual funds for 12 years before retiring. What the author pointed out to this couple were the following facts:

- They were focusing only on a single factor – taxes.

- They ignored all of the taxes they paid on their mutual fund portfolio prior to retirement. Over the last 12 years of owning their mutual funds they paid $18,000 to the IRS. At the $400 annual differential the clients calculated, it will take 45 years for the mutual fund portfolio, at its lower income tax, to close this tax gap.

- Because of annual taxes and higher annual ownership costs, the mutual fund portfolio contained less in it than the similar variable annuity portfolio would because of the variable annuity's tax deferral.

- The biggest mistake these clients made was not considering all of the present and past costs and taxes that would be incurred if a mutual fund or variable annuity portfolio were purchased. They also ignored the fact that the 15% long-term capital gains rate will most likely increase in the future.

After taking into consideration all of the costs and taxes that could be incurred, the author was able to show this couple that they would have been better off had they invested their money in a variable annuity portfolio than the mutual fund portfolio they actually purchased. Their only comment was that they were going to make sure their children did not make the same mistake.

§1514. THE LUMP SUM PROBLEM

Whenever net ending values of variable annuities and mutual funds are compared, it is assumed that the variable annuity owner will liquidate their entire variable annuity holdings and pay taxes at the highest rates possible. In reality this rarely occurs. People are much more likely to withdraw money from any nest egg only as they need it. If a variable annuity grows from $100,000 to $400,000 over twenty years and is cashed out all at one time the income taxes on such a transaction could easily be in the 30% range. However, if the variable annuity owner needs to withdraw only $40,000, then the tax on this money could be as little as 15% depending on whether the variable annuity owner has any other income.

Calculating net ending values of mutual funds and variable annuities by assuming the owners of these investments will take a lump sum and pay taxes all at one time is useful because it does show what these investments will net after *all* income taxes are paid. For example, if $100,000 is invested in a mutual fund and variable annuity for the same period of time earning the same rate of return and are cashed out ten years from now the mutual fund may have a net ending value of $193,000 while the variable annuity might have a net ending value of $189,000 after all costs, taxes, tax deferral, etc., are factored in. The problem with such lump sum comparisons is the income tax rate used for the variable annuity will almost always be larger than the income tax liability that would be paid if the variable annuity owner took withdrawals

121

over a period of time which is what happens in most cases. This may not be the case for mutual funds. The current capital gains rate of 15% would be applied to a lump sum gain of $300,000 or to smaller withdrawals taken over time. If a lump-sum net ending value of a variable annuity is $189,000 and a similar mutual fund has a net ending value of $193,000, the income tax liability will drop for the variable annuity if smaller withdrawals are taken rather than a lump sum. This will cause the net ending value to increase and could make the variable annuity a better investment.

§1515. IRC §1035 AND VARIABLE ANNUITIES

As mentioned earlier, many people believe that because of the capital gains/ordinary income tax myth, that mutual funds make better investments than variable annuities. As this chapter has shown, the lower costs and tax deferral provided by a variable annuity will, over a period of time coupled with annual mutual fund taxation, often close the gap between long-term capital gains and ordinary income taxes. In addition to tax deferral, variable annuities have other tax advantages that mutual funds do not. One such advantage is the availability of IRC §1035 to variable annuity owners. This tax law allows a variable annuity owner to exchange one variable annuity for another without having to pay income taxes on any gain at the time of the exchange. Mutual fund owners can not do this. This single tax law can have a dramatic impact on variable annuity and mutual fund investments.

Example

Dave was 50 when he invested $50,000 in ABC Mutual Fund seven years ago. He wants to get out of ABC and into XYZ Mutual Fund for three years at which time he is going to retire. Dave sold ABC and netted $70,747[2] after all taxes and costs. He reinvested this amount into XYZ Mutual Fund. With the same costs as discussed in §312 below except that his 5% commission dropped to 3.5%, Dave's mutual fund had a net value of $80,483 after the three years it was held in XYZ Mutual Fund.[3]

Example

Kim was 50 when she invested $50,000 in ABC Variable Annuity. She held it for seven years. At the end of seven years her variable annuity was worth $80,447.[4] Kim exchanged her ABC Variable Annuity for an XYZ variable annuity by taking advantage of IRC §1035. Three years later Kim's variable annuity was worth $98,634.[5] If Kim's gain of $48,634 is taxed at an ordinary income rate of 25% her after-tax variable annuity value will be $86,475. Kim's variable annuity produces nearly $6,000 more than Dave's mutual fund. Much of this difference can be attributed to Kim's ability to avoid taxes by using IRC §1035 to exchange her variable annuities on a tax-deferred basis.

---

[2] $50,000 - 5% commission = $47,500 x 7 years x 6.064% = $71,725 - $978 liquidation tax = $70,747.

[3] 6.064% x 3 years x $67,917 ($70,747 - 3½%) = $81,073 less liquidation costs of $590 = $80,483

[4] 7.03% x 7 years x $50,000 = $80,447. See §312 below

[5] 7.03% x 3 years x $80,447 = $98,634.

§1516. TAX-DEFERRED TRADING AND VARIABLE ANNUITIES

Another advantage variable annuity owners have over mutual fund owners is the fact that they can change investments within their variable annuity without triggering any tax liability on any gain made. The same investment changes in a mutual fund will trigger income taxes.

Example

Frank purchased a low turnover mutual fund for $65,000. His sister Fran invested $65,000 in a variable annuity on the same day. Frank and Fran invested their $65,000 in small cap equities. Fifteen months later both accounts had grown to $105,000. Frank and Fran both decided to get out of their small cap investments in favor of international equities. When Frank made this change within his mutual fund it required him to report his $40,000 gain and pay $6,000 in taxes on the gain. When Fran made the same change in her variable annuity, her $40,000 was not reportable as income and therefore generated no income taxes.

§1517. THE INCOME TAX DEDUCTION FOR VARIABLE ANNUITY LOSSES

When a variable annuity is sold at a loss, the owner receives a full income tax deduction for the loss. This deduction reduces *ordinary* income. When a mutual fund generates a capital loss, the deduction, if not offset by realized capital gains, may only be deducted in $3,000 increments over what can be several years.

Example A:

Ellen recently sold a mutual fund she purchased three years ago. Her cost basis in the fund was $90,000. The proceeds from the sale were $69,000, resulting in a $21,000 loss. Ellen has no other capital gains or losses. Ellen's loss deduction is limited to $3,000 for the current tax year. The remaining $18,000 may be written off on future tax returns for six years at the rate of $3,000 a year.[6]

Example B:

Dave recently sold a variable annuity he purchased for $90,000 three years ago. The proceeds from the sale were $69,000, resulting in a $21,000 loss. Dave is entitled to deduct this entire loss and use it to offset his ordinary income.[7] Variable annuity losses, according to the IRS, must be reduced by 2% of a taxpayer's adjusted gross income (AGI). For example, if Dave's AGI is $100,000, his variable annuity loss deduction would be $21,000 less $2,000 or $19,000. Many tax professionals disagree with the position taken by the IRS regarding the 2% reduction based on the taxpayer's AGI and do not reduce it.[8] IRS Revenue

---

[6] This assumes that there are no gains now or in the future to offset losses.

[7] There is no requirement that such variable annuity losses be offset by capital gains. The alternative minimum tax can be triggered by large variable annuity losses that are reduced by 2% of a taxpayer's AGI. A tax professional should be consulted when deducting variable annuity losses. See Chapter 29. Also see "The Deductibility of Variable Annuity Losses" in the May/June (2003) issue of *Variable Product Specialist* magazine.

[8] These tax professionals deduct the variable annuity loss as an above the line deduction without a 2% AGI offset. There is at least one Revenue Ruling supporting this position. The IRS has nothing supporting their position that variable annuity losses are subject to the 2% AGI threshold. Above the line deductions avoid any alternative minimum tax (AMT) problems. Some tax professionals deduct variable annuity losses on Line 14 of the IRS Form 1040 and support it with a Schedule 4797. See Chapter 29 for a full discussion of this issue.

Ruling 61-201 supports the position of the tax professionals. The IRS has nothing supporting their position.

A deduction against ordinary income will always save a taxpayer more than a deduction for a long-term capital loss. The deductibility of variable annuity losses is discussed more fully in Chapter 29.

§1518. MUTUAL FUNDS ARE SUBJECT TO INCOME TAXES EVEN WHEN THEY LOSE VALUE.

Investors owning actively traded mutual funds must keep in mind that these funds are the only equity investments sold that can generate an income tax liability in a year when the fund loses value. Few investors realize how this unusual characteristic of mutual funds can cause the tax liability of fund ownership to increase dramatically.

Example
Ken purchased two mutual funds for $100,000 each. The first fund went up $20,000 in value and required Ken to pay $1,400 in income taxes on its initial distribution. The second fund went down in value by $17,200, but also resulted in a distribution that required Ken to pay $1,400 in income taxes. A year after buying his funds and incurring these taxes, Ken sold both funds. His total gain was $2,800 but his total income tax paid on these funds was $2,800. Ken's tax liability is 100% of his gain.[9]

Mutual fund investors who paid income taxes each year as their mutual funds lost value during the 2000-2002 bear market may want to question what impact a similar market decline might have on their income tax liability in the future. Investors must realize that an investment, such as a mutual fund, that imposes an annual income tax whether the investment goes up, down or sideways will, in many cases, result in an actual tax liability that can be much larger than a similar investment, such as a variable annuity, which imposes an income tax only once at the time of liquidation and then only on the annuity's net gain.

§1519. THE CURRENT 15% LONG-TERM CAPITAL GAINS RATE IS SCHEDULED TO EXPIRE AT THE END OF 2010

Mutual fund investors must keep in mind the current long-term capital gains rate of 15% is temporary. Under current tax law this rate expires and increases to 20% at the end of 2010. The combination of a growing federal deficit and the costs associated with multiple military campaigns around the world does not favor an extension of the 15% capital gains tax rate beyond 2010. Add to this the increasing costs of medicare, health care and soaring state deficits and the likelihood of the current 15% capital gains rate lasting through 2010 becomes even more questionable.

In order to ensure a 15% long-term capital gains tax on investment gain, investors will

---

[9] Stocks, bonds, variable annuities and other investments do not require the payment of taxes when they lose value.

124

have to liquidate their portfolios by December 31, 2010. After paying a 15% tax, the remaining proceeds, if reinvested, will later be subject to a 20% long-term capital gains rate. Such a transaction makes little financial sense. A future increase in the long-term capital gains rate to 20% would make the tax advantage of purchasing variable annuities instead of mutual funds more pronounced than it is today. Mutual fund owners who purchased mutual funds to obtain a 15% long-term capital gains rate only to find these rates increased in the future may question the wisdom of investing in mutual funds in the first place. (After December 31, 2010, dividends paid to mutual fund owners would be taxed at ordinary income tax rates that could reach 35%).

§1520. SWITCHING MUTUAL FUNDS AND INCOME TAXATION

Another income tax advantage of variable annuities is that an owner can switch from one sub-account in his variable annuity to another without triggering any tax consequences. In addition, by complying with §1035 of the Internal Revenue Code, one variable annuity can be exchanged for a completely different variable annuity without generating an income tax.[10] The inability of a mutual fund owner to obtain similar income tax treatment can be costly as the following example demonstrates:

Example

Ten years ago, Judy purchased an index fund for $10,000 and recently decided to switch from her index fund to a growth fund in a different mutual fund family. At the time of this transaction, the index fund had grown in value to $50,000. The income tax on this transaction was $6,000. The $44,000 after-tax balance was reinvested in the growth fund. Fourteen months later, Judy sold her growth fund for $52,000 and switched to an international fund in the same fund family. The income tax on the $8,000 gain in growth fund was $1,200. These two transactions will result in a total income tax burden to Judy of $7,200.[11] Had Judy made the same two transactions while owning her investments within a variable annuity, her income tax liability would have been completely deferred. In addition, the purchase of the growth fund may have required the payment of a commission. Variable annuities allow commission-free trading among the sub-accounts within the annuity.

Mutual fund proponents compare their funds with variable annuities as if the owners of both of these investment vehicles rarely make changes to their holdings. Advisors must impress upon their clients that, in reality, this is rarely the case. Both mutual fund and variable annuity owners buy, sell, switch and transfer investments with some regularity. When the income tax burden and other costs of these transactions are factored into investment decisions, owning variable annuities in order to avoid these taxes and expenses may be worth considering.

---

[10] Section 1035 exchanges should be considered only if there will be no significant surrender charges incurred in the exchange. If the annuity being considered for exchange has lost value, the death benefit available in the current variable annuity should be considered before the exchange is made.

[11] $50,000 - $10,000 = $40,000 x 15% = $6,000 + 15% of $8,000 = $1,200. $1,200 + $6,000 = $7,200.

§1521. THE NET ENDING VALUE ACID TEST – REVISITED

Chapter 11 made the point that no investment decision should be made by looking at any single expense, tax, fee, cost, etc. Only when all of these elements are *totaled* and deducted to obtain a net ending value can an investor begin to understand which investment would be the best one for the investor. Chapter 11 should be reviewed at this point.

§1522. QUESTIONS TO ASK

- Do my clients understand that paying taxes on an investment that is a mix of long-term capital gains rates and ordinary tax rates every year whether the investment goes up, down or remains the same, can produce a heavier tax burden than an ordinary income tax rate that is applied only to the gain in an investment after several years of tax deferral?[12]

§1523. SOURCES

See the footnotes to this chapter.

§1524. REVIEW QUESTIONS

Explain how tax-deferred ordinary income taxes can be less than a combination of long-term capital gains taxes and ordinary income taxes paid annually.

§1525. CONCLUSION

A mutual fund investment that is taxed every year at both capital gains rates and ordinary income tax rates regardless of whether the fund is growing, losing value or remaining constant will often result in a greater income tax burden than a variable annuity investment that is taxed at an ordinary income tax rates following several years of tax deferral. It is important that clients realize that tax treatment of an investment is only one cost to be considered. Financial professionals are encouraged to conduct a net-to-net analysis factoring in *all* the costs of owning competing investments, including taxes, so that they can help their clients determine which investment will *net* them the most when they liquidate their investments in the future.

---

[12] This concept is discussed in *The Wall Street Journal*, "Protecting Your Retirement No Matter Who's President," by Jonathan Clements, p. D1, February 20, 2008.

– CHAPTER 16 –
THE LIQUIDITY, CONTROL AND FLEXIBILITY MYTHS– SUMMARY DISCUSSION
§1601. INTRODUCTION

Many investors, media people and others believe that variable annuities are less liquid than mutual funds and other investments. They also believe investors have better control and flexibility with investments like mutual funds rather than variable annuities. These beliefs are all unfounded myths.

§1602. LIQUIDITY

A variable annuity, mutual fund or stock investment all have the *same* liquidity. Each investment can be sold and converted to cash within a matter of a few days. The real issue is the *cost* of liquidity. Here again, investors and others believe the cost of liquidating a variable annuity is always greater than for a mutual fund or stock investment. This is another unfounded myth. Some investors and others who know little about variable annuities believe that once a variable annuity is purchased it *must* be held for several years or else the annuity's liquidation will be subject to a large penalty. This is a myth.

§1603. CONTROL AND FLEXIBILITY

The belief that variable annuities offer less control and flexibility than similar investments such as mutual funds is without merit. It is just another unsupportable myth.

§1604. CONCLUSION

The liquidity, control and flexibility one obtains with a variable annuity often provides to be significantly better than that which one can receive with a mutual fund. Chapter 17 demonstrates that for those investors who want liquidity, control and flexibility with their investments they may be much better off with variable annuities rather than mutual funds.

– CHAPTER 17 –

THE LIQUIDITY, CONTROL AND FLEXIBILITY MYTHS– DETAILED DISCUSSION

§1701. INTRODUCTION

The investing public often believes that purchasing a variable annuity requires the buyer to accept some illiquidity as a price for making such an investment decision. A common complaint heard from prospective variable annuity purchasers is that they do not want to be "locked" into a variable annuity. This illiquidity myth is exactly that – a myth. The liquidity of variable annuities is rarely any different than it is for mutual funds.

§1702. WHAT IS LIQUIDITY?

Although many investors believe variable annuities are less liquid than mutual funds, few of these investors understand exactly what constitutes liquidity. According to general accounting principles, an asset is liquid if it can be converted into cash within a short period of time without losing a significant amount of its value.[1] Based on this definition, all of the following investments would be considered liquid:

- Common stock
- A B-share mutual fund with a contingent deferred sales charge
- A variable annuity with a contingent deferred sales charge
- A newly purchased five-year bank certificate of deposit
- A corporate bond maturing in seven years
- An A-share mutual fund

The reason the above investments are considered liquid is that they can be converted into cash on short notice without losing a significant amount of their value. For example, a recently purchased bank CD that matures in five years is considered liquid because it can be converted into cash anytime after its purchase without losing a significant amount of its value. The fact that there may be an early withdrawal penalty imposed at the time of its liquidation does not diminish the CD's *liquidity*. The early withdrawal penalty only impacts the *cost of liquidation*.

Not all investments are liquid. Examples of investments that may present liquidity problems include:

- Real estate in a soft market (e.g., Detroit)
- U.S. savings bonds (during first six months of ownership)
- Real estate limited partnerships
- Restricted corporate stock
- A minority interest in closely held corporate stock

The reason the above investments are considered illiquid is that they cannot quickly be

---

[1] Some definitions of liquidity state a time frame in which an asset should be able to be sold. Typically these time periods range from one to two months.

converted into cash without losing a significant portion of their value or they cannot be legally sold at all. For example, a minority ownership interest in the stock of a closely held corporation, as a general rule, may be sold by its owner. However, there is rarely a market for such shares unless a deep discount is offered to the potential buyer. For this reason such stock is deemed illiquid. Restricted corporate stock is similarly illiquid because such stock cannot legally be sold by the owner during the restriction period.

§1703. THE COST OF LIQUIDATION – THE REAL ISSUE

Whether a variable annuity is more or less liquid than a mutual fund is not the issue. As mentioned above, both provide the same degree of liquidity. The real issue is the *cost of liquidation*. Nearly all investments have a cost associated with their liquidation. When A-share mutual funds are liquidated, the up-front, out-of-pocket commission paid to purchase the fund is lost as are any annual ownership fees that have been paid by the owner prior to liquidation. When B-share mutual funds and variable annuities are liquidated, the sellers may be charged a surrender fee if these investments have not been held for an agreed period of time. The fact that commissions are charged, surrender penalties are imposed or some other financial loss is incurred when an investment is sold does not mean the investment is illiquid. As mentioned above, both mutual funds and variable annuities are considered liquid because they can be converted into cash for close to their market value on short notice. It is rarely a good idea to buy mutual funds or variable annuities for short-term investing. However, if the sale of a mutual fund or variable annuity is necessitated due to an emergency or for some other unforeseen reason, both mutual funds and variable annuities will have a nearly identical *costs* of liquidation. Although many investors believe that the costs associated with liquidating a variable annuity are greater than for mutual funds, this rarely proves to be the case as the following example demonstrates:

Example

Betty, who is 60, invested $10,000 in an A-share mutual fund that charged a 5½% commission. On the same day, Chad, who is 60, invested $10,000 in a B-share mutual fund. The B-share mutual fund imposed a 6% contingent deferred sales charge (CDSC) that declined 1% a year. On the same day, Dave, who is 60, invested $10,000 in a variable annuity that imposed a 6% declining CDSC identical to the B-share mutual fund except that the variable annuity allowed surrender charge-free withdrawals of 15% a year on the annuity's account balance. A month later, due to emergencies, all three investors sold their investments which still had a market value of $10,000.[2] Table #1 reflects the cost of liquidation.

---

[2] Due to the short holding period, annual expenses are ignored. However, even if it were assumed that annual expenses were charged, the difference between the net check received at the sale of the A-share mutual fund and variable annuity would be less than $100. It is interesting to note that the variable annuity would most likely be less costly to liquidate than the B-share mutual fund because B-share mutual funds usually have annual expense ratios that are larger than those of variable annuities. Because there is no gain the 10% IRS penalty would not be applicable and no income tax liability would arise.

TABLE #1: COST OF LIQUIDATION

INVESTOR	INVESTMENT	COST OF LIQUIDATION
Betty	A-Share Mutual Fund	$550[3]
Chad	B-Share Mutual Fund	$600[4]
Dave	Variable Annuity	$510[5]

As Table #1 demonstrates, the cost of liquidation is the lowest with the variable annuity investment.

§1704. THE TWO MAJOR COSTS OF OWNING A-SHARE MUTUAL FUNDS

When an investor buys an A-share mutual fund he pays an up-front, out-of-pocket commission which is usually in the 5% to 5½% range for purchases of $25,000 or less and declines if larger investments are made. These reduced commissions for larger investments are referred to as break points. In addition to this commission, the A-share mutual fund investor must pay an ownership fee to the mutual fund company for each year the mutual fund is owned. On average, this fee, commonly referred to as an annual expense ratio, amounts to 1.5% of the mutual fund's total value.[6]

§1705. THE TWO MAJOR COSTS OF OWNING B-SHARE MUTUAL FUNDS

B-share mutual funds do not require an investor to pay an up-front, out-of-pocket commission. Instead, the investor is charged an increased annual expense ratio that is typically 0.9% to 1% more than the A-share's annual expense ratio. B-share mutual funds also impose a contingent deferred sales charge (CDSCs) commonly referred to as a back-end load or surrender fee. These CDSCs average 6% and, as a general rule, decline 1% a year until they reach zero. For example, if an investor sells his B-share mutual fund in the first year of ownership he will lose 6% of his original purchase price to the CDSC.[7] If the sale occurs in the fifth year, he would lose 1% of his sales proceeds. After six years, the CDSC would disappear. When CDSCs terminate, the B-share mutual fund's annual expense ratio drops to the normal A-share annual expense ratio for that fund which, as mentioned above, is usually in the range of 1.5%.

§1706. THE TWO MAJOR COSTS OF OWNING A VARIABLE ANNUITY

Like B-share mutual funds, variable annuities do not charge up-front, out-of-pocket commissions. Variable annuity companies charge annual ownership fees that averages 2.3%.[8] They also impose a contingent deferred sales charge (CDSCs) which is more commonly referred

---

[3]   5½% of $10,000 = $550.

[4]   6% of $10,000 = $600.

[5]   85% of 6% of $10,000 = $510.

[6]   Annual expense ratios include 12b-1 fees. These fees are usually collected quarterly. For ease of math, annual expenses are collected at year-end in the examples used in this report.

[7]   Some mutual fund companies base CDSCs on account value at liquidation while others use the initial investment to determine CDSCs.

[8]   *NAVA Outlook,* November/December 2005, p. 6.

to as a surrender charge. These surrender charges average 6% and, like B-share mutual funds, generally decline 1% a year until they reach zero. Unlike B-share mutual funds, variable annuity companies generally do not reduce their annual ownership costs when CDSCs terminate. As a general rule, variable annuity issuers allow total annual withdrawals by variable annuity owner's of up to 15% of an annuity's account value without having to pay a surrender charge (CDSC).[9] If an investor sells his variable annuity in the first year of ownership he will lose 6% of 85% of his initial purchase to surrender charges.[10] If the sale occurs in the fifth year, he would lose 1% of 85% of his account value to surrender charges. After six years, the surrender charges (CDSCs) would disappear. Variable annuity surrender charges are discussed in more detail below.

§1707. VARIABLE ANNUITY SURRENDER CHARGES

The reason for the perception that variable annuities have higher costs associated with their liquidation than A-share mutual funds is that, as discussed above, variable annuities impose surrender charges if they are sold before the expiration of an agreed holding period. The problem with this perception is twofold. First, the perception ignores the fact that, unlike A-share mutual funds, there are no up-front, out-of-pocket commissions associated with the purchase of the typical variable annuity and second, the perception fails to account for the fact that surrender penalties, unlike up-front, out-of-pocket commissions, decline over time and eventually completely disappear. In addition, most variable annuities allow annual withdrawals of 15% on a surrender charge-free basis. Once investors factor in these three variable annuity attributes, it usually becomes apparent that the cost of liquidating both variable annuities and mutual funds is nearly identical. Where there is a difference, it is usually the variable annuity that proves to be the least expensive of the two investments to liquidate as the next section points out.

§1708. COMPARING LIQUIDATION COSTS

Based just on the information discussed above, a basic comparison of liquidation costs can be made between variable annuities and mutual funds as the following example demonstrates:

Example
Three years ago, Jack transferred an existing $25,000 IRA savings account to an A-share mutual fund. His commission was 5%. His brother Bob, on the same day, transferred an existing $25,000 IRA savings account to a B-share mutual fund. On the same day, Jack's sister Sue transferred an existing $25,000 IRA savings account to a variable annuity. After three years, all three investors liquidated their investments and transferred them to other advisors. Based on the costs of ownership discussed above and a 10% gross rate of return, these three investors would receive the following after expense account values after liquidating their investments at the end of three years:

---

[9] Some variable annuity issuers base penalty-free withdrawals on the initial investment rather than account value. Some base penalty-free withdrawals on the lesser of account values or initial investment, while other companies do just the opposite.

[10] 15% of the variable annuity's value may be taken free of any surrender charge with most variable annuities.

TABLE #2: LIQUIDATION COSTS AFTER THREE YEARS

INVESTOR	AFTER EXPENSE PROCEEDS
Jack (A-share mutual fund)	$30,210[11]
Bob (B-share mutual fund)	$30,008[12]
Sue (variable annuity)	$30,239[13]

What Table #2 demonstrates is that there is very little difference in the cost of liquidation between an A-share mutual fund, B-share mutual fund and variable annuity. In fact, as Table #2 points out, Sue, the variable annuity owner, would actually have the lowest cost of liquidation among the three investors. (Taxes and penalties were avoided because this was an IRA direct transfer).

§1709. SELECTING AN APPROPRIATE SURRENDER PERIOD

One of the advantages of buying variable annuities is that the buyer can select a holding period that best reflects his investment time horizon. For example, if an investor knows he will hold his variable annuity for only three years, he can purchase a variable annuity with a three year CDSC. This will reduce his costs of liquidation. B-share mutual funds do not offer this same degree of flexibility with their surrender periods.

§1710. OTHER FACTORS TO CONSIDER

Table #2 above took into consideration only basic commissions, CDSCs and annual expense ratios in calculating the cost for liquidating an A-share mutual fund, B-share mutual fund and variable annuity. There are four other costs that should be considered when comparing liquidation expenses. These other costs include:

- Trading costs
- Income taxes
- Mutual fund trailing commissions
- The 10% IRS penalty for pre-age 59½ withdrawals

Each of these four additional factors are discussed in the sections that follow.

§1711. TRADING COSTS

Mutual funds are in the business of trying to make a profit for their investors by buying and selling stock. Like all buyers and sellers of stock, mutual fund companies must pay brokerage commissions to the stock brokerage firms with whom they do business. These trading costs are ultimately paid by the owners of the mutual fund. Currently, the SEC does not require

---

[11] $25,000 - 5% + 10% - 1.5% - $23,750 = $1,983 ÷ $23,750 = 8.35% x 3 years x $23,750 = $30,210.

[12] $25,000 + 10% - 2.4% = $1,840 gain ÷ $25,000 = 7.36% x 3 years x $25,000 = $30,936 less a 3% CDSC = $30,008. (Assumes CDSC imposed on sale proceeds).

[13] $25,000 + 10% - 2.3% = $1,867.50 gain ÷ $25,000 = 7.47% x 3 years x $25,000 = $31,031 less a 3% CDSC on 85% of $31,031 = $30,239. (Assumes CDSC imposed on sale proceeds).

that a mutual fund company's trading costs be disclosed to fund investors. However, pending legislation may change this rule in the near future. An investor can find information about the trading costs incurred by his mutual fund company (and passed on to him) by obtaining a statement of additional information for his mutual fund.[14] Trading costs have not changed significantly in the past ten years. The annual trading costs for the typical actively managed mutual fund is approximately 1%.[15] Trading costs for variable annuities are about 30% less than those charged by mutual fund companies. Thus, the average actively managed variable annuity will have a trading cost of approximately 0.70 basis points.[16] The reason for this slight variation is due to the fact that mutual fund companies trade slightly more than variable annuity companies because mutual fund companies must consider the impact that annual income taxes might have on their fund owners. Trading by mutual fund companies for income tax purposes occurs every quarter but is most visible at year-end when mutual fund companies are trying to sell losing positions to off-set capital gains generated by their funds during the year and ultimately taxed to the fund owners. The sale of losing funds also creates the appearance that the investments selected by the fund managers are performing well. Such selling is referred to as a "window dressing" in the mutual fund industry. Because variable annuity owners are not affected by annual income taxes, trading for tax purposes does not occur with variable annuities. This is the primary reason that trading costs are slightly lower for variable annuities. Trading costs are rarely disclosed or set out in any comparison of variable annuities and mutual funds, including potential liquidation cost comparisons. However, when trading costs are factored into such comparisons, their impact is to slightly increase the overall cost for owning mutual funds. This in turn reduces the fund's returns and therefore increases the cost of these mutual funds. In this report, trading costs will be set at a more conservative 0.7% for mutual funds and 0.5% for variable annuities.

§1712. INCOME TAXES

Income taxes are a major factor to be considered when comparing the liquidation costs of variable annuities and mutual funds. Mutual funds are taxed each year based on the mutual fund's turnover ratio. The average turnover ratio for the typical stock mutual fund according to several sources, is 118 which means that the average mutual fund turns over its portfolio every

---

[14] Mutual fund companies do not generally like to provide supplemental prospectuses [technically called Statements of Additional Information (SAI)]. No one should invest in a mutual fund without reading this material as it contains additional information regarding the costs of mutual fund ownership.

[15] *Your Money, Your Choice...Mutual Funds - Take Control Now and Build Wealth Wisely*, Professor Charles Jones (North Carolina State University), Prentice Hall, 2003.

[16] Trading costs (i.e. commissions) are the expenses incurred by both mutual fund and variable annuity companies when they buy stock from brokerage firms. Because variable annuity companies tend to trade slightly less than mutual fund companies, their trading costs are approximately 30% less than those of mutual fund companies. The average trading cost for a mutual fund is 0.7%. For the variable annuity it is 0.5%.

ten months.[17] This, in turn, means that a large part of the capital gain build-up in the average stock mutual fund is short-term which, generally speaking, generates ordinary income taxes for the fund's owners. Because of this, the annual income tax liability for mutual fund owners can exceed the 15% capital gains rate they believe is the maximum tax liability they can face each year.   In short, investors have little control over the amount or nature of the taxes generated each year by his mutual fund. Several studies have found that the owner of the average mutual fund held in a taxable account will lose an average of 2% of his gain each year to income taxes.[18] For example, an investor with a $100,000 mutual fund portfolio that earns a 10% gross rate of return will send 2% of this gain or $2,000 to the IRS in a typical year. In addition, mutual funds are the only investment that can generate an income tax even when they are losing value. During the 2000-2002 bear market, many mutual fund investors learned of this negative mutual fund characteristic firsthand. (Variable annuities and mutual funds held in retirement accounts are subject to identical tax treatment.) Mutual funds also have, in addition to an annual income tax liability, an income tax liability on unrealized capital gains that become realized at the time of sale. The total gain in the average mutual fund will usually consist of unrealized capital gains of approximately 30%. These gains are usually taxed at the long-term capital gains rate of 15%. This report will use these figures in its comparisons unless stated otherwise.

Variable annuities grow tax-deferred and therefore have no *annual* income tax liability. Any taxation owed on a variable annuity's gain is due only when that gain is withdrawn from the variable annuity. Variable annuity gains do not receive capital gains treatment but are taxed as ordinary income. The variable annuity's tax deferral advantage can often overcome the lower capital gains rates received by mutual fund owners. The following example *isolates* and compares *only* the income tax liability for a mutual fund and variable annuity investment:

Example

Jim made a mutual fund investment of $20,000 that averaged a 10% rate of return for 10 years. The mutual fund investment lost 2% of its gain each year to capital gains taxes. At the end of 10 years, Jim sold his mutual fund investment and received an after-tax proceeds check of $43,178.[19] (Taxes on unrealized capital gains generated by the mutual fund upon liquidation are ignored). Jena made a $20,000 variable annuity investment at the same time that Jim bought his mutual fund. Her variable annuity investment grew at 10% a year because it was tax-deferred. After 10 years, Jena sold her investment and paid income taxes on the

---

[17] *The Educated Investor* (Winter 2001) page 2 (118%); William Harding (Morningstar) bankrate.com 2002 (130%); Special Report by Stan Luxenberg (118%) wealth.bloomberg.com. *As Turnover Skyrockets, Investor's Costs Take Off* by Amy Crane citing a 118.6% turnover ratio. Bogle Financial Markets Research Center (118%).

[18] Lipper recently determined in an April 2005 study that mutual fund gains are reduced by an average of 2% each year for federal income taxes.

[19] 8% x 10 years x $20,000 = $43,178.

gain in her variable annuity at her average ordinary income tax rate of 20%. Jena received an after-tax check for $45,500.[20]

As the above example demonstrates, Jim's annual income tax treatment of his fund's gain produces a lower net return than Jena's ordinary income tax liability on her tax-deferred variable annuity investment. The reason for this is that the variable annuity's tax deferral allows compounding of growth. Such compounded growth often produces a larger after-tax return than annually taxable investments such as mutual funds even where the income tax rate for the tax-deferred variable annuity investment is higher than for the taxable mutual fund investment.

§1713. MUTUAL FUND TRAILING COMMISSIONS

Mutual fund companies typically pay annual trailing commissions on A- and B-share mutual funds of approximately 25 basis points (¼%) to the financial professionals who sell their funds. These trailing commissions, which are in *addition* to all other stated commissions, usually begin 13 months after the initial sale and continue as long as the mutual fund is held by the owner. The cost of these trailing commissions is paid for the mutual fund owner. Variable annuities do not pay trailing commissions in addition to normal commissions.[21] In some cases a financial professional may elect to take part of his variable annuity commission over time in the form of a trailing commission. When this is done the cost of such commission is paid by the issuing company and not the variable annuity owner. Additionally, a variable annuity's CDSC is not affected by trailing commissions because the CDSC will disappear at the end of the surrender period. This is true even if the financial professional who sold the variable annuity is receiving an ongoing trailing commission. Because mutual fund trailing commissions are not significant in the short-term, they have been ignored in the comparisons made in this report unless it is specifically stated that they are included. In actual comparisons, mutual fund trailing commissions should be accounted for.

§1714. THE 10% IRS PENALTY

Variable annuities and other similar tax-deferred retirement accounts are long-term investments designed for retirement. Because variable annuities provide the benefit of tax deferral, the IRS imposes a 10% penalty on any *gain* withdrawn from the variable annuity by an owner prior to the owner turning 59½.[22] There are exceptions to imposition of this penalty. For example, when a variable annuity is transferred to a different variable annuity issuer pursuant to IRC §1035, the 10% IRS penalty does not apply. A mutual fund may not be transferred to a

---

[20] $20,000 x 10 years x 10% = $51,875 less 20% tax on $31,875 in gain ($6,375) = $45,500.

[21] Some financial professionals who sell variable annuities may chose to receive their commission over time from the issuing company. For example, instead of a 6% up-front commission, a financial professional might elect to take 2% up-front and 1% a year after the second year of ownership for as long as the variable annuity is held by the owner. Because this method of compensation is fully paid by the annuity issuer, it would in no way impact an investor's cost of owning the variable annuity or its 6% CDSC. The 6% CDSC will still decline to zero over time.

[22] IRC §72.

different mutual fund company pursuant to IRC §1035. The liquidation of an A-share mutual fund held in a taxable account and subsequent purchase of a different fund usually triggers either income taxes or new commissions or both. The tax deferral provided by variable annuities, in many cases, will offset the 10% IRS penalty as the following example demonstrates.

Example

Al, who turned 59 in October, invested $10,000 in an A-share mutual fund seven years ago that had a 9% average annual rate of return over the entire time Al held his fund. The fund charged a 5¼% commission and had 1.5% annual expense ratio. Trading costs were 0.7%. Income taxes reduced Al's return each year by 2.0%. Al's fund grew to $13,453 in seven years at which time he sold the fund.[23] At the same time, Al's twin sister Alma invested $10,000 in a variable annuity with an annual expense ratio of 2.3%. Trading costs were 0.5% and the average annual rate of return was 9%. The variable annuity had a 7% CDSC that declined 1% a year. Alma's average tax bracket is 20%. Alma's variable annuity grew to $15,093 over the same seven-year period before taxes and an IRS penalty.[24] After income taxes *and* a 10% IRS early withdrawal penalty are imposed, Alma's variable annuity account would be worth $13,565 or $112 more than Al's mutual fund.[25] It is important to note that any potential capital gains taxes owed on the sale of the mutual funds owned by Al are ignored in this calculation. Additionally, in a real world situation Alma would most likely wait a few months before liquidating her variable annuity to avoid the 10% IRS penalty. In doing so, her variable annuity would outperform her brother's mutual fund investment by more than $600.[26]

§1715. ALL FACTORS CONSIDERED

Earlier in this report, Tables #1 and #2 demonstrated that when only commissions and contingent deferral sales charges were considered, the liquidation costs for a variable annuity were *less* than for a similar A- or B-share mutual fund. However, a comparison of the liquidation costs for mutual funds and variable annuities must include trading costs, income taxes, IRS penalties and trailing commissions. When liquidation costs for a variable annuity and a mutual fund are compared and any (or all) of the four additional factors mentioned above are included along with commissions and contingent deferred sales charges (CDSCs), the overall cost for liquidating a variable annuity will often prove to be less than for an equivalent mutual fund. The following example demonstrates this:

Example

Paul is 50 and plans to make a $20,000 investment in either an A-share mutual fund, B-share mutual fund or a variable annuity. He is concerned about liquidity three years and six years from now should he have to cash out of his investment.

---

[23] $10,000 - 5¼% = $9,475 + 9% = $10,395 - 2.2% = $10,101 - $9,475 = $626 x 0.77778% = $487 ÷ $9,475 = 5.14%. 5.14% x 7 years x $9,475 = $13,453.

[24] $10,000 + 9% = $10,900 - 2.7% = $10,606 - $10,000 = $606 ÷ $10,000 = 6.06%. 6.06% x 7 years x $10,000 = $15,093.

[25] $15,093 - $10,000 = $5,093 in gain x 20% tax = $1,019. $15,093 - $1,019 = $14,074 - $509 (10% penalty) = $13,565.

[26] $14,074 - $13,453 = $601.

Paul's average income tax bracket is 22%. Paul's financial planner informed Paul that all three of the investments considered by Paul were highly liquid because all of them could be converted to cash in a matter of days. Paul's financial planner also told Paul the real issue he should be concerned with was not liquidity but the *cost* of liquidity. Paul's financial planner obtained the following information on the three investments Paul was considering:

A-Share Mutual Fund: 5% up-front commission and an annual expense ratio of 1.5% (including 12b-1 fees and miscellaneous expenses). Trading costs were 0.7%. The annual income tax loss is 2.0% of the fund's gain. The assumed average annual rate of return is 8.5%. The fund has no trailing commissions.

B-Share Mutual Fund: No up-front commission but an annual expense ratio of 2.4% (including 12b-1 fees and miscellaneous expenses). Contingent deferred sales charges of 6% declining 1% over six years and are imposed on the initial investment amount. Trading costs are 0.7%. Annual income tax loss is 2.0% of the fund's gain. The assumed average annual rate of return is 8.5%. The fund has no trailing commissions.

Variable Annuity: No up-front commission. Annual expense ratio of 2.2%. Contingent deferred sales charges of 6% declining 1% over six years. Trading costs of 0.5%. The assumed average annual rate of return is 8.5%. Surrender penalties are imposed on premiums paid. Surrender charge-free withdrawals of 15% are allowed each year. The variable annuity grows tax-deferred until liquidation. There is an IRS penalty for withdrawal before age 59½ in the amount of 10%. The annuity has no administrative costs that are not included in the annual expense ratio. Based on the above information, Paul's financial planner created Table #3 below:

TABLE #3: LIQUIDATION COSTS AFTER THREE AND SIX YEARS

INVESTMENT	NET VALUE AFTER 3 YEARS	NET VALUE AFTER 6 YEARS
A-SHARE MUTUAL FUND	$21,791[27]	$24,992[28]
B-SHARE MUTUAL FUND	$21,776[29]	$25,201[30]
VARIABLE ANNUITY	$21,892[31]	$25,228[32]

[27] $20,000 less 5% + 8½% less 1.5% less 0.7% less taxes of 2.0% of gain = a net annual rate of return of 4.675%. 4.675% x 3 years x $19,000 = $21,791.

[28] $20,000 less 5% + 8½% less 1.5% less 0.7% less taxes of 2.0% of gain = a net annual rate of return of 4.675%. 4.675% x 6 years x $19,000 = $24,992.

[29] $20,000 + 8½% less 2.4% less 0.7% less taxes of 2.0% of gain = annual rate of return of 3.928%. 3.928% x 3 years x $20,000 = $22,450 - 3% surrender penalty = $21,776.

[30] $20,000 + 8½% less 2.4% less 0.7% less taxes of 2.0% of gain = annual rate of return of 3.928%. 3.928% x 6 years x $20,000 = $25,201.

[31] $20,000 + 8½% less 2.2% less 0.5% = an annual rate of return of 5.571%. 5.571% x 3 years x $20,000 = $23,532. This $23,532 figure would be reduced by a 3% surrender penalty on 85% of $20,000 or $510, income taxes of $777 on a gain of $3,532 at 22% and a 10% IRS penalty of $353 on a gain of $3,532 for a net value of $21,892.

[32] $20,000 x 8½% less 2.2% less 0.5% = an annual rate of return of 5.571%. 5.571% x 6 years x $20,000 = $27,688. This $27,688 figure would be reduced by income taxes of 22% on a gain of $7,688 or $1,691 and a 10% IRS penalty of $769 on a gain of $7,688 for a net value of $25,228.

What Table #3 demonstrates is that if any of the investments considered by Paul were liquidated at either three or six years, the liquidation costs would favor the variable annuity investment by a small amount. Liquidations occurring beyond six years will produce progressively higher net ending values for the variable annuity than for the A- or B-share mutual fund. It is important to note that the results in Table #3 reduce the variable annuity's value by a 10% IRS penalty and ignore any capital gains taxes that would be owed upon the sale of the mutual funds involved.

§1716. CONTROL AND FLEXIBILITY

The first part of this report addressed the cost of liquidity as it pertained to variable annuities and mutual funds. Hopefully, the first part of this report demonstrated that both variable annuities and mutual funds are liquid and that the costs of liquidating either investment are usually very close. Where there is a difference in liquidation costs it is often in favor of the variable annuity. The second part of this report addresses the issue of control and flexibility as they relate to variable annuities and mutual funds. Just as there is a perception by the investing public that variable annuities are less liquid than mutual funds, there is also a perception that variable annuities provide less control and flexibility than mutual funds. However, as with the liquidity issue, an examination of both variable annuities and mutual funds will usually show that variable annuities provide more control and flexibility to their owners than mutual funds as the following sections demonstrate.

§1717. INABILITY TO CONTROL INCOME FLOW AND INCOME TAXES

The state and federal income tax liability that might be generated by an investment is usually an important concern for most investors. Variable annuities provide complete control of income taxes because such annuities are tax-deferred. Like 401(k)s, IRAs and other retirement accounts, variable annuities are not taxed until the annuity owner decides to withdraw gain from the annuity. Mutual funds do not provide a similar benefit outside of a qualified account. Mutual fund owners can not control the income generated by their mutual funds. Each year mutual fund owners receive 1099 distribution notices requiring them to pay income taxes on their funds. Frequently such taxes much be paid even where the mutual fund generating the tax is losing value. During the 2000-2002 bear market, investors became painfully aware of the fact that only mutual funds can force income on fund owners resulting in an income tax obligation even though the mutual fund is losing value. In short, mutual funds force taxable income on fund owners who then lose the ability to control the taxation on this income. Additionally, the *nature* of the income forced on mutual fund owners cannot be controlled. A mutual fund company may decide to sell a stock after owning it for less than a year. This will result in a short-term transaction that may cause an increase in a fund owner's ordinary income which is taxed at rates that can be more than *twice* the current 15% long-term capital gains rate. Along the same line, mutual fund owners have no control over whether the dividends received by their mutual fund company will qualifying for the current 15% tax treatment. This too can result in increased income tax liability. When mutual funds experience net redemptions by existing investors, remaining fund investors may see their income tax liability increase. The reason for this is the annual tax liability generated by mutual funds is divided proportionally among all of the fund's owners who are remaining in the fund at the end of the tax year. Net redemptions result in the tax liability of a mutual fund distribution often being divided among fewer of the fund's shareholders. This in turn increases the income taxes the remaining investors must pay. New mutual fund investors often find themselves saddled with an income tax liability created by investors who have already left the mutual fund. This problem is referred to as the embedded gain problem and is unique to mutual fund investing.

Variable annuity owners can completely control how much income they receive from their variable annuities by simply deciding when to take withdrawals of income from their annuities. In addition, they do not have to worry about redemptions or embedded gains because their tax liability is deferred. Many investors today have variable annuities that they have owned for many years and have never paid any income taxes on them. Although the variable annuity's ability to provide complete control over when taxable income is received is undisputed, some make the point that any income received from a variable annuity is always treated as ordinary income while lower long-term capital gains tax rates can be obtained by investors who purchase mutual funds. By deferring taxes for long periods of time, variable annuity owners are able to accumulate more in their variable annuities than mutual fund owners can because mutual funds are taxed annually. Even after these larger amounts are reduced for income taxes, the *after-tax* values received by variable annuity owners will often be greater than the after-tax value of a mutual fund as the following two examples demonstrate.

Example

Paula has invested in mutual funds for 20 years. She and her husband are now 60 and retired. She invested $10,000 a year over this 20 year period and earned a 10% average rate of return each year. Trading costs for her funds averaged 0.7%. Commissions averaged 5%, annual expenses were 1.5% and taxes amounted to 2.0% of her annual gain. Paula was never able to control the receipt of income from her funds or the amount or nature of the income taxes she had to pay on the funds. Today, Paula's mutual fund portfolio is worth $351,877.[33] She and her husband supplement their $76,000 pension income by taking $12,000 in taxable distributions from their mutual funds each year. Paula and her husband have itemized deductions and exemptions of $19,400, leaving a taxable income of $68,600. Paula believes she made the right choice when she invested in

---

[33] $10,000 - 5% + 10% - 1.5% - 0.7% = $10,220 - $9,500 = $720 x 0.8 = $576 ÷ $9,500 = 6.064%. 6.064% x 20 years x $9,500 in annual investments = $351,877. (Investments were made at year-end).

mutual funds because they now provide a supplemental retirement income that is taxed at what she believes is 15% (this rate is scheduled to increase to 20% after December 31, 2010). Paula often makes fun of her twin brother Paul who started investing when she did, but decided to put his money in variable annuities instead. Paula believes that because Paul's variable annuity withdrawals are treated as ordinary income, his income tax burden is greater than hers. As the next example points out, this is not the case.

Example

Paul started investing $10,000 a year in variable annuities 20 years ago. All of the variable annuities had seven year contingent deferred sales charges. Paul's average rate of return was 10% and his annual expense ratio was 2.2%. Trading costs were 0.5%. He and his wife are now 60 and retired. Paul's variable annuities have grown to $411,300.[34] Paul and his wife have pension income of $76,000 and supplement it with $12,000 taxable withdrawals from Paul's variable annuities. Their itemized deductions and exemptions amount to $19,400, leaving a taxable income of $68,600. The tax on their taxable income is $9,998 (2007). Paul and his wife have a *total* income tax liability of 14.57% on *all* of their retirement income including Paul's variable annuity withdrawals.[35] In addition, Paul received the following benefits from investing in variable annuities:

- Paul's variable annuity portfolio is worth $411,300 after 20 years while Paula's mutual fund account was worth only $351,877. Tax deferral is responsible for a large portion of this difference.

- If Paul paid 28% tax on his variable annuity gain at one time he would net $352,136, which is more than Paula's mutual fund value *before* she pays taxes on her unrealized capital gains if she sold her funds all at one time.

- Paul can continue to control his variable annuity income in retirement while Paula cannot.

- Paul never paid taxes on his variable annuities while they were growing. Paula paid taxes each year regardless of whether her funds went up, down or sideways.

- Marginal income tax rates are not scheduled to increase in the future for middle income earners so Paul's 14.57% income tax liability will most likely remain constant in the future or go down slightly due to inflation indexing. Capital gains rates are scheduled to increase to 20% after 2010, which will significantly increase Paula's income tax liability starting in 2011.

- Paul can, if he elects to do so, take advantage of the exclusion ratio while Paula cannot.

As the above examples demonstrated, an investment that is subject to annual income taxation will grow to a much smaller amount than an identical investment that is allowed to

---

[34] $10,000 + 10% - 2.7% = $703 in gain ÷ $10,000 = 7.03%. 7.03% x 20 years x $10,000 annual payment = $411,300. (Investments were made at year-end).

[35] $9,998 ÷ $68,600 = 14.57%.

grow and compound on a tax-deferred basis. This often results in a investor receiving a larger *after-tax* income from a tax-deferred investment than he would receive by owning an investment that is taxed each year. When larger investments are made over longer periods, the advantage of variable annuity ownership increases dramatically.

§1718. INABILITY TO CONTROL SOCIAL SECURITY TAXATION

Social Security retirement income is not subject to income taxation unless a recipient reports other income that causes his total income to exceed certain limits. Most retired people in their mid-sixties receive Social Security checks as part of their retirement income. For many retired people, Social Security can make up a large portion of their retirement income. Mutual fund distributions frequently raise income levels for retired people resulting in the taxation of their Social Security. Because variable annuities do not make distributions, the mere ownership of a variable annuity, unlike mutual funds, cannot cause an owner's Social Security to be taxed. In short, variable annuity investors, unlike mutual fund investors, can control their variable annuity income and therefore avoid unintended Social Security taxation. Single taxpayers who have provisional incomes of $25,000 or more and married couples who have provisional incomes of in excess of $44,000 are subject to having from 50% to as much as 85% of their Social Security retirement income subject to ordinary income taxes. Provisional income is gross income plus tax-free income plus one half of one's Social Security retirement income. The unintended taxation of Social Security can be a major problem for retirees who own mutual fund portfolios. The following example demonstrates this problem:

> **Example**
> Jack is 65-years old and has pension income of $24,000 a year. He has a mutual fund portfolio worth $150,000. He and his wife receive $20,000 a year in combined Social Security retirement income. Jack and his wife do not have a need for any income above Jack's pension and their Social Security. Although Jack and his wife do not have a need for any additional income, Jack's mutual fund, on average, distributes $15,000 in capital gains to him each year. This mutual fund distribution increases the annual income of Jack and his wife to $59,000. Because of this, a large part of the Social Security income received by Jack and his wife will be subject to income taxes.

In the above example, had Jack held his mutual funds within a variable annuity, none of the Social Security retirement income he and his wife received would be subject to income taxes. The reason for this is that gains made within variable annuities are tax-deferred and do not count in determining whether Social Security retirement income will be taxed. Retired persons who find themselves in a situation like that of Jack and his wife frequently ask if shifting their mutual funds to a tax-free bond fund would solve their problem. The answer is no. The reason for this is that, unlike tax-deferred income, tax-free income must be taken into consideration when determining whether Social Security retirement income will be subject to income taxes.

One of the best ways for retired persons to protect their Social Security retirement income from taxation would be to convert their mutual fund holdings to a variable annuity. The problem with this is that commissions and income taxes due on the sale of mutual funds could be quite large. Preparing for retirement by owning variable annuities instead of mutual funds in the first place eliminates this problem.

§1719. INABILITY TO CONTROL ACCOUNT VALUE AT DEATH

Mutual funds go up and down in value as the stock market fluctuates. The problem with this is that if a mutual fund owner dies when his mutual funds are down in value, his beneficiaries will only receive the diminished value of the funds. For example, mutual funds purchased for $100,000 that are worth $70,000 at the owner's death will pass to the owner's beneficiaries at the $70,000 value. If the mutual funds were worth $130,000 at death this is the value the beneficiaries would receive. Mutual fund owners have no control over what mutual fund value they will pass to survivors. They are at the mercy of an ever-fluctuating stock market. On the other hand, variable annuity owners have complete control over what variable annuity value passes to their beneficiaries at death. When a variable annuity owner dies his beneficiaries receives the greater of the variable annuity's account value or the total amount invested in the variable annuity.[36] For example, a variable annuity purchased for $100,000 that has dropped in value to $70,000 by the time of the owner's death results in $100,000 being paid to the deceased owner's beneficiaries. If the variable annuity were worth $130,000 at death, the deceased owner's beneficiaries would receive this larger figure. Many variable annuity issuers provide a ratcheting death benefit that increases the value of a variable annuity by 5% to 7% for each year it is owned as the next example demonstrates:

Example
Frank purchased a $100,000 variable annuity twelve years ago that had a 7% ratcheting death benefit. He recently died. His variable annuity had a market value of $150,000, but his family received $225,219 due to a 7% ratcheting death benefit Frank's variable annuity offered. Had Frank owned mutual funds his family would have received only $150,000.

The owner of a variable annuity that does not have a ratcheting death can obtain a similar benefit by exchanging his annuity pursuant to IRC §1035.

Example
Tom purchased a variable annuity for $100,000. Seven years later the stock market spiked and Tom's account was worth $250,000. Tom exchanged his variable annuity for a new variable annuity with a three year surrender period. By doing so his death benefit immediately increased to $250,000. Two years later the market corrected and Tom's new variable annuity dropped in value to $150,000. Tom died shortly afterwards. Tom's family would receive $250,000. A mutual

---

[36] Any lifetime withdrawals from the annuity will reduce the death benefit.

fund exchange, based on the identical facts, would only pay $150,000 *before* costs to a mutual fund owner's beneficiaries at his death.

§1720. INABILITY TO CONTROL POTENTIAL LOSSES

Mutual fund owners have no way to avoid potential market losses due to the nature of mutual funds. Mutual funds are like stocks and most other equity based investments – they can lose value. The bear market of 2000-2002 painfully demonstrated this point. Unlike mutual funds, variable annuities allow investors to invest in such a way as to reduce or eliminate downside market risk. Many of the country's best variable annuity issuers offer riders that protect investors against potential losses. This report could not possibly discuss all of these riders, however the following example demonstrates their value and how they provide variable annuity owners with a way to control risk that is unavailable to mutual fund investors.

Example

Max was considering investing an old $30,000 IRA in a variable annuity that had a seven year holding period. The annuity had a rider that would protect Max in case his annuity's value was less than $30,000 seven years from now. At the end of seven years, if the value of the variable annuity is up, Max gets to keep the gain less his investment costs. If the account value is down, the issuing company will refund to Max his entire original investment of $30,000. No costs of any kind are imposed in this last situation. The total annual cost for this annuity, including the money back guarantee, is 2.9% a year. Max was also considering a mutual fund that had a total annual cost of 2.9% (1.5% annual expense ratio, 0.7% annualized commission and 0.7% trading costs). Although the variable annuity and mutual fund have the same annual ownership costs, the mutual fund does not provide Max with any protection if the stock market were to decline over the next seven years.

What the above example demonstrates is that variable annuity investors can control their market risk. This benefit is not available to mutual fund investors. The additional cost of a variable annuity rider to protect against a potential stock market decline will rarely be more than that of the typical mutual fund that provides no similar bear market protection.

§1721. INABILITY TO CONTROL RETIREMENT ACCOUNT RESTRICTIONS

Mutual fund ownership may disqualify taxpayers from taking advantage of the tax benefits that come with converting a traditional IRA to a Roth IRA. Additionally, the ability to fund an IRA and obtain a valuable income tax deduction can be lost to the owners of mutual funds. The ownership of variable annuities does not result in a similar loss of tax advantages. The following example demonstrates how mutual fund ownership can cause the forfeiture of tax benefits normally available to those who desire to fund retirement accounts:

Example

Al and Betty have an adjusted gross income of $80,000. Betty has a traditional IRA containing $250,000 that she would like to convert to a Roth IRA. Al and Betty have a $200,000 mutual fund portfolio. This year, Al and Betty received an annual distribution from their mutual fund portfolio of $22,000. Due to the distribution, Al's and Betty's adjusted gross income will exceed $100,000, making Betty ineligible to convert her traditional IRA to a Roth IRA. This forfeiture would not have occurred if Al and Betty owned their funds inside of a variable annuity. Al and Betty can sell off some of their funds so next year their distribution will be smaller. This might make Betty eligible to convert her IRA to a Roth IRA but they may incur commissions and taxes when the mutual funds are sold. Al and Betty need to be careful if they elect to do this because the sale of the mutual funds may also generate disqualifying capital gains.

§1722. LOSS OF FLEXIBILITY REGARDING MEDICAID QUALIFICATION

Mutual fund ownership may pose a serious problem if the owner of such funds, or his spouse, needs Medicaid assistance should they go into a nursing home. The reason for this is that most states do not count the value of annuities that have been annuitized and are making payments to either or both spouses as an asset for Medicaid eligibility. All states count the full value of mutual funds in determining eligibility for nursing home coverage under Medicaid. A few thousand dollars worth of mutual funds can result in Medicaid disqualification as the following examples demonstrate:

Example

Mary, age 72, went into a nursing home three years ago. Her only asset at that time was a variable annuity worth $144,000 that she purchased ten years ago. Mary has a handicapped spouse that she is concerned about. Shortly before going into the nursing home, Mary annuitized her annuity and started receiving $1,222 per month for life with payments being guaranteed for ten years.[37] Mary had to use this income toward her nursing home care expenses of $4,000 a month. Medicaid only counts annuity *income* to determine Medicaid eligibility. Mary recently died. Her spouse will receive the remaining monthly annuity payments of $1,222 for seven years, for a total of more than $100,000.[38]

Example

Mark, age 72, went into a nursing home three years ago. His only asset at that time was a mutual fund portfolio worth $144,000 that he purchased ten years ago. Mark has a handicapped spouse that he is concerned about. The cost of Mark's nursing home care was $4,000 per month. Medicaid requires that both the *income* and *principal* of mutual fund portfolios be exhausted before Medicaid will pay for nursing home care. Mark made each month's nursing home payment from his mutual fund portfolio. Mark recently died. Mark used the entire $144,000 value of his mutual fund portfolio for his nursing home care over the three years he was

---

[37] For Medicaid purposes, annuity payments may not extend beyond the owner's life expectancy.

[38] Some people are concerned that estate recovery statutes could be applied to proceeds of a variable annuity after the owner's death. Estate recover statutes generally apply to *probate* property only. Because variable annuities are non-probate property, most estate recovery statutes cannot be used to recover variable annuity proceeds passing to the beneficiaries of a variable annuity. Recent changes in Medicaid laws do allow states to claim a lien on annuity proceeds upon the death of a Medicaid recipient unless the proceeds are paid to a spouse or other qualified recipient.

in the nursing home. His spouse will receive nothing. Mark could have liquidated his fund portfolio and bought an annuity but he would have had a smaller nest egg and would have incurred transaction costs and income taxes that Mary, in the prior example, avoided because she had invested her money in a variable annuity initially. In addition, many states require that a variable annuity must have been purchased from 36 to 72 months prior to applying for Medicaid.

§1723. LOSS OF FLEXIBILITY WITH LATE YEAR PURCHASES

Mutual funds must distribute realized gains to fund owners each year in order that these distributions can be reported for income tax purposes by the funds' owners. Mutual fund companies usually make distributions to fund owners of record in November or December. Distributions are broken down into dividends, long-term capital gains and short-term capital gains. These distributions are reported on 1099-DIV forms which are usually sent to investors with other information concerning the distribution. For the uninformed, the purchase of a mutual fund late in the year just before a fund makes a distribution can result in a significant tax disadvantage. The following example demonstrates this problem:

Example

Judy recently inherited $400,000. She wanted to invest the money for her retirement. In late November, after much research, she selected an aggressive Internet mutual fund with a track record of returning 25% a year. Judy invested her $400,000 by purchasing 20,000 shares of the fund at $20 per share. Two weeks later, Judy received a distribution notice from the fund company for $5 per share or $100,000. This $5 represented the per share growth in the Internet fund for the *entire* year. Half of the distribution was ordinary income and half was long-term capital gain. The price of the fund was adjusted downward by the amount of the distribution. Thus, the fund's market value fell from $20 to $15 per share. After the distribution, Judy owned 20,000 shares of the fund worth $300,000 ($15 x 20,000) plus a distribution of $100,000 (20,000 x $5) for a total investment value of $400,000. Although Judy reinvested the distribution, she had to report the $100,000 distribution as income. She paid $25,000 in income taxes on the distribution. After paying the taxes, Judy's net fund investment stood at $375,000, reflecting an immediate $25,000 income tax loss even though her mutual fund did nothing more than make a required distribution. Had Judy put her $400,000 inheritance into similar investments within a variable annuity, she would not have suffered a $25,000 tax loss.

§1724. INABILITY TO CONTROL THE IMPACT ON TUITION ASSISTANCE

The ownership of a mutual fund portfolio may prove problematic for parents with college-bound children. Parents who have applied for college financial aid are learning that large mutual fund holdings may disqualify them, in whole or part, from obtaining such aid. What many parents do not realize is that most financial aid sources do not count assets held in variable annuities when determining eligibility for financial aid if these annuities are in the accumulation phase. The Free Application for Federal Student Aid (FAFSA) used by public colleges and the

CSS/Financial Aid Profile used by many private colleges do not require life insurance or variable annuities to be listed as assets but do require mutual funds to be listed. The following examples demonstrate how ownership of mutual funds may result in the loss of tuition assistance.

Example

Jane's parents applied to obtain college financial aid to put Jane through college. Their total income for each of the past thee years was $50,000. Of this amount, $15,000 was a distribution from a mutual fund. Their mutual funds were worth $250,000. Because of their income level and the value of their mutual fund portfolio, Jane's parents could not obtain college tuition assistance for Jane. Had their investment been in a variable annuity, their reportable income would have been $35,000. In addition, variable annuities are not required to be reported as assets while they are in the accumulation phase. In short, with variable annuity ownership, Jane's parents would have been able to obtain tuition assistance for their daughter.

§1725. INABILITY TO CONTROL THE LOSS OF CREDITS, EXEMPTIONS AND DEDUCTIONS

Mutual fund ownership may cause the owner to lose valuable income tax credits, exemptions and deductions. Under current income tax law, credits, exemptions and deductions are phased out at certain income levels. A taxpayer who receives a forced income distribution from his mutual fund may find that the distribution reduces or eliminates an income tax credit, exemption or deduction. Because variable annuities do not force income on their owners like mutual funds do, a similar loss of income tax benefits do not arise. The following example demonstrates the negative impact forced income distributions might have on mutual fund owners:

Example

Don and Judy have an adjusted gross income (AGI) of $82,500. Among other deductions, Don and Judy have an $11,350 casualty loss deduction. Casualty deductions are limited to amounts above 10% of AGI plus $100. Normally, Don and Judy would be entitled to a $3,000 casualty loss deduction ($11,350 - $8,250 - $100 = $3,000).[39] However, they received a mutual fund distribution of $30,000 which raised their AGI to $112,500. This caused Don and Judy to lose their $3,000 casualty deduction. In effect, the mutual fund distribution caused Don and Judy to lose a $3,000 deduction. At a 20% average tax rate, this lost deduction would cost Don and Judy $600. This loss would not have occurred if Don and Judy had invested in a variable annuity instead of a mutual fund. In addition, Don and Judy must pay income taxes on the $30,000 distribution. This tax burden could range from $4,500 to $6,000 or more.

§1726. INABILITY TO CONTROL COMMISSION COSTS

Variable annuity purchasers do not pay up-front, out-of-pocket commissions. They agree to hold their variable annuities for a specified holding period and if the annuity is liquidated

---

[39] $82,500 x 10% = $8,250. $11,250 - $8,250 = $3,000.

before expiration of the agreed holding period, a declining surrender charge (technically called a contingent deferred sales charge) is imposed. For example, if a variable annuity with a six year holding or surrender period is purchased and liquidated within one year, the owner must pay a six percent surrender fee to the variable annuity issuer from his sale proceeds. A sale occurring after holding the variable annuity for three years would result in a surrender charge of three percent. If the variable annuity is held for six years or beyond, no surrender charge is imposed. Variable annuities are available with holding or surrender periods ranging from zero to ten years. Investors are free to select the holding period that best fits their investment time horizon. If an investor believes he will hold his variable annuity for only three years he can select a variable annuity with a three year holding or surrender period. By doing so, an investor is able to control the commission he pays to buy his variable annuity.

A-share mutual funds do not offer investors the ability to avoid commissions. The reason for this is that A-share mutual funds charge up-front, out-of-pocket commissions which, once paid, are forever lost regardless of how long a mutual fund is held. B-share mutual funds have commission structures that mirror closely that of the variable annuity. However, the standard B-share mutual fund has a six-year declining contingent deferred sales charge that is usually inflexible. Rarely do B-share mutual funds offer holding or surrender periods of less than five or six years. The following example demonstrates how an investor can control commissions by using the flexibility provided by variable annuities.

Example

Tom is sixty years old and has $20,000 in an old 401(k) to invest. He wants to transfer it to an IRA. He plans to invest for several years but may need to liquidate his IRA in three years to help his elderly mother with nursing home expenses. Tom is considering a variable annuity that has a three year surrender period and has a 2.4% annual expense ratio. Trading costs are 0.5%. He is also looking at an A-share mutual fund that imposes a 5½% commission and has an annual expense ratio of 1.5%. Trading costs are 0.7%. A third investment Tom is considering is a B-share mutual fund that has a 6% CDSC that declines 1% over a six year surrender period and an annual expense ratio of 2.4%. Trading costs are 0.7%. Tom's financial planner created the following table to help Tom decide which investment would provide the most control and flexibility regarding commissions, surrender fees and other costs. It is assumed that Tom's investment selections will return 10% a year for three years. Mutual fund trailing commissions are ignored.

INVESTMENT	INITIAL UP-FRONT COMMISSIONS	THREE YEAR EXPENSES	SURRENDER FEES AFTER THREE YEARS	TOTAL THREE YEAR COSTS
A-Share Mutual Fund	$1,100[40]	$1,479[41]	-0-	$2,579[42]
B-Share Mutual Fund	-0-	$2,184[43]	$727[44]	$2,911[45]
Variable Annuity	-0-	$2,047[46]	-0-	$2,047[47]

Based on the above table, Tom elected to buy a variable annuity because it allowed him to control his commission cost because the annuity provided a surrender period that matched his potentially short three-year holding period and therefore generated the largest gain for Tom of the three investments compared.

§1727. LOSS OF FLEXIBILITY REGARDING WITHDRAWALS

Only variable annuities allow owners to withdraw specific amounts of money from their investment each year without incurring a charge for doing so. Such withdrawals are usually allowed for amounts up to 10% to 15% of the annuity's account value.[48] Although A-share mutual funds allow owners to withdraw any amount of their investment at anytime, it must be remembered that the payment of an up-front, out-of-pocket, non-refundable commission will always negatively impact this right of withdrawal. With B-share mutual funds, a contingent deferred sales charge is imposed on *any* withdrawals made during the holding period of the fund. B-share mutual funds do not offer surrender charge-free withdrawals.

The following example demonstrates the flexibility and savings of the surrender-free withdrawal feature provided by variable annuities:

Example

Andy, who is 53, purchased a $20,000 A-share mutual fund a year ago. He was charged a 5¼% commission. The fund had a 1.5% annual expense ratio. Trading costs are 0.7% a year. Annual income taxes reduced Andy's gain by 2.0%. Betty, who is 53, purchased a $20,000 B-share mutual fund that imposed a 6% contingent deferred sales charge (CDSC) that declined 1% a year for six

---

[40] 5½% of $20,000 = $1,100.

[41] $20,000 - 5½% = $18,900 + 10% = $20,790 - 1.5% - 0.7% = $457.40. $457.40 + $491.20 + $530.40 = $1,479.

[42] $1,110 (note 249) + $1,479 (note 37) = $2,579.

[43] $20,000 + 10% = $22,000 less 3.1% = $682. $682 + $727 + $775 = $2,184.

[44] $20,000 + 10% = $22,000 less 3.1% = $21,318 - $20,000 = $1,318 ÷ $20,000 = 6.59%. 6.59% x 3 years x $20,000 = $24,220 x 3% = $727.

[45] $727 (note 256) + $2,184 (note 255) = $2,911.

[46] $20,000 + 10% = $22,000 x 2.9% = $638. $638 + $681 + $728 = $2,047.

[47] See note 258 *supra*.

[48] For complete liquidation, surrender fees are based on total premiums paid in many cases.

years. The fund charged a 2.4% annual expense ratio. Trading costs are 0.7% a year. Annual taxes reduced Betty's gain by 2.0%. Chad, who is 53, purchased a $20,000 variable annuity that had a 6% CDSC that declined 1% a year. The variable annuity had a 2.3% annual expense ratio. The variable annuity allows withdrawals of up to 15% a year of the annuity's account value without imposing surrender penalties. Chad is in a 22% average tax bracket. The 10% IRS penalty for pre-59½ withdrawals would apply. Trading costs are 0.5% a year. Each investor earned 10% a year on his or her investment. At the end of three years each investor withdrew $3,000 from his or her account. Annual mutual fund taxation will be held to 15% although it could be greater. Table #5 summarizes the account balances for the three investors after factoring in the costs associated with these withdrawals:

TABLE #5: THREE YEAR ENDING BALANCE AFTER WITHDRAWALS

INVESTOR	ENDING BALANCE	WITHDRAWN AMOUNT	WITHDRAWAL COSTS	INCOME TAXES	POST W/D VALUE
ANDY (A-Share M.F.)	$22,611[49]	$3,000	$0	$450[50]	$19,161[51]
BETTY (B-Share M.F.)	$23,333[52]	$3,000	$90[53]	$437[54]	$19,806[55]
CHAD (Variable Annuity)	$24,445[56]	$3,000	$0[57]	$960[58]	$20,485[59]

As Table #5 demonstrates, the three-year ending balance for the variable annuity investor is higher than for either of the mutual fund investors because:

- A-share mutual funds charge an up-front, out-of-pocket commission that is non-refundable regardless of how much or how little is ultimately withdrawn from the fund;

- B-share mutual funds charge surrender fees on all withdrawals in any amount; and

- The variable annuity allows annual withdrawals of up to 15% of the account value free of any surrender charge.

---

[49] $20,000 - 5¼% = $18,950 + 10% = $20,845 - 2.2% = $20,386.40 - $18,950 = $1,436.40 - 20% = $1,149 ÷ $18,950 = 6.064%. 6.064% x 3 years x $18,950 = $22,611.

[50] $3,000 x 15% tax = $450.

[51] $22,611 - $3,000 - $450 = $19,161.

[52] $20,000 - 10% = $22,000 - 3.1% = $21,318 - $20,000 = $1,318 - 20% = $1,054 ÷ $20,000 = 5.272%. 5.272% x 3 years x $20,000 = $23,333.

[53] $3,000 less 3% surrender fee = $90.

[54] $3,000 - $90 surrender fee = $2,910 x 15% = $437.

[55] $23,333 - $3,000 - $90 - $437 = $19,806.

[56] $20,000 + 10% = $22,000 - 2.8% = $21,384 - $20,000 = $1,384 ÷ $20,000 = 6.92%. 6.92% x 3 years x $20,000 = $24,445.

[57] Withdrawals of up to 15% or $3,667 may be made without a surrender charge.

[58] $3,000 x 22% income tax = $660 + 10% IRS penalty of $300 = $960.

[59] $24,445 - $3,000 - $960 = $20,485.

§1728. LOSS OF TAX PLANNING FLEXIBILITY REGARDING CAPITAL GAINS TAXATION AT LIQUIDATION

Earlier in this report it was pointed out that mutual fund owners cannot control the amount or nature of the income generated by their mutual funds on an *annual* basis. This in turn results in the inability of mutual fund owners to control the tax liability generated by their funds. Many investors assume that by purchasing mutual funds today they will be taxed at 15% capital gains rates when they sell their funds in the future. The problem with this assumption is that capital gains rates are *not* applied when *purchases* are made – they are determined and applied by the tax law in effect at the time of *sale*. Simply put, an investor does not receive capital gains treatment when they buy an investment but only when they sell it. The capital gains rate in effect at the time of the investment's sale is the rate that is critical. Current tax legislation increases the present 15% capital gains rate to 20% after December 31, 2010. Mutual fund investors who hold their investments beyond 2010 may not receive the 15% capital gains rates that motivated them to purchase their mutual funds in the first place. The likelihood that this increase will occur is heightened for two reasons:

- The federal deficit is large and gets larger daily. Revenues will be needed to combat this deficit. [NOTE: The primary reason Congress refuses to eliminate the universally hated alternative minimum tax (AMT) is because they are faced with a soaring federal deficit]; and

- Initial sources of additional revenue to combat high deficits have traditionally come from the rich. Capital gains taxes benefit the rich more than any other economic class and are a prime target for an increase that could come earlier than December 31, 2010.

Some investors believe they can obtain the benefit of the 15% capital gains rates by selling their mutual funds before December 31, 2010 and then reinvesting their after-tax proceeds in new investments. The likelihood that this strategy will work is not great as the following examples demonstrate:

Example
Steve invested $100,000 in an index fund in 2006. By December of 2010 his account doubled to $200,000. He sold his fund to get the 15% capital gains rate. After paying taxes, his account was worth $185,000 which he reinvested. By 2014 his account doubled again to $370,000. He sold the account and paid 20% tax on the $185,000 gain leaving a net account value of $333,000. (This calculation ignores commissions and other costs).

Example
Sara invested $100,000 in an index fund in 2006. By December of 2010 her account doubled to $200,000. Sara did not sell. By 2014 her account doubled again to $400,000. Sara sold her account in 2014. The $300,000 in gain was taxed at 20% leaving a net account value of $340,000. (This calculation ignores commissions and other costs).

What the above examples demonstrate is that many investors who are eligible for 15% capital gains treatment available up to December 31, 2010 may be better off forfeiting this lower tax rate and paying the higher 20% capital gains taxes in the future. If this is the case, one must ask of what value is the 15% capital gains rate in effect today?

§1729. LOSS OF FLEXIBILITY REGARDING BENEFICIARIES INCOME TAX BURDEN

Many mutual fund investors purchase mutual funds in order to pass them at their death to other family members (usually children or grandchildren). The reason for choosing mutual funds is that they *currently* provide an income tax advantage to beneficiaries who inherit such funds. This tax advantage is technically referred to as a step-up in basis. Simply stated, a step-up in basis allows beneficiaries to treat inherited mutual funds as if they bought the funds for their market value on the day the owner died. This would allow beneficiaries to sell the funds upon inheritance and avoid any income taxes. The step-up in basis would also allow beneficiaries to sell the funds in the future and be taxed only on the difference between their inherited value and the amount received from their sale. The following example demonstrates how the current step-up in basis rule works:

Example

Abel purchased a mutual fund for $10,000. At his death, the fund was worth $20,000. Abel left the fund by will to his daughter Betty. Shortly after receiving the mutual fund, Betty sold it for $20,000. Betty will not incur any income tax liability on the sale of the fund because she is allowed to treat the inherited mutual fund as if she purchased it for its $20,000 fair market value determined as of the date of her father's death. Stated another way, Betty's cost basis in her inherited mutual fund for income tax purposes would be stepped-up from her father's cost basis of $10,000 to the $20,000 date of death value. If the fund were sold by Betty for more than $20,000, she would be obligated to pay long-term capital gain taxes only on those sale proceeds that exceeded $20,000.

Example

Carla purchased a variable annuity for $10,000. At Carla's death, the variable annuity was worth $20,000 and passed to her son Dave who was named as the beneficiary of the variable annuity. Dave will be required to pay ordinary income taxes on those proceeds he received that exceeded his mother's initial $10,000 purchase price for the variable annuity. Assuming Dave is in a 20% average tax bracket, his tax liability will be $2,000. This tax liability arises because Dave is not entitled to a step-up in the $10,000 original cost basis of the annuity purchased by his mother. In short, Carla's $10,000 purchase price for her variable annuity is carried over or transferred to Dave. Although Dave's tax liability is $300 more than Abel paid, the costs of mutual fund ownership are greater than variable annuity ownership and would most likely exceed the $300 tax differential mentioned.

A major problem with the current step-up in basis rule is that IRC§1022 significantly reduces the step-up in basis benefit beginning January 1, 2010. Like many of the recent tax law changes, this law is automatically repealed on January 1, 2011 *unless* extended or made permanent by Congress. Recently, several of the tax laws that were created within the last few years were scheduled to be repealed earlier than 2011. Most of them have been extended by Congress. The President wanted them to be made permanent. Most tax experts predict that the estate tax exemption will be significantly increased by 2010. This will virtually ensure that IRC §1022 will be extended or more likely made permanent for two reasons:

- The loss in revenue from increasing the estate exemption will have to be made-up from some other source. Extending or making permanent the reduction in the step-up in basis benefit currently addressed in IRC §1022 would be a logical source; and

- With the federal deficit at record levels and growing daily, the government must seek new sources of revenue. Under current law the government receives no income tax revenue when capital assets such as mutual funds pass from deceased owners to their beneficiaries. In the next decade it is estimated that ten to twelve *trillion* dollars in assets will pass to the next generation by way of inheritance. The government cannot afford to ignore this huge source of revenue. By extending or making IRC §1022 permanent, the government will be able to levy an income tax on the ten to twelve trillion dollars mentioned above to help reduce the federal deficit.

Investors who are purchasing mutual funds to obtain the benefit of a step-up in basis for their beneficiaries cannot control what Congress will do with IRC §1022 over the next few years. Variable annuities do not provide a step-up in basis to beneficiaries who inherit them. However, tax professionals have developed tax strategies for avoiding both death taxes and income taxes that beneficiaries might owe upon inheritance of such annuities. These tax strategies not only provide the same benefit as the step-up in basis but do so while eliminating any possible estate tax on the variable annuity's value at death. In addition, unlike mutual funds, there are no existing tax laws that propose any limitations on the ability of variable annuity owners to avoid death taxes on their variable annuities while passing their full value to beneficiaries income-tax free. As the following example demonstrates, variable annuity owners have significantly more flexibility and control in taking advantage of the potential estate and income tax savings available to them:

Example:
Jack and his wife, both 68, have an estate worth $5,000,000. One million dollars of this estate is a variable annuity owned by Jack of which half consists of contributions and half is growth. The remainder of the estate, which consists of a house, vacation property, investments, car, etc., is worth $4,000,000. Jack and his wife each own half of these assets. Each has a will containing a credit shelter trust. Jack and his wife need $60,000 a year to supplement their other retirement income. At their death, Jack and his wife want their entire estate to

pass to their three children without estate taxes or income taxes if possible. Basic tax planning can accomplish this. Jack should have his children purchase (and own) a $1,000,000 second-to-die life insurance policy on the lives of Jack and his wife. Annual premiums would be approximately $30,000. After the policy is in place, Jack should transfer his variable annuity tax free (via §1035) to an annuity company in exchange for an immediate joint lifetime annuity (i.e., no guarantee other than lifetime payments). The immediate annuity will pay Jack and his wife approximately $90,000 a year for life. Jack can give $30,000 to his children gift-tax free each year to enable them to pay the premiums on the life insurance they purchased. This leaves Jack and his wife with the $60,000 they need each year to supplement their other retirement income. The exclusion ratio will shelter much of the $90,000 annuity payments made to Jack and his wife from taxation. If either spouse dies tomorrow the annuity will continue to pay the surviving spouse for his or her lifetime. At the second spouse's death the estate will be worth $4,000,000 and will pass to the children estate tax free by applying the current $2,000,000 exemption (2008) together with the credit shelter trust. Jack's immediate annuity would be valued at zero because it is a lifetime annuity that ceases to have any value at the second spouse's death. In addition to the $4,000,000 estate, the children will receive $1,000,000 estate and income-tax free from the insurance company in the form of insurance proceeds. In short, a combination of annuitization, basic estate planning and asset substitution will allow the children to inherit $5,000,000 free of all estate and income taxes. (Any unrecovered portion of the annuity can be treated as an income tax deduction on the deceased owner's final income tax return). Each year Jack and his wife will receive $90,000. In eleven years they will receive their $1,000,000 annuity purchase back and still be entitled to $90,000 payments for life.

There are numerous advantages that beneficiaries obtain when they receive variable annuities from a deceased owner that will oftentimes provide them with an economic benefit that is greater than that which arises with a step-up in basis when mutual funds are inherited. A summary of these advantages include:

- Mutual funds, unlike variable annuities, are subject to a step-down in basis.
- Variable annuities provide low-cost riders that will often provide more value to beneficiaries than will a step-up in basis with mutual funds.
- Spousal continuation, available only with variable annuities, will often provide a benefit greater than a step-up in basis with a mutual fund.
- Annuitization of a variable annuity often provides a greater economic gain than a step-up in basis with a mutual fund.
- Lifetime transfers under IRS §72(e)(4)(c)(i) will often provide a larger benefit than the step-up with mutual funds.
- Tax deferral coupled with IRC §691 will often provide a larger benefit than the step-up in basis with mutual funds.
- The ratcheting death benefit provided by variable annuities may outperform a

mutual fund's step-up in basis.

- The use of IRC §1035 with a variable annuity may outperform a mutual fund's step-up in basis. The following examples demonstrate the use of IRC §1035 to obtain a benefit that could exceed that provided by a mutual fund:

Example

Dana, a widow, purchased a mutual fund for $350,000 when she was 55. Dana is now 70 and in poor health. Dana wants her son to inherit her mutual fund. Dana's mutual fund went up in value to a high of $700,000 several years ago, but when Dana died her mutual fund was only worth $500,000. At her death, Dana's son inherited the mutual fund. Due to the step-up in basis, Dana's son did not have to pay income taxes on the mutual fund's gain and therefore received the full $500,000 value of his mother's mutual fund.

Example

Steve, a widower, purchased a variable annuity for $350,000 when he was 55. Steve is now 70 and in poor health. Steve wants his daughter to inherit his variable annuity. His annuity increased in value to $700,000 several years ago. Steve's financial advisor suggested that Steve take advantage of IRC§1035 and transfer his variable annuity to another similar variable annuity company. This could be accomplished without costs or income taxes. The benefit of the transfer would be that Steve's original death benefit of $300,000 provided by his first annuity would increase to $700,000 with the new variable annuity. This would guarantee that Steve's daughter would never receive less than $700,000 at Steve's death. Steve followed his advisor's suggestion. When Steve died his variable annuity had gone down in value to $500,000. Steve's daughter received a check from the annuity company for $700,000. She had to pay 30% in taxes on the $350,000 in gain in the variable annuity which left her with a *net* (after-tax) inheritance of $595,000. This is $95,000 more than Dana left her son in the prior example even though the son received a step-up in basis. [Note: The fact that Dana may have paid income taxes and higher annual ownership costs for her fund when she owned it was ignored in these examples].

§1730. LOSS OF FLEXIBILITY UPON REINVESTMENT

When a mutual fund owner elects to reinvest his fund he *must* sell the fund, pay taxes and reinvest the proceeds. If the proceeds are reinvested in a different fund family, additional commissions or surrender charges may be imposed. Variable annuity owners, by taking advantage of IRC §1035 (tax-free exchanges) can transfer one variable annuity to an entirely different one without incurring income taxes or having to pay out-of-pocket commissions. This flexibility and control provided by the variable annuity is demonstrated in the following example:

Example

Judy, who is 45, plans to invest $20,000 for her retirement in 15 years. She wants to invest all of her $20,000 in an A-share mutual fund, B-share mutual fund or variable annuity. She asked her financial professional which investment would be best if she elected to move to a similar fund or annuity after seven years. Judy assumes that any transfer would be to a new mutual fund family or a variable annuity issuer. Judy was concerned with the potential income taxes and commissions that would be involved in such a transaction. Judy's financial planner prepared the following table for Judy:

TABLE #6: CONSEQUENCES OF REINVESTING MUTUAL FUNDS AND VARIABLE ANNUITIES

INVESTMENT	OUT-OF-POCKET COMMISSIONS ON PURCHASE	INCOME TAX ON GAIN AT TRANSFER	NEW COMMISSION UPON RE-INVESTMENT
A-SHARE MUTUAL FUND	YES	YES	YES
B-SHARE MUTUAL FUND	NO	YES	NO
VARIABLE ANNUITY	NO	NO	NO

After reviewing the above table Judy was leaning toward the purchase of a variable annuity. However, because Judy is in a 25% average tax bracket, she was also interested in the *net* ending value of the three investments she was considering if she does change investments in seven years. She believes that the market will provide an average annual rate of return of 10% over the next 15 years. Her financial planner found that both the mutual fund and variable annuity that Judy was considering had the following expenses:

A-Share Mutual Fund: 5% initial commission and a 4½% commission on reinvestment. The annual expense ratio was 1.5%, trading cost were 0.7% and the annual income tax loss was 2.0% of gain.

B-Share Mutual Fund: No out-of-pocket commission. The annual expense ratio was 2.4%, trading cost were 0.7%. The fund had a contingent deferred sales charge (CDSC) of 6% that declined 1% a year.

Variable Annuity: No out-of-pocket commission. The annual expense ratio was 2.3%, trading cost were 0.5%. The annuity had a contingent deferred sales charge (CDSC) of 7% that declined 1% a year.

Based on the data she gathered, Judy's financial planner determined that the *net* ending value of the three accounts in 15 years would be:

- A-share mutual funds: $43,881[60]
- B-share mutual funds: $44,204[61]
- Variable annuity: $45,924[62]

If Judy is concerned about out-of-pocket commissions, income taxes and net returns if she changes investments seven years from now, the variable annuity will offer her the most flexibility and control over these costs. The primary reason for this result is that IRC §1035 may be used by variable annuity investors but not mutual fund investors. If Judy decides to hold any of the three investments discussed until her retirement, the variable annuity will provide the largest net gain.

§1731. INABILITY TO CONTROL TRANSACTION COSTS

One of the major advantages of variable annuities is that they frequently offer dozens of sub-accounts managed by investment experts representing numerous money management companies. This allows variable annuity owners to diversify their investment among many money managers. Generally, mutual funds offer a choice of different funds that are managed by various mutual fund money managers. If a mutual fund investor wants to reinvest money in his mutual fund in a different fund offered by another company, they are faced with transaction costs that variable annuity investors do not encounter. Transaction costs generally include income taxes and additional commissions that investors incur when moving from one investment to another. As mentioned above, one of the major advantages of investing in variable annuities is that changing investments among the variable annuity's diverse sub-accounts triggers neither income taxes nor additional commissions. Mutual fund investing does not provide this benefit. If a fund investor sells a fund he owns and purchases a new fund from a different mutual fund company, both income taxes and additional commissions are frequently encountered.[63] Many mutual fund and variable annuity investors understand the importance of rebalancing and reallocating their holdings over time. Such rebalancing and reallocating can be done automatically among the various sub-accounts offered by variable annuities without generating income taxes or incurring additional commissions. Mutual fund investors often face new income taxes and additional

---

[60] $20,000 - 5% + 10% - 1½% - 0.7% less 20% in income taxes on gain = 6.064% x $19,000 x 7 years = $28,690 - 4.5% = $27,399 + 10% - 1½% - 0.7% less 20% in annual income taxes on gain = 6.064% x $27,399 x 8 years = $43,881. [This net ending result ignores income taxes on *unrealized* gain in the mutual fund that would be due at the time of the initial *and* second sale. Trailing commissions are also ignored.]

[61] $20,000 + 10% - 2.4% - 0.7% less 20% in income taxes on gain = 5.272% x $20,000 x 6 years = $27,221 + 10% - 1.5% (reduced A-share annual expense ratio) - 0.7% less 20% in annual income taxes on gain = 6.064%. 6.064% x 1 year x $27,221 = $28,872 + 10% - 2.4% - 0.7% less 20% tax = 5.272%. 5.272% x $28,872 x 6 years = $39,294 + 10% - 1.5% (reduced annual expense ratio) - 0.7% less 20% tax = 6.064%. 6.064% x 2 years x $39,294 = $44,204. [This net ending result ignores income taxes on *unrealized* gain in the mutual fund that would be due at the time of the initial *and* second sale.]

[62] $20,000 x 10% - 2.3% - 0.5% = 6.92% x $20,000 x 15 years = $54,565 less 25% tax on $34,565 in gain = $45,924.

[63] With A-share mutual funds, the sale of one mutual fund and purchase of another within the same family usually will trigger an income tax liability but generally can be accomplished without having pay a new commission. If B-share mutual funds are sold and a new B-share mutual fund from a different mutual fund company is purchased, the sale will usually generate income taxes while the purchase may result in new (and usually longer) surrender period.

commissions when rebalancing and reallocating their mutual funds. The loss of the ability to control transaction costs can prove to be very expensive over time for mutual fund investors as the following example demonstrate:

Example

Tom, who is 50, has $100,000 to invest for his retirement in 15 years. He is considering a mutual fund and a variable annuity. Tom believes in rebalancing his holdings and likes the freedom of moving out of poorly performing investments and into investments that are better performers. For diversification, Tom selected a portfolio of five mutual funds and a portfolio of five variable annuities as two possible investments. He determined the average costs of owning each portfolio would be as follows:

Mutual Fund Portfolio: 5% commission, annual expense ratio of 1.5%, trading costs of 0.7%, annual income tax liability of 2.0%, 10% annual rate of return.

Variable Annuity Portfolio: Annual expense ratio of 2.3%, trading costs of 0.5%, 10% annual rate of return, average income tax liability of 25% on withdrawals of gain.

Based on the above data, Tom determined that his mutual fund portfolio would be worth $229,743[64] in fifteen years. The variable annuity portfolio would be worth $277,066 before taxes and $232,799 after taxes.[65] These figures unrealistically assume no buying, selling, reallocation or rebalancing occurs with the mutual fund. If Tom moved as little as 1/10 of his mutual fund portfolio to funds in other fund families each year, income taxes and new commissions would conservatively add ½% to his tax liability and ½% to his annual commission expense. Factoring in these costs, his mutual fund portfolio would be worth $205,328 in 15 years.[66] This is over $27,000 less than the variable annuity portfolio would produce after-taxes.[67] It is important to note that Tom would not incur any new commissions or income taxes for doing the same amount of trading or rebalancing in his variable annuity account. Additionally, the mutual fund investments were not reduced for unrealized capital gains that would be due when they were sold. Trailing commissions were ignored also.

§1732. LOSS OF FLEXIBILITY IN DEDUCTING INVESTMENT LOSSES

When a variable annuity is sold at a loss, the owner receives a full income tax deduction for the loss. This deduction reduces *ordinary* income. When a mutual fund generates a long-term capital loss, the deduction, if not offset by capital gains, may only be taken in $3,000 increments over what can be several years as the following examples demonstrate.

---

[64] 6.064% x 15 years x $19,000 = $49,948.74 x five funds = $229,744.

[65] 7.03% x 15 years x $20,000 = $55,413 x 5 variable annuities= $277, 066 less 25% tax on $177,066 = $132,799 + $100,000 = $232,799.

[66] 5.2725% x 15 years x $19,000 = $41,066 x 5 mutual funds = $205,328.

[67] $232,799 - $205,328 = $27,471.

Example

Ellen recently sold a mutual fund she purchased three years ago. Her cost basis in the fund was $90,000. The proceeds from the sale were $69,000, resulting in a $21,000 loss. Ellen has no other capital gains or losses. Ellen's loss deduction is limited to $3,000 for the current tax year. The remaining $18,000 may be written off on future tax returns for six years at the rate of $3,000 a year.[68]

Example

Dave recently sold a variable annuity he purchased for $90,000 three years ago. The proceeds from the sale were $69,000, resulting in a $21,000 loss. Dave is entitled to deduct this entire loss (including any surrender charges) and use it to offset his *ordinary* income.[69] The IRS takes the position that variable annuity losses should be reduced by 2% of a taxpayer's adjusted gross income (AGI). For example, if Dave's AGI is $100,000, his variable annuity loss deduction would be $21,000 less $2,000 or $19,000. (Many tax professionals disagree with the position taken by the IRS regarding the 2% reduction based on the taxpayer's AGI).[70]

Being able to fully deduct the loss one has in a variable annuity provides greater control over one's taxes than the long-term capital gain deduction of $3,000 a year allowed to mutual fund owners. In addition, a deduction against ordinary income will always save a taxpayer more than an equivalent long-term capital loss deduction even if the long-term capital loss is fully deductible.

§1733. INABILITY TO CONTROL ALTERNATIVE MINIMUM TAX (AMT) LIABILITY

Distributions from mutual funds can trigger the dreaded alternative minimum tax (AMT). When this happens the effective long-term capital gains rate applicable to mutual funds increases to 22% or more. Because mutual fund investors cannot control the timing, size or nature of mutual fund distributions, they are unable to avoid triggering the AMT. Because variable annuities are tax-deferred and do not force unwanted income on annuity investors, the AMT cannot be triggered by the ownership of variable annuities.

§1734. QUESTIONS TO ASK

Does the liquidity myth have any significant merit?

§1735. SOURCES

See the footnotes to this chapter for other sources to consult.

---

[68] This assumes that there are no gains now or in the future to offset losses.

[69] There is no requirement that such variable annuity losses be offset by capital gains. The alternative minimum tax can be triggered by large variable annuity losses that are reduced by 2% of a taxpayer's AGI. A tax professional should be consulted when deducting variable annuity losses. See "The Deductibility of Variable Annuity Losses" in the May/June issue of *Variable Product Specialist* magazine.

[70] These tax professionals deduct the variable annuity loss as an above the line deduction without a 2% AGI offset. There is case law and at least one Revenue Ruling supporting this position. The IRS has nothing supporting their position that variable annuity losses are subject to the 2% AGI threshold. Above the line deductions avoid any alternative minimum tax (AMT) problems.

§1736. REVIEW QUESTIONS

Explain why variable annuities have an advantage when a client needs liquidity, control and flexibility with his investments.

§1737. CONCLUSION

Variable annuities are every bit as liquid as mutual funds. In most cases, the cost of liquidating a variable annuity will usually be no greater than the cost for liquidating a mutual fund and in many cases will be much less. The argument that variable annuities offer less control and flexibility than mutual funds is simply not accurate. When the elements of investment control and flexibility are examined for both variable annuities and mutual funds it is usually the variable annuity that provides greater control and flexibility.

– CHAPTER 18 –
THE STEP-UP IN BASIS MYTH – SUMMARY DISCUSSION
§1801. INTRODUCTION

One of the most costly myths believed by the media and investors alike is that because mutual funds receive a step-up in basis when inherited they make better wealth transfer investments than variable annuities that do not provide a step-up in basis to beneficiaries. This is a myth in most cases.

§1802. THE STEP-UP IN BASIS RULE – A REVIEW

If one buys a non-qualified mutual fund and dies with the fund, any gain in the fund up to the owner's date of death escapes income taxes in the hands of the beneficiaries of the mutual fund. The reason for this is that the adjusted cost (i.e., basis) in the mutual fund is stepped-up to the date of death value of the mutual fund. This step-up results in the elimination of income taxes for beneficiaries on any gain in the mutual fund up to the owner's death. Variable annuities do not receive a step-up in basis when the owner dies. Beneficiaries of a variable annuity must pay ordinary income taxes (at their rate) on any untaxed gain in any variable annuity they inherit. This difference in tax treatment is responsible for the myth that beneficiaries inherit less with variable annuities than with a similar mutual fund investment. This is not always the case.

§1803. TWO TEST QUESTIONS

Before we move on with the step-up in basis myth, readers should take time to answer the following two questions.

- You have been offered two jobs. Except for salary, the jobs are identical. The first job pays $20,000 and the second pays $90,000. At $20,000, because of exemptions and deductions, your salary is tax-free. At $90,000 you would have an income tax liability each year of $10,000. Which job would you take?

- You have $300,000 to invest. You can invest it tax-free in municipal bonds paying 4% or invest it in taxable corporate bonds paying 6%. The 6% corporate bond income will lose 25% of its value to income taxes. Which bond is the best investment?

For the question dealing with the salary offered for two jobs, the author hopes that readers opted for the $90,000 job. All rational people know there is no way one can be economically worse off by increasing their income. The fact that the $20,000 salary would be tax-free is immaterial. The only issue to consider is which salary *nets* more income after taxes. In this case, the taxable salary will *net* more income than the tax-free salary.

In the question dealing with bonds, the correct answer again is not whether one bond is taxable and one is not, but which bond, *after-taxes*, will net more to the bondholder. Simple math tells us the taxable bond will *net* more income (4½%) to the bondholder than the tax-free bond paying 4% even after income taxes are considered.

§1804. THE NET ENDING VALUE ACID TEST – A REVIEW

In Chapter 11, the net ending value acid test was discussed. This test states that the best investment choice between two investment alternatives, where risk is the same, is the one that produces the largest value (over the same period of time) for the investor when *all* taxes, fees, costs and other factors have been deducted from all investments being compared.

In trying to determine whether beneficiaries would be better off inheriting mutual funds or variable annuities, the step-up in basis received by mutual funds is only one factor to consider. When *all* taxes, fees, costs and other factors are considered, the variable annuity, more often than not, will *net* more to beneficiaries than will a similar mutual fund investment. The primary reason for this is that mutual funds are taxed annually and have ownership costs that typically are higher than variable annuities which grow tax-deferred. The following examples, although overly simplistic show why this is true.

> **Example**
> Ken invested $25,000 in a mutual fund that grew at 10% a year. His ownership costs and taxes are average for the typical mutual fund (see §312 above). Seven years later Ken died. His mutual fund was worth $35,682 at his death.[1] The mutual fund passed to Ken's daughter who sold the mutual fund for $35,682. Because Ken's daughter received a step-up in basis, the $35,682 was not subject to any income taxation.

> **Example**
> Larry invested $25,000 in a variable annuity that grew at 10% a year. His ownership costs and taxes are average for the typical variable annuity (See §312 above). Seven years later Larry died. His variable annuity was worth $40,223 at his death.[2] The variable annuity passed to Larry's son who surrendered it for $40,223. The gain in the variable annuity of $15,223 was taxed as the son's tax rate of 25% because no step-up was available to Larry's son. The *net* value received by the son, after paying income taxes, was $36,417.[3] This is more than Ken's daughter got with her mutual fund and the step-up in basis.

§1805. IRC §691 – THE VARIABLE ANNUITY TAX ADVANTAGE

People who point out that beneficiaries who inherit non-qualified mutual funds receive a step-up in basis almost never mention that the beneficiaries of non-qualified variable annuities receive a tax benefit not available to those who inherit mutual funds. The IRS allows the beneficiaries of a non-qualified variable annuity, where a taxable estate is involved, to take a large income tax deduction when they report the gain on their inherited variable annuity on their income tax returns. This deduction is provided by IRC §691 and is referred to as the income in respect of a decedent deduction or IRD deduction. This deduction, in many cases, can provide as

---

[1] $23,750 x 6.064% x 7 years = $35,862.

[2] $25,000 x 7.03% x 7 years = $40,223.

[3] $40,223 - $3,806 = $36,417.

much tax benefit to beneficiaries who inherit variable annuities as those who inherit mutual funds and receive the step-up in basis. Those who inherit non-qualified mutual funds *cannot* use IRC §691. IRD is discussed in §1913.

§1806. ESTATE PLANNING AND VARIABLE ANNUITIES

Even where a taxable estate is not involved, basic estate planning can provide a more significant tax advantage than can the step-up in basis. An example of such estate planning is discussed in §1917.

§1807. CONCLUSION

There are many other reasons why investors need to be wary of the step-up in basis rule. The next chapter discusses all of these reasons and demonstrates why the step-up in basis is not nearly the benefit that mutual fund investors have been led to believe.

– CHAPTER 19 –

THE STEP-UP IN BASIS MYTH – DETAILED DISCUSSION

§1901. INTRODUCTION

For the past several years, the Internal Revenue Code has provided an unlimited step-up in the cost basis of mutual funds to beneficiaries who inherited them.[1] The same step-up in cost basis rule is not available to beneficiaries who receive variable annuity proceeds from a *deceased* annuity owner.[2] Cost basis, or more simply basis, refers to the original cost of a mutual fund or variable annuity together with any upward or downward adjustments in such cost. The concept of a stepped-up cost basis allows beneficiaries who inherit mutual funds purchased with *non-qualified* money to treat such funds as if they purchased them on the decedent's date of death for their fair market value on that date.[3] When beneficiaries later sell these mutual funds, they will pay long-term capital gains taxes only on the difference between the sale price and the fair market value of the funds on the date the transferring decedent died. This is true even though the decedent may have paid much less for the funds. The following examples demonstrate application of the stepped-up basis rule where a mutual fund and variable annuity owner have died:

Example A

Abel purchased a mutual fund for $10,000. At his death, the fund was worth $40,000. Abel left the fund by will to his daughter Betty. Shortly after receiving the mutual fund, Betty sold it for $40,000. Betty will not incur any income tax liability on the sale of the fund because she is allowed to treat the inherited mutual fund as if she purchased it for its $40,000 fair market value determined as of the date of her father's death. Stated another way, Betty's basis in her inherited mutual fund for income tax purposes would be stepped-up from her father's basis of $10,000 to the $40,000 date of death value.[4] If the fund were sold by Betty for more than $40,000, she would be responsible for paying long-term capital gain taxes only on those sale proceeds that exceeded $40,000.[5]

---

[1] IRC §1014 and §1015. This benefit was limited by Economic Growth and Tax Relief Reconciliation Act of 2001 (EGTRRA), See note 294.

[2] Variable annuity proceeds are considered income in respect of a decedent under IRC §691. Income in respect of a decedent is not eligible for a step-up in basis at the owner's death. Variable annuities purchased or added to prior to October 20, 1979 receive a step-up in basis at the owner's death.

[3] The alternate valuation date, which is six months after death may also be used. See IRC §2032. Variable annuities, qualified plans and accounts (e.g., IRAs) do not get a step-up in basis at an owner's death.

[4] The $10,000 original basis may have changed somewhat due to reinvestment of distributions, etc. The fund's value could be set at the alternate valuation date (six months after the owner's death) if this date were elected for estate tax purposes. (See IRC §2032).

[5] If the funds were sold for less than $40,000, resulting in a loss, Betty would owe no income taxes. However, she would not be able to take any income tax deduction for the loss. Betty would not owe any income taxes on any gain from her basis up to $40,000. Betty could keep the mutual fund portfolio to avoid income taxes and *might* be able to pass it on to her beneficiaries with a stepped-up basis at her death. The sale of assets that receive a stepped-up basis as a result of an owner's death are always taxed at long-term capital gains rates regardless of how long a beneficiary holds the inherited funds.

Example B
Carla purchased a variable annuity for $10,000. At Carla's death, the variable annuity was worth $40,000 and passed to her son Dave who was named as the beneficiary of the variable annuity. Dave will be required to pay ordinary income taxes on those proceeds he receives that exceed his mother's initial $10,000 purchase price for the variable annuity.[6] This is true whether the variable annuity is sold or held by Dave. This tax liability arises because Dave is not entitled to a step-up in the $10,000 original cost or basis of the annuity purchased by his mother. In short, Carla's $10,000 purchase price for her variable annuity is carried over or transferred to Dave.[7]

The perceived benefit of a step-up in basis to those who inherit mutual funds has frequently been cited as a major reason for investing in mutual funds rather than variable annuities. However, a close analysis of the stepped-up basis rule, especially following the recent tax law changes,[8] indicates that this rule is not nearly as beneficial as investors and their families have been led to believe. The following sections discuss this issue.

§1902. TAX LEGISLATION MAY ERODE THE BENEFIT OF THE STEPPED-UP BASIS RULE

It is no secret that Congress is not a proponent of the stepped-up basis rule. Efforts to reduce or eliminate the rule have received significant support in Washington over the past few years. Congress recently passed legislation that has eliminated the unlimited step-up in basis rule and replaced it with a reduced stepped-up basis rule.[9] Many mutual fund owners who purchased funds years ago relying on the unlimited stepped-up basis rule to provide their beneficiaries with an income tax benefit may be surprised to learn that this benefit is under legislative attack. The following example demonstrates how recent tax law changes (see IRC §1022) may reduce the benefit of a step-up in basis for many beneficiaries who might inherit mutual funds in 2010 and possibly beyond.

Example
Ed, who is a 80-year old widower, has real estate and stocks worth $1,300,000. He also has a mutual fund portfolio he recently purchased for $500,000. If these assets double in value and Ed dies in 2010, his heirs will *not* be entitled to an unlimited step-up in basis in his million dollar mutual fund portfolio. Their income tax liability could be $200,000.[10]

---

[6] Annuitization or spreading out payments from the variable annuity over time would reduce the impact of the income taxes owed.

[7] If the variable annuity were worth less than $10,000 at Carla's death, a deduction on her final income tax return would be allowed.

[8] Economic Growth and Tax Relief Reconciliation Act of 2001 (EGTRRA) and the Jobs and Growth Tax Reconciliation and Reliefs Act of 2003 (JGTRRA).

[9] See IRC §1022. This code section will only be in effect for 2010 unless extended or made permanent.

[10] In 2010, Ed's heirs or beneficiaries will receive a maximum step-up in basis of $1,300,000. If this step-up is taken in Ed's real estate and stocks, his heirs will not get a step-up in basis in Ed's mutual fund Portfolio. If Ed's heirs elected to do so, they could take a $500,000 step-up in the basis of Ed's mutual funds but would lose an offsetting $500,000 step-up in basis in Ed's other assets. Beginning on January 1, 2010, the long-term capital gains rates are scheduled to increase to 20%.

IRC §1022 is currently scheduled to apply only for 2010. Many tax professionals, including the author, believe IRC §1022 will be extended or made permanent. Repeal of IRC §1022 is not likely. If this were to occur, trillions of dollars would pass from one generation to the next over the next decade without being subject to income taxes. The likelihood that Congress would support such a large loss of revenue is remote at best. Many tax experts predict further erosion of the stepped-up basis rule over the next few years because of the soaring federal deficit.

§1903. THE STEPPED-UP BASIS S AN ILLUSION

The assumption that a mutual fund portfolio, because it receives a step-up in basis, will provide beneficiaries with a larger inheritance than a variable annuity is not always true. In many instances, the opposite proves to be the case. The reason for this is that the tax-deferred growth provided by a variable annuity will, in many cases, offset or exceed the tax savings provided by the step-up in basis received by beneficiaries who inherit mutual funds at an owner's death. The following two examples, applying a net-to-net analysis (Chapter 11), demonstrate this:[11]

Example A

Sixteen years ago, Ellen invested $100,000 in a mutual fund portfolio that grew at 10% annually. Each year taxes on her distributions reduced Ellen's rate of return by 2%.[12] The annual cost of owning the mutual fund was 1.5% and trading costs were 0.7%.[13] The commission paid by Ellen was 2½%. These expenses reduced Ellen's net rate of return to 6.064%.[14] Ellen recently died and left her mutual fund, now worth $250,088,[15] to her four young grandchildren. Ellen had no other assets. The fund was sold soon thereafter for $250,088. The grandchildren avoided capital gains taxes on unrealized gains because the cost basis of the mutual fund in their hands was stepped-up to $250,088. In short, the grandchildren received the full $250,088 value of the inherited mutual fund unreduced by capital gains taxes.

Example B

Sixteen years ago, Frank purchased a variable annuity for $100,000. The annuity grew at the net rate of 10% but due to annual ownership expense and trading costs of 2.7% associated with owning the annuity, Frank's net rate of return was reduced to 7.03%.[16] Frank recently died leaving his annuity, now worth $296,543,[17] to his four young grandchildren. Frank had no other assets. The annuity proceeds paid out to the grandchildren were subject to a total of $30,216 in *ordinary* income

---

[11] This paper compares mutual funds and variable annuities that are sold by financial professionals. If no load mutual funds or variable annuities are involved, adjustments for commissions paid and other costs of ownership must be made.

[12] The average mutual fund loses approximately 2% of its total annual gain to income taxes according to studies by the Lipper, Inc., and others.

[13] The average A-share mutual fund has an annual expense ratio of 1.5% and trading costs of 0.7%.

[14] $100,000 - $2,500 = $97,500 + 10% = $107,250 - 2.2% = $104,894 - $97,500 = $7,391 x 0.8 = $5,913 ÷ $97,500 = 6.064%.

[15] 6.064% x $97,500 x 16 years = $250,088.

[16] Annual ownership costs are 2.2% and trading costs are 0.5%. $100,000 + 10% = $110,000 - 2.7% = $107,030 - $100,000 = $7,030 ÷ $100,000 = 7.03%.

[17] $100,000 x 7.03% x 16 years = $296,543.

taxes on the annuity's growth of $196,543, thus reducing their inheritance from $296,543 to $266,327.[18] This is $16,239 more than in the first example where a stepped-up basis was obtained.

As the above examples indicate, beneficiaries of variable annuities can frequently be better off financially than beneficiaries who receive mutual funds from a decedent even after factoring in the claimed income tax advantage of the step-up in basis available to those who inherit mutual funds.

§1904. THE TAX SAVINGS MUTUAL FUND OWNERS MIGHT OBTAIN FROM A STEP-UP IN BASIS IS NOT THAT LARGE

Many mutual fund owners measure the gain in their mutual fund by subtracting the original cost of the fund from the current market value. Doing so distorts the potential tax savings that a step-up in basis actually provides. The following example demonstrates this:

Example A

Ten years ago Jack purchased a mutual fund for $10,000. Today it is worth $22,500. Jack needs some money but is reluctant to sell his mutual fund. He believes there is $12,500 in gain in the fund and he wants to pass this gain to his children income tax-free by taking advantage of the step-up in basis rule. What Jack does not realize is that by paying taxes each year on his mutual fund and reinvesting his mutual fund distributions, which most mutual fund investors do, his original $10,000 cost basis is adjusted annually to reflect the taxes Jack paid each year on these reinvested distributions. Jack's current *upwardly adjusted* basis in his mutual fund could be as much as $20,000. This means that if Jack died, any potential tax liability owed by his beneficiaries would be imposed on $2,500, not $12,500. The income tax Jack would save his beneficiaries on this $2,500 by providing a step-up in basis would, at best, amount to a few hundred dollars.

Very few mutual fund owners really understand how little income tax they actually save their beneficiaries when mutual funds are inherited. The following example demonstrates this:

Example B

Quinn, a widower, purchased a conservative bond mutual fund several years ago for $100,000 and it grew to $200,000 by 2000. It has remained at this $200,000 value for the last several years. Quinn considered giving the fund to his daughter but decided not to sell the fund because he wanted to pass the mutual fund to his daughter and provide her with a step-up in basis. Including the mutual fund, Quinn's net estate is valued at just under $2,000,000. If Quinn dies in 2006 while his fund is worth $200,000, he will only have saved his daughter the income taxes that would have been due had Quinn given his daughter the fund while he was alive. Assuming Quinn had paid income taxes every year on his mutual fund

---

[18] $296,543 - $100,000 = $196,543 ÷ 4 = $49,136 per grandchild. Less $5,150 for each grandchild's single standard deduction for 2006 = $43,986. It is assumed that personal exemptions are not available due to the age of the grandchildren. The tax tables for 2006 show the tax on $43,986 is $7,554 for a single person. The four grandchildren will pay a total tax of $30,216 (4 x $7,554), leaving a net inheritance of $266,327 ($296,543 - $30,216).

distributions and these distributions were reinvested, any tax liability would be based only on the *unrealized* capital gains that have built up inside of Quinn's mutual fund. Assuming the unrealized gain in Quinn's mutual fund amounts to 30%, the tax liability on the fund would be calculated by applying the 15% long-term capital gains rate to $30,000 (30% of $100,000 in growth) yielding a total tax of $4,500.[19] In short, the benefit that the step-up in basis would provide Quinn's daughter on a $200,000 bequest would amount to a mere $4,500. If given the choice of receiving $195,500 ($200,000 - $4,500) in 2000 or letting $200,000 sit in a stagnate conservative bond fund for several more years, most people would take the $195,500 and forego the "benefit" of a stepped-up basis. (No estate taxes would be due).

§1905. THE STEP-UP IN BASIS – THE TRUE INCOME TAX COST

The step-up in basis rule states that when a beneficiary inherits mutual funds from a deceased owner, any income tax liability owed on the mutual fund's gain up to the fund's value on the owner's date of death is eliminated regardless of how much gain has built up in the fund. This rule does not in any way limit the income taxes that the owner had to pay prior to his death. Simply stated, income taxes are paid on mutual funds by their owners prior to death so their beneficiaries can inherit these funds without an income tax liability when the owner dies. Variable annuities are not subject to income taxes while the owner his alive, but places the burden of paying income taxes on the beneficiaries who inherit them. This raises an interesting question – is it better to inherit a mutual fund without an income tax liability because the deceased owner paid income taxes on the funds while he was alive, or inherit a variable annuity with an income tax burden because the deceased owner did not have to pay income taxes while owning the variable annuity? As the following examples demonstrate, the latter choice often proves to be the best:

Example A

Don purchased a mutual fund for $50,000 twenty years ago. His commission was 4%. Annual expenses and trading costs for the fund were 2.2%. The fund grew at an average of 10% a year but lost 2.3% of its value on average to annual income taxes. Don's net rate of return was 5.8366%.[20] Don recently died. His mutual fund was worth $149,265.[21] Don's daughter Ellen inherited the fund and sold it for $149,265. Due to the step-up in basis rule, she paid no income taxes on the $149,265. However, Ellen calculated that her father paid $57,656 in income taxes during the period he owned the mutual fund.[22]

---

[19] The daughter can use her father's eight-year holding period to obtain long-term capital gains treatment.

[20] $50,000 - $2,000 = $48,000 + 10% = $52,800 - 2.2% = $51,638 - $48,000 = $3,638 x .77 = $2,802 ÷ $48,000 = 5.8366%. It must be remembered that both long-term capital gains rates and ordinary income tax rates were *significantly* higher in the past than they are today.

[21] 5.8366% x 20 years x $48,000 = $149,265.

[22] $50,000 - $2,000 = $48,000 + 10% = $52,800 - 2.2% = $51,638 - $48,000 = $3,638 ÷ $48,000 = 7.5792% x 20 years x $48,000 = $206,921 - $149,265 = $57,656.

Example B

Judy purchased a variable annuity for $50,000 twenty years ago. The fund had combined annual costs and trading costs of 2.7%. The variable annuity grew at 10% a year. Judy's net rate of return was 7.03%.[23] Judy recently died with her variable annuity worth $194,572.[24] She left the variable annuity to her son Ed. The variable annuity had $144,572 in gain in it. Ed liquidated the variable annuity for $194,572 and paid 30% in income taxes or $43,372 on the annuity's gain. He netted $151,200 from the sale. This $151,200 is $1,935 more than Ellen received in the prior example. It is interesting to note that the IRS received $57,656 in income taxes from Don on the mutual fund portfolio in the prior example, but only $43,372 from Ed on his variable annuity inheritance.

What the above example demonstrates is that the tax-deferral provided to beneficiaries of variable annuities can be much more valuable than the step-up in basis provided to those who inherit mutual funds.

§1906. MUTUAL FUNDS, UNLIKE VARIABLE ANNUITIES, ARE SUBJECT TO A STEP-DOWN IN BASIS

Mutual fund owners rarely consider that their beneficiaries are subject to a step-*down* in basis when mutual funds lose value prior to an owner's death. This cannot happen with variable annuities. As the following examples demonstrate, the variable annuity is a superior investment relative to mutual funds when a step-*down* in basis occurs:

Example A

Jim, age 83, purchased a mutual fund portfolio several years ago. He invested $100,000 in the fund. During a recent stock market correction, the value of Jim's fund portfolio dropped to $75,000. Shortly thereafter he died. Jim's 53-year old daughter was the beneficiary of his portfolio. At Jim's death, the daughter had to take the portfolio at the *stepped-down* value of $75,000. The daughter sold the portfolio and reinvested the $75,000 in an index fund. Seven year later, her portfolio doubled in value to $150,000. The daughter then sold the index fund and paid 15% in long-term capital gains taxes ($11,250) on her index fund's increased value of $75,000, netting her $138,750 ($150,000 - $11,250).

Example B

Judy, age 83, purchased a variable annuity several years ago. She invested $100,000 in the annuity. During a recent stock market correction, the value of her annuity dropped to $75,000. Shortly thereafter Judy died. Her 53-year old son was the beneficiary of Judy's annuity and received a check for $100,000 from the annuity issuer as a death benefit. No income taxes were due at this time because there was no gain in the annuity. Judy's son took the $100,000 and purchased a new variable annuity in his name. He invested the proceeds in an index fund within the new annuity. Seven years later his variable annuity doubled in value to $200,000. Judy's son then sold the annuity and paid 25% or $25,000 in income

---

[23] $50,000 + 10% = $55,000 - 2.7% = $53,515 - $50,000 = $3,515 ÷ $50,000 = 7.03%.

[24] 7.03% x 20 years x $50,000 = $194,572.

taxes on his $100,000 gain netting him $175,000 ($200,000 - $25,000). This is $36,250 more than Jim's daughter received in the prior example on essentially identical facts. The under-performance of the mutual fund is a direct result the step-down in basis attributed to the mutual fund.

§1907. VARIABLE ANNUITIES PROVIDE ECONOMICAL RIDERS THAT WILL PAY INCOME TAXES OWED BY BENEFICIARIES

Today, many variable annuity issuers provide riders that will pay the income taxes owed on a decedent's variable annuity when proceeds of the annuity are paid to a beneficiary. This benefit is commonly referred to as an earnings enhancement benefit, or EEB. In short, a variable annuity purchaser may buy a step-up in basis for his beneficiaries if he desires. In the majority of cases, such riders provide a better benefit to the beneficiaries of variable annuities than the step-up in basis rule provides to those who inherit mutual funds. The following examples demonstrate this.

Example A

Andy purchased a mutual fund for $100,000. Andy paid $2,000 in commissions to buy his mutual fund. Ten years later Andy died and left the mutual fund to his son. Andy's gross annual rate of return was 10%. Annual expenses (1.5%) and trading costs (0.7%) totaled 2.2% and income taxes reduced Andy's gain by 2.0%. Andy's net rate of return was 6.064%. When he died, Andy's mutual fund was worth $176,566.[25] A significant portion of this $176,566 was unrealized capital gains. The son received a step-up in basis and therefore did not have to pay any income taxes on the unrealized gain in the mutual fund.

Example B

Betty purchased a variable annuity for $100,000. She paid 40 basis points or 4/10% of her annuity's value each year for an earnings enhancement benefit (EEB) rider that would increase the gain in her variable annuity by 25% to help pay income taxes if Betty died and the proceeds of the annuity were paid to her daughter. Betty's rate of return was 10%. Annual expenses (2.2%), trading costs (0.5%) and the EEB rider (0.4%) totaled 3.1%. Betty's net rate of return was 6.590%. Ten years later, Betty died and left her variable annuity to her daughter. At her death, Betty's variable annuity was worth $189,306.[26] Of this amount, $89,306 was gain. The rider Betty purchased added 25% of this gain to the value of her variable annuity at death providing Betty's daughter with $211,633 in total proceeds rather than the original $189,306.[27] Betty's daughter had to pay income taxes of 25% on the variable annuity's growth of $111,633 which amounted to $27,908. After paying this tax, Betty's daughter received $183,725. This is $7,159 more than Andy's son got in the prior example even though Andy's son received a stepped-up basis in the mutual funds he inherited.

---

[25] $98,000 x 6.064% x 10 years = $176,566.

[26] $100,000 x 6.590% x 10 years = $189,306.

[27] One fourth of $89,306 = $22,327 + $189,306 = $211,633.

The above examples demonstrate that for investors who want to pass their mutual funds to beneficiaries without saddling them with income taxes, the earnings enhancement benefit provided by many variable annuity issuers may do a better job of this than buying mutual funds and hoping that a stepped-up basis will be available in the future (which does not appear to be the case) to shelter beneficiaries from income taxes on inherited mutual funds. The benefit of earnings enhancement riders are dramatically increased when coupled with the spousal continuation benefit that many variable annuity companies provide when a spouse dies (This unique benefit is discussed in the next section). Variable annuity owners need to keep in mind that the earnings enhancement rider may also be coupled with the deduction allowed by IRC §691 (discussed below in §1913) if estate taxes are involved. Two other points should be mentioned. An EEB can be used to pay income *or* estate taxes. A step-up in basis for mutual funds can only reduce income taxes. If an EEB is not needed to pay income or estate taxes it is paid out to beneficiaries in cash. If a step-up in basis for mutual funds is not available to reduce income taxes, it does *not* provide a cash benefit to anyone.

§1908. THE SPOUSAL CONTINUATION BENEFIT OFFERED BY MANY VARIABLE ANNUITY ISSUERS IS BETTER THAN A STEP-UP IN BASIS

Most variable annuity companies allow surviving spouses to take over a deceased spouse's variable annuity and continue the tax-deferred growth of the variable annuity. This benefit is referred to as spousal continuation. Although a spouse who inherits a mutual fund from a deceased spouse may receive a step-up in basis, the spousal continuation benefit provided by variable annuities will frequently prove to be of greater economic benefit than the step-up in basis obtained when mutual funds are inherited. The following examples demonstrate this:

Example A
Ed purchased a mutual fund for $50,000 and held it for five years. Ed paid $2,000 to buy the fund. Ed's rate of return was 10%. Annual expenses were 2.2% (1.5% annual expense ratio and trading costs of 0.7%). Income taxes reduced the gain on Ed's mutual fund by 2.1%. Ed's net rate of return was 5.988%.[28] During this five-year period, the mutual fund grew in value to $64,199.[29] At this point, Ed died and his wife Fran inherited the mutual fund with a stepped-up basis of $64,199. Although the fund contained unrealized gains, the stepped-up basis rule allowed Fran to avoid having to pay any income taxes on any of the gain. Fran held the fund for an additional five years and the fund grew to $85,863 before she sold it.[30]

Example B
Henry purchased a variable annuity for $50,000 and kept it for five years before he died. Henry's rate of return was 10%. Annual expenses were 2.7% (2.2%

---

[28] $50,000 - $2,000 = $48,000 + 10% = $52,800 - 2.2% = $51,638 - $48,000 = $3,638 x 0.79 = $2,874 ÷ $48,000 = 5.988%.

[29] $48,000 x 5 years x 5.988% = $64,199.

[30] $48,000 x 5.988% x 10 years = $85,86

annual expense ratio and trading costs of 0.5%). Henry's net rate of return was 7.03%.[31] Because spousal continuation was available, Henry's wife Jan was able to continue the variable annuity in her name just as if she purchased the annuity. For this reason, Jan would not have to pay any income taxes on the variable annuity's gain at Henry's death. After electing spousal continuation, Jan held the variable annuity for five more years. At the end of the second five-year period, the variable annuity was worth $98,634.[32] If the gain in the variable annuity of $48,634 were taxed at this time at an average tax rate of 22%, Jan would net $87,935 from the variable annuity.[33] This is $2,072 more than Fran obtained in the prior example even though Fran received a stepped-up basis in the mutual funds she inherited at her husband's death.[34] It is also important to note that Fran's $85,863 net mutual fund portfolio value was *not* reduced for income taxes on unrealized gains she incurred on the gain she made following her husband's death.

What the above examples demonstrate is that the tax deferral provided by spousal continuation of a variable annuity can be financially more advantageous than the step-up in basis received when mutual funds are inherited by spouses. When spousal continuation is combined with the earnings enhancement rider (discussed in the previous section) the economic benefit to the surviving spouse can be greatly increased.

§1909. ANNUITIZATION IS A BETTER ALTERNATIVE TO A STEP-UP IN BASIS

Annuitization of a variable annuity by a beneficiary often provides more income than a mutual fund can generate for a beneficiary even if the inherited fund receives a step-up in basis. The following examples demonstrate this:

Example A
Jane, age 65, purchased a variable annuity 20 years ago for $63,850. Jane's gross average rate of return was 10%. Annual expenses were 2.7% (2.2% annual expense ratio and trading costs of 0.5%). Jane's net rate of return was 7.03%.[35] The annuity is now worth $248,469.[36] Jane recently died. Her husband Roy is the beneficiary of her annuity. Roy, who is 65, needs at least $14,700 *after taxes* for rest of his life from Jane's annuity to supplement his other income. Roy elected to annuitize Jane's annuity so that it would provide him with an income stream for his lifetime. It is assumed Roy's life expectancy is 20 years. The annuity company agreed to pay Roy $17,580 a year for his lifetime.[37] At an average income tax rate of 20% and an exclusion ratio of 18.16%, Roy will net $14,703 a year for life.[38] This is a little more than what Roy needs. These annuity payments

---

[31] $50,000 + 10% = $55,000 - 2.7% = $53,515 - $50,000 = $3,515 ÷ $50,000 = 7.03%.

[32] $50,000 x 7.03% x 10 years = $98,634.

[33] $48,634 x 0.22 = $10,699. $98,634 - $10,699 = $87,935.

[34] $87,935 - $85,863 = $2,072.

[35] $63,850 + 10% = $70,235 - 2.7% = $68,339 - $63,850 = $4,489 ÷ $63,850 = 7.03%.

[36] 7.03% x 20 years x $63,850 = $248,469.

[37] A life expectancy of 20 years is assumed. The annuity is guaranteed to pay for 20 years. The interest rate the annuity company is using is 4%. An immediate annuity of $248,469 will pay $17,580 for 20 years before taxes.

[38] $17,580 and an exclusion ratio of 18.16% ($63,850 ÷ [$17,580 x 20]) less 20% tax = $16,889.

are guaranteed for Roy's life and are also guaranteed to be paid for a minimum of 20 years. If Roy should die before 20 years, the $17,580 annuity payments will continue to be paid to his beneficiaries. In short, the variable annuity will provide a *guaranteed* income in excess of Roy's needs for the rest of his life.

Example B

Bob, age 65, purchased a mutual fund 20 years ago for $63,850. The commission to buy the fund was $2,500. Bob's rate of return was 10%. Annual expenses were 2.2% (1.5% annual expense ratio and trading costs of 0.7%). Income taxes reduced the gain on Bob's mutual fund by 2.1%. Bob's net rate of return was 5.988%.[39] Over 20 years this mutual fund grew in value to $196,313.[40] Bob recently died. His wife, Rita, who is 65, inherited Bob's mutual fund and received a step-up in basis to $196,313. Rita needed at least $14,700 *after taxes* from the inherited fund to supplement her other income. Rita's tax rate is 20%. It is assumed Rita's life expectancy is 20 years. Rita was interested in avoiding risk and wanted to obtain a lifetime stream of income and therefore contacted a financial advisor. The advisor told Rita that she could receive $14,700 a year income tax free from a municipal bond fund portfolio if the portfolio earned a consistent return of 4.73% a year.[41] The advisor told Rita that a 4.73% rate of return on a municipal bond fund portfolio for 20 years was not something she should count on. This could cause Rita to outlive her nest egg. He suggested Rita consider buying a lifetime annuity with her $196,313 but soon realized that such an annuity would:

- Provide an annual *after-tax* income of only $13,075 for Rita's lifetime;[42] or

- Provide *after-tax* income of $14,700 for less than 17 years.[43]

What the two examples above demonstrate is that annuitization of a variable annuity will often provide a larger *after-tax, after-expense* stream of income than a mutual fund will even though the mutual fund provides a step-up in basis to beneficiaries who inherit such funds.

§1910. THE RATCHETING DEATH BENEFIT PROVIDED BY VARIABLE ANNUITIES MAY OUTPERFORM A MUTUAL FUND'S STEP-UP IN BASIS

Many variable annuities allow investors to select a death benefit that ratchets up over time at a stated rate that is usually between 5% and 7%. Mutual funds have no similar benefit. In many cases the ratcheting death benefit may result in beneficiaries receiving significantly more from a decedent who owned a variable annuity rather than a mutual fund. This is true even though the mutual fund, unlike the variable annuity, would receive a step-up in basis at the

---

[39] $63,500 - $2,500 = $61,000 + 10% = $67,100 - 2.2% = $65,623 - $61,000 = $4,624 x 0.79 = $3,653 ÷ $61,000 = 5.988%.

[40] 5.988% x $61,350 x 20 years = $196,313.

[41] $196,313 x 4.73% x 20 years = $14,700 annual payments for twenty years.

[42] $196,313 x 4% x 20 years = $13,889. With an exclusion ratio of 70.7% ($196,313 ÷ $277,790) and a 20% tax rate, Rita would receive only $13,075 of the $14,700 she needs to live on.

[43] $196,313 x 4% and withdrawing $15,615 in payments per year would provide after-tax payments of $14,700 for 17 years if a 20% tax rate is combined with an exclusion ratio of 70.7%.

owner's death. The following examples demonstrate this:

Example A

Ben purchased a mutual fund for $200,000 when he was 60. Ben wanted his daughter to inherit the fund. At his death at age 77, his mutual fund was worth $450,000. Ben paid income taxes on the fund annually when he owned it. Ben's daughter inherited the fund and did not have to pay any further income taxes because of the step-up in basis rule.

Example B

Sara purchased a variable annuity for $200,000 when she was 60. Sara wanted her son to inherit the annuity. The annuity had a 7% ratcheting death benefit. When Sara died at age 77, her variable annuity was worth $500,000, but because of the ratcheting death benefit, Sara's son received a check for $631,763. Sara's son paid 30% income tax on the $431,763 gain in the variable annuity. This reduced his net inheritance to $502,234. This is $52,234 more than Ben's daughter received in the prior example even though she received a step-up in basis.

§1911. THE USE OF IRC §1035 WITH A VARIABLE ANNUITY MAY OUTPERFORM A MUTUAL FUND'S STEP-UP IN BASIS

Owners of variable annuities, unlike mutual fund owners, may take advantage of IRC §1035. IRC §1035 allows the tax-free exchange of one variable annuity for another. The appropriate use of this IRS Code provision can result in beneficiaries receiving significantly more from a decedent who owned a variable annuity rather than a mutual fund. This is true even though the mutual fund, unlike the variable annuity, would receive a step-up in basis at an owner's death. The following examples demonstrate this:

Example A

Dana, a widow, purchased a mutual fund for $350,000 when she was 55. Dana is now 70 and in poor health. Dana wants her son to inherit her mutual fund. Dana's mutual fund went up in value to a high of $700,000 two years ago, but when Dana died her mutual fund was only worth $500,000. At her death, Dana's son inherited the mutual fund. Due to the step-up in basis, Dana's son did not have to pay income taxes on the mutual fund's gain and therefore received the full $500,000 value of his mother's mutual fund.

Example B

Steve, a widower, purchased a variable annuity for $350,000 when he was 55. Steve is now 70 and in poor health. Steve wants his daughter to inherit his variable annuity. His annuity increased in value to $700,000 two years ago. At that time, Steve's financial advisor suggested that Steve take advantage of IRC§1035 and transfer his variable annuity to another similar variable annuity. This could be accomplished without costs or income taxes. The benefit of the transfer would be that Steve's original death benefit of $300,000 provided by his first annuity would increase to $700,000 with the new variable annuity. This would guarantee that Steve's daughter would never receive less than $700,000 at Steve's death. Steve followed his advisor's suggestion. When Steve died his variable annuity had gone down in value to $500,000. Steve's daughter received a check from the annuity company for $700,000. She had to pay 35% in taxes on the $350,000 in gain in the variable annuity which left her with a *net* (after-tax) inheritance of $577,000. This is $77,000 more than Dana left her son in the prior example even though the son received a step-up in basis. [Note: The fact that Dana would most likely have paid income taxes on her fund during her ownership was ignored in these examples].

§1912. LIFETIME TRANSFERS OF VARIABLE ANNUITIES RECEIVE A STEP-UP IN BASIS

One of the major benefits of owning a variable annuity is that if an owner gives his annuity away during his lifetime, his donee receives a stepped-up basis, whereas a similar lifetime gift of a mutual fund does not provide the donee with a stepped-up basis.[44] In order to obtain this benefit, the donor of a variable annuity need only report any *gain* in the variable annuity given away on his income tax return for the year of the gift. For example, Ann bought a variable annuity for $100,000 three years ago and gave it to her son when it was worth $120,000. By reporting the $20,000 gain on her income tax return for the year of the gift, Ann's son would receive a step-up in basis in the annuity to $120,000. He could sell the variable annuity for $120,000 without having to pay any income taxes, IRS penalties or surrender charges regardless of his age. Ann's son would be responsible for paying future income taxes only on withdrawals or sale proceeds from the annuity that exceeded $120,000. If Ann gave mutual funds worth $120,000 to her son during her lifetime for which she paid $100,000, her son would *not* receive a stepped-up basis, but rather a carryover in basis. The son's basis would be $100,000. The son would have to pay long-term capital gains taxes on all proceeds above $100,000 when the fund was sold. Knowledge of this beneficial tax treatment of variable annuities allows lifetime gifts of annuities to be made under conditions that are much more advantageous tax-wise than where mutual funds are passed to beneficiaries with a stepped-up basis at the owner's death. The following examples demonstrate this:

Example A
Andy bought a mutual fund portfolio several years ago for $900,000 and it has increased in value to $1,400,000. Andy and his second wife Betty are both 70 years old. Andy has four children who are Betty's step-children. Andy also has fourteen grandchildren. Andy wants his $1,400,000 mutual fund portfolio to pass to his children and grandchildren at his death with a step-up in basis. To ensure a step-up in basis for his children and grandchildren, Andy decided to leave the $1,400,000 portfolio to them in his will. Andy has $2,000,000 in other assets he plans on leaving to his wife. Andy also has $1,100,000 in a bank account he wants to leave his children and grandchildren. Assuming Andy dies in 2008, the

---

[44] IRC § 72(e)(4)(c)(i) governs the step-up in basis for lifetime gifts of variable annuities. Donees of lifetime transfers (i.e., gifts) of mutual funds receive a carryover basis rather than a step-up in basis.

$1,400,000 mutual fund portfolio and the $1,100,000 bank account passing to his children and grandchildren will be subject to an *estate* tax of $225,000,[45] netting them $2,275,000.[46] No *income taxes* will be due on the mutual fund portfolio at Andy's death due to application of the stepped-up basis rule. The remaining assets would pass to Andy's wife without any *estate tax* by applying the unlimited marital deduction.

Example B

Bob bought a variable annuity years ago for $900,000 and it has increased in value to $1,400,000. Bob and his second wife April are 70 years old. Bob has four children who are April's step-children. Bob also has fourteen grandchildren. Bob wants his children and grandchildren to receive his annuity. Bob also has $2,000,000 in other assets he wants to leave to his wife. Bob has a bank account containing $1,100,000 that he also wants to pass to his children and grandchildren if possible. In early 2008, Bob and his wife decided to give the $1,400,000 annuity to their 18 children and grandchildren. They will report the $500,000 gain in the transferred annuity on their 2008 income tax return and will pay 35% in ordinary income taxes, or $175,000, on this gain. This tax will be paid from the $1,100,000 bank account. After making the gift, the children and grandchildren will receive a stepped-up basis of $1,400,000 in the annuity. The 10% IRS penalty would not apply because the annuity has no gain due to the step-up on which to impose the penalty. There will be no gift taxes on this transaction. Of the $1,400,000 gift, $432,000 is untaxed because of the split gifts made by Bob and his wife to their children and grandchildren (i.e. $24,000 x 18 = $432,000). The $968,000 excess gift is untaxed because it is more than covered by the $1,000,000 exemption amount available in 2006 for gifts. Assuming Bob dies in 2008. His remaining assets would pass to his wife without estate taxes by applying the unlimited marital deduction. The children and grandchildren would receive $2,325,000 (the $1.4 million variable annuity plus the $925,000 bank account). This $2,325,000 transfer would not be subject to estate taxes (The taxable gift of $968,000 plus the $925,000 bank account are less than the 2008 exemption amount of $2,000,000). By giving the variable annuity away during life, Bob and his wife were able to pass $2,325,000 to Bob's children and grandchildren. This is $50,000 more than Andy passed to his children and grandchildren in the previous example even though Andy's children and grandchildren received a step-up in basis in Andy's mutual fund portfolio.[47]

It is important to note that in the examples discussed above, the owners of the mutual funds would have saved their beneficiaries a significant amount in estate or income taxes (or both) by giving their mutual funds away during their lifetime. The major problem with this is

---

[45] $2,500,000 will generate a death tax of $1,005,800 less a credit of $780,800 (2007) = $225,000.

[46] $2,500,000 - $225,000 = $2,275,000.

[47] $2,325,000 - $2,275,000 = $55,000. This example ignores the fact that the variable annuity, because of tax deferral, would grow to a larger amount. If any of the children or grandchildren sold their interests in the variable annuity, they would not be required to pay a 10% penalty for being under 59½ years old because this penalty is only applied to investment growth. With a step-up in basis there is no growth.

that many investors are told that a step-up in basis for mutual funds is available only if they die with the fund's in their estate. These investors rarely seek advice regarding lifetime transfers of their funds. When the issue of lifetime transfers of mutual funds is discussed, many financial advisors advise against such transfers by pointing out that they will often generate income taxes and will result in forfeiture of the step-up in basis offered by mutual funds. All of this raises an interesting question – if maximum tax savings can be obtained, in most cases, by giving variable annuities and mutual funds away during an owner's lifetime, is the step-up in basis touted by mutual fund proponents a real benefit?

In the above examples, all of the beneficiaries received a step-up in basis in the mutual funds and variable annuities they received. However, the beneficiaries of the variable annuity were subject to a smaller *total* tax burden than the recipients of the mutual fund portfolio. More importantly, to pass a stepped-up basis to beneficiaries with mutual funds, the owner of the funds must die first and therefore will never have the opportunity to see the benefit the bequest of his mutual funds might provide. With a variable annuity, a step-up in basis can be provided to donees by way of a *lifetime* gift made by the variable annuity owner. Not only does the lifetime transfer of a variable annuity save taxes, but it allows the donor to see the benefits provided by his gift (e.g., houses being bought, grandchildren being educated, etc.). In short, variable annuity ownership allows the owner to choose when to make a gift of his annuity, when to pass a step-up in basis to his beneficiaries and when to make available those benefits that will flow from making such a transfer. The owner of a mutual fund has none of this flexibility. As a general rule, the longer a mutual fund owner lives, the less benefit his beneficiaries will derive from a mutual fund inheritance. For example, if the owner of a mutual fund portfolio lives to 90, his children could be in their late sixties. An inheritance received by one who is in his late sixties is not nearly as useful as a gift received by one who is in his forties.

Another advantage of transferring a variable annuity during life is that ordinary investment losses may be used to offset any gain in the variable annuity. This can't be done with mutual funds as the following two examples demonstrate:

Example C
Jack had an annuity worth $15,000 for which he paid $12,000 seven years ago. Jack gave the annuity to his daughter and reported the $3,000 gain on his tax return. Jack also had a $3,000 ordinary (short-term) loss from the sale of some stock. Jack used the $3,000 loss to offset the gain in the annuity given to his daughter. This kept Jack from paying any taxes on the transfer of the annuity. Not only was Jack able to avoid a potential income tax liability, but Jack's daughter would still receive a step-up in basis in the annuity to $15,000. The daughter could sell the annuity for $15,000 and have no taxable gain. She would not have to pay the standard 10% IRS penalty even if she was under age 59½ because this penalty is only imposed on investment *gain*. A variable annuity transfer provides

a stepped-up basis and therefore generates no gain on which to impose a 10% penalty. All surrender charges have expired.

Example D:

Tara had a mutual fund worth $15,000 for which she paid $12,000 seven years ago. Tara transferred the fund to her son. Tara also had a $3,000 short-term stock market loss. The son would not get a stepped-up basis in the transferred mutual fund and Tara could not use her $3,000 stock market loss to offset the $3,000 gain in the mutual fund she transferred to her son. If the son sells the fund in the future he will have to pay income taxes on all proceeds received from a sale of the fund that exceed $12,000.[48]

§1913. THE INCOME IN RESPECT OF A DECEDENT DEDUCTION (IRC §691)

Although mutual funds qualify for a step-up in basis when inherited by beneficiaries, they cannot take advantage of IRC §691. This code provision, referred to as the income in respect of a decedent or IRD provision. Unlike mutual fund owners, this IRS Code provision is available to those who inherit variable annuities from a decedent. The IRD provision allows an income tax deduction for any portion of a variable annuity that must be reported by beneficiaries as income. The deduction is equal to the estate taxes generated by that portion of a variable annuity that will have to be reported as income by the beneficiaries who receive the variable annuity. This income tax deduction, in conjunction with income tax deferral, can be quite large in some cases and can often provide the beneficiaries of a variable annuity with a larger net inheritance than mutual funds can, even though mutual funds provide a step-up in basis. The following two examples demonstrate the positive impact the IRD deduction has on net variable annuity proceeds received from a decedent:

Example A

Jim purchased a $50,000 mutual fund ten years ago. The commission to buy the mutual fund was $2,000. Jim's gross annual rate of return was 10%. Annual expenses were 2.2% (1.5% annual expense ratio and trading costs of 0.7%). Income taxes reduced the gain on Jim's mutual fund by 2.0%. Jim's net rate of return was 6.064%.[49] Jim's mutual fund had a current value of $86,481. [50] Jim had other assets worth $2,000,000. Jim died in 2008. Jim left his mutual fund portfolio to his four grandchildren. His total net estate was worth $2,086,481 and was subject to an estate tax of $38,916.[51] This left a net value of $2,047,565 to Jim's beneficiaries. Because of the step-up in basis there were no income taxes due on the mutual fund portfolio gain.

---

[48] Tara could sell the mutual fund and offset the $3,000 gain with her $3,000 loss. She could then give the $15,000 in proceeds to her son to purchase the fund she sold. This would put her son in the same position as Jack's daughter in the prior example. The difference would be that Tara and her son would most likely incur transaction costs not incurred by Jack and his daughter.

[49] $50,000 - $2,000 = $48,000 + 10% = $52,800 - 2.2% = $51,638 - $48,000 = $3,638 - 20% (2% of 10%) = $2,911 ÷ $48,000 = 6.064%. Note that a 2.0% tax burden is used although tax rates were higher in the past than they are today.

[50] $48,000 x 6.064% x 10 years = $86,481.

[51] $86,481 x 0.45 = $38,916. ($780,000 exclusion for 2008).

Example B

Donna purchased a $50,000 variable annuity ten years ago. Donna's gross annual rate of return was 10%. Annual expenses were 2.7% (2.2% annual expense ratio and trading costs of 0.5%). Donna's net rate of return was 7.03%.[52] Donna died in 2008. She left her variable annuity to her four grandchildren. Her variable annuity was worth $98,634 at that time.[53] The rest of Donna's estate was worth $2,000,000 making Donna's net estate worth $2,098,634. Estate taxes were $44,385 reducing Donna's estate to $2,054,249.[54] There was a $48,634 gain in the variable annuity that, at an average income tax rate of 24%, will reduce the net value received by Donna's beneficiaries by $11,672 to $2,042,577. This is $4,988 less than Jim's beneficiaries received when they inherited Jim's mutual funds. This difference is attributed to the step-up in basis received by Jim's grandchildren. However, the above comparison does not consider the IRC §691 IRD deduction available to beneficiaries who inherit non-qualified variable annuities but not to beneficiaries inheriting non-qualified mutual funds. In short, Donna's grandchildren would not pay income taxes at 24% on the variable annuity gain of $48,634 but would be allowed an income tax deduction for that portion of the estate tax paid attributable to the portion of Donna's annuity that was subject to income taxes. Estate taxes on the variable annuity's full $98,634 value was $44,385.[55] Of the $98,634, $48,634 is the portion of the variable annuity subject to income taxes. This $48,634 represents 49.308% of the $98,634 full value. Therefore, 49.308% of the estate tax of $44,385 or $21,885 is an *income* tax deduction available to Donna's grandchildren. Donna's grandchildren would pay income taxes on $26,749 ($48,634 - $21,885) not $48,634. At a 24% tax rate, Donna's grandchildren would have an income tax liability of $6,420, not $11,672. By adjusting for the IRD deduction, Donna's grandchildren will receive a net estate of $2,047,829,[56] which is more than Jim's grandchildren received (in Example A above) even though they received a step-up in basis.

What the above examples demonstrate is that a combination of the IRD deduction and income tax-deferral available to beneficiaries who receive variable annuities from a deceased owner can be more valuable than the step-up in basis available to beneficiaries who inherit mutual funds from a decedent. The reason for this is that the mutual fund owner had to pay annual income taxes during the ownership of his fund and his beneficiaries could not take advantage of IRC §691.

§1914. HOLDING A MUTUAL FUND IN AN ESTATE IN ORDER TO OBTAIN A STEP-UP IN BASIS IS OFTEN A COSTLY MISTAKE

It is critical for investors to understand that the "benefit" of a step-up in basis for mutual funds can *only* be obtained by dying and passing these funds to beneficiaries. By keeping such

---

[52] $50,000 + 10% = $55,000 - 2.7% = $53,515 - $50,000 = $3,515 ÷ $50,000 = 7.03%.

[53] $50,000 x 7.03% x 10 years = $98,634.

[54] $98,634 x 0.45 = $44,385. $2,098,634 - $44,385 = $2,054,249.

[55] $98,634 x 0.45 = $44,285.

[56] $2,098,634 - $44,385 - $6,420 = $2,047,829.

funds in one's estate to obtain a stepped-up basis for beneficiaries, mutual fund owners frequently generate estate taxes that more than negate any perceived income tax benefit from providing a stepped-up basis to beneficiaries. The following examples demonstrate this:

Example A

Sam, a 60 year-old widower, purchased a variable annuity three years ago for $200,000. When it was worth $275,000, he gave it to his daughter Paula. Sam paid 25% in income taxes, or $18,750 on the $75,000 growth in the annuity. Sam died in 2008 with a $2,000,000 estate. The annuity held by his daughter has grown in value to $1,000,000. Sam's estate tax obligation would be $118,350. [57] Sam's income and estate tax burden together would be $137,100 (i.e., $118,350 + $18,750). Assuming Paula sold the variable annuity for $1,000,000 and paid income taxes on the annuity's $725,000 growth since she received it, she would owe $253,750 in income taxes using a 35% tax rate.[58] The total tax burden for Sam and his daughter would be $390,850 (i.e., $137,100 + $253,750).

Example B

Betty, a 60 year-old widower, purchased a mutual fund three years ago for $200,000. When the fund was worth $275,000 she contemplated giving it to her son Jack, but decided against the gift because it would result in Jack not receiving a step-up in basis. Without a step-up in basis, Jack would have to pay income taxes on any sale proceeds representing gain. Betty decided to keep the fund and pass it to Jack at her death, thus providing Jack with a stepped-up basis. Betty died in 2008 with $2,000,000 in assets in addition to the mutual fund which had grown to $1,000,000. Her $3,000,000 estate was left to Jack. If Jack, as the beneficiary of the mutual fund, sold the fund for $1,000,000, he would owe no income taxes because he would have received a stepped-up basis in the fund. However, the estate tax burden on Betty's $3,000,000 estate would be $450,000.[59] This is $59,150 more in taxes than those paid by Sam and his daughter in the previous example.

Holding on to mutual funds for the possibility that they might be passed to beneficiaries with a step-up in basis can result in increasing estate taxes by more than any potential income tax benefit a step-up in basis might provide to beneficiaries. It must also be remembered that IRC §1022 may greatly reduce any benefit currently provided by the step-up in basis rule. (See Section 1 above). It is important to note that the above examples assumed a mutual fund and variable annuity, if initially funded with identical amounts, would both grow to $275,000 in three years. In fact, the variable annuity would grow to a larger amount than the mutual fund due to the income tax deferral provided by the variable annuity.

---

[57] $275,000 gift - $12,000 annual exclusion (2008) = $263,000 (Sam's net gift to his daughter that must be included on his death tax return to determine the death tax). When this $263,000 is added to his current assets of $2,000,000 it will equal $2,263,000. The estate tax on $2,263,000 for 2008 is $118,350 (45% of $263,000)

[58] $1,000,000 - $275,000 = $725,000 x 35% = $253,750.

[59] $1,000,000 taxable estate x .45 = $450,000.

§1915. COMPLETE REPEAL OF ESTATE TAX WOULD BENEFIT VARIABLE ANNUITY OWNERS

President Bush has promised to end the federal estate tax. Most tax experts believe that estate taxes could be repealed in the near future for all but the very wealthy. Any repeal, whether partial or full, would most likely result in the elimination of the stepped-up basis rule for those who inherit mutual funds. Variable annuity owners will not be affected because annuities do not currently receive a step-up in basis at an owner's death. The following examples compare a mutual fund investment with a variable annuity investment as if both estate taxes and the step-up in basis rule have been repealed.

Example A

Twelve years ago, Ed invested $75,000 in a mutual fund. Ed's gross annual rate of return was 10%. Annual expense were 2.2% (1.5% annual expense ratio and trading costs of 0.7%). Income taxes reduced the gain on Ed's mutual fund by 2.0%. Ed paid $2,000 to purchase his fund.[60] Ed's net rate of return was 6.064%.[61] Ed recently died and left his mutual fund, now worth $147,958,[62] to his four grandchildren. Of the $72,958 in gain, $23,104 was unrealized. Ed had no other assets. The fund was sold soon thereafter and the grandchildren had to pay total *long-term* capital gains taxes of $3,466 on the inherited funds because their was no step-up in basis.[63] The net amount passing to the grandchildren was $144,942.

Example B

Twelve years ago, Fran purchased a variable annuity for $75,000. Fran's rate of return was 10%. Annual expenses were 2.7% (2.2% annual expense ratio and trading costs of 0.5%). Fran's net rate of return was 7.03%.[64] Fran recently died leaving her annuity, now worth $169,484,[65] to her four grandchildren. Fran had no other assets. The $169,484 in annuity proceeds paid out to the grandchildren were subject to a total of $9,372 in *ordinary* income taxes on the annuity's growth of $94,484, thus reducing their inheritance from $169,484 to $160,112.[66] This is $15,630 more than Ed's grandchildren got in the previous example.

What the above examples demonstrate is that if a repeal of the estate tax occurs, the variable annuity may prove to be a better investment than mutual funds for long term investors. [NOTE: There is no legislation existing that in any way impacts the unlimited step-up in basis

---

[60] Actual commissions could be 3%.

[61] $75,000 - $2,000 = $73,000 + 10% = $80,300 - 2.2% = $78,533 - $73,000 = $5,533 - 20% (2% of 10%) tax = $4,427 ÷ $73,000 = 6.064%.

[62] $73,000 x 12 years x 6.064% = $147,958.

[63] The unrealized gain of $23,104 was taxed at 15% long-term capital gains rates. This tax would be $3,466.

[64] $75,000 + 10% = $82,500 - 2.7% = $80,273 - $75,000 = $5,273 ÷ $75,000 = 7.03%.

[65] $75,000 x 7.03% x 12 years = $169,484.

[66] $169,484 - $75,000 = $94,484 ÷ 4 = $23,631 per grandchild. Less $5,350 for each grandchild's single standard deduction for 2007 = $18,281. It is assumed that personal exemptions are not available. The tax tables for 2007 show the tax on $18,281 is $2,343 for a single person. The four grandchildren will pay a total tax of $9,372 (4 x $2,343), leaving a net inheritance of $160,112 ($169,484 - $9,372).

available to variable annuity owners who want to make lifetime transfers of their annuities].

§1916. NON-SPOUSAL ANNUITIZATION

All of the examples discussed above had the beneficiaries of a variable annuity liquidating the annuity on receipt and paying all income taxes due at one time. In reality, this would be a very rare scenario. Beneficiaries of variable annuities have several options for paying income taxes other than in a lump sum upon receipt of the annuity. One option is to annuitize the annuity and take lifetime payments. This option provides three benefits:

- Income taxes are reduced (because payments are received over time);
- The exclusion ratio can be used;
- A lifetime stream of income is guaranteed.

A mutual fund beneficiary may annuitize his inherited mutual fund but is unlikely to generate a net (after-tax) income as large as the variable annuity will produce. The following two examples demonstrate this:

Example A

Ed invested $10,000 a year in a mutual fund portfolio for 25 years starting at age 60. Ed's gross average rate of return was 10%. His annual tax loss was 2.0%. Annual expenses and trading costs totaled 2.2%. Commissions were 5%. Ed's net return was 6.064%.[67] Ed died at age 85. At his death his fund was worth $557,828.[68] Ed's 65-year old daughter Betty inherited the fund. The step-up in basis rule eliminated any income taxes. Ed did not have a taxable estate for death tax purposes.

Example B

Jane invested $10,000 a year in a variable annuity for 25 year starting at age 60. Jane's gross average rate of return was 10%. Annual cost to own the annuity were 2.7%. Jane's net return was 7.03%.[69] Jane recently died at age 85 with her variable annuity worth $679,877.[70] Jane's 65-year old son Sal inherited the annuity. Sal's taxable retirement income is $63,700. Jane did not have a taxable estate for death tax purposes. Sal would have to pay income taxes on the gain in his mother's variable annuity in the amount of $136,185 for 2007 resulting in an after-tax value of $544,692.[71] This is less than the mutual fund value Betty received in the previous example.

The real likelihood that Sal would elect to pay income taxes all at one time at the highest possible tax rate upon receiving Jane's variable annuity is unlikely. If Sal wanted to, he could annuitize the annuity and receive annual payments of $48,102[72] for his life expectancy of 20

---

[67] $10,000 - 5% = $9,500 + 10% = $10,450 - 2.2% = $10,220 - $9,500 = $720 - 20% (2% of 10%) = $576 ÷ $9,500 = 6.064%.

[68] 6.064% x 25 years x $9,500 annual investment = $557,828.

[69] $10,000 + 10% = $11,000 - 2.7% = $10,703 - $10,000 = $703 ÷ $10,000 = 7.03%.

[70] 7.03% x 25 years x $10,000 annual investment = $679,877.

[71] $679,877 - $250,000 investment + $63,700 taxable income = $493,577 - $349,700 = $143,877 x 0.35 = $50,357 + $94,601 = $144,958 - $8,773 tax on $63,700 in taxable income = $136,185. $679,877 - $136,185 = $543,692.

[72] $679,877 for 20 years at 4% = $48,102/year.

years. His exclusion ratio would be 26%.[73] Based on this, Sal's after-tax annual payment from the variable annuity will be $39,202.[74] Betty, in the previous example, could annuitize her $557,827 for her 20 year life expectancy. Betty would receive $39,467 a year in pre-tax income.[75] Her exclusion ratio would be 70.67%.[76] Based on this, Betty would receive $36,573[77] in after-tax annual income or $2,629[78] a *year* less than Sal would receive.

Many investors do not like to annuitize assets. In this case, such investors may want to elect to take annual payments from an inherited annuity based on their life expectancy. This election provides an alternative way to avoid having to pay income taxes in a lump sum on an inherited variable annuity. Results similar to annuitization are possible without having to annuitize. This election is commonly referred to as "stretching" a non-qualified variable annuity.

§1917. VARIABLE ANNUITIES CAN BE EASILY STRIPPED OF ALL POTENTIAL ESTATE AND INCOME TAXES

The supposed benefit of a step-up in basis with a mutual fund is that beneficiaries can inherit such funds without paying income taxes if the funds are sold for no more than their inherited value which is set at the decedent's date of death. To obtain a step-up in basis with a mutual fund portfolio one may expose the full value of the funds to estate taxes. Often, these taxes can be greater than any income taxes saved by those who inherit the funds. As was discussed in Chapter 18, variable annuities lend themselves to being easily stripped of all potential income taxes beneficiaries may have to pay as well as all potential estate taxes. In light of this characteristic, it becomes a moot issue as to whether or not a variable annuity can receive a stepped-up basis at an owner's death. The following example demonstrates how variable annuities can be stripped of all potential estate and income taxes:

Example

Jack, age 67, a widower, has an estate worth $3,000,000. One million dollars of his estate is a variable annuity of which half consists of his contributions and half is growth. If Jack died in 2008, his estate taxes would be $450,000. Income taxes owed by beneficiaries on the variable annuity could reach $175,000. Combined, these taxes could be as much as $625,000.[79] The other $2,000,000 of Jack's estate consists of his house, car, etc. Jack wants to retire but needs to supplement his pension by at least $50,000 (after taxes) each year in order to do so. Jack wants his entire estate to pass to his three adult children without death or income taxes if possible. The solution for all of Jack's concerns can be resolved easily. Jack

---

[73] $250,000 ÷ $962,049 = 26%.

[74] $48,102 - 26% = $35,595. The income tax on $35,595 would be $8,899 at 25%. $48,102 - $8,899 = $39,202. If payments were made for more than 20 years the exclusion ratio would not be available and the entire $48,102 annual payment would be taxable.

[75] $557,828 x 4% x 20 years = $39,467.

[76] $557,828 ÷ $789,345 ($39,467 x 20) = 70.67%.

[77] Of $39,467 only 29.33% or $11,576 would be taxed. The tax would be $2,894 at 25%, netting Betty $36,573.

[78] $39,202 - $36,573 = $2,629.

[79] $450,000 + $175,000 = $625,000.

should have his children purchase (and own) a $1,000,000 life insurance policy on Jack's life. The premiums on this policy will be approximately $27,000 a year. After the policy is in place, Jack should convert his variable annuity to an immediate straight life annuity (i.e., no guarantee other than lifetime payments). The immediate annuity will pay Jack approximately $90,000 a year for his lifetime (assumed to be 15 years). The exclusion ratio will shelter 37% of this income from taxation for several years.[80] Jack is in a 20% average tax bracket. The after-tax annuity payment Jack will receive will be $78,660.[81] Jack can give his children $27,000 each year to pay the premiums on the life insurance they purchased. (No gift taxes would be due because of the $12,000 annual per person exclusion for 2008). This leaves Jack with more than the $50,000 in additional income he needs each year. If Jack dies in 2008, his estate will be worth $2,000,000 and will pass to his children estate tax free due to the $2,000,000 exemption applicable in 2008. The immediate annuity would be valued at zero because it is a straight life annuity that ceases to have any value at death. In addition, the children will receive $1,000,000 estate and income tax free from the insurance company. (Estate taxes are avoided because the insurance is not in Jack's estate. In addition, insurance proceeds are not subject to income taxation.) In short, a combination of annuitization and asset substitution eliminates all estate and income taxes for Jack's children and enables them to inherit Jack's entire $3,000,000 estate tax-free. Any unrecovered portion of the annuity may be taken as a deduction on Jack's final income tax deduction.

§1918. QUESTIONS TO ASK

- If there are several ways for a client to own a variable annuity and pass more of its value to the next generation than would an equivalent mutual fund, don't I have the obligation as a financial professional to understand how this can be done and share this information with my clients?

§1919. SOURCES

See the footnotes to this chapter for other sources to consult regarding the step-up in basis.

§1920. REVIEW QUESTIONS

Discuss four ways variable annuities can pass more to beneficiaries than mutual funds can even though the step-up in basis is available to those who inherit mutual funds.

§1921. CONCLUSION

In many cases the net amount received by donees or beneficiaries who receive variable annuities as gifts or inheritances may be larger than that provided by a step-up in basis when mutual funds are inherited. The step-up in basis provided by lifetime transfers of variable annuities may be more tax efficient than the step-up in basis provided by mutual funds. Many IRS Code provisions available to variable annuity owners are of greater benefit than the step-

---

[80] $500,000 ÷ [$90,000 x 15] = 37%.

[81] $90,000 x 0.63 = $56,700 x 0.20 = $11,340. $90,000 - $11,340 = $78,660.

up in basis provided by mutual funds. The ability of variable annuity owners to eliminate all potential estate, gift and income taxes for their beneficiaries with basic estate planning can provide a better result than can be obtained with the step-up in basis available to those who inherit mutual funds. The estate planning technique discussed in §1917 above offers such a good opportunity for financial professionals to help their variable annuity clients (present or future) save a significant amount in taxes, an additional chapter (Chapter 20) has been added to this book to explain this tax savings technique in detail.

– CHAPTER 20 –

ELIMINATING ESTATE, GIFT AND INCOME TAXES FROM
VARIABLE ANNUITIES

§2001. INTRODUCTION

One of the largest assets owned by individuals today is their retirement accounts. Common examples include individual retirement accounts (IRAs), 401(k)s, 403(b)s, Simplified Employee Plans (SEPs), variable annuities and the like. Many estates contain one or more of these retirement accounts. Gains made in retirement accounts, because they are deemed to constitute income in respect of a decedent under IRC §691, do not receive a step-up in basis at death like mutual funds, stocks and other capital assets. For this reason, retirement accounts can be exposed to both federal estate taxes, which are an obligation of the decedent's estate, gift and federal income taxes, which are paid by those who receive assets from a decedent's estate. (State death, gift and income taxes, although a potential liability, will not be specifically addressed in this report).[1] Financial advisors should be aware that many of their clients who own one or more retirement accounts are probably subject to this double tax. (The term financial advisor is used generically and includes insurance professionals also). At a minimum, competent financial advisors should warn their clients of the costly tax consequences of passing retirement accounts to beneficiaries and inform them that proper planning can eliminate *all* potential estate, gift and income taxes from these retirement accounts. To the extent possible, financial advisors should make an effort to inform the public of this potential tax liability as well as how it can be eliminated. The following example demonstrates the potential tax loss facing an individual who has not been advised of the tax consequences they face when they pass their retirement accounts to their beneficiaries at death.

Example

John, a widower, had an estate worth $3.1 million when he died in 2007. One of the assets that made up part of John's estate was an IRA worth $1.1 million. John's entire estate passed to his daughter. His estate had to pay $495,000 federal death taxes on this $3.1 million dollar estate.[2] In addition, his daughter would ultimately be responsible for paying income taxes on the IRA she inherited from her father. This income tax liability could exceed $150,000.[3] Combined federal

---

[1] The elimination of federal estate and income taxes by using asset substitution as outlined in this report will often eliminate state death and income taxes also. Where the asset substitution technique is not used, state death and income taxes may compound the federal estate and income tax loss.

[2] $1,230,800 tax on $3,000,000 + $45,000 tax on $100,000 = (45% of $100,000) = $1,295,800 - $780,800 = $495,000.

[3] The daughter would be able to take advantage of IRC §691 which would provide her with an *income tax deduction* of $495,000 which could be used to reduce the impact of paying income taxes on the $1.1 million IRA. Generally, IRC §691 allows an income tax *deduction* for the *estate* taxes paid on the asset that generates income in respect of a decedent. For example, if the full $1.1 million IRA were taken as income shortly after John's death, his daughter could take an IRC §691 income tax deduction of $495,000 to off-set the $1.1 million in income. This would reduce the amount subject to income taxes from $1,100,000 to $605,000. This would in turn reduce the maximum potential income tax liability from $385,000 (at 35%) to $211,000 (at 35%). (The impact of state death taxes are ignored). If the $1,100,000 variable annuity proceeds are taken over several years, the $495,000 IRC §691 income tax deduction would have to be prorated based on the income actually reported each year for tax purposes.

estate and income taxes on these facts could reach $706,000.[4] This amounts to 64% of John's $1.1 million IRA.

§2002. TRADITIONAL SOLUTIONS

In an effort to avoid the double taxation of retirement accounts at death, financial professionals have relied on a few tax planning techniques with mixed results. The most common techniques designed to reduce the impact of the double taxation problem mentioned above are briefly discussed below:

- **Charitable Transfers** - This technique involves direct gifts to charities, the use of charitable remainder trusts and similar transfers to charitable entities. The problem with these transfers, in addition to their inflexibility and complexity, is that beneficiaries do not always receive the full value of a decedent's estate when they are used. Additionally, income taxes may be triggered when retirement accounts are transferred to charitable entities during the lifetime of the account owner. (During 2007 these potential income taxes could be avoided for direct, charitable IRA contributions of $100,000 or less if certain IRS rules were followed. This rule will may be extended for 2008 and beyond.).

- **Stretching Programs** - This technique recommends that a retirement account owner take minimum distributions from his retirement account over his life expectancy. The surviving spouse, if any, does the same thing when they inherit the retirement account. Successive beneficiaries of these retirement accounts are likewise encouraged to repeat this process. With each generation taking only minimum distributions, it is hoped that the original retirement account will grow to a very large sum for future generations. Such stretching techniques do not eliminate estate taxes and, at best, merely postpone some of the income tax liability owed on the retirement account until it is ultimately inherited by future beneficiaries. One factor that reduces the effectiveness of the stretching technique is the fact that some retirement accounts may not allow for the stretching out of distributions. Additionally, many beneficiaries may need (or want) to take more money from an inherited retirement account than a stretching technique might allow.[5]

- **Life Insurance Funding** - This technique suggests that a retirement account owner use his retirement account to fund life insurance that is purchased and owned by his beneficiaries or a trust for the beneficiaries' benefit. This technique has a few drawbacks. If the account owner dies shortly after funding the insurance purchase, a large part of his retirement account may still be held by the account owner and therefore would be subject to estate taxes even though the insurance purchased will pass tax-free to beneficiaries. Retirement account withdrawals used to fund the insurance are subject to income taxes (and possibly IRS penalties) while the owner is alive and may

---

[4] $495,000 + $211,000 = $706,000.

[5] If a beneficiary lives to an old age (i.e. 90+) the current IRS required minimum distribution rules will subject a very large part of the inherited retirement account to income taxes.

also generate income taxes for beneficiaries who inherit any excess retirement account assets not used to purchase life insurance. If the retirement account owner needs (or wants) income from his retirement account, this technique may not work. Another problem with this technique is that a bear market could reduce the ability of the account owner to make planned insurance premiums.

- **Roth Conversion** - This technique recommends that the owner of an eligible qualified retirement account transfer the account to a traditional IRA. The traditional IRA is then converted to a Roth IRA. This will eliminate any income tax liability for beneficiaries who inherit the Roth in the future. However, to get this result the IRA owner must pay all income taxes owed on the traditional IRA at the time of conversion. Another problem to consider is the fact that Roth IRA's do not escape estate taxes. Currently, if an owner's modified adjusted gross income level is more than $100,000, they are not be eligible to make a Roth IRA conversion. [When all tax issues are considered it is often determined that Roth conversions rarely deliver the tax savings their proponents claim are available].

- **Gifting** - Some financial professionals recommend that retirement accounts be given away using the $12,000 annual gift tax exclusion (2008) and other similar exemptions.[6] The problem with this recommendation is that the donor will have to pay income taxes on withdrawals from his retirement account before giving them away. Additionally, depending on the size of the donor's estate and its investment performance, the gifts may only have a minimal effect on reducing estate and income taxes at the owner's death. Gifts in excess of $12,000 may reduce the applicable credit amount (i.e., old unified credit) at the donor's death.

§2003. ASSET SUBSTITUTION

There is a tax strategy that can eliminate the double taxation currently imposed on retirement accounts. This report refers to this tax strategy as asset substitution because a life insurance policy and an immediate annuity are substituted (on a tax-free basis) for the retirement account that is subject to double taxation. This simple exchange results in the elimination of estate and income taxes from the retirement account. Retirement accounts, whether qualified or not, have a dual purpose. First, they provide income to the owner while he is alive and secondly, they provide wealth to be passed on to the next generation at the owner's death. The asset substitution technique ensures these two functions are maintained. By substituting an immediate annuity and a life insurance policy for the retirement account, the owner receives a *guaranteed lifetime* stream of income from the annuity while the life insurance *guarantees* a *tax-free* source of wealth to be passed to the next generation. In most cases, asset substitution provides the following three benefits to clients who own one or more retirement accounts:

---

[6] Other exemptions would, for example, include transfers to educational entities under IRC §2503(e), etc.

189

1) It will eliminate both federal estate taxes owed by an owner's estate and income taxes owed by beneficiaries on any retirement accounts ultimately passing to them;

2) It will increase the net value of the estate passing to beneficiaries; and

3) It will provide an increased current income stream for the account owner without diminishing the value of the owner's estate.

As mentioned above, asset substitution is a simple, cost effective estate planning technique that removes from a client's estate any retirement account (qualified or not) that could potentially generate an estate tax or impose an income tax on beneficiaries and replaces it with a life insurance policy coupled with an immediate annuity.[7] The benefit of using the asset substitution technique as part of an overall tax plan is that all potential estate taxes and all income taxes the beneficiaries might ultimately owe on a retirement account can be completely eliminated. Additionally, as mentioned above, the size of the decedent's net estate passing to beneficiaries is increased while providing the retirement account owner with an increased stream of income while alive.

The following problem demonstrates the potential estate and income tax savings that can result from using the tax planning technique of asset substitution:

Problem:

Jack, who is 67 and a widower, has an estate worth $3,000,000. Jack has three adult daughters. One million dollars of his estate is a non-qualified variable annuity of which $240,000 represents Jack's contributions and $760,000 constitutes his investment gain. The remainder of Jack's estate, which consists of his house, car, etc., is worth $2,000,000. If Jack dies in 2008, his estate tax would be $450,000.[8] The income taxes owed on the variable annuity inherited by his three adult daughters could exceed $137,000.[9] This combined tax liability of over $587,000 will cause approximately 59% of the variable annuity's value to be lost to the IRS.

Jack has the following concerns:

1. He does not want his estate to be exposed to federal death taxes of $475,000;

2. He wants to pass the full value of his $1,000,000 variable annuity to his three children but does not want them to have to pay income taxes on the annuity;

---

[7] The concept of asset substitution for tax planning is not new. For example, to reduce a client's current income tax liability, many tax advisors, in the right circumstances, recommend ownership of municipal bonds to clients rather than taxable investments. Variable annuities, because of their tax deferral advantage, are often recommended by tax advisors as substitutes for investments that are currently taxable for those clients who need to defer income taxes. In both cases one asset is substituted for another in order to reduce the owner's tax liability.

[8] $1,005,800 + $225,000 (45% of $500,000) = $1,230,800 - $780,800 = $450,000.

[9] $760,000 in annuity gain = 76% of $1,000,000. 76% of $450,000 in estate taxes provides a $342,000 IRC §691 income tax deduction. $760,000 - $342,000 = $418,000 x 33% (assumed tax rate) = $137,940.

3. He wants his daughters to inherit his $3,000,000 estate without any reduction for taxes; and

4. He wants to receive a *guaranteed, after-tax* income of $40,000 a year from his annuity for as long as he lives.

A financial advisor using the asset substitution technique would be able to help Jack overcome all of his concerns. The four steps necessary to accomplish this are set out below:

Solution:

Step 1. Jack's three adult children, with Jack's assistance, should apply for and become the owners of a life insurance policy on Jack's life for at least one million dollars. The annual premium will be approximately $27,000. Such premiums are usually payable for 10-12 years. [An irrevocable life insurance trust *may* be needed under certain circumstances.][10]

Step 2. Once the life insurance policy has been issued, Jack should transfer his variable annuity tax-free (via IRC §1035) to the immediate annuity company that will provide Jack with the largest annual income possible.[11] The immediate annuity, as a general rule, should *not* provide for any guarantees other than payments for life.[12] It will be assumed that Jack could receive $80,000 a year for life from such an immediate annuity.

---

[10] A whole life or variable policy would be appropriate. The premium is based on the assumption that the policy issued to Jack is for a standard non-smoker. Today, many insurance companies can guarantee both premiums and death benefits. A policy for more than $1,000,000 could be purchased to cover inflation, the expected investment gain if the retirement account were kept, etc. The premium does not have to be Jack's burden alone. In some cases, the ultimate beneficiaries may pay some (or even all) of the premiums due. An irrevocable life insurance trust (ILIT), although not necessary for the asset substitution technique to work, could be used if the facts indicated such a trust would be beneficial. By purchasing the insurance so that it is owned by the ultimate beneficiaries, IRC §2035 is avoided. IRC §2035 requires the inclusion in a decedent's gross estate for the value of any life insurance *transferred* to others within three years of the transferor's death. [Special attention has to be paid to who owns the new policy, who the beneficiaries are, what percentages of the proceeds they are entitled to and how the new application is written. Proper issuance for a life insurance policy at its inception is critical in order to avoid inadvertently exposing the death benefit to income taxation. It is important to remember that while the asset substitution strategy is rather straight forward, its implementation can be fraught with pitfalls for the uninitiated. It is also important to understand that all immediate annuities are not the same. Different annuity companies will most likely quote different guaranteed payments. Advisors should always work with tax professionals.

[11] The financial strength of the immediate annuity company is an important factor to consider. Stronger issuers will make annuity payments that are slightly smaller than less financially sound issuers. An insurance professional can help determine the appropriate level of financial security for an annuity issuer by considering other factors such as the limits of coverage provided by state insurance guaranty funds.

[12] As a general rule, the immediate annuity purchased as part of the asset substitution technique should not provide for payments beyond the owner's lifetime. Guaranteed payments made after an owner's death are subject to estate and income taxes. To the extent income is not needed from the immediate annuity, the retirement account owner should consider increasing the life insurance purchased as part of the asset substitution technique. Some clients may be uncomfortable with the idea that annuity payments will cease upon their death especially if they should die shortly after completing an asset substitution strategy. Some clients may feel more comfortable knowing that some minimum number of payments will be received by them or their heirs (i.e. payments for the first ten years or some other specified period). The following are negative aspects of selecting a guaranteed payout period: 1) the remaining value of the guaranteed annuity payments would be added to the estate tax and income tax calculations; 2) The amount of each payment would be less than what the annuitant would receive if he or she had chosen a life-only immediate annuity; 3) The difference in annuity payments from a life-only immediate annuity and an annuity with a guaranteed period will not be available to purchase additional insurance that could be received by the beneficiaries tax free; 4) if the annuitant lives beyond the guaranteed period of the annuity, he or she will continue to pay a premium for that minimum guaranteed payout long after the benefit no longer exists. It is very important that the pros and cons of the various annuity selections be completely discussed with clients.

Step 3. The $80,000 annual payment received by Jack from the immediate annuity will be tax favored due to application of the exclusion ratio available to immediate annuity owners.[13] Of Jack's $80,000 annual immediate annuity payment, only $64,000 will be subject to income taxes.[14] The income tax liability on $64,000, at a 20% average tax rate, will be $12,800 leaving an after-tax annual income of $67,200.[15]

Step 4. In 2008, Jack can make total annual gifts of $36,000 ($12,000 x 3) to his three daughters without incurring a gift tax.[16] Thus a $27,000 gift made by Jack to his daughters to pay the insurance premiums would not be subject to gift taxes. After giving $27,000 to his children, Jack will receive an after-tax stream of income from his immediate annuity in the amount of $40,200 which is slightly more than he requires.[17] Because Jack now owns an immediate annuity, these payments are guaranteed for Jack's life.

Once the four steps discussed above are in place, Jack will have eliminated any possible federal estate tax on his present $3,000,000 estate. The reason for this is that an immediate annuity with no period of guaranteed payments, other than lifetime payments, has no value for estate tax calculation purposes.[18] This would result in Jack's estate being valued at $2,000,000 rather than $3,000,000. No estate taxes would be due because the current estate tax exemption amount is $2,000,000 (2007-8). In addition to this, Jack's three daughters will receive $1,000,000 in life insurance proceeds free of both estate[19] and income taxes.[20] The end result of asset substitution tax planning would be that Jack's children would receive the full value of his $3,000,000 estate without losing any of it to the IRS. Additionally, if Jack lives for 12½ years he will receive back in annual immediate annuity payments the full $1,000,000 cost of his immediate annuity.[21] After that he would continue to receive $80,000 a year from his annuity for the rest of his life.

---

[13] IRC §72.

[14] Assuming Jack's life expectancy is 82, he will receive 15 payments of $80,000 or $1,200,000. His contributions to his variable annuity were $240,000. This creates an exclusion ratio of 20% ($240,000 ÷ $1,200,000). The $80,000 in payments received each year from the immediate annuity will receive the advantage of the 20% exclusion ratio. This means that for each $80,000 annuity payment Jack receives each year, $16,000 or 20% will be excluded from income taxation while $64,000 will be subject to income taxes. This will continue for 15 years to allow Jack to recover his $240,000 in contributions tax-free. (15 x $16,000 = $240,000). After that, each payment of $80,000 made to Jack will be fully subject to ordinary income taxes.

[15] $64,000 x 20% = $12,800. $80,000 - $12,800 = $67,200.

[16] A $12,000 (2007) annual gift tax exemption for each of the three children exceeds the $27,000 gift to the children.

[17] $67,200 - $27,000 = $40,200. It is important to note that Jack did not need all of the money generated by the immediate annuity he purchased. If a client does need all of the income generated by an immediate annuity the asset substitution technique may not be a viable estate planning tool. If the client's children are willing to pay the insurance premiums involved with this technique then it could still be used.

[18] IRC §2039.

[19] The insurance proceeds are not subject to estate taxes because the decedent did not own the policy at death or have any incidents of ownership in the policy at his death. IRC §2035 would not apply because no insurance policy was *transferred*.

[20] As a broad general rule, insurance proceeds are not subject to income taxes.

[21] 12½ years x $80,000 = $1,000,000. Any unrecovered immediate annuity payments would be an income tax deduction on the final income tax return of the deceased variable annuity owner and would not be subject to the 2% AGI threshold.

The above asset substitution technique may also be used for married couples even if one of the spouses is uninsurable.[22] The following example demonstrates the potential tax savings available in such a situation:

Example:

Paul and his wife, Jan, both 68, have an estate worth $5,000,000. They have two adult sons. One million dollars of their estate is a Simplified Employee Plan (SEP) set up by Paul several years ago. Paul, due to health problems, is not insurable. The remainder of the estate, which consists of a house, vacation property, investments, car, etc., is worth $4,000,000. Paul and his wife each own half of these assets. Paul and his wife each have a will containing a credit shelter (by-pass) trust provision. Paul and his wife need to supplement their other retirement income by at least $50,000 a year (before taxes) from the SEP in order to live comfortably in retirement. At their death, Paul and his wife want the full value of their $4,000,000 estate and $1,000,000 SEP to pass to their two children without estate or income taxes reducing this $5,000,000 value. If nothing is done, estate and income taxes could reach several hundred thousand dollars. The ability to eliminate this potential tax liability is quite simple. Paul and his wife should have their two children purchase (and own) a $1,000,000 second-to-die life insurance policy insuring Paul and Jan's lives. Only one spouse needs to be insurable with a second-to-die insurance policy. The premium for such a policy will be approximately $27,000 a year.[23] After the policy is in place, Paul should transfer his SEP tax-free to an annuity company in exchange for an immediate lifetime joint survivor annuity (i.e., no guarantee other than lifetime payments to Paul and his wife).[24] The immediate annuity will pay Paul and his wife approximately $80,000 a year for as long as either lives. Paul and his wife can give $27,000 to their children gift tax-free each year to enable them to pay the premiums on the life insurance they purchased. This leaves Paul and his wife with $53,000 in pre-tax annual income for their retirement. (A SEP does not provide an exclusion ratio because it is a qualified retirement account on which no income taxes have been paid). If either spouse dies tomorrow the annuity will continue to pay $80,000 to the surviving spouse for his or her lifetime. This will provide $53,000 in pre-tax income while also providing $27,000 a year to the children to pay the insurance premium. At the second spouse's death the remainder of the estate (i.e. $4,000,000) will pass to the children estate tax-free by coupling the current $2,000,000 exemption (2008) with the credit shelter (by-pass) trusts that were included in Paul and Jan's wills. At the second spouse's death, the immediate annuity is valued at zero because it is a lifetime annuity that ceases to have any value at the second spouse's death. In addition, the children will receive $1,000,000 estate and income tax free from the life insurance company in the form of insurance proceeds. In short, basic asset substitution will allow

---

[22] Only one spouse needs to be insurable in order to obtain a second-to-die life insurance policy.

[23] For second to die policies, the premiums are usually set for 10 to 12 years only. See note 376 above on premium amount.

[24] Any qualified retirement account (other than a Roth IRA) can be transferred to an IRA within an immediate annuity on a tax-free basis similar to an annuity-to-annuity transfer pursuant to IRC §1035.

the children to inherit their parents' entire $5,000,000 estate free of all death and income taxes.

§2004. ADVANTAGES OF ASSET SUBSTITUTION FOR CLIENTS

There are many advantages that flow to clients who elect to use the asset substitution tax planning technique. Among them are:

(1) All estate taxes on the retirement accounts involved are eliminated.

(2) The full value of any retirement accounts involved is passed on to beneficiaries without imposing any income tax liability on them.

(3) The technique is simple to explain to clients and implement.

(4) The technique is effective. It can avoid estate and income tax losses on a retirement account that can be between 60% to 70%.

(5) The technique is cost efficient.

(6) Any unrecovered portion of the immediate annuity used with the asset substitution technique is deductible by the decedent's executor against income taxes owed by the decedent.[25]

(7) The technique provides a guaranteed lifetime stream of income to the retirement account owner and his spouse if married.

(8) Non-qualified variable annuities qualify for the exclusion ratio.

(9) The asset substitution technique can save taxes even for estates that are not currently subject to estate taxes or later become exempt due to increasing exemption amounts.[26]

§2005. ADVANTAGES OF ASSET SUBSTITUTION TO THE FINANCIAL ADVISOR

Financial advisors who recommend and implement the asset substitution technique can often help their clients save hundreds of thousands of dollars in estate and income taxes. Additionally, they can establish a sizeable guaranteed lifetime stream of income for their clients that may be eligible for the exclusion ratio. Financial advisors who implement the asset substitution technique for a single $1,000,000 retirement account will need to put in place two insurance products – a $1,000,000 life insurance policy and a $1,000,000 immediate annuity.

§2006. MALPRACTICE TRAP

Financial advisors should be aware that the likelihood that their clients will die with one or more retirement accounts is quite high. Failure to recommend a tax planning technique that will eliminate all potential estate and income taxes from a client's retirement account could result in a malpractice claim by survivors. At a minimum, financial professionals should inform their clients of the fact that estate and income taxes on retirement accounts can easily be avoided. If, after being informed of this, a client elects not to take advantage of such planning,

---

[25] IRS Pub. No. 529, p. 10.

[26] An estate made up entirely of a $2 million retirement account in 2007 would not be subject to estate taxes but the beneficiaries would face a large income tax liability. If the retirement account were converted to an immediate annuity to fund life insurance, the potential income tax liability would be eliminated.

documentation of this refusal should be placed in the client's file.[27] Financial advisors, who are
not tax experts, should *always* have a CPA or tax attorney assist them in implementing an asset
substitution plan for a client.

§2007. SHARING YOUR PROFESSIONAL FINANCIAL KNOWLEDGE

Many attorneys and CPAs are not aware of how beneficial asset substitution can be
for their clients. Financial advisors should do everything possible to inform these other
professionals about the benefits of asset substitution. If a client elects to eliminate potential
estate and income taxes from their retirement accounts by using the asset substitution technique,
attorneys and CPAs usually understand how important it is to seek the services of a financial
advisor. Attorneys and CPAs will almost always obtain insurance and annuity policies needed to
implement asset substitution from the financial advisors who initially helped them understand the
benefits of this tax saving technique. Attorneys and CPAs know that a mistake in the structure
or timing of the insurance or annuity substituted for the client's retirement account can result in
significant financial losses.[28] The following are just a few examples of actual errors that have
been made when the asset substitution technique was attempted without the assistance of experts
familiar with the insurance and annuities required to properly implement the asset substitution
technique:

(1) A *term* life insurance policy was purchased in an attempt to effectuate asset
substitution. The policy lapsed just before the owner died resulting in a $1.2 million
tax loss. Whole life, guaranteed universal life or some similar type of life insurance
should be used with the asset substitution technique.

(2) A client's retirement account was exchanged for a straight-life immediate annuity
before the application for life insurance was approved. The client proved to be
uninsurable and died a short while later. This resulted in a $950,000 forfeiture of the
annuity premium. Life insurance must be in place *before* an immediate annuity is
purchased when the asset substitution technique is used.

(3) The immediate annuity purchased with an IRA in an attempt to effectuate asset
substitution was set up with a *refund* feature. The client died shortly after the
immediate annuity was purchased resulting in the full value of the annuity being
included in the decedent's estate. This in turn resulted in the imposition of a large
estate tax. Additionally, the beneficiaries had to pay income taxes on the annuity
proceeds they inherited. Although elimination of both of these taxes was what the
client was seeking, neither came about.[29]

(4) Rather than have the children buy insurance on the life of their father, a tax
professional advised the father to transfer an existing life insurance policy to the

---

[27] A document signed by a client indicating they have declined to take advantage of the asset substitution technique after it was fully
explained to them is the best protection against allegations by beneficiaries at a later time that proper estate planning was not done.

[28] See notes 376 and 278 above.

[29] Although the beneficiaries were better off because of the decedent's actions, they did not get the full advantage of the asset substitution
technique due to the timing issue.

children. He died two years later and IRC §2035 required inclusion of the insurance policy's full $1.4 million value in the father's estate (The same result can occur if the retirement account owner purchases and owns the life insurance policy purchased as part of the asset substitution technique).

(5) Failure to consider income needs and the loss of control issue with the retirement account owner. If the account owner needs all of the income he can obtain from his retirement account or would be uncomfortable losing control of such an account, the asset substitution technique should not be used.

§2008. CONCLUSION

Retirement accounts are one of the largest and most common assets financial advisors encounter in their practices. Retirement accounts can be subject to both estate and income taxes that can result in a tax loss of 60% or more of the value of these retirement accounts if proper tax planning is not done. Failure to inform clients that both estate and income taxes can be eliminated from retirement accounts can, at best, result in embarrassment and, at worst, can precipitate litigation. Financial advisors, together with attorneys and CPAs, should work as a team in an effort to help clients take advantage of the asset substitution technique.

– CHAPTER 21 –
THE LONG BREAK-EVEN MYTH

§2101. INTRODUCTION

Many investors and others believe that the purchase of a variable annuity only makes sense if it is held for nearly twenty years because it would take that long for the variable annuity's tax deferral to overcome a similar mutual fund investment. This is a myth.

§2102. THE BREAK-EVEN POINT

If money is invested in a mutual fund and variable annuity at the same time and both earn the same gross rate of return over the same time period, the net ending value of the variable annuity investment will usually lag behind that of the mutual fund for a certain period of time. However, at some point in time, due to tax deferral, the declining contingent deferred sales charge (CDSC) and lower costs, the variable annuity value will overcome that of the mutual fund. This point of crossover is referred to by financial professionals as the break-even point. Many years ago a hack reporter compared a typical variable annuity to an index mutual fund and concluded that the break-even point for the variable annuity was close to twenty years. Ever since this defective apples-to-oranges comparison was made, the myth that variable annuities have a twenty year break-even point when compared to a similar mutual fund investment has persisted. This myth has no merit to it, the truth is that the current break-even point for the typical variable annuity and mutual fund is closer to six or even seven years. The following example computes the break-even point for a mutual fund and variable annuity and concludes that the break-even point is six years. This is true even though the variable annuity investment would require the payment of a small contingent deferred sales charge (CDSC) and a 10% pre-age 59½ IRS penalty. Notice that *all* of the costs, fees, taxes, penalties and other factors were considered in order to obtain a net ending value for the variable annuity and mutual fund. The net ending value acid test discussed in Chapter 11 should be reviewed.

> **Example**
> Jim, who is 53, is considering a $20,000 investment in a mutual fund or a variable annuity. He is concerned about surrender charges and the 10% IRS penalty for pre-59½ withdrawals. How long must Jim hold his variable annuity to overcome these surrender charges and the 10% IRS tax penalty?

1. Mutual Fund Portfolio
   A. Amount to be invested $20,000
   B. Commission 5.0%
   C. Annual management fee, 12b-1 fee 1.6%
   D. Assumed rate of return.. 8%
   E. Annual income tax loss... 1.6%
   F. Expected holding period .... 6 years
   G. Trading costs.. 0.7%
   H. Value of Portfolio after six years
      after all expenses and taxes.................................... $24,411[1]

2. Variable Annuity Purchase
   A. Amount to be invested $20,000
   B. Assumed rate of return.. 8%
   C. Annual cost of variable annuity ownership................... 2.3%
   D. Average income tax rate.. 22%
   E. Anticipated holding period .... 6 years
   F. IRS penalty on growth if withdrawn before age 59½..... 10%
   G. 7% CDSC (Declines 1% each year)................................ 1%
   H. Trading costs.. 0.5%
   I. Value of variable annuity after six years
      after all expenses and taxes.................................... $24,430[2]

§2103. CONCLUSION

By conducting a basic net-to-net analysis (see Chapter 11) a financial professional can determine the true break-even point for a variable annuity and mutual fund.

---

[1] $20,000 - 5% =$19,000 x 8% = $20,520 - 2.3% = $20,048. $20,048 - $19,000 = $1,048 gain x 20% tax (1.6% of 8%) = $838 ÷ $19,000 = 4.41263%. $19,000 x 4.41263% x 6 years = $24,619 - $208 capital gains tax ($4,619 gain x 0.30 x 0.15) = $24,411
[2] $20,000 x 8% = $21,600 - 2.8% = $20,995 - $20,000 = $995 in gain ÷ $20,000 = 4.976%. $20,000 x 4.976% x 6 years = $26,765. Surrender penalty of $170 (0.85% of withdrawal of initial premium). Value after surrender penalty = $26,595. Income taxes of 22% on the gain of $6,765 = $1,488. 10% IRS penalty = $677 (10% of $6,765). Net value of the variable annuity after 6 years = $26,765 - $170 - $1,488 - $677 = $24,430. The 15% surrender charge-free withdrawal benefit is assumed for the variable annuity.

– CHAPTER 22 –
THE HIGH COMMISSION MYTH – SUMMARY DISCUSSION
§2201. INTRODUCTION

People who know little about variable annuities, which includes the media, often claim that the commissions paid to purchase a variable annuity are higher than the commissions paid to purchase similar investments. These same people believe that financial professionals who sell variable annuities do so because variable annuities provide them with more income than similar investment products. Neither of these claims are true–both are myths.

§2202. AN ANALOGY

Frank is considering two restaurants to take his wife to for dinner this weekend. Both restaurants are identical by all regards and serve identical steak dinners. Restaurant #1 charges a total of $125 for two people to eat a steak dinner at their restaurant. Restaurant #2 charges $160 for the exact same meal. Which restaurant is the best economic choice? Based only on the information provided, Restaurant #1 is the better choice. What if Frank's brother and his wife want to take Frank and his wife to Restaurant #2 and the brother has agreed to pay for everyone's meal. Should Frank and his wife now consider going to Restaurant #2? Absolutely! Although Restaurant #2 is more expensive, it will cost Frank and his wife nothing to eat there because someone else is paying for the meal.

§2203. VARIABLE ANNUITY COMMISSIONS

Variable annuity commissions are similar to the restaurant analogy discussed above. If one has a choice of investing $25,000 in a mutual fund and paying a 5% commission or investing $25,000 in a variable annuity that has a 6% contingent deferred sales charge (CDSC), which is the better economic choice? *If* the full 5% or 6% commission is going to be paid by the *investor*, the mutual fund would be the best choice. However, variable annuity commissions are *not* paid by the investor like the up-front, out-of-pocket commission paid to buy a mutual fund. The variable annuity commission is paid or advanced by the variable annuity issuer. For each year a variable annuity is held the CDSC usually declines by 1% a year until it disappears at the end of the holding period. The advanced commission is recouped in the annual charges imposed by the variable annuity issuer.

If a variable annuity is not held by the investor for an agreed holding period (averaging six years) the investor must repay all or part of the advanced commission. This is called a contingent deferred sale charge or CDSC.

Many people argue that because the commission that is advanced by the variable annuity issuer is built into the cost of owning the variable annuity, the variable annuity is more expensive to own on an annual basis. This is not true. As Chapters 9 and 10 pointed out, the annual cost of owning a variable annuity, including the built in cost for recouping any advanced commissions, in many cases is less than the cost of a mutual fund.

§2204. SURRENDER CHARGES

Another myth about variable annuities is that when a variable annuity is surrendered there is always a surrender fee that must be paid. This is not true. All surrender fees (CDSCs) disappear when a variable annuity has been held for its agreed holding period. Many variable annuities can be purchased that do not impose any surrender fee (CDSC) under any circumstances.

§2205. CONCLUSION

Once investors understand how commissions are paid when mutual funds and variable annuities are purchased, they will be in a better position to make a proper investment choice. Chapter 23 discusses commissions in detail including surrender fees.

– CHAPTER 23 –
THE HIGH COMMISSION MYTH – DETAILED DISCUSSION
§2301. INTRODUCTION

Both variable annuities and mutual funds sold by financial professionals generate commissions in one form or another. These commissions are designed to compensate selling professionals for their services and expertise in selecting, monitoring and providing ongoing advice and service to the owners of these two important investments. Many investors have been led to believe that the commissions paid to purchase variable annuities negatively affect returns more so than for an equivalent mutual fund purchase. In addition, many investors are under the impression that variable annuity owners must always pay some surrender charge when they sell their variable annuities. Neither of these assumptions are correct. This report compares the affect of commissions on the returns of variable annuities and mutual funds sold by financial professionals and reaches the conclusion that the affect of commissions charged to purchase an average variable annuity, together with any surrender charges, will frequently be less than for an equivalent mutual fund purchase.

Variable annuities and mutual funds are two popular investments sold by financial professionals. Various commission structures are used to compensate the professionals who sell these investments. Because these commission structures are somewhat complicated, many investors do not fully understand how they impact variable annuity and mutual fund returns. This can lead to faulty investment decisions. This chapter examines how the various commission structures imposed on purchasers of actively managed variable annuities and mutual funds impact the returns generated by these two investments.[1] Hopefully, this chapter will provide investors with information about commission charges that will help them make better investment decisions when considering the purchase of either a variable annuity or mutual fund.

§2302. COMPARISON DATA

All of the comparisons made in this report are based on average or typical investments made in variable annuities and mutual funds. Investors should use the comparisons discussed in this report as a guide only. Actual data for any potential investment should be substituted for the hypothetical data used in this report. For example, this report might use a typical A-share commission of 5% for an average mutual fund investment of $30,000. However, if an investor is considering the purchase of a mutual fund that imposes a 4½% commission on a $50,000 investment, then the 4½% and $50,000 figures should be used when trying to determine whether the mutual fund or a similar variable annuity will be the better investment.

---

[1] The report limits its comparisons to actively managed mutual funds and variable annuities sold by financial professionals.

§2303. NON-COMMISSION RELATED COSTS

Both variable annuities and mutual funds impose or generate expenses that are unrelated to commissions. One of the major difficulties encountered in comparing the impact that commissions have on the returns produced by variable annuities and mutual funds is ensuring that these non-commission related costs are properly excluded before any comparisons are made. In an effort to isolate commission costs in this report, all non-commission related expenses have, to the extent possible, been ignored. For example, federal income taxes increase the annual cost of owning mutual funds. However, these taxes are *not* part of the commission structure of mutual funds. For this reason, the federal income tax liability incurred each year for owning mutual funds has been ignored in this report by assuming such funds are held in a qualified account like an IRA or basing results on pre-tax returns. Likewise, potential IRS penalties associated with early withdrawals from variable annuities may increase the cost of owning annuities. However, because such penalties are not part of the commission structure of variable annuities, they too are excluded when comparing commission costs. On the other hand, surrender charges *actually* imposed on buyers of variable annuities and B-share mutual funds are part of the commission structure of owning these two investments and therefore are included in the comparisons made in this report. Non-commission costs such as annual taxation of mutual funds and IRS penalties imposed on variable annuity owners are important cost factors that one should weigh when considering the purchase of either variable annuities or mutual funds. For this reason, these expenses are discussed separately at the end of this report. The next section discusses more fully what constitutes a commission for the comparisons made in this report.

§2304. COMMISSION - A WORKING DEFINITION

Because this report deals exclusively with a comparison of variable annuity and mutual fund commissions, a working definition of this term is important. As used in this report, the term commission refers to:

1. Any up-front, out-of-pocket payment made by an investor to the seller of a mutual fund or variable annuity at the time of purchase;

2. Any contingent deferred sales charge (CDSC) actually paid by the owner of a variable annuity or mutual fund when either of these investments are partially or completely liquidated;

3. Any recurring annual fee or charge imposed by a variable annuity or mutual fund company to the extent they are designed to recoup commissions advanced by the mutual fund or variable annuity company. (These fees or charges are included as part of the annual expense or ownership fees);

4. Any trailing commissions paid to a financial professional that are recouped from the owner of a mutual fund or variable annuity (i.e., 12b-1 fees); and

5. Any expenses or trading costs incurred by a variable annuity or mutual fund company to buy investments to the extent these expenses or costs are passed on to the owners of

the variable annuity or mutual fund.

§2305. THE VARIABLE ANNUITY COMMISSION STRUCTURE

Media reporters and others who know little about variable annuities claim that purchasers of variable annuities not only incur up-front, out-of-pocket commissions when they buy variable annuities, but are also required to pay surrender fees when they sell their annuities. Neither of these claims is true. The few variable annuities that charge an up-front, out-of-pocket commission do *not* also impose surrender charges. The overwhelming majority of variable annuities sold by financial professionals today *do not* impose any up-front commission that investors must pay out of their pocket at the time of purchase. Instead, variable annuity issuers actually impose what is technically called a contingent deferred sales charge or CDSC. With the CDSC commission structure, the financial professional selling a variable annuity is paid a commission by the issuing annuity company and *not* by the investor who purchases the annuity.[2] The issuing company advancing the commission will require reimbursement of part of all of the advanced commission from the annuity purchaser *only* if the purchaser sells his annuity before expiration of an agreed holding period. Reimbursements by variable annuity investors of advanced commissions are called surrender charges. For basic variable annuities, CDSCs typically range from 5% to 7% and, as a general rule, decline approximately 1% a year until they completely disappear.[3] CDSCs are imposed on either total premiums (investments) made in the variable annuity or on the value of the account at the time of a withdrawal. The prospectuses for all variable annuities specify which method is used. This report will specify which method is used in its examples and will alternate the methods. There is a major exception to the rule that a full surrender fee is charged for the early liquidation of all or part of a variable annuity. Nearly all variable annuities allow withdrawals from 10% to 15% of the annuity's value each year without the variable annuity owner having to incur a surrender penalty. Complete surrender charge-free withdrawals are frequently allowed for hardships such as entry into a nursing home, unemployment, permanent disability or terminal illness.

It is critical for potential variable annuity investors to fully understand the CDSC commission structure applicable to variable annuity sales. The letters 'SC' in CDSC stand for sales charge, which is synonymous with commission. The letter 'D' stands for deferred. This means that no up-front, out-of-pocket sales charge or commission is required of a variable

---

[2] Commissions are technically paid by variable annuity and mutual fund companies to the financial entity employing the financial professional selling the annuity or mutual fund who in turn is paid by his employer. To avoid an unnecessary technicality, this report will have commissions paid to the financial professional selling the variable annuity or mutual fund involved.

[3] Holding periods generally range from three to seven years. There are zero holding period variable annuities. Variable annuities offering the most attractive living benefits usually have holding periods that range from five to ten years. CDSCs do not necessarily decline 1% a year. For example, a variable annuity with a six year holding period could decline as follows: 7%, 7%, 6%, 6%, 5%, 1%. Regardless of how a CDSC declines over time, at the end of the holding period the CDSC will *always* be zero. This is another reason why it is important to select variable annuities that have holding periods that match ones investment time horizon.

annuity investor at the time of purchase. Instead, any potential commission is deferred and paid, if at all, at sometime in the future. The letter 'C' is the most important component of the CDSC and stands for contingent. This means that the deferred sales charge or delayed commission may or may not have to be paid by the annuity purchaser. The contingency that determines whether a variable annuity purchaser will ever have to pay a full or partial sales charge or commission out of his pocket is whether the annuity purchaser holds his annuity for an agreed period of time before it is sold.[4] This time period, as mentioned above, is referred to as the holding or surrender period. This period, which is selected by the annuity purchaser, can range from zero to ten years with the average holding period being six years. This average holding period is used in this report unless a longer period is specified. Under the CDSC commission structure, commissions, if they must be paid back, are usually reimbursed to the issuing company on a declining scale. CDSCs generally decline 1% a year and completely disappear when the holding period expires.[5] The following example demonstrates how the CDSC commission structure of the variable annuity operates:

Example
Betty just invested $50,000 in the Zenith Horizon Variable Annuity. Zenith's CDSC table, which is found in the company prospectus, appears below:

TABLE OF SURRENDER FEES FOR THE ZENITH SIX YEAR CDSC VARIABLE ANNUITY

YEARS HELD	SURRENDER CHARGE
Less than 1	6%
> 1 but < 2	5%
> 2 but < 3	4%
>3 but < 4	3%
> 4 but < 5	2%
> 5 but < 6	1%
More than 6	0%

As the above table indicates, Zenith, the company issuing the Horizon Variable Annuity, has a holding or surrender period of six years. Based on this information, if Betty sells her annuity in its first year of ownership, she will have 6% of her $50,000 initial investment or $3,000 withheld from her sale proceeds at the time of surrender to offset the commission advanced by the issuing company to the financial professional who sold the Zenith Horizon Variable Annuity to Betty.[6] If the variable annuity is held by Betty for a little more than three years and then sold, a 3% CDSC, based on Betty's initial investment, will be withheld

---

[4] The term sold includes both a liquidation or sale as well as an exchange pursuant to IRC §1035.

[5] See note 3 above.

[6] The CDSC can be imposed on the initial investment or the account value (asset base) at the time of surrender. This report alternates these two methods in the examples discussed.

from Betty's sale proceeds at the time of surrender.[7] Betty would not have to pay any surrender charges on the first 10% to 15% of this or any withdrawal taken in a given year. It is important to note that if the Zenith Horizon Variable Annuity is held by Betty for one day beyond six years, she will pay no commission out of her pocket for buying her variable annuity. Had Betty purchased an A-share mutual fund with a 4½% commission, she would have paid an up-front, out-of-pocket commission of $2,250 at the time of purchase. Whether Betty held this fund for one day or one decade, she would be out-of-pocket $2,250 when she sold her mutual fund. The variable annuity gives Betty the opportunity to avoid having to pay any up-front, out-of-pocket commissions and completely avoid any CDSC by simply holding her annuity for the holding period she selects.

Variable annuity companies also impose annual ownership fees for owning their variable annuities. These annual ownership fees, as determined by the SEC and others, will average between 2.1% to 2.3%, including administrative, (e.g., 12b-1 fees) and mortality fees together with other miscellaneous fees.[8] This report will use an average annual ownership cost of 2.2% for variable annuities. These annual ownership fees cover the salaries of the variable annuity investment managers and the other ongoing expenses of operating the variable annuity. These annual fees are set in such a way as to allow variable annuity companies recoup commissions they advance to the financial advisors who sell their variable annuities if annuity purchasers hold their annuities long enough to avoid the CDSC. In summary, the variable annuity CDSC commission structure operates as follows:

1 When an investor buys a variable annuity, the investor will not pay any up-front, out-of-pocket commission to purchase his variable annuity if he holds the annuity;

2. When an investor buys a variable annuity, the annuity company advances a full commission to the financial professional selling their annuity;

3. For every year of ownership, the variable annuity purchaser will be charged an annual ownership fee that averages 2.2%. A portion of this ownership fee is designed to recoup commissions paid out by the variable annuity company to the professionals who sell their variable annuities. This 2.2% ownership fee is deducted from the value of the annuity each year on a quarterly basis;[9]

4. If the investor purchasing the variable annuity surrenders part of all of his variable annuity before the agreed holding period expires, he will have to reimburse the issuing annuity company part or all of the commission the company advanced to the selling professional when the annuity was initially purchased (this is accomplished by imposition of the CDSC);

---

[7] *Id.*

[8] Joint SEC/NASD report on variable insurance products (June 9, 2004, page 6). This report states the average annual expense of owning a variable annuity ranges from 1.3% to 2.2%. The higher figure is used by the author. Morningstar sets this annual expense ratio at 2.06%.

[9] Annual expenses are imposed by variable annuity and mutual fund companies on a quarterly basis. For the sake of arithmetic simplicity, this report will impose them on an annual basis.

5. Trading costs are separately charged each year to cover the commissions paid by the annuity company to buy and sell investments for the variable annuity. Trading costs, in this report, are set at 0.5% for the variable annuity. (Trading costs are discussed below); and

6. The first 10% to 15% of any withdrawal made each year from a variable annuity is not subject to a surrender charge. (Surrender charges are usually waived if the variable annuity owner becomes terminally ill, unemployed, disabled, needs nursing home care, etc.)

In short, the money received by a variable annuity company by imposing a CDSC and charging an increased annual ownership fee will ensure that between the two, the variable annuity company will recover any commissions it advances to the financial professionals who sell their variable annuities. If a variable annuity purchaser sells his variable annuity shortly after its purchase, the CDSC will recoup most or all of the commission advanced by the issuing company. In this case, annual ownership costs will be ineffective in recouping advanced commissions because the variable annuity would not held long enough to allow full recoupment of any advanced commissions. On the other hand, if a variable annuity is held by its owner long enough to avoid most or all of the declining CDSC, the issuing company will recoup its advanced commission primarily through recurring annual ownership costs. If an annuity is sold at some mid-point, the issuing company will recoup its advanced commission through a combination of a declining CDSC and collection of annual ownership costs over a few years.

§2306. THE MUTUAL FUND COMMISSION STRUCTURE

Mutual funds have several commission structures. The most common of these are the A- and B-share commission structure. A complete coverage of the differences between these two commission structures cannot be accomplished in a short report and no such attempt will be made here. The basic characteristics of the two major types of mutual fund commission structures is briefly discussed here so that potential mutual fund purchasers can compare these commission structures to those imposed by variable annuities.

The A-share mutual fund commission structure imposes an up-front, out-of-pocket commission that, for the typical mutual fund investor, runs between 4% and 5.75% depending on several factors including the amount invested in the fund.[417] This report will use a 5% commission on mutual fund purchases of less than $30,000. This up-front, out-of-pocket commission is imposed on the initial purchase price of the mutual fund. For example, a 4% up-front, out-of-pocket commission on a $50,000 mutual fund purchase would result in $48,000 being invested in the mutual fund and $2,000 being paid to the financial professional selling the fund. As a general rule, when an A-share mutual fund is later sold by the owner, no additional commission is imposed at the time of sale. Sales and re-purchases of funds taking place within

---

[10] Large mutual fund investments made in A-share mutual funds are usually entitled to a break-point or reduced up-front commission.

the same fund family do not generally generate new commissions. In addition to charging an up-front, out-of-pocket commission, A-share mutual fund companies charge annual ownership fees. These ownership fees are expressed as a percentage of a mutual fund's total year-end net value and are referred to as annual expense ratios. The annual expense ratio for an A-share mutual fund will, on average, range from 1.5% to 1.6%.[11] These figures include 12b-1 marketing fees. Except for 12b-1 fees, which usually amount to 0.25%, the annual expense ratio for an A-share mutual fund does not include an amount designed to recoup commissions advanced by the mutual fund company to those who sell their mutual funds because such advanced commissions do not arise where A-share mutual funds are purchased. In short, when an A-share mutual fund is purchased, the buyer pays a one-time, up-front, out-of-pocket commission and is charged a small annual 12b-1 fee primarily to pay trailing commissions to the financial professional who sold the mutual fund.

The B-share commission structure does not require a mutual fund purchaser to pay an up-front commission out of his pocket. For example, if $50,000 is invested in a B-share mutual fund, the purchaser's entire $50,000 is invested in his mutual fund unreduced by any up-front, out-of-pocket commission. When a B-share mutual fund is initially sold by a financial professional, the mutual fund company will advance to that professional a commission as compensation for selling the mutual fund. This advanced commission typically ranges from 4% to 5.75% on average. This report assumes a 5% advanced commission on purchases of less than $30,000. When a B-share commission is chosen by a mutual fund purchaser, the annual expense ratio for the A-shares sold by the mutual fund is usually increased by approximately 0.80% so that the mutual fund company can, over time, recoup the commission it advances to the financial professionals who sell their mutual funds. In addition to paying an increased annual expense ratio, the B-share mutual fund commission structure imposes a contingent deferred sales charge (CDSC) that operates much like the CDSC applicable to variable annuity purchases.[12] The major difference between the two is that variable annuities allow annual withdrawals of 10% to 15% of the annuity's value without imposing a surrender charge. B-share mutual funds do not provide this benefit. Like variable annuity CDSCs, B-share mutual fund CDSCs are designed to decline over a period of time. With a CDSC, if a B-share mutual fund is sold by the owner before the expiration of a certain period of time, usually about six years, the mutual fund seller will be required to reimburse the fund company for some or all of the commission the company

---

[11] *The Great Mutual Fund Trap*, Gary Gensler (Former Undersecretary of the U.S. Treasury 1999-2001) and Gregory Baer (Former Assistant Secretary for Financial Institutions for the U.S. Treasury) Broadway Books, New York, 2002, p 102. *Your Money, Your Choice...Mutual Funds - Take Control Now and Build Wealth Wisely*, Professor Charles Jones, Prentice Hall, 2003, p 32.

[12] CDSCs should not be confused with a rarely used commission structure called a back-end load. With a back-end load, a flat commission equal to an A-share commission is charged on the original investment amount when the fund is *sold*. This commission does *not* decline over time.

advanced at the time the fund was purchased. The CDSC is used to obtain this reimbursement. For example, if a B-share mutual fund with a six-year, 6% CDSC is sold by its owner in the first year of ownership, the mutual fund company would deduct 6% of the initial investment from the sale proceeds.[13] If the same fund is sold in the second year of ownership, a 5% CDSC, based on the initial investment, would be deducted from the sale proceeds and so on. If the B-share mutual fund is held for the entire six year holding period, the CDSC disappears and no CDSC is imposed if the fund is sold by the owner after that point. In short, CDSC's are imposed to help offset the initial commission advanced by the mutual fund company to the financial professionals who sell the company's mutual funds if the owner of the fund sells the fund before the expiration of the holding period required by the CDSC. In summary, the money received by a mutual fund company from imposing a CDSC and increasing its annual expense ratio will ensure that between the two, the mutual fund company will recover any commissions they advance to those professionals who sell their mutual funds. If a mutual fund owner sells his fund early on, the mutual fund company will not receive much in the way of an increased annual expense ratio but will recoup advanced commissions via their CDSC. If a fund owner holds his fund for several years the CSDC will disappear while the increased annual expense ratio will allow the fund company to recoup any commissions it advanced. If a mutual fund is sold at some mid-point, the issuing company will recoup its advanced commission through a combination of the declining CDSC and the collection of increased annual ownership fees.

As mentioned above, a typical annual expense ratio for an A-share mutual fund sold by a financial professional will be in the range of 1.5% to 1.6%. B-share mutual funds usually impose an annual expense ratio that is approximately 0.80% more than the typical A-share mutual fund.[14] For this reason, the annual expense ratio for an average B-share mutual fund will be in the range of 2.3% - 2.4%. This report will use the 2.3% figure. The 0.80% increase in the annual cost for owning a B-share mutual fund is usually temporary. Unlike variable annuities, when the CDSC for a B-share mutual fund expires the annual expense ratio is usually reduced from the higher B-share level to the lower A-share annual expense ratio for the mutual fund. For example, Judy invested $30,000 in a B-share mutual fund. The fund had a six-year holding or surrender period. The fund's annual expense ratio for its A-share fund is 1.6%. Because this is a B-share fund purchase, it will be assumed that the annual expense ratio will be increased for the first six years of ownership to 2.4%. After six years, if the fund is still owned, the 2.4% annual expense ratio for the B-share mutual fund will usually drop to the A-share level of 1.6%. The SEC mandates that mutual fund B-shares must be converted to A-shares no later than the end of the eighth year of a fund's ownership.

---

[13] CDSCs are usually imposed on the amount originally invested.

[14] www.Adamsfin.com.

§2307. OTHER MUTUAL FUND SHARE CLASSES

As discussed above, the most common classes of mutual funds are the A- and B-share classes. However, like variable annuities, mutual funds have many other share classes.[15] Mutual fund share classes, other than the A-and B-share classes, are rarely purchased by typical mutual fund investors. After A- and B-share classes, the most common mutual fund share class is the C-share. As a general rule, C-share mutual funds have annual expense ratios that are approximately 0.80% higher than the A-share class for the same mutual fund. When a C-share mutual fund is first purchased, the selling professional typically receives a 1% commission which is paid by the issuing mutual fund company. For each year, after the first, the selling professional will receive an additional 1% annual commission paid by this issuing mutual fund company. Such commissions are called trailing commissions. Once the mutual fund is sold by the fund owner, trailing commissions stop. Unlike B-share mutual funds, which convert to A-shares after a period of time, C-share mutual funds do not convert to a less expensive share class. A few C-share mutual funds also impose a small up-front, out-of-pocket commission of approximately 1%. Nearly all C-share mutual funds impose a contingent deferred sales charge (CDSC) for the initial year or year and a half of ownership. This short-term CDSC is usually in the range of 1%. C-share mutual funds can be a better choice than an A- or B-share fund for investors who plan to hold their mutual funds for only one to two years at most. Because of minimal utilization, this report will not examine C-share mutual funds or other lesser known mutual fund share classes. If an investor plans to buy a mutual fund share class other than A- or B- shares, he can, for comparison purposes, easily add the commission cost data relating to such a purchase to the tables and examples discussed in this report.

§2308. MUTUAL FUND HOLDING PERIODS

Much like variable annuities, an investor will want to select a mutual fund share class that best reflects his or her investment time horizon. The availability of different share classes is not as great with mutual funds as it is with variable annuities. As a *general* rule, long-term investors (e.g., eight years or more) are usually better off owning A-share mutual funds. For holding periods of three to seven years, B-share mutual funds usually prove to be the better buy. (C-share mutual funds are usually a better buy for investors who plan to sell their mutual funds within a few years.) These general rules can be altered by several factors, including the size of investment, trading activity, stock market fluctuations, etc.

§2309. MUTUAL FUND AND VARIABLE ANNUITY TRAILING COMMISSIONS

Earlier, trailing commissions were included in the definition of what constitutes a commission. Mutual fund companies frequently pay annual trailing commissions on A- and B-share mutual funds of approximately 25 basis points (¼%) to the financial professionals who sell

---

[15] Some examples include D-, F-, I-, J-, M-, N-, Y-, R-, and H-shares.

their funds. These trailing commissions are reflected in the fund's annual expense ratio as 12b-1 fees. They usually begin 13 months after the initial mutual fund sale and continue as long as the fund is held by the owner. The cost of these trailing commissions is paid for by the mutual fund owner. Some variable annuities pay trailing commissions also.[16] When this is the case, variable annuity issuers charge 12b-1 fees to cover these trailing commissions. These 12b-1 fees are included in the annual expense ratio charged by the variable annuity issuer.

§2310. MUTUAL FUND AND VARIABLE ANNUITY TRADING COSTS

Earlier in this report the term commission was defined to include: "...[a]ny expenses or trading costs incurred by a variable annuity or mutual fund company to buy investments to the extent these expenses or costs are passed on to the owners of the variable annuity or mutual fund." Trading costs are a major component of the commission cost of both variable annuities and mutual funds. Trading costs are the commissions that variable annuity and mutual fund companies pay to stock brokerage firms to buy and sell the investments that make-up the sub-accounts and underlying investments managed by variable annuity and mutual fund companies. Because these costs are fully deducted from gains made by variable annuity and mutual fund companies, the owners of variable annuities and mutual funds pay these trading costs or commissions. Trading costs are, in the truest sense, a pure commission cost for both owners of variable annuities and mutual funds. Trading costs are rarely disclosed to the public and few investors even know they exist, much less that they actually pay these commissions. Trading costs do *not* appear in the prospectuses for either variable annuities or mutual funds, nor do they appear in annual reports or other documents generally available to the investing public. In fact, the SEC does not require the sellers of variable annuities or mutual funds to disclose trading costs to investors. The only mention of trading costs appears in a document known as a Statement of Additional Information or SAI. The Statement of Additional Information is commonly referred to as a supplemental prospectus. Trading costs or commissions can add up to 1% of the annual cost of owning mutual funds.[17] Because mutual fund companies, as a general rule, trade more frequently than variable annuity companies, especially at year's end, their trading costs or commissions are slightly higher.[18] This in turn translates into higher trading costs for mutual fund owners than for variable annuity owners. It is estimated that the average variable

---

[16] Some financial professionals who sell variable annuities may chose to receive their commission over time from the issuing company. For example, instead of a 6% up-front commission, a financial professional might elect to take 2% up-front and 1% a year after the second year of ownership for as long as the variable annuity is held by the owner. This election would in no way impact the cost of owning the variable annuity or its 6% CDSC. The 6% CDSC will still decline to zero over time.

[17] Plexis Group. See *Better Investing*, July 2001, p. 29.

[18] The average turnover ratio for a mutual fund in 2004, according to Morningstar, was 118. The average turnover ratio for a variable annuity is 84. The difference between these two ratios is 28.8%. It would follow that the trading costs for variable annuities would be approximately 28.8% less than for mutual funds. Average trading costs for mutual funds (according to the Plexis Group) is 1%. Therefore, the average trading costs for a variable annuity would be 0.712% or approximately 30 basis points less than the mutual fund.

annuity has trading costs that are 30% lower than mutual funds.[19] When this differential is added to the other commission related costs of mutual funds, it increases the negative impact these costs have on mutual fund performance more than for an equivalent variable annuity investment. In this report, trading costs for mutual funds are set at a conservative 0.70% and for variable annuities at 30% less or 0.50%. Because trading costs can be significant, investors should make an effort to determine what the trading costs are for any variable annuity or mutual fund they are considering for purchase. Once this is accomplished, investors should include these costs in any comparison they make between variable annuities and mutual funds.

§2311. TOTAL COMMISSION COSTS - THE COMPONENTS

As discussed above, investors who purchase mutual funds or variable annuities pay annual ownership fees that are usually expressed as a percentage of the account value of the owner's mutual fund or variable annuity. (Although these fees are usually assessed quarterly, for ease of computation they will be treated in computations as if they are assessed annually.) These recurring ownership expenses are commonly referred to as annual expense ratios and include 12b-1 marketing fees. These 12b-1 fees, as mentioned above, help offset trailing commissions paid by mutual fund and, to some extent, variable annuity companies. A-share mutual funds impose up-front, out-of-pocket commissions. B-share mutual funds and variable annuities do not charge up-front, out-of-pocket commissions, but rather impose CDSCs. Both mutual funds and variable annuities have trading costs. In short, total commissions paid by investors who buy mutual funds or variable annuities are composed of one or more of the following:

1. Up-front, out-of-pocket commissions;
2. Contingent deferred sales charges (CDSCs);
3. Annual ownership fees that include amounts designed to recoup advanced commissions;
4. 12b-1 fees charged to offset trailing commissions paid by mutual fund and variable annuity companies; and
5. Trading costs.

Investors who buy A-share mutual funds will pay commissions based on a combination of items 1, 3, 4 and 5 above. Investors who buy B-share mutual funds will pay commissions based on a combination of items 2, 3, 4 and 5. Purchasers of variable annuities pay commissions based on items 2, 3, 4 and 5. Mutual fund and variable annuity companies rarely use a commission structure that combine items 1 and 2.[20] Investors considering the purchase of variable annuities or mutual funds should determine the affect that commissions will have on their potential investment returns before committing money to either investment. Investors should not

---

[19] *Id.*

[20] A C-share mutual fund, if liquidated in the first 12-18 months of ownership may result in both imposition of a CDSC and a small up-front, out-of-pocket commission.

automatically assume that the commission structure of the variable annuity will result in a lower net investment returns than a similar investment in mutual funds or vice versa. The following section reviews the various commission structures of both variable annuities and mutual funds and examines how they affect the net investment results of these two investment vehicles. The comparisons made in this report, because of their widespread use among investors, will be limited to A- and B-share mutual funds and B-share variable annuities.

§2312. COMMISSIONS INCLUDED IN ANNUAL EXPENSE RATIOS

As mentioned above, A-share mutual funds, B-share mutual funds and variable annuities all impose annual ownership expenses (technically called annual expense ratios). To some degree, as discussed above, annual ownership expenses include an amount designed to cover advanced commission or pay for future trailing commissions for both mutual funds and variable annuities. A review of these commissions is set out below:

- **A-Share Mutual Funds** – A-share mutual funds are purchased with up-front, out-of-pocket commissions. For example, a $20,000 A-share mutual fund purchase subject to a 5% commission will result in $19,000 being invested for the buyer and $1,000 being paid to the financial professional selling the mutual fund. Because an up-front commission is charged when A-share mutual funds are purchased, no additional cost is added to the annual ownership expense to generate further commission income. Because trailing commissions are commonly paid each year to the financial professional who sold the mutual fund to compensate him for helping the mutual fund purchaser in the future, a 12b-1 fee is added to the annual expense ratio of the typical A-share mutual fund. This 12b-1 fee is usually 0.25%. The combined annual expense ratio and 12b-1 fee for the average equity mutual fund is 1.5%.[21] This figure is used in this report. A-share mutual funds impose trading costs also. This report will use an A-share mutual fund trading cost of 0.70%.

- **B-Share Mutual Funds** –B-share mutual funds do not impose up-front, out-of-pocket commissions. Instead, a contingent deferred sales charge (CDSC) is imposed to enable the mutual fund company, over time, to recoup the commission they advanced to the financial professional selling their mutual fund. In addition, 12b-1 fees are added to the annual expense ratio to cover previously advanced as well as trailing commissions to be paid to the financial professional who will monitor and assist the mutual fund purchaser in the future. B-share mutual funds have annual expense ratios, including 12b-1 fees that are approximately 0.80% larger than the average mutual fund. Thus, B-share mutual funds have combined annual expense ratios and 12b-1 fees of approximately 2.3%. This report will use this figure. (As mentioned earlier, B-share annual expense ratios and 12b-1 fees revert to the A-share level after approximately six years). B-share mutual funds impose trading costs also. This report will use an B-share mutual fund trading cost of 0.70%.

---

[21] *NAVA Outlook*, Nov/Dec 2005, p. 6. See *Investment News*, "Fund Fees Baffle MBA Students" by David Hoffman, April 24, 2006.

- **Variable Annuities** –Much like B-share mutual funds, variable annuities impose no up-front, out-of-pocket commissions. Instead, their annual ownership expense includes an amount designed to recoup the commissions the variable annuity company advances to the financial professionals who sell their annuities. Variable annuities also include 12b-1 fees in their annual ownership cost. The average variable annuity will have a total annual ownership expense of 2.2% (including 12b-1 fees). This 2.2% figure is used in this report. Unlike B-share mutual funds, this figure does not drop after expiration of any applicable holding period. Variable annuities also impose trading costs. This report assumes such trading costs to be 0.50%.

As can be determined from the above summary, variable annuity and B-share mutual fund annual expense ratios (including 12b-1 fees) are respectively 0.70% to 0.80% larger than the average A-share mutual fund's annual expense ratio and 12b-1 fees of 1.5%. This 0.70% to 0.80% difference reflects additional fees designed to recoup advanced commissions and must be considered when comparing variable annuity commissions with either A- or B-share mutual funds. When such comparisons are made, it is common to factor in the *entire* annual expense ratio and 12b-1 fees for the mutual fund or variable annuity being compared rather than just the 0.70% to 0.80% differential discussed above. Mathematically, the comparison, for example, of an A-share mutual fund with a 1.5% annual expense ratio and 12b-1 fees to a variable annuity with a 2.2% annual expense ratio and 12b-1 fees will yield essentially the same end result as a comparison showing a variable annuity with an annual expense ratio and 12b-1 fees that are 0.70% larger than an A-share mutual fund. By factoring in *total* annual expense ratios and 12b-1 fees for any mutual fund or variable annuity compared in this report, not only will the additional commission related costs of these investments will be reflected but investors will have a better idea of how overall expenses impact their net investment returns.

§2313. THE VARIABLE ANNUITY COMMISSION STRUCTURE – TWO ADVANTAGES

The variable annuity CDSC commission structure provides two major benefits not offered to mutual fund investors:

1. Any investor buying a variable annuity can select a holding period that matches his expected investment time horizon and if he holds his variable annuity for this holding period, he will be able to avoid having to pay any up-front, out-of-pocket commission to buy his annuity (B-share mutual funds do not allow investors to select holding periods); and

2. Because variable annuity companies charge no up-front, out-of-pocket commissions to investors, 100% of the annuity purchaser's investment starts working for him immediately.

These two important concepts are discussed in the next two sections.

§2314. CHOOSING AN APPROPRIATE HOLDING PERIOD TO AVOID SURRENDER CHARGES

One of the major advantages of owning variable annuities is that they can be purchased with holding or surrender periods that match a buyer's investment time horizon. By matching holding periods and investment time horizons, a variable annuity investor can avoid both – paying an up-front, out-of-pocket commissions and contingent deferred surrender charges. There are some variable annuities today that have no surrender periods associated with their purchase. Many variable annuities have surrender periods of three or four years. Most variable annuities have surrender periods of six to seven years, although some can have surrender periods of as much as ten years. As a general rule, the shorter a variable annuity's surrender period the larger the annual ownership fee will be for owning the annuity. Conversely, a variable annuity with a longer surrender period will usually have lower annual ownership costs. For example, if Apex Variable Annuity Company sells a variable annuity with a seven-year surrender period and charges an annual ownership fee 2.1% of the annuity's value each year to own such an annuity, they might charge 2.4% a year to a purchaser of the same variable annuity who only wants a three-year surrender period. Another general rule regarding variable annuities is that the longer the surrender period the more benefits the variable annuity will usually offer to the purchaser.

In light of the fact that a variable annuity investor can completely avoid having to pay any up-front, out-of-pocket commission or surrender charges if he holds his variable annuity for an agreed holding period, it is important for investors contemplating the purchase of a variable annuity to select an annuity with a surrender period that they can reasonably expect to meet. This concept of matching a holding period to one's investment time horizon to obtain a higher return or greater benefits is not unique to the variable annuity industry. For example, it plays a central role in the purchase of bonds. A new issue of corporate bonds maturing in ten years will almost always have a higher yield than a similar bond maturing in five years. This time-value concept is also found in other investment settings as the following example demonstrates:

Example
Sara is considering the purchase of a bank CD. The bank offers three CDs with different maturities and annual interest rates. They are:

- One-year CD paying 4%
- Three-year CD paying 5½%
- Five-year CD paying 6%

The bank imposes a penalty for early withdrawal. If a CD is liquidated prior to its maturity, the interest rate for the actual period of time the CD was held will apply and, as a penalty, this rate will be reduced by one percent. For example, if Sara purchases a five-year CD and liquidates it shortly after three years, she will receive the annual rate of 6% less a 1% penalty or 5% on her CD for each of the three years she held it. If Sara believes she can only hold a CD for three years, she would be better off buying a three-year CD and receiving an annual 5½% rate of return over her three-year holding period.

For investors, the ability to have investment commissions paid by the issuing company rather than themselves can be a tremendous benefit. Most people would agree that if an investor is looking at two identical investments that charge the same commission, all else being equal, both investments will cost the same to purchase. However, this conclusion is based on the assumption that the investor will pay the stated commission out of his pocket regardless of the investment selected. If either commission is paid by a third party, then a different conclusion would have to be reached. The following example, using a non-investment analogy, demonstrates this point:

Example

Dr. Smith is a dentist. He lives with his wife and two young children in El Paso, Texas. He and his wife want to move back to Tampa, Florida where their parents live. In preparation for their move, Dr. Smith and his wife have contacted a real estate broker to sell their $300,000 house. The broker will charge a 6% commission to sell the house. Dr. Smith interviewed with two dental partnerships in Tampa and both have offered him a job and both are offering the same salary. In trying to make up his mind as to which practice to work for, Dr. Smith asked both partnerships what, if anything, they would contribute to his relocation expenses. The first partnership said they would contribute nothing while the second partnership agreed to pay the real estate broker's commission that Dr. Smith would incur upon the sale of his house. As a condition to paying the real estate commission, the second partnership would require Dr. Smith to work for the partnership for at least six years. If Dr. Smith leaves his employment with the second partnership before this six year period is up, he would have to reimburse the 6% real estate commission to the partnership on a pro-rata basis according to the schedule set out in the table below:

REIMBURSEMENT OF
REAL ESTATE BROKER'S COMMISSION

YEARS OF EMPLOYMENT	AMOUNT OF COMMISSION TO BE REIMBURSED
1 or less	6%
> 1 but < 2	5%
> 2 but < 3	4%
> 3 but < 4	3%
> 4 but < 5	2%
> 5 but < 6	1%
More than 6	0%

If there are no significant differences in working for either partnership, Dr. Smith would be better off working for the second partnership. If he stays with them for the agreed six years, he will avoid an $18,000 real estate commission. Even if he leaves after as little as one year of employment, his reimbursement to the second partnership will be less than the $18,000 broker's commission he would have had to pay out of his pocket to sell his house if he elected to work for the first partnership. Regardless of who Dr. Smith decides to work for, the real estate broker will still receive a 6% commission. However, the important thing to keep in mind is that Dr. Smith's *out-of-pocket* real estate commission can be reduced to zero and this will put him in the position of possibly saving $18,000 if he elects to work for the second partnership for at least six years. If Dr. Smith elects to work for the first partnership, the $18,000 commission he would pay is an economic loss that he can never recover.

The situation involving Dr. Smith in the above example arises everyday in the financial world as the following example demonstrates.

Example

Dr. Baker is a 54 year-old physician. She is married and has two children. She has a $20,000 IRA bank account she wants to invest for the next six or seven years. She initially considered a mutual fund that charged a 5¼% A-share commission that she would have to pay out of her pocket at the time she bought the mutual fund. Dr. Baker realized the impact of this commission would be to reduce her $30,000 investment to $18,850. Later, Dr. Baker looked at a variable annuity that carried a 6% commission. The professional selling the variable annuity informed Dr. Baker that the 6% commission charged for purchasing the variable annuity would be advanced by the issuing company. This would allow 100% of Dr. Baker's money to be invested. The 6% advanced commission declined 1% a year over a six year period. If Dr. Baker did not sell or transfer her variable annuity to another investment for six years she would not be required to pay any commission out of her pocket to own the annuity. If she did sell or transfer the variable annuity before the agreed six-year holding expired, she would have to repay some or all of the advanced commission on a pro-rata basis according to the CDSC provision in the variable annuity prospectus. It is important to note that after one year any CDSC imposed by the variable annuity issuer would be less than the 5¼% commission she would pay up-front to own the above mentioned mutual fund.

§2315. PUTTING 100% OF AN INVESTMENT TO WORK

As discussed above, the first advantage of the variable annuity commission structure is that is that it gives a long-term investor the ability to completely avoid having to pay any up-front, out-of-pocket commission or CDSC to purchase a variable annuity. The second significant advantage of the variable annuity commission structure is that all of an investor's money immediately begins working for the investor because there are no up-front, out-of-pocket commissions imposed at the time a variable annuity is purchased. This advantage is most obvious when variable annuities are compared to investments, such as A-share mutual funds, that do charge up-front, out-of-pocket commissions. The combination of a variable annuity's declining CDSC and the fact that 100% of a variable annuity investment goes to work for the annuity investor will frequently produce a larger investment return than will a similar mutual fund investment that is subject to an up-front, out-of-pocket commission.

Example

Ann, who is 54, wanted to transfer an old $30,000 401(k) to a new IRA account. She wants to invest for at least six years. She is considering an A-share mutual fund that charges a 5% up-front, out-of-pocket commission. The annual expense ratio for the mutual fund is 1.5%. Trading costs are 0.70%. She was also interested in a variable annuity that charges no up-front, out-of-pocket commission but imposes an annual ownership expense of 2.2% and trading costs of 0.50%. The variable annuity also imposes a 6% CDSC that declines 1% over six years.[22] Ann assumes both investments will return 8% a year. Ann's financial advisor determined that the variable annuity would have an ending account value of $40,396 after six years.[23] The mutual fund would provide an ending value of only $39,575.[24] The variable annuity outperforms the mutual fund primarily because the mutual fund investment is reduced at the time of purchase by an up-front, out-of-pocket commission while the variable annuity is not. [The difference in net results was also a function of the declining nature of the variable annuity's CDSC].

§2316. THE VARIABLE ANNUITY DEATH BENEFIT - COMMISSION RELATED OR NOT?

Variable annuities provide a form of portfolio insurance that guarantees that the beneficiaries of a deceased owner's variable annuity will receive all net investments made in the annuity if the account value of the annuity is less than net investments made in the annuity by the owner prior to his death. The cost of this death benefit, which averages 0.20%, is included in the 1.3% mortality and expense figure which is itself included in the 2.2% average annual cost of owning the typical variable annuity.[25] The following example examines the death benefit provided by variable annuities:

Example

In late 1999, Jane and her twin brother Jack both had $50,000 IRAs held in bank CDs that they wanted to rollover their IRAs into equities because the stock market

---

[22] CDSCs do not necessarily decline 1% a year. For example, a variable annuity with a six year holding period could decline as follows: 7%, 7%, 6%, 6%, 5%, 1%. Regardless of how a CDSC declines over time, at the end of the holding period, the CDSC will *always* be zero. This is another reason why it is important to select variable annuities that have holding periods that match ones investment time horizon.

[23] $30,000 + 8% = $32,400 - 2.7% = $31,525 - $30,000 = $1,525 ÷ $30,000 = 5.084%. $30,000 x 5.084% x 6 years = $40,396.

[24] $30,000 - 5% = $28,500+ 8% = $30,780 - 1.5% - 0.70% = $30,103 - $28,500 = $1,603 ÷ $28,500 = 5.624% x 6 years x $28,500 = $39,575.

[25] *The New Life Insurance Investment Advisor* by Ben Baldwin, CLU, ChFC, CFP, pg. 353.

was soaring. Jane invested her IRA in a variable annuity that had a six year CDSC that declined 1% a year. In addition, Jane's variable annuity imposed a 2.2% annual ownership cost that included a basic death benefit. Trading costs for the variable annuity were 0.50%. Jack invested his $50,000 in an A-share mutual fund that imposed a reduced break-point commission of 4% in addition to an annual expense ratio of 1.5% and trading costs of 0.70%. During the three year bear market from 2000 to 2002, Jane and Jack lost 14% of their investment each year. By the end of 2002, Jane's annuity was worth $29,296[26] while Jack's mutual fund was worth $28,560.[27] In early January of 2003, Jane and Jack were killed in an automobile accident. Jane's family received an income tax-free check for $50,000 from the liquidation of her annuity while Jack's family received $28,560 from the liquidation of his mutual fund. On these facts, the annuity provided $21,440 more to beneficiaries than the mutual fund did. [It is also interesting to note that prior to death, Jane's variable annuity out-performed Jack's mutual fund].

Some financial professionals feel the cost of the death benefit provided by variable annuities is a charge made solely to provide insurance coverage and therefore is not a commission. For this reason, it is often argued that this insurance cost should be excluded when the affect of commissions on variable annuity and mutual fund returns are compared. Other financial professionals argue that the variable annuity's death benefit is rarely paid out and therefore the charge made for this benefit ultimately becomes an additional source of revenue for companies that issue variable annuities. For this reason it is argued that the variable annuity's insurance cost should be treated as a commission cost. This latter argument does not contain a great deal of merit. For proof of this, one need only realize that the variable annuity industry paid out $2.8 billion in death benefits between 2001 and 2003 as a result of the 2000-2002 bear market.[28] The mutual fund industry paid out zero. The fact that one pays for insurance that he never uses does not mean the insurance has no value or did not serve its function. If one pays a thousand dollars a year for fire insurance on his house for thirty years and never has a fire, can it be said that the insurance was an unwise purchase? Certainly not.

Regardless of the persuasive argument that the charge made for the variable annuity death benefit is *not* commission related, this report will treat it as if it were. This position has been adopted, in part, because the annual ownership costs quoted for variable annuities almost always includes the cost of providing a death benefit. Investors should keep in mind that variable annuities do provide a death benefit that is not available with mutual funds when comparing the commission costs of these two financial products.

---

[26] $50,000 x -.14 = $43,000 - 2.7% = $41,839 - $50,000 = -$8,161 ÷ $50,000 = -16.32%. -16.32% x $50,000 x 3 years = $29,296.

[27] $48,000 x -.14 = $41,280 - 2.2% = $40,372 - $48,000 = -$7,628 ÷ $48,000 = -15.89%. -15.89% x $48,000 x 3 years = $28,560.

[28] NAVA press release dated September 28, 2004.

§2317. THE VARIABLE ANNUITY COMMISSION STRUCTURE VS. THE MUTUAL FUND COMMISSION STRUCTURE

As discussed above, before investors commit money to either mutual funds or variable annuities, they should determine what impact total commissions will have on their potential investment results. The following example demonstrates how this can be accomplished:

Example

Paul, who is 60, has $30,000 from an old 401(k) that he wants to invest for the next six years.   He is considering an A-share mutual fund that charges a 5% up-front, out-of-pocket commission and also imposes a 1.5% annual expense ratio. The A-share mutual fund has annual trading costs of 0.70%. Paul is also interested in the same fund with a B-share commission structure that has no up-front, out-of-pocket commission but has a 2.3% annual expense ratio. In addition, the B-share mutual fund imposes a contingent deferred surrender charge (CDSC) of 6% that declines 1% a year over six years. The B-share mutual fund has annual trading costs of 0.70%. Paul is also considering a standard variable annuity that has a sub-account that is nearly identical to the mutual fund he is considering. The variable annuity has no up-front, out-of-pocket commission but has a 6% CDSC that declines 1% a year over six years. This surrender charge is imposed on the ending account value of the variable annuity.[436] Surrender-free withdrawals of 15% based on account value are allowed each year. This annuity also imposes a 2.2% annual expense ratio. The variable annuity has annual trading costs of 0.50%. Paul believes all three investments will grow at an 8% average annual rate of return. He plans to invest until his retirement at age 66. Paul wants to know what impact commissions will have on these investment choices. Paul's financial advisor ran this data through his computer and obtained the results found in Table #1 below:

TABLE #1 - NET INVESTMENT RESULTS FOR A- AND B-SHARE MUTUAL FUNDS VS. A VARIABLE ANNUITY ($30,000 INVESTMENT AT 8%)

INVESTMENT	NUMBER OF YEARS THE INVESTMENT IS HELD					
	1	2	3	4	5	6
A-SHARE MUTUAL FUND	$30,103[30]	$31,796[31]	$33,584[32]	$35,472[33]	$37,468[34]	$39,575[35]
B-SHARE MUTUAL FUND	$29,928[36]	$31,724[37]	$33,591[38]	$35,533[39]	$37,752[40]	$39,655[41]
VARIABLE ANNUITY	$30,185[42]	$32,002[43]	$33,924[44]	$35,960[45]	$38,115[46]	$40,396[47]

[30] $30,000 - 5% = $28,500 x 8% increase = $30,780 - 2.2% (annual expenses, trading costs and 12b-1 fees) = $30,103 - $28,500 = $1,603 ÷ $28,500 = 5.624% x $28,500 x 1 year = $30,103.

[31] $30,000 - 5% = $28,500 x 8% increase = $30,780 - 2.2% (annual expenses, trading costs and 12b-1 fees) = $30,103 - $28,500 = $1,603 ÷ $28,500 = 5.624% x $28,500 x 2 year = $31,796.

[32] $30,000 - 5% = $28,500 x 8% increase = $30,780 - 2.2% (annual expenses, trading costs and 12b-1 fees) = $30,103 - $28,500 = $1,603 ÷ $28,500 = 5.624% x $28,500 x 3 year = $33,584.

[33] $30,000 - 5% = $28,500 x 8% increase = $30,780 - 2.2% (annual expenses, trading costs and 12b-1 fees) = $30,103 - $28,500 = $1,603 ÷ $28,500 = 5.624% x $28,500 x 4 year = $35,472.

[34] $30,000 - 5% = $28,500 x 8% increase = $30,780 - 2.2% (annual expenses, trading costs and 12b-1 fees) = $30,103 - $28,500 = $1,603 ÷ $28,500 = 5.624% x $28,500 x 5 year = $37,468.

[35] $30,000 - 5% = $28,500 x 8% increase = $30,780 - 2.2% (annual expenses, trading costs and 12b-1 fees) = $30,103 - $28,500 = $1,603 ÷ $28,500 = 5.624% x $28,500 x 6 year = $39,575.

[36] $30,000 + 8% = $32,400 - 3.0% (annual expenses and 12b-1 fees) = $31,428 - $30,000 = $1,428 ÷ $30,000 = 4.76%. $30,000 x 4.76% x 1 year = $31,428 - 5% of $30,000 = $29,928.

[37] $30,000 + 8% = $32,400 - 3.0% (annual expenses and 12b-1 fees) = $31,428 - $30,000 = $1,428 ÷ $30,000 = 4.76%. $30,000 x 4.76% x 2 year = $32,924 - 4% of $30,000 = $31,724.

[38] $30,000 + 8% = $32,400 - 3.0% (annual expenses and 12b-1 fees) = $31,428 - $30,000 = $1,428 ÷ $30,000 = 4.76%. $30,000 x 4.76% x 3 year = $34,491 - 3% of $30,000 = $33,591.

[39] $30,000 + 8% = $32,400 - 3.0% (annual expenses and 12b-1 fees) = $31,428 - $30,000 = $1,428 ÷ $30,000 = 4.76%. $30,000 x 4.76% x 4 year = $36,133 - 2% of $30,000 = $35,533.

[40] $30,000 + 8% = $32,400 - 3.0% (annual expenses and 12b-1 fees) = $31,428 - $30,000 = $1,428 ÷ $30,000 = 4.76%. $30,000 x 4.76% x 5 year = $37,852 - 1% of $30,000 = $37,752.

[41] $30,000 + 8% = $32,400 - 3.0% (annual expenses and 12b-1 fees) = $31,428 - $30,000 = $1,428 ÷ $30,000 = 4.76%. $30,000 x 4.76% x 6 year = $39,655.

[42] $30,000 + 8% = $32,400 - 2.7% = $31,525 - 30,000 = $1,525 ÷ $30,000 = 5.084%. $30,000 x 5.084% x 1 year = $31,525 - 5% of 85% of $31,525 = $30,185.

[43] $30,000 + 8% = $32,400 - 2.7% = $31,525 - 30,000 = $1,525 ÷ $30,000 = 5.084%. $30,000 x 5.084% x 2 year = $33,128 - 4% of 85% of $33,128 = $32,002.

[44] $30,000 + 8% = $32,400 - 2.7% = $31,525 - 30,000 = $1,525 ÷ $30,000 = 5.084%. $30,000 x 5.084% x 3 year = $34,812 - 3% of 85% of $34,812 = $33,924.

[45] $30,000 + 8% = $32,400 - 2.7% = $31,525 - 30,000 = $1,525 ÷ $30,000 = 5.084%. $30,000 x 5.084% x 4 year = $36,582 - 2% of 85% of $36,582 = $35,960.

[46] $30,000 + 8% = $32,400 - 2.7% = $31,525 - 30,000 = $1,525 ÷ $30,000 = 5.084%. $30,000 x 5.084% x 5 year = $38,442 - 1% of 85% of $38,442 = $38,115.

[47] $30,000 + 8% = $32,400 - 2.7% = $31,525 - 30,000 = $1,525 ÷ $30,000 = 5.084%. $30,000 x 5.084% x 6 year = $40,396.

What Table #1 demonstrates is that when annual ownership expenses (including trading costs and 12b-1 fees) are added to up-front, out-of-pocket commissions or CDSCs to account for all commission costs, the overall after-commission returns for the variable annuity can be greater than that of an equivalent A- or B- share mutual fund investment over a one to six year period. It is also important to note that the returns determined in Table #1 above include the fees charged by the variable annuity company for insurance as if they were commission charges rather than insurance premiums.

§2318. OTHER FACTORS IMPACTING RETURNS

The material discussed above demonstrates that after factoring in all commission costs, the purchaser of a typical variable annuity will frequently obtain investment returns that are larger than he would obtain with a similar mutual fund investment. However, in order to fully understand variable annuity and mutual fund returns, several other issues must be addressed. The sections that follow discuss these issues.

§2319. THE LENGTH OF INVESTMENT

The length of time that an investment is held may alter the impact that commissions might have on the performance of the investment. For example, a 5% up-front, out-of-pocket commission paid for an A-share mutual fund will affect a three-year investment more than a ten-year investment in the same mutual fund because the 5% commission is spread over more years with the ten year investment. Similarly, the annual expense ratio of a B-share mutual fund usually declines to the A-share level of the same fund once the CDSC period expires and therefore total commission costs will drop for a B-share mutual fund if it is held beyond its CDSC period. Much like B-share mutual funds, many variable annuities reduce their annual expense ratios after their CDSC holding periods expire. Thus, the total commission cost for owning such variable annuities will also decline if held until the CDSC holding period lapses. The following example demonstrates how the length of time an investment is held can alter commission costs and therefore the return an investor might obtain on a potential investment:

Example
Nancy, who is 57, is about to rollover an old 403(b) account into an IRA. The 403(b) account contains $30,000. She is considering investing her $30,000 in a mutual fund or a similar variable annuity. Nancy's financial planner told her that the performance of the mutual fund and variable annuity she was considering has been similar over the past few years and he feels these returns should average 8% over the next several years. Nancy plans to hold her IRA for at least six years but could hold it for as many as nine years and as few as three. She wants to know what her ending IRA account balance will be with the A- and B-share versions of the mutual fund she is considering as well as with the variable annuity she is looking at. The A-share mutual fund charges an up-front, out-of-pocket commission of 5% and has an annual expense ratio of 1.5% and trading costs

of 0.70%. The B-share mutual fund has a 6% CDSC that declines 1% a year for six years. It also has an annual expense ratio of 2.3% and trading costs of 0.70%. After six years the annual expense ratio for the B-share drops from 2.3% to the A-share level of 1.5%. The variable annuity has no up-front, out-of-pocket commission but imposes a 6% CDSC that declines over six years. The annual expense ratio for the variable annuity is 2.2% and not reduced regardless of how long the variable annuity is held. The variable annuity has a trading cost of 0.50%. The variable annuity allows annual surrender charge-free withdrawals of 15% of the variable annuity's current value. Nancy's financial planner created Table #2 below to help Nancy make the best investment choice.

TABLE #2 - NET INVESTMENT RESULTS FOR A- AND B-SHARE MUTUAL FUNDS AND A VARIABLE ANNUITY ($30,000 INVESTMENT AT 8%)

INVESTMENT	NUMBER OF YEARS THE INVESTMENT IS HELD		
	3 years	6 years	9 years
A-SHARE MUTUAL FUND	$33,584[48]	$39,575[49]	$46,635[50]
B-SHARE MUTUAL FUND	$33,591[51]	$39,655[52]	$45,592[53]
VARIABLE ANNUITY	$33,924[54]	$40,396[55]	$46,876[56]

What Table #2 demonstrates is that if Nancy plans to hold her IRA for either three, six or nine years, or anywhere in between, she will maximize her net return with the variable annuity. The results in Table #2 assume the variable annuity does not reduce its annual expense ratio in a manner similar to B-share mutual funds which many variable annuities do. It is also important to note that the figures in Table #2 include the fee charged by the variable annuity company for insurance protection as if it were a commission cost which it is not. The figures in Table #2 impose CDSCs on the variable annuity's ending account value rather than the initial premium which often occurs.[57] If adjustments were made for these factors, the variable annuity would clearly prove to be the better investment choice for Nancy at the three year mark or

---

[48] See note 32 above.

[49] See note 35 above.

[50] $30,000 - 5% = $28,500 x 8% increase = $30,780 - 2.2% = $30,103 - $28,500 = $1,603 ÷ $28,500 = 5.624%. $28,500 x 5.624% x 9 years = $46,635.

[51] See note 38 above.

[52] See note 41 above.

[53] $39,655 + 8% increase = $42,827 - 3.0% = $41,542 - $39,655 = $1,888 gain ÷ $39,655 = 4.76%. 4.76% x $39,655 x 3 years = $45,592.

[54] See note 44 above.

[55] See note 47 above.

[56] $30,000 + 8% = $32,400 - 2.7% = $31,525 - $30,000 = $1,525 ÷ $30,000 = 5.084%. 5.084% x 9 years x $30,000 = $46,876.

[57] See note 6 above.

beyond. If Nancy could find a mutual fund with a commission less than 5%, the mutual fund might produce a net return that would be closer to the ending value of the variable annuity. It is important to understand that mutual funds are rarely held for nine years. Mutual fund investors, on average, hold their mutual funds for approximately three years before selling them.[58] Variable annuity investors tend to hold their variable annuities longer because of the surrender charges associated with these investments. If an investor buys and sells investments in three year cycles, commission-wise, he will be better off purchasing variable annuities than mutual funds as the following example demonstrates:

Example

Dan, who is 52, and his twin sister Donna, are typical investors. They have a history of rarely holding an investment for more than three years. Dan and Donna both have $25,000 IRAs they want to rollover into new investment accounts. Dan has chosen an A-share mutual fund charging a 5% commission and imposing a annual ownership fee of 1.5%. Donna has chosen a variable annuity with a 6% CDSC that declines 1% a year and, in addition, imposes a 2.2% annual ownership fee. Trading costs for the mutual fund are 0.70% and 0.50% for the variable annuity. Each year Donna can withdraw 15% of her variable annuity's account value without surrender charges. If Dan buys the mutual fund and rolls it over into different funds in three year cycles, nine years from now his mutual fund account will contain $41,369 assuming a 10% annual rate of return.[59] On the same facts, Donna's variable annuity will contain $44,905.[60]

§2320. THE SIZE OF INVESTMENT

A-share mutual funds offer break-points or reduced up-front, out-of-pocket commissions for large investments. B-share mutual funds and variable annuities do not, as a general rule, offer similar break-points or commission discounts. It is assumed by some, that at larger investment levels, the variable annuity is a more expensive investment to own than an A-share mutual fund. Such an assumption is not always correct and can prove to be a costly mistake as the following example demonstrates:

Example

Ben has $50,000 in an IRA. He wants to transfer it to another IRA. He is interested in an A-share mutual fund that will give him a break-point commission of 4.25% on a mutual fund purchase of $50,000. The fund has an annual expense

---

[58] *The Great Mutual Fund Trap*, Gary Gensler (Former Undersecretary of the U.S. Treasury 1999-2001) and Gregory Baer (Former Assistant Secretary for Financial Institutions for the U.S. Treasury) Broadway Books, New York, 2002, p. 101 citing a three year holding period. Dalbar, Inc. In a 2003 report titled "Quantitative Analysis of Investor Behavior" found the holding period of the average equity fund to be 29.5 months.

[59] $25,000 less 5% = $23,750 x 10% = $26,125 less 2.2% = $25,550 - $23,750 = $1,800 ÷ $23,750 = 7.58%. 7.58% x 3 years x $23,750 = $29,570 - 5% = $28,092 x 10% = $30,901 - 2.2% = $30,221 - $28,092 = $2,79 ÷ $28,092 = 7.58% x 3 years x $28,399 = $34,977 - 5% = $33,228 x 10% = $36,550 - 2.2% = $35,746 - $33,228 = $2,518 ÷ 33,228 = 7.58% x 3 years x $33,228 = $41,369.

[60] $25,000 x 10% = $27,500 less 2.7% = $26,757 - $25,000 = $1,758 ÷ $25,000 = 7.03% x 3 years x $25,000 = $30,652 - 3% of 85% of $30,652 = $29,871. $29,871 x 10% = $32,858 - 2.7% = $31,971 - $29,871 = $2,099 ÷ $29,871 ÷ 7.03% x 3 years x $29,871 = $36,624. $36,624 x 10% = $40,286 - 2.7% = $39,199 - $36,624 = $2,575 ÷ $36,624 = 7.03% x 3 years x $36,624 = $44,905.

ratio of 1.5% and trading cost of 0.70%. The other investment option Ben is considering is a variable annuity that has a 6% CDSC that declines 1% a year and imposes a 2.2% annual expense ratio. The variable annuity has a 0.50% trading cost. Ben is 54 and plans to invest until he is 60. He is assuming that the rate of return he will earn with either investment will average 8% per year. Based on this data the value of the mutual fund account in six years will be $69,385[61] while the ending account value of the variable annuity will be $69,429.[62]

Investors should not assume that a break-point commission offered by an A-share mutual fund will always yield a better investment result than a variable annuity. It takes only a few minutes to determine which investment will provide the largest net return over time.

§2321. BONUS VARIABLE ANNUITIES

Many variable annuities today offer buyers premium bonuses of 1% to 5% which are added to their initial variable annuity investment. When bonuses are offered, the annual cost of owning the variable annuity is usually increased by 20 to 40 basis points (2/10% to 4/10%). This increase allows the issuing company, over time, to recoup some or all of the bonus they provide. Although a variable annuity bonus should be viewed more as a loan than a gift, it can still have a positive effect on the net investment results where variable annuities are purchased. In some cases, a bonus variable annuity may even outperform a large mutual fund investment that provides a significant break-point commission as the following example demonstrates:

Example
George purchased a $100,000 mutual fund that charged a 3% A-share break-point commission and had a 1.5% annual expense ratio. The fund had trading costs of 0.70%. Ellen, at the same time purchased a variable annuity for $100,000 that had a 6% CDSC that declined 1% a year over six years. The normal annual expense ratio for the variable annuity was 2.2%. The annuity had trading costs of 0.50%. Ellen elected to receive a 5% bonus at the time she purchased her annuity. Due to this election, the variable annuity's annual expense ratio was increased from 2.2% to 2.5%. George and Ellen are 54 years old and will hold their investments for six years. Assuming a 9% pre-tax rate of return for both investments the mutual fund will grow to $142,336,[63] while the bonus annuity will grow to $146,683.[64]

What the above example demonstrates is that a bonus variable annuity will often outperform an A-share mutual fund even where the mutual fund provides a reduced break-point commission. Whenever an investor is considering a mutual fund or a variable annuity purchase, he should take into consideration any bonus paid by the variable annuity. In many cases, such a

---

[61] $50,000 less 4¼% = $47,875 x 8% less 1.5% = $50,929 - $47,875 = $3,054 ÷ $47,875 = 6.38% x 6 years x $47,875 = $69,385.

[62] $50,000 x 8% less 2.2% = $52,812 - $50,000 = $2,812 ÷ $50,000 = 5.624% x 6 years x $50,000 = $69,429.

[63] $100,000 - 3% = $97,000 x 9% = $105,730 - 2.2% = $103,404 - $97,000 = $6,404 ÷ $97,000 = 6.6%. $97,000 x 6.6% x 6 years = $142,336.

[64] $100,000 + 5% = $105,000 x 9% = $114,450 - 3.0% = $111,017 - $105,000 = $6,017 gain ÷ $105,000 = 5.73%. 5.73% x 6 years x $105,000 = $146,683.

bonus can increase the return of the variable annuity.

Another major advantage of obtaining a bonus when purchasing a variable annuity is that the bonus can dramatically reduce surrender charges as the following example demonstrates:

Example

Sarah, who is 60, purchased a variable annuity for $30,000 with an old 403(b). The annuity credited Sarah with a 5% bonus. The annuity had a 7% annual declining surrender charge that was imposed on all premiums paid. After ten months of a flat market, Sarah sold her annuity. She had to pay a 7% surrender charge on her initial $30,000 premium. Withdrawals of up to 15% incur no surrender charges. Her net proceeds from the sale were $29,715 or 99.05% of her original $30,000 investment.[65] In effect, Sarah's surrender penalty was less than 1% not 7% primarily because of the 5% bonus she received at the time she purchased her variable annuity. On the same facts, had Sarah purchased an A-share mutual fund with a 5% up-front commission, her sale proceeds check would have been $28,500, reflecting a *full* 5% commission loss. A B-share mutual fund with a 6% CDSC would have reduced Sarah's investment to $28,200, reflecting a *full* 6% CDSC loss.

§2322. MONEY MARKET AND FIXED ACCOUNTS

If a variable annuity is purchased and the owner transfers any part or all of his account balance into a money market or other fixed account, the annuity's annual expense ratio is reduced by all money management fees. In some cases mortality and expense (M&E) charges are also reduced or eliminated. In light of the fact that these two fees make up the largest part of a variable annuity's annual expense ratio, the annual cost of owning such an annuity will drop dramatically. If a fixed account is purchased in a mutual fund and, for example, an A-share commission of $2,500 was paid to purchase the fund, money management fees may be reduced but *none* of the $2,500 commission is rebated to the fund purchaser.

§2323. THE INCOME TAX COST OF OWNING MUTUAL FUNDS AND VARIABLE ANNUITIES

Income taxes are an important cost to be considered by those contemplating the purchase of variable annuities and mutual funds. However, because income taxes are not part of the commission paid for either of these investment products, they must be examined separately. Studies have shown that equity based mutual funds lose, on average, 20% of their gain each year to income taxes. This means that a mutual returning 10% will net the investor 8% *before* considering any other costs or commissions. In addition, there is a capital gains tax due upon the sale of a mutual fund on any unrealized gains that are realized at the time of sale. Variable annuities grow tax-deferred. For this reason there are no *annual* income taxes that must be paid by variable annuity investors. However, at the time of sale, all of the gain in a variable annuity is subject to taxation at ordinary income tax rates. For mutual funds and variable annuities held in

---

[65] $30,000 + $1,500 = $31,500 - 7% of 85% of $30,000 or $1,785 = $2,100 = $29,715. $29,715 ÷ $30,000 = 99.05%.

qualified accounts (e.g., IRAs, 401(k)s, etc.) the tax treatment of these two investment products is identical.

Where non-qualified (i.e., taxable accounts) are concerned, investors should factor in income taxes. It should be kept in mind that such taxes are *not* commission costs. The following examples compare the net returns of both a mutual fund and a variable annuity after *including* the income tax liability of each investment.

Example

Tom, who is 60, purchased a mutual fund for $40,000 fifteen years ago. The fund had a 4% commission and a 1.5% annual expense ratio. Trading costs were 0.70%. The income tax liability averaged 2.0% of the fund's gain each year. The fund grew at 10% a year. The fund is worth $92,864 today.[66]

Example

Vicky, who is 60, purchased a variable annuity for $40,000 fifteen years ago. The annuity had a 7% CDSC that declined over seven years and an annual expense ratio of 2.2%. Trading costs were 0.50%. All income taxes were deferred. The annuity grew at 10% a year. The annuity is worth $110,826 today.[67] Assuming Vicky is currently in a 20% average tax bracket, the annuity's after tax value would be $96,661[68] or $3,797 more than the mutual fund in the last example.[69]

The above calculations ignore the income tax liability that would be owed on the mutual fund's unrealized capital gains at sale and assumes a 15-year holding period for a mutual fund, which is unlikely. Adjusting for these factors would further increase the variable annuity's return over the mutual fund.

§2324. ALL COSTS CONSIDERED

If the commission and other costs of owning a variable annuity are indeed less than for owning mutual funds and tax deferral is really a significant benefit, one would expect that in the long run, variable annuities would outperform mutual funds by a wide margin. In fact, this is exactly what happens in most cases where mutual funds and variable annuities are compared on a net (after-cost, after-commission) basis.

§2325. CAVEAT TO INVESTORS

Although any comparison of the effect that commissions might have on variable annuity and mutual fund returns will usually show that variable annuity returns will be larger than for an equivalent mutual fund purchase, there will continue to exist, as there has been in the past, a few individuals who will continue to claim that variable annuity commissions affect variable annuity returns more than mutual funds. This situation usually arises when a commentator, reporter or

---

[66] $40,000 - 4% = $38,400 + 10% = $42,240 - 2.2% = $41,311 - $38,400 = $2,911 - 20% tax = $2,329 ÷ $38,400 = 6.064%. $38,400 x 6.064% x 15 years = $92,864.

[67] $40,000 + 10% = $44,000 - 2.7% = $42,812 - $40,000 = $2,812 ÷ $40,000 = 7.03%. $40,000 x 7.03% x 15 years = $110,826.

[68] $110,826 - $40,000 = $70,826 less 20% tax = $56,661 + $40,000 = $96,661.

[69] $96,661 - $92,864 = $3,797.

other misinformed individual:

1. Compares an actively managed variable annuity sold by financial professionals with a no-load or passively managed index mutual fund sold directly to the public by the issuing fund company;

2. Compares a mutual fund that has no options, riders or other benefits with a variable annuity that provides options, riders and other benefits to an investor who wants and is willing to pay an additional fee for these options, riders and benefits; or

3. Attempts to treat as part of a variable annuity's commission structure unrelated costs that can be completely avoided by a variable annuity purchaser.

Each of these topics is discussed in the sections that follow.

§2326. INACCURATE COMPARISONS

In years past, a few misinformed individuals have compared the affect of commissions imposed by *actively* managed variable annuities sold by financial professionals with no- or low-load or *passively* managed index funds *not* sold by financial professionals. Such comparisons are like comparing apples to oranges and can be misleading. For example, it is not difficult to find people who see nothing wrong with comparing variable annuities with a 6% CDSC that declines over six years and having an average annual ownership expense of 2.2% to no- or low-load mutual funds that have annual expense ratios well under 2.2%. The problem with such comparisons is that these two investments provide entirely different benefits to purchasers. For example, variable annuities sold by financial professionals come with the benefit of ongoing advice and assistance provided by the selling professional. The less expensive no- or low-load fund provides no such advice or assistance. Frequently, comparisons of variable annuities and no- or low-load or index funds are made intentionally in an attempt to indicate that *all* mutual funds have lower commission costs than variable annuities. This is not the case and investors must be wary of such inaccurate comparisons. If one is going to compare a no- or low-load passively managed mutual fund, like an index fund, then a no- or low-load variable annuity or equity-linked index annuity should be used in the comparison. Investors must ensure that whenever a comparison of any two investments is made, the investments being compared are similar in the benefits and services they provide. If not, an improper and costly investment decision may result.

§2327. INCOMPLETE COMPARISONS

Another way in which mutual fund commissions and annual expense ratios are improperly compared with variable annuity CDSCs and annual expense ratios occurs when a basic mutual fund is compared with a variable annuity that provides an additional benefit that an annuity purchaser has elected to buy that is not available with the mutual fund. If an auto dealer compared his $25,000 basic sedan, without options, to a competitor's $27,000 sedan that had $3,000 worth of options desired and paid for by the buyer, most people would spot such a price comparison as deceptive. However, it is not uncommon for the commission and annual expense ratio of a basic mutual fund to be compared to a variable annuity with a higher CDSC and expense ratio without any disclosure being made that these higher costs include fees designed to pay for options the annuity provides that the mutual fund does not. For example, some variable annuities offer an option that will guarantee the investor will get back 100% of his investment after a certain period of time even his variable annuity account value declines in value over this period. This principal protection feature should not be confused with the *death* benefit provided by variable annuities. The money back guarantee referred to is a living benefit. Living benefits are paid to *living* variable annuity owners. If a variable annuity containing a living benefit has a 7% CDSC that declines over seven years and has an annual expense ratio of 2.85%, it would be unfair to compare it to a B-share mutual fund that has a 6% CDSC declining over six years and an annual expense ratio of 2.55% but offers no similar protection against loss of principal.

Investors who purchase variable annuities with additional riders may actually position themselves to eliminate all commissions and other costs of ownership as the next example demonstrates:

Example

Nate, who is 53, wanted to invest a $30,000 401(k) he owned in equities. Nate narrowed his potential investments to a mutual fund and variable annuity. The mutual fund was an A-share fund that charged a 5% up-front, out-of-pocket commission and had an annual expense ratio of 1.5%. Trading costs were 0.7%. The variable annuity had no up-front, out-of-pocket commission but did impose a seven year CDSC that declined 1% a year. In addition, the annuity had a 2.3% annual expense ratio. Trading costs are 0.5%. For 25 basis points more, Nate purchased a rider that would guarantee him that at the end of seven years he would, at a minimum, receive back his $30,000 if the stock market went against him. Nate's financial advisor determined that the mutual fund would be worth $44,586 after seven years assuming an average annual growth rate of 9%.[70] The variable annuity with the principal protection rider would grow to $44,470 on the same facts.[71] However, if the stock market went down an average of 6% over the same seven year period of time the mutual fund would be worth less than $16,000.[72] The variable annuity, due to its refund feature, would be worth $30,000. It is important to note that, in the case of such a loss, Nate's total annual ownership costs of 2.2% a year for seven years, all trading cost and the 25 basis points paid for the guarantee would be reduced to zero.[73]

---

[70] $30,000 - 5% = $28,500 + 9% = $31,065 - 1.5%- 0.7% = $30,382 - $28,500 = $1,882 gain ÷ $28,500 = 6.602%. $28,500 x 6.602% x 7 years = $44,586.

[71] $30,000 + 9% = $32,700 - 2.2% - 0.5% - 0.25% = $31,735 - $30,000 = $1,735 gain ÷ $30,000 = 5.78%. $30,000 x 5.78% x 7 years = $44,470.

[72] $30,000 less 5% = $28,500 - 9% = $26,790 - 1.5% - 0.7% = $26,201 - $28,500 = -$2,299 ÷ $28,500 = -8.068%. -8.068% x 7 years x $28,500 = $15,816.

[73] Some variable annuity companies will fully refund the cost of protective riders if they are not used.

§2328. FACTORING IN AVOIDABLE EXPENSES

Some misinformed individuals attempt to include as an *actual* commission cost the *potential* 10% IRS penalty that may be incurred when an annuity owner surrenders his annuity early or makes large withdrawals from profits generated by his annuity before reaching the age of 59½. This is misleading. Avoidable penalties are not an out-of-pocket cost that increases the CDSC or annual expense ratio imposed for the purchase of a variable annuity. Nearly all workers today fund retirement accounts such as 401(k)s, 403(b)s, IRAs, etc. Each of these retirement accounts may impose a *potential* 10% IRS penalty for liquidations or withdrawals made prior to age 59½. Whenever the cost of funding a 401(k), IRA or other retirement account is calculated, the annual expense of owning these accounts does not include any potential IRS penalty. The reason for this is that it is assumed that people who contribute to their retirement accounts will hold them long enough to avoid any IRS penalty. This same assumption should apply to variable annuities. Most people who buy variable annuities with a *potential* 10% IRS penalty for early liquidation or withdrawal plan to hold their investment long enough to keep from having to pay this penalty. Even if one is faced with having to liquidate or take an early withdrawal from their variable annuity, there are numerous ways to avoid this penalty (See IRC §72). In addition, IRC §1035 allows a variable annuity owner to exchange his non-qualified variable annuity for another without triggering the 10% IRS penalty for pre-age 59½ withdrawals or surrenders. §1035 is *not* available for similar exchanges with non-qualified mutual fund portfolios. Where tax deferred accounts are involved (e.g., IRA, 401(k)s, etc.) the mutual fund is subject to the same potential 10% IRS penalty as would variable annuities. It is important to note that there are several *avoidable* costs associated with owning mutual funds that are much *more* likely to arise than the triggering of the 10% IRS penalty associated with the liquidation or early withdrawal from a variable annuity. For example, buying and selling different mutual funds within a multi-fund portfolio, which is commonly done, can result in additional commissions. This is true whether the account is qualified or not. When mutual funds are purchased it is usually assumed that a fund investor will not trade in his account in such a way as to increase the commission cost of owning his funds. For this reason, fund trading that *might* generate *potential* commissions is not factored into the commission cost of owning mutual funds. Likewise, the *potential* of having to pay an IRS penalty for an early liquidation or withdrawal of gains from a variable annuity should not be factored into the CDSC or annual cost of owning a variable annuity.

The 10% IRS penalty imposed for early liquidations or withdrawals of gain from variable annuities prior to age 59½ is usually offset or nearly offset within six years by the tax deferral provided by variable annuities. One contemplating the purchase of a variable annuity that may need to be liquidated or drawn on prior to age 59½ should, at a minimum, plan to hold the variable annuity for that period of time that will allow the variable annuity's tax deferral to offset any potential 10% IRS penalty. The following example discusses this matter:

Example

Don is a 25 year-old teacher and has $25,000 to invest. He is thinking about going to graduate school in five years and wants to invest for that purpose. His options are a mutual fund or variable annuity. He is considering a variable annuity with a five-year contingent deferred sales charge (CDSC) that declines 1% over six years and imposes a 10% IRS penalty on any gain withdrawn from the variable annuity prior to age 59½. The mutual fund, because it is an A-share fund, has no surrender charge or 10% IRS penalty but does have a 5% up-front, out-of-pocket commission. Don plans to sell his investment five years from now. He believes the market will provide a 10% gross rate return over the next five years. An initial investment of $25,000 in the mutual fund would be reduced to $23,750 by a 5% commission. Don's 10% return on the mutual fund would be further reduced by a 1.5% annual expense ratio, 0.7% in trading costs and taxes at 20% of his gain. Five years from now Don's mutual fund investment would be worth $31,879.[74] If the variable annuity is purchased, all of Don's $25,000 investment will go to work for him. The 2.3% annual cost of owning the variable annuity and trading costs of 0.5% will reduce his 10% gross rate of return to a net 7.03%. In five years, Don's variable annuity investment would grow to $35,113.[75] A sale at this point would result in a 1% surrender charge of $351 and a 10% IRS penalty of $976 on the $9,762 in gain Don made in his variable annuity, thus reducing Don's sale proceeds from $35,113 to $33,786.[76] A surrender fee of income taxes at 19% on the gain of $9,762 would further reduce this variable annuity investment by another $1,855 to $31,931.[77] However, this final figure still produces a net result which is larger than the mutual fund investment would yield even though Don had to pay a surrender charge and a 10% IRS penalty for selling his variable annuity prior to age 59½.[78] It is also important to note that the above calculation does not include the tax liability that would be owed by Don on the unrealized capital gains that would be due at the time he sold his mutual fund.

§2329. QUESTIONS TO ASK

• In light of the fact that commissions have an impact on net investment results, don't I have an obligation as a financial professional to understand and share with my clients exactly how the commission structure of various investment products are applied?

§2330. REVIEW QUESTIONS

Explain why the commission earned or paid when variable annuities are purchased are usually no more than those earned or paid with other equity investments.

---

[74] $25,000 - 5% = $23,750 + 10% = $26,125 less 1.5% less 0.7% = $25,550 less 20% tax on a gain $1,800 = $1,440 ÷ $23,750 = 6.064%. $23,750 x 6.064% x 5 years = $31,879.

[75] $25,000 + 10% = $27,500 - 2.2% - 0.5% = $26,758 - $25,000 = $1,758 ÷ $25,000 = 7.03%. $25,000 x 7.03% x 5 years - $35,113.

[76] $35,113 - $351 - $976 = $33,786.

[77] $33,786 - 19% of $9,762 or $1,855 = $31,931.

[78] $31,931 - $31,879 = $52.

§2331. SOURCES

See the footnotes to this chapter for other sources to consult regarding commissions..

§2332. CONCLUSION

The purpose of this report was to show investors how to compare the impact of commission costs on potential variable annuity and mutual fund returns over time. By using average or common mutual fund commissions, variable annuity CDSCs and annual ownership costs, this report hopefully demonstrated that the impact that commissions have on either variable annuity or mutual fund returns are very similar. Investors who want to understand the impact of commissions on variable annuity and mutual fund returns must understand the difference between an up-front, out-of-pocket commission and one that is paid by a third party. The key to reducing CDSCs on variable annuity and mutual fund transactions is for investors to match their investment time horizon to the holding period of the annuity or fund to be purchased. If an investor is comfortable that he can hold a variable annuity for six years, he should select a variable annuity or mutual fund with a six-year surrender period. If his investment time horizon is only three years, a variable annuity with a three-year surrender period should be selected. By selecting an appropriate surrender or holding period and taking time to understand the commission structures of both variable annuities and mutual funds, investors will be in a better position to select that investment that will provide them with the best after-commission investment returns.

– CHAPTER 24 –
THE TAX DEFERRAL MYTH – SUMMARY DISCUSSION

§2401. INTRODUCTION

Many investors believe that the tax deferral offered by variable annuity is not a major benefit because the variable annuity's tax-deferred gain is subject to ordinary income taxes while mutual funds receive at least some long-term capital gains treatment during the accumulation phase and are usually taxed upon liquidation at the long-term capital gains rate. This belief usually proves to be a myth.

§2402. OTHER CONSIDERATIONS

When comparing a mutual fund to a variable annuity it is important to realize that there are other considerations that must be factored into any such comparisons. These important considerations are:

- Although mutual fund owners usually pay income taxes each year to own their mutual funds, the fact that a variable annuity owner could invest an equal amount in a separate investment account is frequently ignored; and

- The after-tax, after-cost results of mutual fund and variable annuity investments assumes that variable annuity investors would elect to liquidate their variable annuities all on one day and pay a lump sum income tax on the gain at their highest marginal tax rate. In reality, this rarely occurs.

- It is also assumed in most long-term comparisons of mutual funds and variable annuities that the investments made in the mutual funds will not be changed and therefore no additional income taxes will result.

The primary issue that should be considered when comparing a mutual fund to a variable annuity is the ability of a variable annuity owner to invest the same amount of money that would be used to pay annual taxes had he owned a mutual fund if the money used to pay these taxes comes from sources other than the mutual fund.

§2403. CONCLUSION

When all the economics and tax factors are considered, the tax deferral provided by a variable annuity will often result in a net value that is larger than could be obtained with a similar mutual fund.

– CHAPTER 25 –
THE TAX DEFERRAL MYTH – DETAILED DISCUSSION

§2501. INTRODUCTION

When comparing taxable investments, such as mutual funds, to tax-deferred investments, such as variable annuities, investors make a common mistake – they compare only the after-tax investments results. These results, standing alone, can lead to incorrect and costly investment decisions. What is often ignored in these comparisons is what economists refer to as opportunity cost. When a tax-deferred investment is made, the concept of opportunity cost calculates the value of the investment gain that can be obtained on the money that is not used to pay income taxes that would have been owed had a taxable investment been purchased. This chapter examines the concept of opportunity cost and its importance when considering the purchase of either a taxable or tax-deferred investment. Although current tax law sets income tax rates for qualifying mutual fund dividends and long-term capital gains at 15%, many long-term investors may be better off purchasing variable annuities that provide the advantage of tax deferral. Such tax deferral, in many cases, may offset the 15% long-term capital gains tax rates applicable to mutual fund dividends and long-term capital gains.

§2502. TAX HISTORY

The Jobs and Growth Tax Reconciliation and Recovery Act of 2003 (JGTRRA) lowered the income tax rates on both qualifying dividends and long-term capital gains to 15%. This rate was set to expire on December 31, 2008 but was recently extended under the Tax Increase Prevention Re-conciliation Act (TIPRA) of 2005 (signed in 2006) for two additional years to December 31, 2010. Other than reducing marginal income tax rates, JGTRRA did not provide any specific tax relief for variable annuity owners who pay ordinary income tax rates on variable annuity gains. Many financial professionals, as well as members of the investing public, believe that due to the difference in tax treatment, investing in mutual funds will result in larger after-tax returns than investing in variable annuities. Before making such an assumption, advisors and investors alike should take the time to determine their actual tax liability for any potential purchase of either a mutual fund or variable annuity as well as the economic benefit that tax deferral provides. This two-step process will frequently demonstrate that the variable annuity may be a better investment than a comparable investment made in a mutual fund.

§2503. IMPACT OF TAX LAW CHANGES

The tax laws passed in the last several years have crated many issues that would be important for financial professionals to understand. Under current tax law, an investor contemplating an investment in mutual funds must consider the following issues:

- Annual distributions from mutual funds will *require* the owner to pay income taxes on these distributions whether or not the owner initiates any activity in his or her account.

- Depending on an investor's tax bracket, the *annual* income tax liability on mutual fund distributions can be higher than 15%.

- Tax reporting may become more cumbersome due to the complexity of the current IRS rules relating to the taxation of dividends and capital gains.

- The deduction of investment related expenses will be allowed only if the advantage of the 15% tax rates for capital gains and dividends is waived by the investor thus requiring him to use higher pre-JGTRRA tax rates.

- Records must be kept in order to track annual adjustments in the cost basis for all mutual funds owned. These records will be needed for tax reporting when the mutual funds are sold.

- Annual mutual fund distributions may result in income taxation even if the mutual fund goes *down* in value.

- Unrealized long-term capital gains do not receive 15% income tax treatment unless the mutual funds involved are sold before December 31, 2010. If mutual funds are sold in late 2010 to obtain the 15% capital gains tax rate before this tax rate expires, the proceeds that are reinvested in new mutual funds will be subject to income taxation at the increased 20% long-term capital gains rate that goes into effect after December 31, 2010.

- Any trading among different mutual fund companies may result in income taxation ranging from 15% to 35% depending on how long the liquidated mutual fund was held. Such trading may also generate new commissions.

- The 15% tax rate for dividends does not apply to all dividends. Only qualified dividends receive the 15% tax rate under current tax law.

- The 15% tax rate for dividends earned on mutual fund holdings is not available unless the underlying stock is held for a specific period of time after the dividend is received.

- The 15% tax rate for dividends expires at the end of 2010 and is scheduled to increase to as much as 35% starting after December 31, 2010.

- Dividends, which are paid yearly, result in annual income taxes that will increase each year as these dividends are reinvested.

- The selection of mutual funds will be limited for investors seeking large dividend pay-outs because most mutual funds pay relatively little or no dividends at all.

- The receipt of tax-advantaged dividends or long-term capital gains can expose an investor to the alternative minimum tax (AMT).

- Taxpayers subject to the alternative minimum tax (AMT) may face paying an effective tax rate in excess of 20% on long-term capital gains and dividends rather than a 15% tax rate.

Investors who decide to purchase a variable annuity will not have to deal with any of the issues listed above that negatively impact mutual funds because variable annuities grow on a tax-deferred basis. However, variable annuity purchasers will have to be concerned about paying *ordinary* income taxes on the ultimate withdrawal of gains from their variable annuity in the future.

HYPOTHETICAL CASE STUDY #1

To analyze the impact of income taxes on an investment in a mutual fund and variable annuity, the following hypothetical case study will be used:

> Bob and Linda are 53 years old. Their gross income is $110,000 and their taxable income is $79,500. They plan to retire in seven years and want to be able to liquidate any investment they purchase today at that time. Currently, their average tax rate is 16% and their marginal tax rate is 25%. Bob and Linda have $100,000 in a bank account they want to invest. They are interested in obtaining the 15% income tax rate on qualifying dividends and capital gains provided by current tax law to mutual fund purchasers. They are considering an investment in a mutual fund portfolio holding dividend paying stocks as well as the possible purchase of a variable annuity with their $100,000. Bob and Linda have sought the assistance of a CPA to compare the tax cost of owning the mutual fund and variable annuity they are considering. Because they only want to know what their income tax liability will be, non-tax costs have been ignored in the comparison. This hypothetical case study is designed to isolate the impact of income taxes on a potential mutual fund and variable annuity investment. Although non-tax costs are ignored, it should be noted that the annual non-tax costs of owning the average actively managed mutual fund are usually *higher* than that of the average actively managed variable annuity. This issue is discussed below. The assumed average, annual pre-tax rate of return for either investment will be 10%. Any investment selected will be deemed made on January 1, 2008 and will be held for seven years until the end of 2014 when the investment will be sold. For a mutual fund investment, the 10% return will be comprised of 1.8% in qualifying dividends, 2.2% long-term capital gains, 2% short-term gains and 4% unrealized capital gains. All dividends, distributions and gains will be reinvested and any income taxes due on distributions will be paid from sources other than the mutual fund. For a variable annuity investment, income taxes will be deferred until the end of 2014 when the annuity will be liquidated. Ordinary income taxes of between 25% and 28% will be due on the variable annuity's gain. Bob and Linda have a bank account containing enough money to pay any taxes that would be due upon the sale of a variable annuity should they elect to purchase a variable annuity.

Bob and Linda, the hypothetical investors, want to know whether they should invest their $100,000 in a mutual fund or a variable annuity. To determine the right investment, they decided to compare their income tax liability for both a mutual fund and variable annuity investment for their holding period of seven years. For the three year period from January 1, 2008 to December 31, 2010, both long-term capital gains and dividends distributed by mutual funds will be taxed at 15% while short-term capital gains are taxed at ordinary income tax rates. For Bob and Linda this latter rate will be 25% (i.e. their marginal tax rate). On December 31, 2010, the long-term capital gains tax rate is scheduled to increase to 20%. Dividend income and short-term capital gains will be taxed at ordinary income tax rates. For Bob and Linda, their ordinary income tax rate after 2010 will be 25%. For a variable annuity investment, Bob and Linda will have no tax liability between 2008 and the end of 2014 due to the fact that variable annuities grow on a tax-deferred basis. Based on the hypothetical facts discussed above, the income tax liability for a $100,000 investment made in a mutual fund and variable annuity from January 1, 2008 to the end of 2010 is set out in Table #1.

TABLE #1: ANNUAL TAX LIABILITY 2008-2010

INVESTMENT	2008	2009	2010	TOTAL
Mutual Fund	$1,100[1]	$1,215[2]	$1,331[3]	$3,646[4]
Variable Annuity	-0-	-0-	-0-	-0-

On December 31, 2010, considering only income taxes, both the mutual fund and variable annuity investment will have a value of $133,100.[5] The variable annuity will have grown to this amount tax-deferred while the mutual fund will have grown to the same amount because the income tax liability of $3,646 is assumed to have been paid from other sources which is common with mutual fund investing.

In order to take advantage of the 15% tax rate applicable to long-term capital gains, a mutual fund investment would have to be sold no later than December 31, 2010. As mentioned above, under current tax law, the 15% tax rate for long-term capital gains expires on December 31, 2010 and increases to 20% on January 1, 2011. The 15% tax rate applicable to dividends also expires on December 31, 2010. Starting on January 1, 2011, dividends will be taxed at ordinary income tax rates along with short-term capital gains. If the hypothetical mutual fund portfolio mentioned above is sold on December 31, 2010 to benefit from the lower long-term capital gains tax rate before it expires, a tax of $1,986 will be due on the $13,240 in unrealized capital gains that built up in the mutual fund portfolio that were not taxed during the first three years that the fund portfolio was held.[6] As mentioned, *annual* income taxes paid on the mutual fund

---

[1] For 2008, long-term capital gains and dividends are $4,000 (2.2% + 1.8% = 4% of 10% of $10,000 [$110,000-$100,000]) x 15% = $600. Short-term capital gains of $2,000 (2% of 10% of $10,000) x 25% = $500. Total tax liability for 2008 is $1,100. Unrealized capital gains would be 4% of 10% of $10,000 or $4,000.

[2] For 2009, long-term capital gains and dividends are $4,400 (2.2% + 1.8% = 4% of 10% of $11,000[$121,000 - $110,000]) x 15% = $660. Short-term capital gains of $2,220 (2% of 10% of $11,000) x 25% = $555. Total tax liability for 2009 is $1,215. Unrealized capital gains would be 4% of 10% of $11,000 or $4,400.

[3] For 2010, long-term capital gains and dividends are $4,840 (2.2% + 1.8% = 4% of 10% of $12,100[$133,100-$121,000]) x 15% = $726. Short-term capital gains of $2,420 (2% of 10% of $12,100) x 25% = $605. Total tax liability for 2010 is $1,331. Unrealized capital gains would be 4% of 10% of $12,100 or $4,840.

[4] $1,100 + $1,215 + $1,331= $3,646.

[5] $100,000 x 10% x 3 years = $133,100.

[6] For 2008 unrealized capital gains were 40% (i.e. 4% of 10%) of $10,000 or $4,000. For 2009 they were 40% (i.e. 4% of 10%) of $11,000 or $4,400. For 2010 they were 40% (i.e. 4% of 10%) of $12,100 or $4,840. The total of unrealized capital gains for the three year period 2008-2010 would be $13,240. At 15%, the income tax liability on this $13,240 would be $1,986.

portfolio up to the end of 2010 would be $3,646 (from Table #1). This $3,646 and the $1,986[7] in liquidation taxes will yield a total tax liability of $5,632 from January 1, 2008 through December 31, 2010.[8] The variable annuity investment would have grown on a tax-deferred basis and would have no income tax liability until sold at the end of 2014. Table #2 summarizes the above data.

TABLE #2: INCOME TAX LIABILITY (2008-2010)

INVESTMENT	ANNUAL INCOME TAXES	2010 LIQUIDATION TAX	TOTAL INCOME TAXES
Mutual Fund	$3,646[9]	$1,986[10]	$5,632[11]
Variable Annuity	-0-	-0-	-0-

§2504. INCOME TAX LIABILITY FOR 2011-2014

If the proceeds of the mutual fund portfolio (i.e. $133,100) are reinvested in similar mutual funds on January 1, 2011, the income tax liability for the mutual fund investment for 2011 through 2014 must now be determined. Table #3 reflects this tax liability. (Because of tax deferral, the variable annuity will have no income tax liability).

TABLE #3: ANNUAL INCOME TAX LIABILITY FOR 2011-2014

INVESTMENT	2011	2012	2013	2014	TOTAL
Mutual Fund	$1,851[12]	$2,035[13]	$2,239[14]	$2,463[15]	$8,588[16]
Variable Annuity	-0-	-0-	-0-	-0-	-0-

---

[7] See notes 4 and 6 *supra*.

[8] $3,646 + $1,986 = $5,632.

[9] See Table #1.

[10] See note 6 *supra*.

[11] See note 8 *supra*.

[12] For 2011, long-term capital gains will be 22% (2.2% of 10%) of $13,310 ($146,410 - $133,100) or $2,928 x 20% = $586. Dividend income will be 18% (1.8% of 10%) of $13,310 or $2,396 x 25% = $599. Short-term capital gains are 20% (2% of 10%) of $13,310 or $2,662 x 25% = $666. The total income tax liability for 2011 will be $1,851 ($586 + $599 + $666). Taxation of unrealized capital gains is not included. This calculation appears in note 17 *infra*.

[13] For 2012, long-term capital gains will be 22% (2.2% of 10%) of $14,641 ($161,051 - $146,410) or $3,221 x 20% = $644. Dividend income will be 18% (1.8% of 10%) of $14,641 or $2,635 x 25% = $659. Short-term capital gains are 20% (2% of 10%) of $14,641 or $2,926 x 25% = $732. The total income tax liability for 2011 will be $2,035 ($644 + $659 + $732). Taxation of unrealized capital gains is not included. This calculation appears in note 17 *infra*.

[14] For 2013, long-term capital gains will be 22% (2.2% of 10%) of $16,105 ($177,156 - $161,051) or $3,543 x 20% = $709. Dividend income will be 18% (1.8% of 10%) of $16,105 or $2,899 x 25% = $725. Short-term capital gains are 20% (2% of 10%) of $16,105 or $3,221 x 25% = $805. The total income tax liability for 2012 will be $2,239 ($709 + $725 + $805). Taxation of unrealized capital gains is not included. This calculation appears in note 17 *infra*.

[15] For 2014, long-term capital gains will be 22% (2.2% of 10%) of $17,716 ($194,872 - $177,156) or $3,898 x 20% = $780. Dividend income will be 18% (1.8% of 10%) of $17,716 or $3,188 x 25% = $797. Short-term capital gains are 20% (2% of 10%) of $17,716 or $3,543 x 25% = $886. The total income tax liability for 2013 will be $2,463 ($780 + $797 + $886). Taxation of unrealized capital gains is not included. This calculation appears in note 17 *infra*.

[16] $1,851 + $2,035 + $2,239 + $2,463 = $8,588.

§2505. LIQUIDATION OF INVESTMENTS ON JANUARY 1, 2015

In keeping with the hypothetical facts involving Bob and Linda, a comparison of the ending value of the mutual fund and variable annuity investment following their liquidation needs to be made. The only tax liability imposed on the mutual fund at liquidation on January 1, 2015 will be for $4,942 which represents a 20% long-term capital gains income tax on $24,708 of unrealized capital gains that built up in the fund during 2011 through 2014.[17] The variable annuity investment must be reduced by *ordinary* income taxes on the annuity's entire gain of $94,872 ($194,872 - $100,000) that accumulated on a tax-deferred basis from 2008 through 2014. That tax liability would be $25,006.[18] Table #4 summarizes the income taxes due on the hypothetical mutual fund and variable annuity investment only at their *liquidation* on January 1, 2014.

TABLE #4: JANUARY 1, 2015 LIQUIDATION INCOME TAX

INVESTMENT	LIQUIDATION TAX
Mutual Fund	$4,942[19]
Variable Annuity	$25,006[20]

Table #5 combines the annual income tax liability of the mutual fund and variable annuity investment with their respective liquidation tax liability for the period 2008-2014.

TABLE #5: TOTAL MUTUAL FUND AND VARIABLE ANNUITY TAXES 2008-2014

INVESTMENT	ANNUAL INCOME TAXES	LIQUIDATION TAXATION	TOTAL INCOME TAX LIABILITY
Mutual Fund	$12,234[21]	$6,928[22]	$19,162
Variable Annuity	-0-	$25,006[23]	$25,006

---

[17] Unrealized capital gains for 2011 were 40% (4% of 10%) of $13,310 [$146,410 - $133,100] or $5,324. Unrealized capital gains for 2012 were 40% (4% of 10%) of $14,641 [$161,051 - $146,410] or $5,856. Unrealized capital gains for 2013 were 40% (4% of 10%) of $16,105 [$177,156 - $161,051] or $6,442. Unrealized capital gains for 2014 were 40% of $17,716 [$194,872 - $177,156] or $7,086. $5,324 + $5,856 + $6,442 + $7,086 = $24,708 x 20% = $4,942.

[18] $100,000 x 10% x 7 years = $194,871 - $100,000 = $94,871 gain. $51,950 ($131,450 - $79,500 current taxable income) taxed at 25% = $12,988 and $42,922 ($94,872 - $51,950) taxed at 28% = $12,018. $12,988 + $12,018 = $25,006. This calculation is based on today's tax rates. They may differ seven years from now.

[19] See note 17 *supra*.

[20] See note 18.

[21] See Table #1 ($3,646) and note 16 *supra* ($8,588). $3,646 + $8,588 = $12,234.

[22] See note 6 ($1,986) and note 17 *supra* ($4,942). $1,986 + $4,942 = $6,928.

[23] See note 18 *supra*.

§2506. INVESTMENT VALUE ON DECEMBER 31, 2013

On December 31, 2013, the account values of the mutual fund and variable annuity would both be $194,872.[24] The variable annuity would grow to this amount because it generated no income tax liability from 2008 to the end of 2014. However, the income tax liability (paid from other sources) for the mutual fund investment through December 31, 2014, as Table #5 indicates, would be $19,162.[25] The income tax liability for the variable annuity would be $25,006.[26]

Table #6 summarizes the before and after-tax values of the hypothetical mutual fund and variable annuity investment after seven years:

TABLE #6: SUMMARY OF TOTAL INCOME TAX LIABILITY FOR 2008-2014

INVESTMENT	ORIGINAL INVEST.	VALUE AFTER 7 YRS @ 10%	TOTAL INCOME TAXES PAID	NET AFTER-TAX VALUE
Mutual Fund	$100,000	$194,872	$19,162	$175,710[27]
Variable Annuity	$100,000	$194,872	$25,006	$169,866[28]

From Table #6, Bob and Linda, the hypothetical investors, might conclude that their $100,000 should be invested in mutual funds inasmuch as the funds appear to provide an after-tax return that is $5,844 ($175,710 - $169,866) larger than a similar investment in a variable annuity. The problem with this conclusion is that it ignores a critical income tax factor. The $100,000 in-vested in the variable annuity grew tax-deferred, therefore there were no income taxes paid on the variable annuity for the seven year period it was held. The money that was ultimately used to pay the income taxes on the variable annuity (i.e. $25,006) was, according to the hypothetical case study, *fully* available for investment for 88½ months (January 1, 2008 to April 15, 2015). On the other hand, the mutual fund investment required the payment of income taxes each year. These tax payments were not fully available for investment. This dichotomy is referred to by economists as an opportunity cost and must be taken into consideration when an investor is trying to determine whether to invest in a mutual fund or a variable annuity.

As mentioned above, the $25,006 income tax payment ultimately used to pay income taxes on the variable annuity gain could have been invested for 88½ months. Assuming an 8% *after-tax* rate of return, this $25,006 would have produced a gain of $19,105 over this 88½ month period.[29] This investment gain must be added to the net value of the variable annuity investment

---

[24] $100,000 x 10% x 7 years = $194,872.

[25] Table #5.

[26] Table #5 and note 18 *supra.*

[27] $194,872 - $19,162 = $175,710.

[28] $194,872 - $25,006 = $169,866.

[29] $25,006 x 8% x 88½ months = $44,111 - $25,006 = $19,105 in gain.

on its liquidation date if a correct decision is to be made as to whether a mutual fund or variable annuity will provide the largest after-tax gain.

The income taxes paid on the mutual fund investment were due on April 15th following the first year of ownership and annually each April 15th thereafter. In addition, income taxes on unrealized capital gains were also due on April 15th following each year in which the mutual funds were liquidated (i.e. at the end of 2010 and 2014). For this reason, money used to pay these income taxes would not have been *fully* available for investment if a mutual fund were owned. These funds would be *partially* available for investment and any potential gains on any funds not immediately needed for the payment of income tax should also be considered when attempting to compare the after-tax returns for mutual funds and variable annuities. Table #7 sets out the income tax liability on the hypothetical mutual fund investment. As with the variable annuity investment, it is assumed that an 8% *after-tax* rate of return could have been received by any funds waiting to be used to pay income taxes on the mutual funds.

TABLE #7: TOTAL INCOME TAX LIABILITY AND AFTER-TAX INVESTMENT GAIN ON MONEY HELD TO PAY MUTUAL FUND INCOME TAXES

TAX DUE DATE	TAX PAYMENT[30]	MTHS. AVAIL. FOR INVEST.	ASSUMED RATE OF RETURN	INVESTMT. GAIN
Apl. 15, 2009	$1,100	16½ months	8%	$123
Apl. 15, 2010	$1,215	28½ months	8%	$244
Apl. 15, 2011	$1,331	40½ months	8%	$395
Apl. 15, 2011	$1,986	52½ months	8%	$795
Apl. 15, 2012	$1,851	64½ months	8%	$948
Apl. 15, 2013	$2,035	64½ months	8%	$1,042
Apl. 15, 2014	$2,239	76½ months	8%	$1,418
Apl. 15, 2015	$2,463	88½ months	8%	$1,882
Apl. 15, 2015	$4,942	88½ months	8%	$3,776
	$19,162			$10,623

---

[30] Tax payments due on April 15 of 2009 to April 15 of 2011 come from notes 1-3 *supra*. The final six figures in the column come from Tables #2, #3 and #4.

As Table #7 indicates, the after-tax investment gain that could have been received on money being held to pay mutual fund income taxes was $10,623. As pointed out earlier, the money held to pay income taxes on the variable annuity investment would have been able to generate a total after-tax gain of $19,105.[31] Table #8 adds these investment gains to the amounts determined in Table #6 above.

TABLE #8: REAL AFTER-TAX ENDING VALUES
WITH INVESTMENT GAINS ON TAX PAYMENTS FACTORED IN

INVEST.	ORIG. INVEST. AMOUNT	VALUE AFTER 7 YRS @ 10%	TOTAL INCOME TAXES PAID (-)	NET AFTER-TAX VALUE	GAIN ON TAX PAYMENTS INVEST. (+)	REAL AFTER-TAX ENDING VALUE
Mutual Fund	$100,000	$194,872	$19,162[32]	$175,710	$10,623[33]	$186,333[34]
Variable Ann.	$100,000	$194,872	$25,006[35]	$169,866	$19,105[36]	$188,971[37]

What Table #8 confirms is that when the concept of tax deferral and opportunity cost are factored in, an investment in a variable annuity may provide an after-tax return that his larger than a similar in-vestment made in a mutual fund.

§2507. SINGLE VS. DOUBLE LIQUIDATION

Mutual fund proponents may question whether it makes good financial sense for a fund investor to liquidate his portfolio at the end of 2010 to obtain the 15% long-term capital gains rate before these rates expire and then reinvest their reduced, after-tax proceeds only to subject themselves to 20% long-term capital gains rates for three years. Financially, such an election does not make sense. If the hypothetical mutual fund portfolio discussed above is not liquidated on December 31, 2010 but is liquidated only once, seven years later, on January 1, 2014 the real after-tax ending value will actually be *greater* than if a liquidation occurs at the end of 2010 and

---

[31] See note 29 *supra*.

[32] See Table #7.

[33] See Table #7.

[34] $194,872 - $19,162 + $10,623 = $186,333.

[35] See note 18 *supra*

[36] See note 29 *supra*

[37] $194,872 - $25,006 (Note 18) + $19,105 (Note 29) = $188,971.

again at the end of 2013. Table #9 shows the annual income tax liability for the hypothetical mutual fund portfolio discussed above for the seven year period from January 1, 2008 to the end of 2014 assuming the mutual fund portfolio is not liquidated on December 31, 2010. This table also shows the investment gain that could be earned on money held to pay income taxes on the mutual fund portfolio from 2008 to 2014.

TABLE #9: ANNUAL INCOME TAX LIABILITY AND AFTER-TAX INVESTMENT GAIN ON MONEY HELD TO PAY MUTUAL FUND INCOME TAXES (2008-2014)

TAX DUE DATE	TAX PAYMENT[38]	MO.S AVAIL. FOR INVESTMENT	ASSUMED RATE OF RETURN	INVESTMENT GAIN ON TAX PMT.[39]
Apl. 15, 2009	$1,100	16½ months	8%	$123
Apl. 15, 2010	$1,215	28½ months	8%	$244
Apl. 15, 2011	$1,331	40½ months	8%	$395
Apl. 15, 2012	$1,851	52½ months	8%	$741
Apl. 15, 2013	$2,035	64½ months	8%	$1,043
Apl. 15, 2014	$2,239	76½ months	8%	$1,418
Apl. 15, 2015	$2,463	88½ months	8%	$1,881
	$12,234			$5,845

[38] For years 2008-2010 see Table #1 in conjunction with notes 1-3 ($3,646).

- For 2011 (due April 15, 2012), long-term capital gains will be 22% (2.2% of 10%) of $13,310 ($146,410 - $133,100) or $2,928 x 20% = $586. Dividend income will be 18% (1.8% of 10%) of $13,310 or $2,396 x 25% = $599. Short-term capital gains are 20% (2% of 10%) of $13,310 or $2,662 x 25% = $666. The total income tax liability for 2011 will be $1,851 ($586 + $599 + $661). Taxation of unrealized capital gains is not included. This calculation appears in note 17 *infra*.
- For 2013, long-term capital gains will be 22% (2.2% of 10%) of $14,641 ($161,051 - $146,410) or $3,221 x 20% = $644. Dividend income will be 18% (1.8% of 10%) of $14,641 or $2,635 x 25% = $659. Short-term capital gains are 20% (2% of 10%) of $14,641 or $2,926 x 25% = $732. The total income tax liability for 2013 will be $2,035 ($644 + $659 + $732). Taxation of unrealized capital gains is not included. This calculation appears in note 17 *infra*.
- For 2014, long-term capital gains will be 22% (2.2% of 10%) of $16,105 ($177,156 - $161,051) or $3,543 x 20% = $709. Dividend income will be 18% (1.8% of 10%) of $16,105 or $2,899 x 25% = $725. Short-term capital gains are 20% (2% of 10%) of $16,105 or $3,221 x 25% = $805. The total income tax liability for 2014 will be $2,239 ($709 + $725 + $805). Taxation of unrealized capital gains is not included. This calculation appears in note 17 *infra*.
- For 2015, long-term capital gains will be 22% (2.2% of 10%) of $17,716 ($194,872 - $177,156) or $3,898 x 20% = $780. Dividend income will be 18% (1.8% of 10%) of $17,716 or $3,188 x 25% = $797. Short-term capital gains are 20% (2% of 10%) of $17,716 or $3,543 x 25% = $886. The total income tax liability for 2015 will be $2,463 ($780 + $797 + $886). Taxation of unrealized capital gains is not included. This calculation appears in note 17 *infra*.

[39] Table #7 up to April 15, 2012 = $1,348. For April 15, 2013, $2,035 x 64½ months x 8% = $1,043 in gain. For April 15, 2014, $2,239 x 76½ months x 8% = $1,418 in gain. For April 15, 2015, $2,463 x 88½ months x 8% = $1,881 in gain. $1,348 + $1,043 + $1,418 + $1,881 = $5,690.

§2508. LIQUIDATION OF MUTUAL FUND PORTFOLIO ONCE AT THE END OF 2014

Table #10 shows the income tax liability on the unrealized gain that would built up in the mutual fund portfolio from January 1, 2007 through the end of 2013. This table also reflects the investment gain that could have been earned on the money being held to pay the income taxes on the mutual fund's unrealized gain.

TABLE #10: UNREALIZED MUTUAL FUND CAPITAL GAINS (2008-2014)

UNREALIZED CAPITAL GAIN 2008-14	INCOME TAXES ON UNREALIZED GAIN @ 20%	INVESTMENT GAIN ON MONEY HELD TO PAY CAP. GAINS TAXES
$37,948[40]	$7,590[41]	$5,799[42]

Table #11 consolidates the information from Tables #8 through #10.

TABLE #11: REAL AFTER-TAX ENDING VALUES

WITH INVESTMENT GAINS ON TAX PAYMENTS FACTORED IN

INVEST.	ORIG. INVEST. AMOUNT	VALUE AFTER 7 YRS @ 10%	TOTAL INCOME TAXES PAID (-)	NET AFTER-TAX VALUE	GAIN ON TAX PAYMENTS INVEST. (+)	REAL AFTER-TAX ENDING VALUE
Mutual Fund	$100,000	$194,872	$19,824[43]	$175,048	$11,644[44]	$186,692[45]
Variable Ann.	$100,000	$194,872	$25,006[46]	$169,866	$19,105[47]	$188,971[48]

When Table #11 is compared to Table #8, it can be determined that the hypothetical mutual fund portfolio's after-tax ending value actually *increases* slightly if the portfolio is liquidated only once at the end of 2014 rather than at the end of 2010 *and* again at the end of 2014. The problem with liquidating the mutual fund portfolio only once at the end of 2014 is twofold. First, the 15% income tax rate that was initially available for mutual funds (pre-2011) must be *forfeited* and a 20% long-term capital gains rate accepted in order for a mutual fund investor to obtain a slightly larger ending value on his mutual fund investment. Second, the increased gain obtained when a single liquidation takes place rather than a double liquidation is still not enough to outperform the hypothetical variable annuity purchase on an after-tax basis.

---

[40] See note 6 ($13,240) and note 17 ($24,708) = $37,948.

[41] $37,948 x 20% = $7,590.

[42] $7,590 x 88½ months x 8% = $5,799 in gain.

[43] See Tables #9 and #10. $12,234 + $7,590 = $19,824.

[44] See Tables #9 and #10. $5,845 + $5,799 = $11,644.

[45] $194,872 - $19,438 + $11,489 = $186,923.

[46] See Table #5 and note 18.

[47] See note 29 *supra*.

[48] $194,872 - $25,006 + $19,105 = $188,971.

§2509. CONTINUATION OF THE 15% LONG-TERM CAPITAL GAINS TAX RATES

Many investors express confidence that the current 15% long-term capital gains income tax rate applicable to qualifying dividends and long-term capital gains will not expire on December 31, 2010 even though current tax law (TIPRA) provides for such a repeal. These same investors believe that if these reduced income tax rates do not expire as scheduled, then mutual funds will be a better investment than variable annuities. Such an assumption may prove defective. If it is assumed that the 15% long-term capital gains income tax rate for qualifying dividends and mutual fund gains does not expire in 2010 but will continue through 2014, a variable annuity investment may still produce a larger after-tax return than a similar mutual fund investment. This issue is discussed in the sections that follow.

§2510. INCOME TAX LIABILITY IF THE 15% CAPITAL GAINS TAX RATE IS NOT REPEALED ON DECEMBER 31, 2010

Continuing with the above hypothetical mutual fund case study, the income tax liability for 2008-2014, assuming the current 15% long-term capital gains tax rate is not repealed on December 31, 2010 is reflected in Table #12:

TABLE #12: 2008-2014 ANNUAL INCOME TAX LIABILITY

INVESTMENT	2008-2010	2011	2012	2013	2014	TOTAL
Mutual Fund	$3,646[49]	$1,465[50]	$1,610[51]	$1,771[52]	$1,949[53]	$10,441
Variable Annuity	-0-	-0-	-0-	-0-	-0-	-0-

As was done earlier, the annual income investment gain that could be earned while money is being held to pay income taxes must be calculated. Table #13 shows this investment gain based on the data set out in Tables #1 and #12. The chart also sets out the annual income tax liability for the mutual fund portfolio for the seven year holding period.

---

[49] See Table #1 and notes 1-3 for years 2008-2011.

[50] For 2011, long-term capital gains and dividends are $5,324 (2.2% + 1.8% = 4% of 10% of $13,310[$146,410 - $133,100]) x 15% = $799. Short-term capital gains of $2,662 (2% of 10% of $13,310) x 25% = $666. Total tax liability for 2011 is $1,465. Unrealized capital gains would be 4% of 10% of $13,310 or $5,324.

[51] For 2012, long-term capital gains will be 22% (2.2% of 10%) of $14,641 ($161,051 - $146,410) or $3,221 x 15% = $483. Dividend income will be 18% (1.8% of 10%) of $14,641 or $2,635 x 15% = $395. Short-term capital gains are 20% (2% of 10%) of $14,641 or $2,928 x 25% = $732. The total income tax liability for 2012 will be $1,610 ($483 + 395 + $732).

[52] For 2013, long-term capital gains will be 22% (2.2% of 10%) of $16,105 ($177,156 - $161,105) or $3,543 x 15% = $531. Dividend income will be 18% (1.8% of 10%) of $16,105 or $2,899 x 15% = $435. Short-term capital gains are 20% (2% of 10%) of $16,105 or $3,221 x 25% = $805. The total income tax liability for 2013 will be $1,771 ($531 + $435 + $805).

[53] For 2014, long-term capital gains will be 22% (2.2% of 10%) of $17,716 ($194,872 - $177,156) or $3998 x 15% = $585. Dividend income will be 18% (1.8% of 10%) of $17,716 or $3,189 x 15% = $478. Short-term capital gains are 20% (2% of 10%) of $17,716 or $3,543 x 25% = $886. The total income tax liability for 2014 will be $1,949 ($585 + $478 + $886).

TABLE #13: ANNUAL INCOME TAX LIABILITY AND AFTER-TAX INVESTMENT GAIN OR MONEY HELD TO PAY MUTUAL FUND INCOME TAXES (2008-2014)

TAX DUE DATE	TAX PAYMENT	MTHS AVAIL. FOR INVESTMENT	ASSUMED RATE OF RETURN	INVESTMENT GAIN ON TAX PMT.
Apl. 15, 2009	$1,100	16½ months	8%	$123
Apl. 15, 2010	$1,215	28½ months	8%	$244
Apl. 15, 2011	$1,331	40½ months	8%	$395
Apl. 15, 2012	$1,465	52½ months	8%	$586
Apl. 15, 2013	$1,610	64½ months	8%	$825
Apl. 15, 2014	$1,771	76½ months	8%	$1,122
Apl. 15, 2015	$1,949	88½ months	8%	$1,488
	$10,441			$4,783

At the end of 2014, all unrealized capital gains in the mutual fund investment would be subject to long-term capital gains taxes. The total amount of unrealized capital gains from 2008 through 2014 is set out in Table #14.

TABLE #14: UNREALIZED MUTUAL FUND CAPITAL GAINS 2008-2014

UNREALIZED CAPITAL GAIN 2008-14	INCOME TAXES ON UNREALIZED GAIN @ 15% JANUARY 1, 2014 LIQUIDATION	INVESTMENT GAIN ON MONEY HELD TO PAY TAXES
$37,948[54]	$5,692[55]	$4,349[56]

Table #15 combines the data set out in Tables #13 and #14:

---

[54] Unrealized capital gains for 2008-2010 were $13,240 (See note 6 *supra*). Unrealized capital gains for 2011 were 40% (4% of 10%) of $13,310 [$146,410 - $133,100] or $5,324. Unrealized capital gains for 2012 were $5,856 (40% [4% of 10%] of $14,641), for 2013 were $6,442 (40% [4% of 10%] of $16,105) and for 2014 were $7,086 (40% [4% of 10%] of $17,716). (See note 17 *supra*). $13,240 + $5,324 + $5,856 + $6,442 + $7,086 = $37,948.

[55] $37,948 x .15 = $5,692.

[56] $5,692 x 8% x 88½ months = $4,349 investment gain.

TABLE #15: AFTER-TAX ENDING VALUES WITH INVESTMENT GAINS ON TAX PAYMENTS FACTORED IN (2008-2014)

INVEST.	ORIG. INVEST. AMOUNT	VALUE AFTER 7 YRS @ 10%	TOTAL INCOME TAXES PAID (-)	NET AFTER-TAX VALUE	GAIN ON TAX PAYMENTS INVEST. (+)	REAL AFTER-TAX ENDING VALUE
Mutual Fund	$100,000	$194,872	$16,133[57]	$178,739	$9,132[58]	$187,871[59]
Variable Ann.	$100,000	$194,872	$25,006[60]	$169,866	$19,105[61]	$188,971[62]

Table #15 confirms that even if the 15% tax rate provided by current tax law (TIPRA) does not expire at the end of 2010, the hypothetical variable annuity investment would still be more profitable, on an after-tax basis, than a similar investment in a mutual fund once the advantage of the variable annuity's tax deferral is taken into consideration. This advantage reflects consideration of the economic concept of opportunity cost. In reality, the 15% long-term capital gains tax rate will most likely increase over the next few years.

§2511. EXCESS FUNDS NOT AVAILABLE

The comparison discussed above was based on the assumption that the hypothetical variable annuity investors had $25,006 in liquid assets that were available for investment for seven years before being used to pay income taxes on their variable annuity investment.[63] A question may arise as to whether the benefit of tax deferral offered by a variable annuity can be quantified if variable annuity investors do *not* have excess funds that can be invested until they are needed to pay income taxes in the future. The answer to this question is yes. The advantage of tax deferral offered by variable annuities can be clearly demonstrated even where variable annuity investors do not have large amounts of cash or investments that can be held until needed to pay income taxes in the future. The following hypothetical case study demonstrates the advantage of the tax deferral benefit provided by variable annuities in this latter situation:

---

[57] $10,441 (Table #13) + $5,692 (Table #14) = $16,133.

[58] See Table #13 ($4,783) + Table #14 ($4,349) = $9,132.

[59] $194,872 - $16,133 + $9,132 = $187,871.

[60] See note 18 *supra*.

[61] See note 29 *supra*.

[62] $194,872 - $25,006 + $19,105 = $188,971.

[63] See note 18 *supra*.

HYPOTHETICAL CASE STUDY #2

Zeb and Zelda are 50 years old. Their annual gross income is $80,000. Their taxable income of $65,100 for 2008 is used fully for living expenses each year. They inherited $50,000 in late 2007 and wanted to invest it for ten years. On January 1, 2008, Zeb and Zelda purchased a variable annuity with their $50,000. Later they were told variable annuity gains were subject to ordinary income taxation and that mutual funds were taxed mostly at long-term capital gain tax rates of 15%. They wanted to know whether this difference in taxation made the variable annuity a less desirable investment than a mutual fund. Zeb and Zelda recently met with a financial planner who was able to calculate the total tax obligation they will incur with the variable annuity investment and compare it to a similar mutual fund investment. The financial advisor assumed that the annual return for both investments would be 9%. Of the 9% mutual fund return, 3% will be long-term capital gains and qualifying dividends taxed at 15%. One percent will be short term capital gains taxed at 25%. Five percent will be unrealized capital gains subject to the long-term capital gains tax upon liquidation ten years from now. It was also assumed that Zeb and Zelda would have paid any annual mutual fund tax liability from sources other than mutual funds had mutual funds been purchased. The financial advisor assumed that the 15% long-term capital gains tax rate currently applicable to qualifying dividends and long-term capital gains rates would remain in effect for the next ten years even though they are scheduled to expire on December 31, 2010. (After that date the long-term capital gains rate increases to 20% and dividends will be taxed at ordinary income tax rates of as much as 35%). The following sections examine this hypothetical.

§2512. MUTUAL FUND INVESTMENT

Each year on April 15, Zeb and Zelda, because they have no excess savings, would have paid the annual income taxes owed on their hypothetical mutual fund investment from sources other than their mutual funds had a mutual fund been purchased. Their financial professional prepared Table #16 below to summarize the annual income tax liability Zeb and Zelda would have incurred over the next ten years had they invested in a mutual fund.

TABLE #16: INCOME TAX LIABILITY ON THE MUTUAL FUND INVESTMENT FROM 2008-2017

TAX YEAR	TAX DUE DATE	TAX OBLIGATION
2008	April 15, 2009	$350[64]
2009	April 15, 2010	$381[65]
2010	April 15, 2011	$416[66]
2011	April 15, 2012	$453[67]
2012	April 15, 2013	$494[68]
2013	April 15, 2014	$538[69]
2014	April 15, 2015	$587[70]
2015	April 15, 2016	$640[71]
2016	April 15, 2017	$697[72]
2017	April 15, 2018	$760[73]
		$5,316

[64] The gain for 2008 is 9% of $50,000 or $4,500 ($54,500 - $50,000). The income tax for 2008 will be $350. $1,500 (3/9 of $4,500) long-term capital gain x 15% = $225 plus $500 short-term capital gain (1/9 of $4,500) taxed at 25% = $125. $225 + $125 = $350. Unrealized capital gains are 5/9 of $4,500 or $2,500.

[65] The gain for 2009 is 9% of $54,500 or $4,905 ($59,405 - $54,500). The income tax for 2009 will be $381. $1,635 long-term capital gain (3/9 of $4,905) x 15% = $245 plus $545 short-term capital gain (1/9 of $4,905) taxed at 25% = $136. $136 + $245 = $381. Unrealized capital gains are 5/9 of $4,905 or $2,725.

[66] The gain for 2010 is 9% of $59,405 or $5,346 ($64,751.45 - $59,405). The income tax for 2010 will be $416. $1,782 long-term capital gain (3/9 of $5,346) x 15% = $267 plus $594 in short-term capital gain (1/9 of $5,346) taxed at 25% = $149. $267 + $149 = $416. Unrealized capital gains are 5/9 of $5,346 or $2,970.

[67] The gain for 2011 is 9% of $64,751 or $5,828 ($70,579 - $64,751). The income tax for 2011 will be $453. $1,942 long-term capital gain (3/9 of $5,828) taxed at 15% = $291 plus $648 in short-term capital gain (1/9 of $5,828) taxed at 25% = $162. $291 + $162 = $453. Unrealized capital gains are 5/9 of $5,828 or $3,238.

[68] The gain for 2012 is 9% of $70,579 or $6,352 ($76,931 - $70,579). The income tax for 2012 will be $494. $2,117 long-term capital gain (3/9 of $6,352) taxed at 15% = $318 plus $706 in short-term capital gain (1/9 of $6,352) taxed at 25% = $176. $318 + $176 = $494. Unrealized capital gains are 5/9 of $6,352 or $3,530.

[69] The gain for 2013 is 9% of $76,931 or $6,924 ($83,855 - $76,931). The income tax for 2013 will be $538. $2,308 long-term capital gain (3/9 of $6,924) taxed at 15% = $346 plus $769 in short-term capital gain (1/9 of $6,924) taxed at 25% = $192. $346 + $192 = $538. Unrealized capital gains are 5/9 of $6,924 or $3,846.

[70] The gain for 2014 is 9% of $83,855 or $7,547 ($91,402 - $83,855). The income tax for 2014 will be $587. $2,516 long-term capital gain (3/9 of $7,547) taxed at 15% = $377 plus $839 in short-term capital gain (1/9 of $7,547) taxed at 25% = $210. $377 + $210 = $587. Unrealized capital gains are 5/9 of $7,547 or $4,193.

[71] The gain for 2015 is 9% of $91,402 or $8,226 ($99,628 - $91,402). The income tax for 2015 will be $640. $2,742 long-term capital gain (3/9 of $8,226) taxed at 15% = $411 plus $914 in short-term capital gain (1/9 of $8,226) taxed at 25% = $229. $411 + $229 = $640. Unrealized capital gains are 5/9 of $8,226 or $4,570.

[72] The gain for 2016 is 9% of $99,628 or $8,967 ($108,594 - $99,628). The income tax for 2016 will be $697. $2,989 long-term capital gain (3/9 of $8,967) taxed at 15% = $448 plus $996 in short-term capital gain (1/9 of $8,867) taxed at 25% = $249. $448 + $249 = $697. Unrealized capital gains are 5/9 of $8,967 or $4,981.

[73] The gain for 2017 is 9% of $108,594 or $9,773 ($118,368 - $108,594). The income tax for 2017 will be $760. $3,258 long-term capital gain (3/9 of $9,773) taxed at 15% = $489 plus $1,086 in short-term capital gain (1/9 of $9,773) taxed at 25% = $271. $489 + $271 = $760. Unrealized capital gains are 5/9 of $9,773 or $5,430.

In addition to annual income taxes of $5,316,[74] Zeb and Zelda would have a 15% tax liability on the unrealized capital gains of $37,983 upon the sale of their hypothetical mutual fund portfolio.[75] At 15% this will result in an additional income tax of $5,697.[76] Based on this, the total taxes on Zeb and Zelda's hypothetical mutual fund investment from January 1, 2008 to January 1, 2018 would be $11,013.[77] A $50,000 mutual fund investment returning 9% a year will grow to $118,368 in ten years if income taxes on the mutual fund are paid from another source as is assumed in this hypothetical.[78] Thus, Zeb and Zelda's after-tax mutual fund investment balance would have been $107,355 after ten years had they purchased a mutual fund.[79]

§2513. VARIABLE ANNUITY INVESTMENT

Zeb and Zelda's financial professional pointed out to them that their variable annuity investment would grow tax-deferred for their ten year holding period. A $50,000 variable annuity investment returning 9% will grow tax-deferred to $118,368 over ten years.[80] The gain of $68,368[81] would be subject to income taxes of $17,153.[82] This would result in an after-tax variable annuity investment balance of $101,215 ten years from now.[83] Based on this data, Zeb and Zelda concluded that a mutual fund would have been the better investment tax-wise because it would produce an after-tax investment gain of $6,090 more than their variable annuity investment would produce.[84] Zeb and Zelda's financial professional pointed out that the conclusion they had reached did not consider the amount of money that they could set aside each year that would not be used to pay income taxes on their tax-deferred variable annuity they purchased nor did Zeb and Zelda consider the investment return that they could receive on these funds. The mutual fund investment would require income tax payments every year regardless of whether the mutual funds moved up or down in value. In other words, Zeb and Zelda failed to consider the concept of opportunity cost. This concept is discussed in the next section.

---

[74] See Table #16.

[75] See Notes 64-73 ($37,983).

[76] 15% of $37,983 = $5,697.

[77] Note 76 ($5,697) + Table #16 ($5,316) = $11,013.

[78] $50,000 x 10 years x 9% = $118,368.

[79] $50,000 x 10 years x 9% = $118,368 - $11,013 (Note 77) = $107,355.

[80] $50,000 x 10 years x 9% = $118,368.

[81] $118,368 (Note 80) - $50,000 investment = $68,368 gain.

[82] Zeb and Zelda have a total taxable income of $65,100 (from hypothetical) plus $68,368 variable annuity gain = $133,468. Income tax on first $65,100 of Zeb and Zelda's taxable income = $8,963 (2008). The income tax on the taxable income from $65,100 to $131,450 = $66,380 at 25% = $16,588. The income from $131,450 to $133,468 would be $2,018. This amount would be taxed at 28% resulting in a tax of $565. $16,588 + $565 = $17,153. (Assumes no change in tax rates after 2007).

[83] $118,368 (note 80) - $17,153 (note 82) = $101,215.

[84] $107,355 (note 79) - $101,215 (note 83) = $6,140.

§2514. THE CONCEPT OF OPPORTUNITY COST

Zeb and Zelda's financial professional reminded them that the variable annuity they purchased would not require them to pay income taxes each year like they would have had to do with a mutual fund investment. Zeb and Zelda would be able to set aside an amount each year equal to the mutual fund's annual tax liability and earn a return on these funds. Stated differently, if Zeb and Zelda could come up with income tax money to pay mutual fund income each year, they could come up with the same amount of money if they purchased a variable annuity. The only difference, as mentioned, would be that the money that would normally be used to pay annual mutual fund income taxes could be used to create a secondary investment account that could be funded each year because Zeb and Zelda elected to purchase a variable annuity. In short, the mutual fund investment takes advantage of an opportunity not fully available to mutual fund investors. The gain from any secondary investment account created must be considered when comparing a mutual fund and variable annuity on an after-tax basis. Zeb and Zelda's financial professional created Table #17 for them. This table, set out below, shows amounts that could be invested each year by Zeb and Zelda because these amounts would not be used to pay annual income taxes on a mutual fund portfolio. These are the same amounts that would have been paid each year in income taxes had Zeb and Zelda elected to purchase a mutual fund. Table #17 also shows the investment gain these unused funds could generate. For the purpose of simplicity, Table #17 will assume that Zeb and Zelda will invest these annual payments in a municipal bond portfolio that would provide a conservative after-tax rate of return of 4%.

TABLE #17: INVESTMENT OF MONEY NOT USED TO PAY ANNUAL MUTUAL FUND TAXES IF A VARIABLE ANNUITY IS PURCHASED

TAX YEAR	TAXES DUE	INVESTMENT[85]	YEARS INVESTED[86]	RATE OF RETURN	ACCOUNT BALANCE
2008	Apl. 15, 2009	$350	9	4%	$498
2009	Apl. 15, 2010	$381	8	4%	$521
2010	Apl. 15, 2011	$416	7	4%	$547
2011	Apl. 15, 2012	$453	6	4%	$573
2012	Apl. 15, 2013	$494	5	4%	$601
2013	Apl. 15, 2014	$538	4	4%	$629
2014	Apl. 15, 2015	$587	3	4%	$660
2015	Apl. 15, 2016	$640	2	4%	$692
2016	Apl. 15, 2017	$697	1	4%	$725
2017	Apl. 15, 2018	$760	.375[87]	4%	$771
2017	Apl. 15, 2018	$5,697[88]	.375	4%	$5,781[89]
		$11,013			$11,998

As Table #17 indicates, Zeb and Zelda, by purchasing a variable annuity, can create a separate investment account with the money that they would have used to pay annual income taxes had they chosen to invest in a mutual fund. This secondary investment account would contain $11,998 on April 15, 2018.[90] If Zeb and Zelda add their tax-free secondary investment account balance of $11,998 from Table #17 to their pre-tax variable annuity account value of $118,368[91] they will have a ten-year combined investment balance of $130,367.[92] This figure

---

[85] All of the figures in this column come from Table #16. (See notes 64 to 73 *supra*).

[86] Money that would have been used to pay mutual fund taxes can be invested from 1 to 9 years.

[87] Zeb and Zelda may deposit $761 in their special side account but it will earn interest only for 4.5 months (or .375 years). The reason for this is at the end of 2016 they will liquidate their variable annuity investment. Taxes on this sale will be due 4.5 months later on April 15, 2017. $760 x .375 years x 4% = $771.

[88] The $5,697 figure represents the income taxes that would be due on long term capital gains of $37,948 (note 40) when the mutual fund was sold. $37,983 x 15% = $5,697. See note 87 *supra* as to the .375 year investment period.

[89] This figure represents the income taxes that would have been due on the long-term capital gains that built up in the mutual fund and become due on April 15, 2017 (i.e., $5,697). Because this $5,697 tax obligation was not due with the variable annuity, it grew to $5,781 ($5,697 x .375 x 4%). See note 76 *supra*. See note 87 *supra* as to the .375 year investment period.

[90] See account balance column (total) in Table #17.

[91] See note 78 *supra*.

[92] $11,999 (See note 90) + $118,368 (See note 78 *supra*) = $130,367.

253

must be reduced by the taxes owed on the variable annuity gain. This tax would amount to $17,103.[93] This will leave Zeb and Zelda with an after-tax variable annuity investment account balance of $113,264.[94] This figure is $5,909 *more* than the after-tax value provided by the mutual fund portfolio.[95] This is true even though 100% of Zeb and Zelda's variable annuity gain would be taxed at ordinary income tax rates of between 25% and 28%, while the mutual fund would have produced gains that would have, under the assumed facts, been taxed at the 15% long-term capital gains rate. Instead of creating a low yielding secondary municipal bond investment account, Zeb and Zelda could have invested the money they would have normally used to pay income taxes on a mutual fund in a higher yielding investment (including the variable annuity they initially purchased). Had this been done, the end result discussed above would have made the variable annuity investment an even better choice than the mutual fund investment. It is also important to remember that Zeb and Zelda received 15% income tax treatment on their long-term capital gains and dividends in the years 2011 through 2015 even though this tax rate is set to increase to 20% after December 31, 2010. If this increase takes place, the advantage Zeb and Zelda will receive from investing in their variable annuity over a similar mutual fund investment would be further increased.

§2515. PAYING INCOME TAXES FROM A MUTUAL FUND INVESTMENT

The first hypothetical case study discussed above involving Bob and Linda dealt with a situation where income taxes due on a mutual fund investment or variable annuity investment were paid from an existing separate fund held by the investors. The second hypothetical case study involving Zeb and Zelda dealt with a situation where annual income taxes owed on a mutual fund investment were paid each year as they come due. In this latter case, it was assumed that the investors did not have a separate source of funds available to them to pay income taxes each year. The amount of income taxes paid each year was set aside where the variable annuity was compared. This money earned a return that was later considered when comparing the after-tax value of the mutual fund and variable annuity investment. The only other way investors can purchase actively managed mutual funds and pay the annual income taxes on these funds is to withdraw the taxes owed on the funds each year from the funds themselves. If this rarely used method of paying annual mutual fund taxes is used, the benefit of tax deferral provided by variable annuities will, as in the prior two cases, often provide a larger after-tax return than

---

[93] See note 82 *supra.*

[94] $130,367 (Note 92) - $17,103 (Note 82) = $113,264.

[95] $113,264 (Note 94) - $107,355 (Note 79) = $5,909.

a similar mutual fund investment as demonstrated by the next hypothetical case study. This hypothetical case study will assume that any annual income taxes owed will be paid by the investors by withdrawing these taxes each year from the mutual fund.

HYPOTHETICAL CASE STUDY #3

> Mike and Mindy are 48 years old. Their gross income is $80,000 and their taxable income is $65,100 for 2008. They fully spend their taxable income each year. Mike recently won $50,000 (after-taxes) at a casino in Atlantic City. Mike and his wife want to invest this windfall for the next twelve years. They have found a mutual fund that they believe will return an average of 10% over the next twelve years. Of the 10% annual gain, 30% will be unrealized, 50% will be long-term capital gains taxed currently at 15% and 20% will be short-term capital gains taxed at 25%. Mike and Mindy want to know if the tax deferral they could obtain from a variable annuity would yield a larger after-tax return than they could receive from a mutual fund.

§2516. THE MUTUAL FUND INVESTMENT

Mike and Mindy found a financial advisor who would help them answer their questions concerning the tax deferral offered by variable annuities. The advisor created Table #18 for Mike and Mindy. Table #18 summarizes the gains and income taxes that would be owed on these gains if Mike and Mindy were to purchase a mutual fund with their $50,000 and hold it for eight years.

TABLE #18: MUTUAL FUND GAINS AND INCOME TAXES FOR 2008-2019

TAX YEAR	STARTING BALANCE	ENDING VALUE	TOTAL GAIN	UNREALIZED GAIN	INCOME TAXES WITHDRAWN
2008	$50,000	$55,000	$5,000	$1,500	$625[96]
2009	$54,375	$59,813	$5,438	$1,631	$680[97]
2010	$59,133	$65,046	$5,913	$1,774	$739[98]
2011	$64,307	$70,737	$6,431	$1,929	$804[99]
2012	$69,933	$76,927	$6,994	$2,098	$1,049[100]
2013	$75,878	$83,466	$7,588	$2,276	$1,138[101]
2014	$82,328	$90,560	$8,232	$2,470	$1,235[102]
2015	$89,325	$98,258	$8,933	$2,680	$1,340[103]
2016	$96,918	$106,610	$9,692	$2,680	$1,454[104]
2017	$105,156	$115,672	$10,516	$3,155	$1,578[105]
2018	$114,094	$125,503	$11,409	$3,423	$1,711[106]
2019	$123,792	$136,171	$12,379	$3,714	$1,857[107]
	$134,314			$29,330	$14,211

What Table #18 demonstrates is that after twelve years, Mike and Mindy will have a mutual fund account value of $134,314 which includes a reduction for *annual* income taxes in the amount of $14,211. This $134,314 mutual fund account balance must be further reduced by the unrealized mutual fund gains of $29,330 which become realized when the mutual fund is sold. (See Table #18). If these gains are taxed at the 20% long-term capital gains tax rate that will apply after December 31, 2010 it will result in an income tax liability of $5,866.[108] When this amount is subtracted from $134,314, it yields an after-tax mutual fund account value of $128,448.[109]

---

[96] 50% of $5,000 = $2,500 x .15 = $375. 20% of $5,000 = $1,000 x .25 = $250. $375 + $250 = $625.

[97] 50% of $5,438 = $2,719 x .15 = $408. 20% of $5,438 = $1,088 x .25 = $272. $408 + $272 = $680.

[98] 50% of $5,913 = $2,957 x .15 = $443. 20% of $5,913 = $1,183 x .25 = $296. $443 + $296 = $739.

[99] 50% of $6,431 = $3,216 x .15 = $482. 20% of $6,431 = $1,286 x .25 = $322. $482 + $322 = $804.

[100] 50% of $6,994 = $3,497 x .20 = $699. 20% of $6,994 = $1,399 x .25 = $350. $699 + $350 = $1,045.

[101] 50% of $7,588 = $3,794 x .20 = $759. 20% of $7,588 = $1,518 x .25 = $379. $759 + $379 = $1,138.

[102] 50% of $8,232 = $4,116 x .20 = $823. 20% of $8,232 = $1,646 x .25 = $412. $823 + $412 = $1,235.

[103] 50% of $8,933 = $4,467 x .20 = $893. 20% of $8,933 = $1,787 x .25 = $447. $893 + $447 = $1,340.

[104] 50% of $9,692 = $4,846 x .20 = $969. 20% of $9,692 = $1,938 x .25 = $485. $969 + $485 = $1,454.

[105] 50% of $10,516 = $5,258 x .20 = $1,052. 20% of $10,516 = $2,103 x .25 = $525. $1,052 + $525 = $1,578.

[106] 50% of $11,409 = $5,705 x .20 = $1,141. 20% of $11,409 = $2,282 x .25 = $570. $1,141 + $570 = $1,711.

[107] 50% of $12,379 = $6,190 x .20 = $1,238. 20% of $12,379 = $2,476 x .25 = $619. $1,238 + $619 = $1,857.

[108] $29,330 x .20 = $5,866.

[109] $134,314 - $5,866 = $128,448.

§2517. THE VARIABLE ANNUITY INVESTMENT

If Mike and Mindy elect to purchase a variable annuity with their $50,000, it will grow tax-deferred to $156,921 over the next twelve years.[110] Of this amount, $106,921 is gain.[111] If all of this gain is taxed at rates between 25% and 28%, the variable annuity investment will have an after-tax value of $128,973[112] or $525 more than the mutual fund investment discussed above.[113]

Investors like Mike and Mindy may conclude that the potential after-tax return on a mutual fund investment or a variable annuity investment are so close that it would not really make a difference which investment vehicle they choose. This conclusion over looks several things. Among them are:

- A mutual fund investment would be subject to all of the problems listed at the beginning of this chapter;
- Mutual funds can force income on investors even if they do not want it;
- Mutual funds can generate income taxes even when they are losing value;
- In the case study involving Mike and Mindy, it was assumed that they would not trade in their mutual fund account or rebalance their funds. When this is done, income taxes and additional costs may arise. Intra-variable annuity trading and rebalancing is available on a no cost basis with variable annuities.
- Investors rarely cash out of mutual funds or variable annuities and pay taxes at the highest possible rate. Systematic withdrawals are more common. Such withdrawal would reduce the variable annuity's tax liability but not necessarily the mutual fund's.

Based on these considerations, Mike and Mindy might be better off with a variable annuity.

§2518. ALL COSTS CONSIDERED

The material discussed in this chapter examined only the impact of capital gains taxes for mutual funds as compared to ordinary income taxes for variable annuities. Hopefully, this report demonstrated that due to tax deferral, the after-tax returns for variable annuities will frequently be greater than those of mutual funds even where mutual funds receive the advantage of lower capital gains rates. The reason for this is that the tax deferral available to variable annuity investors will, over time, overcome the long-term capital gains income tax rates available to mutual fund investors.

Both mutual funds and variable annuities have costs associated with them other than income taxes. For example, A-share mutual funds charge up-front commissions whereas

---

[110] $50,000 x 12 years x 10% = $156,921.

[111] $156,921 (note 110) - $50,000 = $106,921.

[112] $131,450 is in the 25% marginal tax bracket - $65,100 taxable income plus $66,350 of variable annuity gain. $66,350 x 25% = $16,587. $40,571 of variable annuity gain taxed at 28% = $11,360. $16,588 + $11,360 = $27,948. $156,921 (note 110) - $27,948 = $128,973.

[113] $128,973 (note 112) - $128,448 (note 109) = $525.

variable annuities do not. Both mutual funds and variable annuities have trading costs associated with their ownership. The trading cost for mutual funds is slightly higher than for variable annuities. Both mutual funds and variable annuities have annual ownership costs. These costs are usually slightly higher for a variable annuity than a mutual fund. When these three non-tax costs are totaled, they come to approximately 3.2% a year for a typical mutual fund[114] and 2.85% for an average variable annuity.[115] If these additional non-tax costs are factored into any of the three hypothetical case studies discussed above, the variable annuity will produce an even larger return than the mutual fund because the tax deferral of the variable annuity already results in the variable annuity outperforming the mutual fund when only tax-related costs are compared.

§2519. QUESTIONS TO ASK

If mutual fund owners take money out of their pocket each year to pay income taxes, shouldn't variable annuity owners be able to invest this same amount each year in a side investment because their variable annuities are tax deferred?

§2520. SOURCES

- See the footnotes to this chapter for sources to consult regarding the variable annuities tax deferral advantage.
- See "Get Going" column by Jonathan Clements in *The Wall Street Journal* for February 20, 2008, p. D1 for a discussion of tax deferral.

§2521. REVIEW QUESTIONS

Explain the concept of opportunity cost as it applies to annual mutual fund taxation and the tax deferral provided by variable annuities.

§2522. CONCLUSION

The purpose of this chapter was to demonstrate that when *all* income tax factors, including the benefit of tax deferral are considered, the variable annuity often proves to be a better investment than a mutual fund. This result occurs frequently even though mutual funds may qualify for 15% long-term capital gains income tax rates while variable annuity gains are taxed as ordinary income. It must be remembered that tax deferral has two aspects. First, a tax-deferred investment compounds without having to adjust the compounding for income taxes. Second, money that would be used to pay income taxes on a taxable investment is available to create a second investment account. Both aspects of tax deferral must be factored into any comparison of mutual funds and variable annuities. Any investor considering an investment in a mutual fund or variable annuity would be well advised to factor in both aspects of the tax deferral benefit provided by variable annuities before finalizing their investment decision.

---

[114] *The Great Mutual Fund Trap*, Gary Gensler (Former Undersecretary of the U.S. Treasury 1999-2001) and Gregory Baer (Former Assistant Secretary for Financial Institutions for the U.S. Treasury) Broadway Books, New York, 2002. This 3.2% figure includes commissions (1%), annual expense ratio (1.5%) and trading costs (0.7%).

[115] This 2.85% figure includes money management fees (1%), M&E fees (1.35%) and trading costs (0.5%).

– CHAPTER 26 –

THE DUPLICATION OF TAX DEFERRAL MYTH – SUMMARY DISCUSSION

§2601. INTRODUCTION

Many investors, the media and even a few financial advisors believe that variable annuities should not be placed in qualified accounts or funded with qualified money. The rationale for this belief lies in the mistaken belief that variable annuity issuers charge a fee to investor for the tax deferral provided by the variable annuities they issue. This is not true.

§2602. HISTORY OF THE MYTH

Several years ago the National Association of Security Dealers (NASD), the self-regulatory body for professionals in the securities business (now FINRA), indicated their concern that some dishonest financial advisors were recommending tax-deferred variable annuities to clients for their qualified accounts based on the fact that variable annuities offered tax deferral. It was not disclosed that all qualified accounts receive tax-deferral. Many broker-dealers and their compliance departments misinterpreted NASD's concern. They believed that NASD was prohibiting the sale of variable annuities in all cases where they were to be placed in qualified accounts or if they would be purchased with qualified money.

It has taken several years for the securities industry to realize that NASD was only concerned with the sale of variable annuities where the *sole* reason for recommending them to potential purchasers with qualified accounts was the tax deferral benefit offered by the variable annuity.

§2603. CHAIRMAN OF THE FEDERAL RESERVE

In the July 26, 2006 issue of *The Wall Street Journal*, it was reported that Ben Bernanke, the Chairman of the Federal Reserve, held over half of his investable assets in variable annuities and that *all* of these variable annuities were held in qualified accounts.

§2604. VARIABLE ANNUITIES AND QUALIFIED ACCOUNTS

Nearly two-thirds of all variable annuities owned today are in qualified accounts. The largest issuer of variable annuities in the United States (TIAA-CREF) places nearly 100% of the variable annuities it sells inside of qualified accounts.

§2605. NASD NOTICE TO MEMBERS 99-35

In 1999, NASD issued Notice to Members 99-35 (NTM 99-35) to clarify those situations where variable annuity sales were appropriate or inappropriate if such sales were directed at potential buyers with qualified accounts. This Notice should be obtained from the Financial Industry Regulatory Authority (FINRA) and read by all financial professionals who sell variable annuities.

§2606. CONCLUSION

Variable annuities may be sold to potential buyers who will place these variable annuities in their qualified plans or purchase them with qualified money if there are appropriate reasons for doing so. Recommending that a variable annuity be placed inside a qualified account or purchased with qualified money based *solely* on the variable annuity tax deferral benefit is fraud. Chapter 27 discusses the duplication of tax deferral myth in detail.

– CHAPTER 27 –

THE DUPLICATION OF TAX DEFERRAL MYTH – DETAILED DISCUSSION

§2701.INTRODUCTION

Over the past two decades, 401(k)s, 403(b)s, IRAs and similar qualified plans and retirement accounts have proliferated. Today, many individuals prepare for retirement by funding one or more of these income tax-deferred retirement vehicles.[1] Recently, articles have appeared in the financial press questioning the practice of selling variable annuities as investments for qualified plans.[2] Those who have challenged the appropriateness of this common transaction attempt to support their position by arguing that:

1. Both variable annuities and qualified plans are income tax-deferred investments. Because tax deferral is duplicated when variable annuities are sold as investments for qualified plans, such transactions are inappropriate;

2. The cost of variable annuities is higher than that of other qualified plan investments. In the long run, these higher costs will reduce overall performance when variable annuities are held in qualified plans; and

3. Regulatory guidelines and rules indicate that the selling of variable annuities as investments for qualified plans is improper.

None of these arguments, when examined closely, have any merit. Each is discussed below.

§2702. THE DUPLICATION ARGUMENT

Proponents of the duplication argument claim that placing a variable annuity inside a qualified plan duplicates the benefit of income tax deferral provided by the qualified plan and therefore such a transaction is improper because the purchaser receives no benefit from it. The duplication argument would have validity only where a variable annuity offered income tax deferral as its *sole* benefit. The problem with this is that anyone with a basic understanding of investing knows that variable annuities offer buyers many benefits other than tax deferral.

The duplication argument is usually made by journalists and commentators who misstate or offer no support for this argument. For example, the author of an article appearing in *The Wall Street Journal,* after making the duplication argument, stated that variable annuity companies charged a premium for the tax deferral offered with their variable annuities.[3] This statement is incorrect. The tax-deferred status afforded to variable annuity owners is not a benefit created by the companies that issue variable annuities, but is the result of congressional mandate. By law, Congress declared decades ago that variable annuities may grow on an income tax-deferred

---

[1] Under recently passed tax legislation, IRAs, SEPs, 401(k)s and 403(b)s are all easily transferrable and interchangeable.

[2] In this article, the term qualified plan will be used generically to refer to all income tax-deferred qualified plans and retirement accounts including 401(k)s, 403(b)s, IRAs, SEPs, etc. Because qualified plans are generally funded for retirement purposes, it will be assumed that all investments are long-term and will remain in place until the owner is at least 59½ years old.

[3] *The Wall Street Journal,* annuities watch column by David Frenecki, July 20, 1998, p. C-20.

basis. No insurance company issuing variable annuities has ever charged anything for the income tax deferral provided by variable annuities.

If purchasing a variable annuity for a qualified plan results in duplicating the benefit of income tax deferral and such duplication costs nothing, it defies logic to claim that the buyer of a variable annuity has somehow been harmed if the annuity provides some benefit the buyer is seeking other than income tax deferral. The defective nature of the duplication argument can easily be demonstrated by applying it to other everyday financial transactions. The following two examples are illustrative:

Example 1

John went to a local building supply store to buy a chainsaw. At the check-out counter the cashier informed John that his purchase entitled him to receive a free pair of safety goggles. John informed the cashier that he had several pairs of safety goggles and did not need another pair. If the argument that a sales transaction is improper if the seller, without cost, duplicates a benefit a buyer already has were meritorious, the building supply store would be acting in an improper manner by attempting to sell a product (chainsaw) to a customer while duplicating a benefit the customer already had (safety glasses). This would be true even if the duplication were cost-free.

Example 2

Sally has a radio in her bedroom and has decided to purchase a newer model. Anyone who owns a radio may use the radio airwaves without cost. Every time one purchases a radio, they receive the benefit of free access to these airwaves. The proponents of the duplicity argument would claim that any department store selling a radio to Sally would be acting improperly because such a sale would duplicate, without cost, an existing benefit already enjoyed by Sally.

In both of the above examples the building supply store and department store provide new products to customers that, if purchased, would duplicate benefits their customers already enjoyed. If the building supply store and department store do not charge customers for the safety goggles they provide or allowing customers to use radio airwaves, any argument that their selling practices could somehow be construed as improper is baseless.

The two examples discussed above involved a duplicated benefit for which, like the tax deferral available with variable annuities, the buyer is charged nothing. Many financial transactions today involve the sale of goods or services where a duplicated benefit is provided to a buyer for an additional charge. In many of these cases, the additional expense of the duplicated benefit can increase the cost of the underlying goods or services by 20% or more. The following example demonstrates this situation:

Example 3

Judy recently rented an automobile at the airport. The rental fee was $39.00 a day. The rental agent suggested that Judy purchase insurance to protect her if she had an accident. Judy purchased the insurance which increased the cost of renting the automobile to $47.00. Judy did not realize that the insurance she purchased duplicated her own automobile insurance. In order for the rental car insurance to pay off, Judy would have to be in an accident that was her fault and would have to *fully* exhaust her personal automobile insurance. Not only has the rental agency duplicated a benefit Judy already had (i.e. auto insurance coverage) but they charged for it knowing that the likelihood the rental agency's policy would ever pay off was remote at best.

The three examples discussed above, although laughable, are no different than the position taken by the proponents of the duplication argument regarding the sale of variable annuities as investments for qualified plans. In short, where a variable annuity provides some benefit sought by a qualified plan owner other than income tax deferral, the duplication argument becomes irrelevant. The following examples demonstrate this:

Example 1

Dave has $100,000 in a SEP (Self Employed Plan) that currently provides him with income tax deferral.[4] Dave lives in a state where SEPs are not protected from creditors although variable annuities are. As a young physician, Dave is concerned about lawsuits and the possibility that his SEPs could be taken by potential judgment creditors. Dave's financial professional suggested that Dave transfer his SEP to a variable annuity to obtain creditor protection. Dave followed this advice even though the variable annuity, without any cost, duplicated the income tax deferral provided by his SEP. Could anyone seriously argue that the recommendation made by the financial professional was somehow improper or unethical? Certainly not.

Example 2

Fred has a $100,000 IRA sitting in a bank CD earning 4%. He needs to get a better rate of return before he retires in ten years but does not want any additional risk. Fred has found a variable annuity that will let him invest in the equities market for ten years and have the opportunity to receive a long-term market rate of return. The annuity company also provides for a small fee, a rider that will return 100% of Fred's $100,000 investment if his account is worth less than $100,000 ten years from now. The availability of this rider would be an excellent reason for Fred to purchase the variable annuity with the funds in his IRA account.

In summary, the decision to include a variable annuity in a qualified plan should not be discounted simply because the benefit of income tax deferral is duplicated without cost by purchasing the variable annuity. The important issue is whether the variable annuity provides a qualified plan owner with some other benefit desired by the plan owner.

§2703. THE HIGHER COST ARGUMENT

Those who question the propriety of placing variable annuities in qualified plans frequently attempt to support this position by claiming that variable annuities are more expensive

---

[4] The principal and income in a SEP grow income tax deferred.

to own than other investments typically held in qualified plans. Making such an argument demonstrates a basic lack of knowledge regarding financial principles. Merely because two products sell for different prices does not necessarily mean the less expensive product is a better buy. In comparing products with different prices one must always take into consideration any additional benefits or value provided by the more expensive product or lacking with the less expensive product. If this were not true, it would be inappropriate for a stockbroker to recommend IBM stock to a client if the broker knew Fly-By-Night Computer stock was available for a lower price. It would be also be improper for a real estate broker to sell a young couple a three bedroom house knowing that a large tent would be a cheaper housing alternative. Following this flawed logic, the local Mercedes dealer would have his morals questioned if he sold a Mercedes to a customer knowing full well that used Ford pick-up trucks could be purchased for much less. As silly as these examples seem, they mirror the position taken by the proponents of the higher cost argument.

When qualified accounts containing variable annuities are compared with qualified accounts containing mutual funds on an annual cost basis it is rarely mentioned that variable annuities often provide valuable additional benefits to their owners that are not available with other investments. The decision to buy a Mercedes or a Honda, a Rolex or Timex, a first class airline ticket or coach ticket is made everyday by consumers. In many cases the more expensive item or service is purchased. This is done because the buyer is receiving some additional value or benefit not provided by the less costly alternative. If a variable annuity provides guarantees, reduces investment risks, adds certainty or offers other benefits not available with less expensive investments, investors should have the economic freedom to decide for themselves whether they want to purchase these benefits.

Example
Gina has $300,000 in an inherited IRA. She, as a recent widow, cannot afford to expose the IRA to risk. She needs to know that her IRA will produce a nest egg of at least $600,000 in the next ten years from which Gina can draw income. The only investment that can provide such a guarantee is a variable annuity with a guaranteed minimum income benefit (GMIB) rider. If Gina uses her $300,000 IRA to purchase such a variable annuity she will be guaranteed a lifetime stream of income from $600,000 under a *worst* case scenario. If the stock market increases her account value to more than $600,000, she can walk away with the larger account value less her costs of investing. No other investment will provide such a guaranteed benefit.

The biggest flaw with the higher cost argument is the incorrect assumption that variable annuities are more expensive to own than other qualified investments such as mutual funds. For example, current research and data from several sources indicates that the average annual cost of owning the typical variable annuity in a qualified account is approximately 2.9%. This 2.9%

figure includes the fees paid to money managers, commissions, trading costs and insurance costs.[5] The average annual cost of owning an A-share mutual fund held in a qualified retirement account is approximately 3.23%. This 3.23% is made up of annual expense, 12b-1 fees, commissions and trading costs.[6] Simply stated, the annual cost of owning the average stock mutual fund held in a qualified retirement account is 33 basis points more expensive to own on an annual basis than a similar variable annuity held in a qualified retirement account. The table below sets these costs out:

ANNUAL COST COMPARISON: AVERAGE A-SHARE EQUITY MUTUAL FUND HELD IN A QUALIFIED ACCOUNT VS. A VARIABLE ANNUITY HELD IN A QUALIFIED ACCOUNT (A 10% GROSS RATE OF RETURN ON A $10,000 INVESTMENT IS ASSUMED)

COST	AVERAGE MUTUAL FUND	AVERAGE VARIABLE ANNUITY
Management and 12b-1 fees[7]	1.50%	0.90%
Mortality and Expense[8]	0.00%	1.30%
Trading Costs[9]	0.70%	0.50%
Commissions[10]	0.83%	0
Misc. Expenses[11]	0.20%	0.20%
Total (Non-taxable Account)	3.23%	2.90%

---

[5] Lipper Analytical.

[6] Baer and Gunsler, *The Great Mutual Fund Trap.*

[7] Mutual funds and variable annuities charge fees to cover the cost of paying their investment managers. Mutual funds and variable annuities also charge 12b-1 fees and administrative fees to help pay for marketing and advertising costs. The average A-share mutual fund charges 1.5% to mutual fund owners to cover investment management and 12b-1 fees. The average variable annuity charges a fee of 0.90% to cover these two expenses.

[8] Mortality and expenses (M&E) fees are charged by variable annuity issuers but not mutual fund companies. This fee is designed to pay for the insurance that guarantees that beneficiaries of a variable annuity never receive less than the net investment made in the variable annuity by the owner when the owner was alive. M&E fees are also used to offset the compensation advanced by variable annuity companies to the financial professionals who sell their variable annuity to investors. M&E fees average 1.3% for the average variable annuity.

[9] Trading costs are the expenses incurred by both mutual fund and variable annuity companies when they buy stock from brokerage firms. Because variable annuity companies tend to trade slightly less than mutual fund companies, their trading costs are approximately 30% less than those of mutual fund companies. The average trading cost for a mutual fund is 0.7%. For the variable annuity it is 0.5%.

[10] Commission figures should be *annualized*. The average A-share mutual fund commission is 4.1% and the average holding period of a mutual fund is 3.3 years. Thus, the average *annualized* commission would be 1.25%. A conservative annual commission of 1% is assumed. If a 5% commission is charged and a fund will be held 6 years, the annualized commission would be .83%. (The figure used in this Table). If B-share funds are sold, the out-of-pocket commission for the buyer is zero but the annual expense ratio increases from 1.5% to approximately 2.4%. Because out-of-pocket commissions are not paid by variable annuity purchasers, this figure is zero.

[11] Both mutual funds and variable annuities charge various administrative fees (i.e. redemption fees, maintenance fees, etc.) Where such fees are charged, they should be taken into consideration as part of the overall cost of owning either investment. The above table assumes both the mutual fund and variable annuity charge a miscellaneous fee of $20 a year on average account balances of $10,000.

Retirement funds held in qualified plans such as 401(k)s may have costs associated with them that may not be fully disclosed. It is no secret that 401(k)s are expensive to set up and maintain. Someone has to bear this expense. Many qualified plan participants believe that their employers absorb these costs. This is not always the case. Employers commonly shift these expenses to their employees.[12] The improper transfer of 401(k) expenses from employers to employees has not gone unnoticed. In the past, the U.S. Labor Department has filed dozens of suits against employers involved in such activities.[13] Studies indicate that qualified plan participants may be paying additional administration, trustee and bookkeeping fees of up to 2.5% a year to maintain their 401(k)s.[14]

If a retired 401(k) participant is paying as little as 1% of the expense of maintaining his 401(k), this cost when added to the other costs of owning mutual funds in the account results in a total cost that can easily exceed that of the variable annuity. The purchase of $25,000 in stock held in an IRA can generate a commission of $350. The sale of the stock can also result in a similar commission. Commissions of $700 paid in a one-year period on a $25,000 stock purchase and sale is equivalent to a 2.8% annual commission. If these buy and sell transactions include repurchase commissions for new stock, total annualized commission costs for such transactions can exceed 4%.

In short, the true cost of owning a variable annuity in a qualified plan in many cases may be *less* than owning similar investments in these plans. Even in those cases where the cost of owning a variable annuity in a qualified plan is slightly higher than the cost of owning other investments, the many benefits offered by the variable annuity may be, for many plan participants, well worth the additional cost. The following material discusses several of the advantages of owning variable annuities in qualified plans that may be worth a slightly higher cost.

§2704. THE DEATH BENEFIT

Variable annuities provide a death benefit that guarantees the owner that regardless of what happens to the value of the underlying investments held in his annuity, should he die, his beneficiaries will receive the greater of the market value of the annuity at his death or the net value of the contributions paid into the annuity.[15]

---

[12] "The Hidden Foes in the 401(k)" by Darrell Preston, *Bloomberg Markets*, March 2001, p. 96-103 and "Workers Pick Up 401(k) Charges", *USA Today*, Monday, October 30, 2000, p. 1B.

[13] "The Hidden Foes in the 401(k)" by Darrell Preston, *Bloomberg Markets*, March 2001, p. 96-103 and "Feds Crack Down on 401(k) Fees that Aren't Legit", *USA Today*, December 5, 1999, Page 1B.

[14] *Id.*

[15] During the last bear market (2001-2003), the variable annuity industry paid out more than $2.8 billion in death benefits as a result of the recent bear market. National Underwriter, *Life and Health*, October 4, 2004, p.7.

Example

Several years ago, Dave went to work for an employer who offered a 401(k).
Dave chose to purchase mutual funds offered through his 401(k). The funds
have been in Dave's 401(k) for 20 years and have increased in value to $500,000.
Dave is now 66 and his health is not good. He retired last year and initially left
his 401(k) with his employer. Dave wants his wife be financially secure should
he die. Based on the advice of his financial planner, Dave liquidated the mutual
funds in his 401(k) and transferred the balance to an insurance company to
purchase a variable annuity. The annuity had more investments to choose from
and many of the investments had better performance records than Dave's prior
401(k) plan. More importantly, if a stock market correction were to occur and
the value of Dave's variable annuity were to drop, for example, from $500,000 to
$300,000, Dave's wife would, if Dave were to die, receive a minimum of $500,000
due to the death benefit provided by the variable annuity. On the same facts,
had Dave elected to keep his 401(k), at his death his wife would only receive the
$300,000 reduced value of the 401(k). The reason for this is that investments,
other than variable annuities, held in qualified plans do not provide a death
benefit. By owning a variable annuity as his retirement vehicle, Dave is able to
provide an extra measure of financial security for his wife.

In recent years, the death benefit offered by variable annuity companies has been greatly
improved. Several annuity issuers now pay a death benefit equal to the highest value that the
annuity reaches before the owner's death. Other annuity issuers provide death benefits that will
automatically adjust or ratchet upward (but never downward) every few years. For example,
a variable annuity might increase the owner's death benefit to match the annuity's increased
account value every three years. This could be a significant benefit, especially in light of the
fact that the death benefit is provided by variable annuity issuers to purchasers without the
requirement of a physical examination or having to prove insurability. Other annuity issuers
allow a variable annuity owner to purchase a death benefit that is guaranteed to increase in value
each year at a set rate. For example, a variable annuity issuer might increase an annuity owner's
death benefit by five to seven percentage points a year. This benefit ensures that the owner's
beneficiaries will always receive proceeds that will exceed contributions made by the annuity
owner.

Example

Jane, who is 70 years old and in poor health, has an IRA containing $510,000.
Her IRA is held in a long-term bank CD paying 4%. She has other assets to live
on and plans on leaving her IRA to her grandchildren. At the recommendation
of her financial planner, Jane purchased a variable annuity that provided a death
benefit that compounds at 7% a year. For the small additional cost of owning
such an annuity, Jane can ensure that she can pass an increasing benefit to her
grandchildren. For example, if Jane dies at age 80 her grandchildren will receive,
at a minimum, more than one million dollars as a death benefit from the variable

annuity she purchased for $510,000. In addition, Jane has the opportunity to invest more aggressively because her death benefit protects her beneficiaries against loss. If Jane's investments do well it is possible that her grandchildren could receive an amount that could easily exceed the million dollar death benefit mentioned above. Under no circumstances would the grandchildren receive less than $510,000 increased by 7% each year until Jane's death.

The death benefit offered by variable annuities is not offered by any other type of investment that can be held in a qualified plan. This benefit, as the next example demonstrates, is so significant that a case for professional malpractice could be made if a financial professional failed to suggest a variable annuity for qualified funds in certain cases.

Example

Ed has had a 401(k) for several years. He has been a conservative investor over the years and his 401(k) now contains $500,000. Ed is 67 years old and retired. He just learned that he has cancer and has a reduced life expectancy. Although the stock market has been extremely volatile lately, Ed feels he must be more aggressive with his 401(k) in order to hopefully leave more than $500,000 to his family. Ed sought the advice of a financial advisor who suggested to Ed that he consider using his 401(k) proceeds to purchase more aggressive mutual funds within a new IRA. Ed asked about the death benefit provided by variable annuities but his advisor warned him not to buy a variable annuity with his 401(k) money because the benefit of tax deferral would be duplicated. Ed followed his advisor's advice. Shortly thereafter, the stock market corrected sharply and Ed's new mutual fund IRA dropped in value to $350,000. Ed died a few months later. Ed's family received the $350,000 held in the IRA. Had the advisor transferred Ed's 401(k) to a variable annuity offering aggressive sub-accounts, Ed would have been placed in a win-win situation. Had the variable annuity gone up in value, his family would have received all of the gain. Had the market gone down, as it did in this case, his family would have received, *at a minimum*, the $500,000 placed in the variable annuity together with all additional contributions less withdrawals. The advisor's failure to assist Ed in purchasing a variable annuity with his 401(k) proceeds, on these facts, could constitute professional negligence. Without a physical exam, Ed would also have been eligible to purchase a rider that would have increased the value of his variable annuity by 5% to 7% a year until his death. The National Association of Securities Dealers has held that the death benefit offered by variable annuities may be an appropriate reason for placing a variable annuity inside of a qualified plan.[16]

Variable annuities not only provide a basic and increasing death benefit for senior investors, but they also provide a way for such investors to increase their death benefit without any additional cost. This benefit is available to senior investors because variable annuity owners, unlike mutual fund owners, may take advantage of IRC §1035 which allows the tax-

---

[16] NASD Notice to Members 99-35. (Available at www.nasdr.org. Also attached to the end of this report)

free exchange of one variable annuity for another. The appropriate use of this IRS Code section can result in beneficiaries receiving more from a decedent who owned a variable annuity than a mutual fund. The following example demonstrates this:

Example

Steve, a widower, purchased a variable annuity for $350,000 when he was 60. Steve is now 70 and in poor health. Steve wants his daughter to inherit his variable annuity. When his annuity increased in value to $700,000 two years ago, Steve's financial advisor suggested that Steve take advantage of IRC §1035 and transfer his variable annuity to another similar variable annuity. This could be accomplished without costs or income taxes. The benefit of the transfer would be that Steve's original death benefit of $300,000 provided by his first annuity would increase to $700,000 with the new variable annuity. This would guarantee that Steve's daughter would never receive less than $700,000 at Steve's death. Steve followed his advisor's suggestion. When Steve died, his variable annuity had decreased in value to $500,000, yet Steve's daughter received a check from the annuity company for $700,000. The fact that using IRC §1035 to increase a death benefit may impose a new surrender period on the owner of the variable annuity is a moot issue if the owner intends to pass the variable annuity to his beneficiaries at this death because surrender charges cease at one's death.

§2705. INCOME TAX REDUCTION

As a general rule, qualified plans are subject to ordinary income taxes in the hands of beneficiaries following the death of the plan owner. One of the major benefits of having a qualified plan held in a variable annuity is the opportunity to reduce or eliminate the income tax burden facing beneficiaries who inherit qualified plans. Of all the investment vehicles available to qualified plan owners only the variable annuity provides a rider for reducing or eliminating income taxes on inherited qualified plans. This rider is most commonly referred to as an earnings enhancement benefit or EEB. Variable annuities offering the EEB rider charge a fee to provide additional cash at the owner's death to help beneficiaries of an annuity to reduce or fully pay all income taxes associated with the inherited annuity.

Example

Judy, who is 55, had a IRA containing $100,000. She recently retired early due to poor health. The IRA was not performing well and Judy transferred it to a brokerage firm. Judy earmarked the IRA for her children because she had other assets to cover her retirement needs. Judy's total estate was worth less than $2,000,000. Judy invested her money in growth mutual funds. At age 65 Judy died. Her IRA was worth $350,000 at her death. Her four children inherited the IRA and each paid 20% in income taxes (i.e. $17,500) on their $87,500 share of the IRA's value, netting each child $70,000.

Example

John, age 55, had an IRA containing $100,000. He recently retired early due to poor health. The IRA was not performing well and John transferred it to a variable annuity company. John earmarked the IRA for his children because he had other assets to cover his retirement needs. John's total estate was worth less than $2,000,000. John purchased a variable annuity that invested in growth oriented investments. The variable annuity contained an EEB rider that provided, at John's death, that 40% of any growth in his variable annuity would be added to the annuity's value to help beneficiaries defray income taxes. This benefit was capped at $100,000. At age 65 John died. His IRA was worth $350,000 at his death. The EEB rider added $100,000 (40% of $250,000 in growth) to the value of the annuity. John's four children each received $112,500 and paid 25% income tax on this amount, netting each child $84,375 or $14,375 more than Judy's children received on identical facts in the previous example.

§2706. PLAN TRANSFER COSTS

Transferring (i.e. rolling over) one qualified plan to another plan is a common transaction today. One of the drawbacks of such transfers is cost. In many cases, when a qualified plan is transferred it frequently must be liquidated for cash. The cash is then transferred to the new plan. The reinvestment of these cash proceeds can often involve the payment of commissions and related expenses. Reinvestment costs do not occur when qualified plans are transferred to variable annuities. All of a participant's plan balance that is transferred to a variable annuity is fully invested and working for the participant from the date of the transfer.

Example

Andy had an IRA containing $300,000 that was not performing well. He transferred it to a local brokerage firm and set up a new IRA. Andy invested the $300,000 by placing half in stocks and half in mutual funds. The commission for funding the IRA with new investments was $9,000. Only $291,000 of Andy's money went into investments. Had Andy transferred his IRA to a variable annuity, his entire $300,000 would have been invested and working for him.

It could be argued that proceeds from the liquidation of a qualified plan could be reinvested in an IRA offering B-share mutual funds, thus providing the same advantage as investing in a variable annuity. This argument is defective for two reasons:

1. B-share mutual funds may not be appropriate for an investor with a $300,000 portfolio. Any financial professional working with Andy would most likely point out that an A-share commission (i.e. front end load) would be more cost efficient; and

2. Many investors who own IRAs, SEPs, etc., outside of variable annuities buy investments other than B-share mutual funds for their qualified plan (i.e. stocks and bonds) that generate commissions when these investments are bought and sold.

§2707. PREMIUM BONUS BENEFIT

Many annuity companies pay premium bonuses of as much as 5% when their annuities are purchased. Some annuity companies charge a fee to provide such a bonus and others charge nothing. In some cases the cost of such bonuses are often recouped by reducing the commission paid to the financial professional selling the variable annuity.[17] Those companies that charge nothing for bonuses usually require that the annuity be held for between seven and ten years to obtain the full benefit of the bonus. For people funding qualified plans, such holding periods are usually not a concern. The benefit of a bonus is demonstrated in the following examples:

Example

Larry had a poorly performing 403(b) that contained $500,000. He decided to transfer his 403(b) to a variable annuity company. Larry's $500,000 deposit was increased by $25,000 due to a 5% bonus paid by the annuity company. Larry's $525,000 was invested in good quality sub-accounts within the variable annuity. Ten years later, Larry's annuity tripled in value to $1,575,000.

Example

Linda had a poorly performing 403(b) that contained $500,000. She transferred the $500,000 balance to a brokerage firm, her $500,000 was reinvested in five good quality mutual funds to obtain diversification. The brokerage firm charged an average A-share commission of 2% on these funds for a total of $10,000. Ten years later Linda's $490,000 net plan balance tripled in value to $1,470,000. This is $105,500 less than Larry received in the previous example. Larry's out-performance was due primarily to receiving a bonus when he purchased his annuity.

§2708. AVAILABILITY OF FIXED RATE INVESTMENTS

401(k)s, 403(b)s and similar qualified plans rarely, if ever, provide investments that guarantee a fixed rate of interest over a long period of time. Frequently, they do offer money market accounts. However, these accounts do not offer a fixed interest rate, but rates that vary according to market conditions. On the other hand, most variable annuities offer investors account options that provide long-term guaranteed rates of return. In some situations, a long-term guaranteed rate of return can be of importance to a qualified plan participant.

Example

Jan, who is 58 years old and single, plans to retire in seven years. She has $666,000 in her 403(b). Jan has determined that to have the type of retirement she has planned, her 403(b) must grow to at least $1,000,000 by the time she retires. None of the investments available to Jan in her 403(b) will guarantee the return Jan needs to reach her retirement goal. Jan, following the advice of her financial advisor, transferred her 403(b) balance to a variable annuity. One of the investment choices available to Jan in the variable annuity was a fixed account offering a 6% rate of return guaranteed for a seven year period. In seven years, the 6% compound return provided by the variable annuity will increase Jan's $666,000 qualified plan balance to just over $1,000,000.[18] In short, by transferring her 403(b) account to a variable annuity, Jan will be *assured* of meeting her retirement goal.

---

[17] In some cases the cost of a bonus may be paid for entirely by the variable annuity purchaser through higher fees or longer holding periods. The cost of any bonus should be examined before opting to elect the bonus.

[18] $666,000 x 7 years x 6% = $1,001,418. It is important to understand that the 4.0% return guaranteed to Jan is a net return. Whether or not additional costs are imposed for owning her variable annuity is immaterial because Jan is guaranteed the 6.0% return she needs.

§2709. TAX SAVINGS AT DEATH

Owning variable annuities purchased with qualified money can provide dramatic estate and income tax savings not often available where other investments are used to hold qualified funds.

Example

Jack, aged 67, a widower, has an estate worth $3,000,000. One million dollars of his estate is a variable annuity purchased with IRA contributions and qualified account rollovers. The remainder of his estate consists of his house, car, etc. which is worth $2,000,000. If Jack dies in 2008, his estate taxes would be $450,000. Income taxes owed by his children (after any §691 deduction) could bring total taxes to $600,000. Jack wants to retire but needs at least $45,000 (after taxes) each year from his annuity to supplement his other retirement income. Jacks wants his entire $3,000,000 estate to pass to his three children without death or income taxes if possible. The solution for all of Jack's concerns can be resolved easily. Jack should have his children purchase (and own) a $1,000,000 life insurance policy on Jack. The premiums on this policy will be approximately $27,000 a year. After the policy is in place, Jack should convert his variable annuity to an immediate lifetime annuity (i.e., no guarantee other than lifetime payments). The immediate annuity will pay Jack approximately $90,000 a year for life. At 20%, income taxes will reduce this figure to $72,000. The after-tax annuity payment will be $72,000. Jack can give his children $27,000 each year to pay the premiums on the life insurance they purchased. (No gift taxes would be due because of the $12,000 annual exclusion). This leaves Jack with more than the $45,000 in income he needs each year. If Jack dies tomorrow, his estate will be worth $2,000,000 and will pass to his children estate tax free due to the current $2,000,000 exemption. The immediate annuity is valued at zero because it is a lifetime annuity that ceases to have any value at death. In addition, the children will receive $1,000,000 estate and income tax free from the insurance company. (Estate taxes are avoided because the insurance is not in Jack's estate. Insurance proceeds are not subject to income taxation.) In short, a combination of annuitization and asset adjustment eliminates all estate and income taxes for Jack's children. They will receive Jack's $3,000,000 estate. (Any unrecovered portion of the annuity premium (if non-qualified) can be treated as an income tax deduction on *Jack's* final income tax return).

In the above example, a combination of annuitization of an existing variable annuity coupled with the purchase of life insurance eliminated all estate taxes and beneficiary income taxes on Jack's three million dollar estate. Additionally, the benefit of a lifetime stream of income for Jack was preserved. If Jack held his IRA in any investment other than a variable annuity, he would not be able to obtain the same tax benefits as the variable annuity provided at the same cost. For example, had Jack kept his $1,000,000 IRA account invested in mutual funds, stocks or other investments, he could have sold these investments and used the proceeds to purchase life insurance and immediate annuity. However, there may be a cost associated with the sale of these investments. A brokerage commission of just 1% to sell a portfolio of stocks could cost $10,000 to obtain a tax benefit variable annuity ownership provided for nothing. Being able to pass a large estate to beneficiaries without a death or income tax burden together with additional savings in commissions may be a benefit that would make owning a variable annuity inside of a qualified plan an excellent financial decision. It is important to note that the variable annuity provides a death benefit while being held. No other IRA vehicle provides this benefit.

§2710. PRINCIPAL PROTECTION

Today, many variable annuities offer a guarantee against loss of invested principal. This benefit should not be confused with the *death* benefit variable annuities provide. The principal protection benefit is referred to as a *living* benefit because the annuity owner receives the benefit during his lifetime. There are several variations of living benefits. In order to obtain a living benefit, annuity owners are required to hold their annuities for a specified period. This period usually ranges from five to ten years. Such holding periods rarely present a problem for people funding qualified plans because such plans are usually long-term investments by their nature. Some annuity companies, but not all, require that the principal protection benefit be annuitized if a living benefit is elected. Like all living benefits provided by variable annuity issuers, the annual cost of such benefits can range from 20 to 70 basis points. Several variable annuity companies allow investors to purchase variable annuities that guarantee *at a minimum* that the investor can withdraw 100% of his principal over a period of time ranging form 8 to 14 years and still have a chance of receiving stock market gains. In some cases the issuing company will guarantee that after a certain period (usually 10 years) 100% of the investor's principal will be returned to him should the stock market decline while giving the investor all of the gain if the stock market goes up over time. The following example discusses this benefit:

Example
Dick is 53 years old and wants to retire at 60. He has $400,000 in his IRA and cannot afford to lose any of this money if he and his wife are to have the retirement they desire. Additionally, Dick also wants the chance to invest more aggressively in equities in hopes of increasing his $400,000 nest egg. Dick transferred his $400,000 IRA to an annuity company that provided a principal guarantee if the annuity owner held his annuity for seven years. There was a small charge made for this benefit. The annuity company does not require annuitization if the principal protection guarantee is elected. If the account moves up in value, Dick would be entitled to the gain less his normal costs of investing. Assume that just before Dick turns 60 that the stock market suffers a reversal and Dick's annuity is only worth $250,000. By opting for the principal protection benefit, Dick and his wife will receive $400,000. Had Dick placed his IRA in an unprotected equity investment, he and his wife would receive $250,000 rather than $400,000.[19]

---

[19] Investors need to discuss any living benefit they might be interested in owning with their financial professional. The cost must be compared to the benefit that will be received.

§2711. ELIMINATION OF ONGOING COMMISSIONS

When qualified plan owners want to change investments, they may be required to pay commissions or other similar costs. Variable annuities do not charge commissions when the annuity owner changes investments within the annuity. Once commissions are taken into consideration, the cost of owning a variable annuity within a qualified plan can frequently be less than owning other types of qualified plan investments.

Example

Jill has an IRA containing $300,000 with North Star Brokerage. The IRA is invested in several different stocks and mutual fund families. Jill's twin brother Jeff, has his IRA, worth $300,000, with Polar Star Insurance Company. Jeff's IRA is invested in a variable annuity. Jeff's IRA is equally divided among several sub-accounts made available to him through his annuity. Jill and Jeff actively trade investments within their IRAs. Jill incurs commissions of $3,000 a year due to the trading she conducts in her IRA. Jeff's trading activity is similar to Jill's, but he pays no commissions on his trades because his IRA is held in a variable annuity. Based on these facts, Jill could lose up to 1% of her IRA's value to commissions each year. This loss will cause Jill's IRA to underperform her brother's IRA over time. Some would argue that Jill could reduce her commission costs by purchasing B-share mutual funds. This argument is unpersuasive for the same two reasons mentioned in §2607.

Individuals who have IRAs, SEPs and similar qualified plans may find that the commissions they are paying may be more costly than they thought. Having a variable annuity hold IRAs, SEPs and similar qualified plans may prove to be a better economic choice.

§2712. ANNUITIZATION BENEFIT

Qualified money held in a variable annuity may be annuitized without cost. Annuitization provides a stream of income that cannot be outlived. Some argue that any investment held in any qualified plan can be transferred to an annuity company in exchange for an immediate annuity at any time. Although this is true, such transfers may not be cost-free.

Example

Ben is 60 and has held his SEP in a variable annuity for the past 30 years. The SEP is now worth $800,000. Ben has elected to annuitize the $800,000. This can be done without any cost. Had Ben, for example, held his SEP in a full-service brokerage firm he could face commissions that could easily reach into five figures in order to liquidate his brokerage account to obtain a guaranteed lifetime stream of income provided by a variable annuity without a commission charge.

In addition, when one buys a variable annuity, all contract expenses are fixed at the time of purchase. Additionally, mortality tables in effect at the time of purchase are used to forecast the lifetime payments that will be made upon future annuitization. For example, a variable annuity purchased just a few years ago might show the life expectancy of a 60-year old to be less than current mortality tables. Someone buying such a variable annuity could receive a larger annuity payment from such an annuity than someone the same age who liquidates mutual funds to buy a variable annuity today. The annuitization benefit and fixed contract expenses offered by variable annuities have been cited by industry regulators as appropriate reasons for placing a variable annuity in a qualified plan.[20]

§2713. GUARANTEED RATES OF GROWTH AND INCOME

Several annuity companies currently guarantee the amount invested in their annuity will grow by a specified rate. This rate is usually 6% to 7%. The guaranteed rate of growth benefit, when elected, is paid out as a lifetime annuity and is only available if the variable annuity purchased is held for a specified amount of time, usually ten years. For persons saving for retirement, such holding periods are usually of little concern. Most annuity companies charge an annual fee of from 30 to 50 basis points of an annuity's account value for this benefit.

Example

Ken, who is fifty-five, has $400,000 in an inactive 401(k) he had with his prior employer. He is currently self-employed. Ten years from now he plans to retire. Ken *must* have a nest egg that will provide at least $45,000 a year in income for his lifetime. Ken transferred his dormant 401(k) to a variable annuity that would *guarantee* that his $400,000 investment would, in a worst case scenario, provide an $800,000 nest egg in ten years that will provide a minimum lifetime stream of income for Ken in the amount of $45,000. Over this ten year holding period, Ken may invest in any or all of the sub-accounts offered by the variable annuity on a no cost basis. If, ten years from now, the value of Ken's account is only worth $250,000 due to a poorly performing stock market, he can elect to receive a lifetime income stream from his $800,000 annuity nest egg that will pay him $45,000 for life. Because of this living benefit, Ken can afford to invest more aggressively. If the stock market does well and Ken's account for example, grows to $1,000,000 in value ten years from now, Ken can opt to take the $1,000,000 in cash, transfer it to another qualified account or elect to annuitize any portion of this larger amount. If Ken places his 401(k) in stocks or mutual funds he will not be able to obtain a similar guaranteed benefit.

There are many other benefits offered to qualified plan owners by variable annuity issuers that may not be available in other types of qualified plans. Space limitations do not allow for a complete discussion of all of them. Three such benefits are set out below in summary form as examples:

1. Many variable annuities offer automatic dollar-cost averaging at no cost while paying above market rates of return on money awaiting investment. For those investors who prefer to dollar-cost average rather than make lump-sum investments, this benefit may be attractive.

2. Many variable annuities offer automatic asset rebalancing or reallocation at no cost. For investors who believe in asset allocation, this may prove to be a valuable benefit.

---

[20] See note 19 *supra*.

Automatic asset rebalancing or reallocation on a no-cost basis is rarely available with investments other than variable annuities.

3. Some states provide creditor protection for variable annuities. This same protection may not be available for certain qualified plans (IRAs, Roth IRAs, etc.). In such cases, creditor protection may be obtained by transferring qualified plan proceeds to a variable annuity.

Even if it is assumed that owning a variable annuity in a qualified plan is more expensive than owning other investments in such plans, the many exclusive benefits provided by the variable annuity may, for many investors, be well worth the additional cost of receiving these benefits. This same concept applies when one chooses to buy a house rather than rent an apartment. The house will cost more, but it provides more.

There are several situations where variable annuities offer benefits that may also be available with other investments. Just because a benefit is provided by both a variable annuity and another investment does not necessarily mean selecting the variable annuity for inclusion in a qualified plan would be an incorrect decision.

Example

Sara had a 403(b) that was performing poorly. She talked to two financial professionals who made similar suggestions. The first professional suggested Sara purchase a more aggressive portfolio of mutual funds in order to obtain better investment results. The second professional suggested Sara purchase a variable annuity offering a couple of aggressive sub-accounts that had a history of providing attractive returns. Just because good rates of return are common to both the mutual fund and variable annuity does not mean that Sara should ignore the variable annuity. She should look at costs, commissions, other benefits, etc. before making her decision.

§2714. THE IMPROPRIETY ARGUMENT

Just like the duplicity argument and the higher cost argument, the argument that there is some government regulation or ethical rule indicating that the sale of variable annuities for inclusion in qualified plans is improper is completely baseless. There is not a single state law, federal statute, government regulation or ethical mandate existing that comes close to supporting the impropriety argument. To the contrary, nearly all guidance dealing with this issue indicates that variable annuities may be considered as possible investments for those looking to invest qualified funds.

It is interesting to note that variable annuities were developed in 1952 *exclusively* for use in qualified plans for college professors.[21] Later, the use of variable annuities, with congressional approval, was expanded to allow their inclusion in other qualified plans. Variable annuities make up a large part of all the 403(b) plans in existence today. In addition, many 401(k) plans are

---

[21] "Why Use a Variable Annuity to Fund a Qualified Plan?" 1997 report issued by the National Association of Variable Annuities.

funded with variable annuities.[22] One of the country's largest financial institutions has a variable annuity designed *exclusively* to attract qualified funds.[23]

The most important document existing today dealing specifically with the topic of selling variable annuities as investments for qualified plans is NASD Notice to Members 99-35 (available at www.nasdr.org or see attachment). Nowhere in this notice is there language that blanketly prohibits the sale of variable annuities as investments for qualified plans. Notice to Members 99-35 is a comprehensive guide designed to help registered representatives comply with four important responsibilities that have existed for many years. They are:

1. A registered representative should never sell a variable annuity to a client based *solely* on the variable annuity's tax-deferred status if the variable annuity will be held in a qualified plan such as a 401(k), IRA, etc.

2. If a registered representative recommends a variable annuity as an investment to be held in a qualified plan (i.e. 401(k), IRA, etc.) the recommendation *must* rest on one or more of the benefits provided by the variable annuity other than tax deferral. When such a recommendation is made the registered representative should inform his client that the variable annuity provides no additional tax benefit and in fact duplicates the tax deferral already enjoyed by the client through his qualified plan.

3. Registered representatives should, in addition to discussing the benefits of variable annuities, fully discuss any potential limitations (e.g. surrender fees, liquidity, etc.) or other material information before recommending a variable annuity (e.g. costs, IRS penalties, treatment of required minimum distributions, etc.). A review of the variable annuity prospectus is a good way to accomplish this.

4. Registered representatives should know, understand and record their clients' financial background so they can better determine the suitability of recommending a variable annuity for inclusion in a client's qualified plan. At a minimum, the basic information obtained from a client for the purchase of any investment (e.g. age, investment experience, investment time horizon, etc.) must be reviewed with the client.

Registered representatives need to understand there may be some situations where placing a variable annuity in a qualified plan may be inappropriate. The following list identifies some of these situations.

1. Short-term investing is contemplated

2. Hardship withdrawals are contemplated

3. Large loans from a qualified plan are contemplated (403(b) loans)

4. Surrender penalties could be triggered (B-share commissions)

5. Liquidity problems may arise

---

[22] In 1996, approximately 50% of variable annuity sales went into qualified accounts. "Why Variable Annuities May Make Sense in a Qualified Account", by Kurt Ohlson, *Financial Advisor Pro*, newsletter, p. 5.

[23] Merrill Lynch created the Merrill Lynch IRA Annuity to capture IRA money sitting in CDs, money market accounts and other low return accounts.

6. Death benefit is not realistic

7. Early retirement is contemplated (see the following example).

Example

Mike recently took an early retirement at age 56. His 401(k) contains $800,000. He needs to withdraw $25,000 a year during retirement. Transferring his 401(k) to a variable annuity which may convert the 401(k) to an IRA may not be appropriate because the IRS imposes a 10% penalty on withdrawals taken from an IRA inside a variable annuity if the owner is under 59½. The IRS does not impose this penalty on 401(k) withdrawals taken by owners if they are retired and over 55 years of age.[24]

Good financial professionals realize how important it is to have written records that reflect why an investment was recommended to a client and the reasoning behind its purchase. The best way for an investor and their financial professional to ensure they have discussed the four responsibilities outlined above is to have a written disclosure form that addresses all of these responsibilities. A suggested disclosure form appears below. Financial professionals and investors must understand that the form provided is merely an example that may need to be modified to reflect the specific variable annuity being considered for inclusion in a client's qualified plan. Use of a modified version of this sample form will provide a written record that will reflect the basis for a client's decision to buy a variable annuity for his or her qualified plan. Such a record protects both the client and the financial advisor.

§2715. SAMPLE TAX DUPLICATION DISCLOSURE DOCUMENT

The form below is a sample disclosure document that should be filled out whenever a variable annuity will be placed in a qualified plan or purchased within qualified funds.

---

[24] Mike could leave $100,000 in his 401(k) and transfer $700,000 to a variable annuity in order to avoid IRS penalties. Additionally, if the variable annuity can be set up in the variable annuity as a 401(k), no penalty would be imposed on withdrawals from the variable annuity. IRC §72(t) (Series of equal periodic payments) might also work in this situation.

MORGAN AND MELLON FINANCIAL ADVISORS

I. Product Description:

The undersigned client is contemplating the purchase of a variable annuity issued by the_____
_____ Insurance Company. The specific name of this annuity is _____
_____. This variable annuity will be purchased with qualified money and will be held as a qualified plan.

II. Type of Qualified Plan or Retirement Account Involved:

The undersigned client is contemplating the purchase of the above-described variable annuity to be held as a qualified plan or retirement account. The specific plan or account involved is a:
☐ 401(k)   ☐ 403(b)   ☐ Traditional IRA   ☐ 457 Plan   ☐ Other_____.

III. Tax Deferral:

The decision to purchase a variable annuity, which is a tax-deferred investment, should not be based *solely* on the variable annuity's tax-deferred benefit if the variable annuity is to be held as a qualified plan or retirement account. Qualified plans, retirement accounts and variable annuities all provide tax deferral. The purchase of a variable annuity for a qualified plan or retirement account should be based on one or more of the other benefits available through variable annuities. These benefits are discussed in item IX below.

IV. Client Background:

Because variable annuities are retirement vehicles, they should be purchased with that in mind. No variable annuity should be purchased until the client and his financial professional have discussed all of the following information and data regarding the client and the client's retirement goals.

* Name:..
* Address: ....
* Phone Number: ....
* Occupation:...
* How long employed:..
* Employer:..
* Marital status:...
* Social Security #:...
* Age:...
* Number of dependents: ....
* Retirement goals:...
* Investment time horizon:...
* Investment objectives: ☐ Growth   ☐ Other...
* Approximate retirement date:..
* Life expectancy at retirement: ....
* Risk tolerance:...
* Marginal tax bracket now:....................% At retirement:... %
* Prior investment experience:..
* Retirement sources other than Social Security:..
* Total net worth:...
* Liquid net worth:...
* Client's annual income: ....
* Spouse's income:...
* Special situations (i.e. special needs child, etc.)? ....
* Bank used:...

- Are you related to anyone in the securities business? ☐ Yes ☐ No
- Other investments: ....
- Liquidity needs: ....
- Life insurance coverage: ....

V.   Surrender Fees:

The annuity contemplated for purchase by the undersigned client imposes a surrender fee that will be in effect until _____. The annuity allows withdrawals of up to ___% a year without a surrender fee. Variable annuities are long-term investments that provide less liquidity than other investments. If withdrawals of more than __ % a year are contemplated or large withdrawals will be required prior to the date set out above, the purchase of the variable annuity should not be considered. If large withdrawals are not required before the date set out above, the surrender fees will have little impact on untaxed withdrawals. All variable annuities and qualified plans, regardless of the investments held in such plans, may be subject to a 10% penalty imposed by the IRS if such investments are withdrawn prior to a specified age (usually 59½). The prospectus more fully discusses the surrender fees involved with the purchase of the above-described annuity and has been discussed with the client.

VI.   Prospectus:

A prospectus is a *detailed* explanation of every aspect of a variable annuity. Variable annuities are subject to market risk. This is set out in detail in the prospectus. Any investor contemplating a variable annuity purchase *must* be given a copy of the prospectus for any variable annuity to be purchased. It should be reviewed by the prospective variable annuity purchaser and his financial advisor. Special attention should be paid to IRS required minimum distributions (RMDs) and surrender charges. The client has received a prospectus and reviewed it with the undersigned financial advisor.

VII. Pricing Structure:

No investment should be considered for purchase unless the prospective purchaser understands the various costs that may be charged for owning the investment. The variable annuity prospectus for the annuity being contemplated for purchase by the undersigned client fully discusses mortality and expense charges, administrative charges, investment advisor fees, etc. The client and financial advisor have completely reviewed the prospectus mentioned above, giving special attention to the expenses and pricing structure. Sub-account choices have been reviewed by the client and financial advisor also.

VIII. Tax Treatment:

All investments held in tax-deferred qualified plans including stocks, mutual funds, variable annuities, etc. receive the same tax treatment under current IRS rules. Withdrawals from all qualified plans and variable annuities funded with before-tax dollars are subject to ordinary income taxes.

IX.   Variable Annuity Features:

For the reason mentioned in item III above, a variable annuity should not be purchased for a qualified plan (401(k), IRA, etc.) *solely* based on the fact that the variable annuity provides tax-deferred growth. The purchase of a variable annuity for a qualified plan should be based on one or more of the other benefits offered by the variable annuity contemplated for purchase. The annuity under consideration by the undersigned client offers the following benefits other than tax-deferred growth. The undersigned client has checked those benefits that are the basis of his/her decision to purchase the variable annuity described above. The undersigned financial professional has discussed each of these benefits fully.

☐ Death benefit (basic or enhanced)
☐ Guaranteed fixed contract expenses
☐ Guaranteed lifetime income with or without annuitization
☐ Potential estate and income tax savings
☐ Guaranteed minimum growth rates
☐ No cost automatic reallocation and rebalancing
☐ No cost dollar-cost averaging of contributions
☐ Eliminate transaction costs
☐ Stretch IRA
☐ Guaranteed increasing death benefit
☐ Guarantee against loss of principal
☐ Premium bonuses
☐ Creditor protection
☐ Spousal continuation
☐ Long-term fixed rates of return
☐ Medicaid planning
☐ College tuition planning
☐ Other...

Variable Annuities may not be appropriate for holding qualified money where:
Each of the following issues have been discussed between the client and financial advisor:
- Large loans from a qualified plan are contemplated
- Surrender penalties could be triggered by RMDs
- Early retirement is a consideration
- Hardship withdrawal may be needed
- Short-term investments are planned
- There may be liquidity concerns
- Benefits limited by age

X.   **Summary:**
Each of the following topics was fully discussed between the undersigned client and financial advisor:
- The specific variable annuity being recommended (see item I)
- The qualified plan that will hold the annuity (see item II)
- The duplication of tax deferral (see item III)
- Client background (see item IV)
- Surrender fees (see item V)
- Prospectus for the variable annuity was delivered to and discussed with the client (see item VI)
- Pricing structure of the variable annuity (see item VII)
- Tax treatment of the variable annuity (see item VIII)
- Variable annuity features (see item IX)

_____   _____
Client   Date

_____   _____
Financial Advisor   Date

§2716. QUESTIONS TO ASK

If no cost is imposed for the tax deferral provided by variable annuities, what loss arises if a variable annuity is funded with qualified funds or if the variable annuity is placed in a qualified account?

§2717. SOURCES

See the footnotes in this chapter for sources to consult regarding placing a variable annuity in a qualified account or funding a variable annuity with qualified money.

§2718. REVIEW QUESTIONS

- Discuss two reasons why there is nothing wrong with placing a variable annuity in a qualified account or selling a variable annuity that will be funded with qualified funds.

- Discuss one situation where selling a variable annuity that will be funded with qualified funds or placed in a qualified account would constitute fraud.

- Discuss three benefits one can obtain with a variable annuity held in a qualified account (other than tax deferral) that are not available with any other investment.

§2719. CONCLUSION

Variable annuities are no different than any other type of investment that a financial professional might recommend to a client for inclusion in the client's qualified plan. The fact that both variable annuities and qualified plans provide tax deferral is of no significance. Clients who elect to have some or all of their qualified money invested in a variable annuity are not charged anything for the duplication of this tax benefit. The recommendation of a variable annuity for inclusion in a qualified plan should always be based on some benefit provided by the variable annuity other than tax deferral. Today, variable annuities exist that respond to nearly every need or concern qualified plan owners might have. These annuities, among other benefits, offer guarantees, eliminate fears and provide certainty. Many benefits offered by variable annuities are rarely, if ever, available with any other type of qualified plan investment. If a financial professional knows of a variable annuity that provides a needed benefit to a client not offered by the client's qualified plan, he or she would be obligated to fully discuss this option with the client. Whether any financial product, including a variable annuity, is an appropriate investment for inclusion in a qualified plan must be determined by what is best for the client.

Variable annuities, for over a half a century, have been one of the most common investments held in qualified plans. Long-term investment in these annuities have laid the foundation for secure and comfortable retirements for millions of Americans. This trend will continue as qualified plan participants begin to learn of the many unique benefits provided by variable annuities.

– CHAPTER 28 –
THE TAX DISADVANTAGE MYTH – SUMMARY DISCUSSION

§2801. INTRODUCTION

Many investors and others believe that variable annuities are not treated as favorably as mutual funds are under our current income tax code. This is a myth.

§2802. VARIABLE ANNUITIES AND THEIR TAX ADVANTAGED TREATMENT

Prior chapters have discussed the many advantages variable annuity owners receive by owning variable annuities. A brief review of these advantages is set out below:

- Tax-free investment trading
- Tax-deferred ownership
- Tax deduction under IRC §691 (IRD)
- Tax-free exchanges under §1035
- Avoidance of income tax phase-outs
- Avoidance of the AMT
- No late year purchase tax penalty

The above list is not complete. Many early chapters dealt with the tax issues of mutual funds and variable annuities discusses the many tax benefits of variable annuity ownership.

§2803. DEDUCTIBILITY OF VARIABLE ANNUITY LOSSES

One of the major advantages of variable annuity ownership is that losses are deductible against ordinary income in the year the variable annuity is surrendered. Mutual fund ownership does not provide this tax benefit. Mutual fund losses, if they can not be offset against gains, may only be taken in $3,000 increments over what can be many years. This tax advantage is so important that it is discussed in the next chapter as a separate topic.

§2804. CONCLUSION

The tax treatment received by variable annuity owners, in many cases, is better than the tax treatment received by mutual fund owners. One example of this is the treatment afforded to loses incurred with variable annuity and mutual funds. The next chapter discusses this difference in tax treatment in detail.

CHAPTER 29

VARIABLE ANNUITY LOSSES
AND TAX DEDUCTIBILITY – DETAILED DISCUSSION

§2901. INTRODUCTION

The owners of non-qualified variable annuities, like the owners of stocks and mutual funds, may liquidate their investment at a loss. The owners of these investments who incur realized losses need to understand how these losses are treated for income tax purposes. This chapter examines this issue.

Many investors purchase and sell mutual funds and stocks on a regular basis. When such investments are sold at a loss, their owners can deduct some or all of these capital losses by reporting them on Schedule D of their personal income tax returns. There are numerous sources available to assist taxpayers in properly deducting these losses.

The owners of non-qualified variable annuities also purchase and sell their annuities with some frequency. However, there is little concrete guidance from the IRS regarding the tax treatment of losses incurred when non-qualified variable annuities are sold.[1] This lack of information has caused tax professionals to reach vastly different conclusions regarding this important tax issue. Some tax practitioners have taken the position that losses resulting from the sale of non-qualified variable annuities are not deductible under any circumstances.[2] Other financial experts who have examined this issue have concluded that such losses are fully deductible without limitation. Many financial professionals believe the proper deductibility of variable annuity losses lies somewhere between these two extremes.

This article reviews IRS Revenue Rulings, tax court cases, tax code provisions, government publications and other related materials to the extent such sources provide guidance regarding the deductibility of variable annuity losses. By combining this data, the author hopes to clarify how losses resulting from the sale of non-qualified variable annuities are properly deducted for income tax purposes.

§2902. PROFIT MOTIVE REQUIREMENT

The starting point in the determination of whether the loss resulting from the sale of a non-qualified variable annuity is deductible or not requires an examination into the motive for the purchase of a variable annuity. The IRS has taken the position that the loss resulting from the sale of a non-qualified variable annuity, for deductibility purposes, must have arisen in the conduct of a trade or business or in some transaction entered into with a profit motive

---

[1] Owners of qualified variable annuities that are funded completely with pre-tax dollars are not allowed an income tax deduction for losses resulting from the surrender of such annuities.

[2] Today, most tax professionals agree that variable annuity losses are fully deductible subject to certain thresholds.

although not necessarily connected with a trade or business.[3] Because few non-qualified variable annuities are purchased as part of a trade or business, the author will limit his examination to those variable annuities purchased by individuals as personal investments. Most variable annuities are purchased with the intent that such annuities will produce a profit for their buyers at some point in the future. For this reason, demonstrating a profit motive regarding a variable annuity purchase is not difficult to do in most cases. However, in some cases the IRS has been successful in showing that a variable annuity was not purchased with a profit motive. When such a determination is made, it will result in the non-deductibility of any loss resulting from the sale of such a variable annuity.[4]

§2903. IRS MESSAGE #1052060

Whenever the IRS responds in writing to taxpayer questions, the response is referred to as an IRS Message. An example of an IRS Message responding to a taxpayer's question concerning the deductibility of variable annuity losses is IRS Message #1052060 issued in December of 2001.[5] The hypothetical facts supplied by the taxpayer on which IRS Message #1052062 was issued appear below:

My annuity is described as a deferred variable annuity by the prospectus. I invested $100,000 three years ago. Since the decline in the [stock] market, it is currently valued at $68,000. The funds invested were [non-qualified] funds. If I request a liquidation of my contract, may I deduct the loss incurred which is the difference [between] the original investment and the net [amount] received from the liquidation on my [tax] return up to my current income for the year?

In response to this question, the IRS held that the taxpayer's $32,000 loss was fully deductible against ordinary income as a miscellaneous itemized deduction to the extent the loss exceeded 2% of the taxpayer's adjusted gross income (AGI).[6] The IRS takes the position that if a taxpayer does not itemize deductions, the loss is not allowed. However, see §2916 below. This loss need not be offset by a taxpayer's long-term capital gains. Based on the facts set out above,

---

[3] A loss deduction can be claimed only if the loss is incurred in connection with the taxpayer's trade or business or in a transaction entered into for profit. IRC §165. This same code provision states, in part, that "[t]here shall be allowed as a deduction any loss sustained during the taxable year and not compensated for by insurance or otherwise."

[4] *Early v. Atkinson*, 175 F.2d 118 (4th Cir. 1949).

[5] It is important to understand that placing a great deal of reliance on an IRS message can be risky. IRS messages do not arise to the level of Private Letter Rulings. Although Private Letter Rulings are at least binding between the IRS and the requesting taxpayer, an IRS message is not binding on the IRS even as to the requesting taxpayer. At best an IRS message does nothing more than report research done by an IRS agent regarding a narrow tax issue.

[6] IRS Message #1052060 states that IRC §165, dealing with losses in general, applies to variable annuity losses assuming that a profit motive for purchasing the variable annuity in question can be demonstrated by the taxpayer incurring the loss. IRC §67(a) holds that this loss deduction is limited to the extent it exceeds 2% of the taxpayer's adjusted gross income (AGI). All deductions that are subject to the 2% AGI threshold are cumulated and deducted as a whole to the extent they exceed 2% of the taxpayer's AGI. Implicit in the statement that a variable annuity loss is a miscellaneous itemized deduction is the fact that such a loss is an *ordinary* loss and not a *capital* loss. Rev. Rul. 61-201, 1961-2 CB 46; *Cohan v. Comm.*, 39 F.2d 540 (2nd Cir. 1930), aff. 11 BTA 743.

if the taxpayers adjusted gross income (AGI) was $100,000, his loss deduction would be limited to $30,000 ($32,000 less 2% of $100,000 = $30,000). The cost basis for calculating losses on variable annuities is the total *after-tax dollar* contributions made to the variable annuity.[7] The net amount received upon surrender is subtracted from the cost basis to determine the loss.[8] (This essentially allows for the deduction of surrender charges.) Any prior withdrawals must also be taken into consideration. For example, Ben paid $30,000 for a non-qualified variable annuity he recently surrendered for $18,000. Ben's basis of $30,000 would be reduced by the surrender proceeds of $18,000 yielding a $12,000 loss that is treated as a miscellaneous itemized deduction subject to a further reduction of 2% of Ben's AGI. If prior to surrendering his variable annuity, Ben withdrew $2,000 from the annuity, this withdrawal would have to be reflected in a downward adjustment of his cost basis from $30,000 to $28,000. Assuming the account balance upon surrender was $18,000 and Sam's basis of $30,000 is reduced to $28,000, this would yield a $10,000 loss that is treated as a miscellaneous itemized deduction subject to a further reduction of 2% of Ben's AGI.

§2904. IRS PUBLICATION 575

IRS Message #1052060 concedes that there are no IRS publications directly addressing the deductibility of variable annuity losses, but indicates that IRS Publication 575 (*Pension and Annuity Income*) may provide, *by analogy*, some guidance on this issue.[9] Publication 575 addresses losses from lump sum distributions (i.e. surrenders) from *qualified plans* by stating that if a participant obtains a lump sum distribution from his *qualified plan* that is less than the participant's cost basis, the resulting loss is deductible.[10] IRS Message #1052060 points out that Publication 575, which it cites for support of the deductibility of losses resulting from the complete surrender of a *non-qualified* annuity, requires such deduction be treated as a miscellaneous itemized deduction. In addition, the deduction may be taken only to the extent it exceeds 2% of the taxpayer's adjusted gross income (AGI) for the year of the distribution.

> **Example:**
> Over the past several years Mike contributed $70,000 in *after-tax dollars* to a *qualified* retirement plan at his place of employment. He recently resigned from his job and elected to take a lump sum distribution from his plan. Upon surrendering his retirement plan, Mike received $40,000. On these facts the IRS, in accord with IRS Publication 575, would allow Mike a $30,000 miscellaneous

---

[7] IRC §1011. Also see *Tax Facts* (1999), p. 39, question 31.

[8] The IRS penalty for withdrawing gain from a non-qualified variable annuity before age 59½ is not relevant regarding the deductibility of a variable annuity loss because this penalty is imposed only on gain. However, as with penalties imposed by the early redemption of a bank CD, the surrender penalty imposed by the issuer of a non-qualified variable annuity is included as part of the loss taken upon the surrender of the variable annuity.

[9] IRS Publication 575 (Cat. No. 15 142B) 2001 issue, p. 19.

[10] A lump sum distribution is essentially equivalent to a complete surrender. A lump sum distribution requires payment in cash or worthless securities or a combination of the two. Cost basis is the total *after-tax dollar* contributions made to the plan.

itemized deduction subject to the 2% AGI threshold.

IRS Message #1052060 states that there should be no distinction made between losses resulting from lump sum distribution of a *qualified plan* and a loss resulting from the complete surrender of a *non-qualified* variable annuity. It is important to understand that a loss deduction for a variable annuity is *realized* only upon a *complete surrender*. Nothing less will do. For example, a §1035 tax-free exchange of one variable annuity for another is *not* a complete surrender and no deduction would be allowed if the first annuity showed a loss at the time of the exchange. Surrendering one variable annuity and using the proceeds to purchase a second would be considered the complete surrender of the first annuity. Partial withdrawals from a variable annuity resulting in an unrealized (i.e., paper) loss are not deductible.

§2905. IRS PUBLICATION 590

IRS Publication 590 (*Individual Retirement Arrangements*) discusses the tax treatment of losses resulting from the liquidation of traditional and Roth IRAs. This publication holds that losses resulting from the surrender of such IRAs are deductible as miscellaneous itemized deductions subject to the 2% AGI threshold where *after-tax* dollars have been used to fund these IRAs.[11]

Example:
Oscar has several deductible and non-deductible IRAs. He recently liquidated all of these IRAs. The amount he received was $40,000 less than the *after-tax* dollar (i.e. non-deductible) contributions he made to these IRAs. Oscar is entitled to a miscellaneous itemized deduction of $40,000 subject to the 2% AGI threshold.

Example:
Nora contributed $16,000 to her only Roth IRA. She recently liquidated it for $10,000. Nora is entitled to a $6,000 miscellaneous itemized deduction subject to the 2% AGI threshold.

§2906. THE 2% ADJUSTED GROSS INCOME THRESHOLD

The real controversy regarding variable annuity losses does not revolve around the general issue of the deductibility of these losses. Such deductibility is clearly allowed by the IRS and used by taxpayers.[12] The real question seems to center on the narrower issue of how these

---

[11] Publication 590 *Individual Retirement Arrangements*. Losses are allowed for traditional IRAs only when *all* traditional IRAs are liquidated and fully distributed to the owner. The same rule applies to Roth IRAs. If one is seeking a loss deduction on a traditional IRA, Roth IRAs need not be liquidated and vice versa. For loss deduction purposes the cost basis in one or more IRAs is the total *after-tax dollar* contributions made to the IRA. Contributions to a traditional IRA are deemed made with *before-tax dollars* to the extent such contributions are deducted for income tax purposes. IRAs may contain non-deductible contributions. The total of these contributions for all of a taxpayer's IRAs would be his cost basis. All contributions to Roth IRAs are deemed made with *after-tax dollars*

[12] Popular financial magazines have reported the position stated in IRS Message #1052060. For example, *Kiplingers Personal Finance,* in its October issue at p. 105 advises taxpayers that variable annuity losses are deductible along the lines stated in IRS Message #1052060. In their *Tax Letter, Kiplingers* advises that Roth IRAs sold at a loss receive similar treatment. (Vol. 77, No.22 and 23). IRS spokesperson Bruce Friedland has been quoted in *Kiplingers Tax Letter* as agreeing with the result set out in IRS Message #1052060.

losses are to be reported to the IRS. As mentioned earlier, many tax professionals, as well as the IRS, have taken the position that the loss incurred on the sale of a variable annuity is treated as a miscellaneous deduction that must be itemized and reported Schedule A of Form 1040. Additionally, this deduction is reduced by the amount the deduction exceeds 2% of a taxpayer's adjusted gross income (AGI).

> **Example:**
> Sara purchased a non-qualified variable annuity for $100,000. She recently sold it for $65,000. Sara's adjusted gross income (AGI) is $150,000. According to the IRS, Sara's variable annuity loss is deductible only if she itemizes her deductions. Additionally, Sara's deduction, according to the IRS, would be limited to the amount $35,000 exceeds 2% of her AGI (i.e. $3,000). In other words, Sara's *net* deduction would be limited to $32,000.

§2907. IRC §67(b)

Proponents of the proposition that variable annuity losses are subject to the 2% AGI threshold frequently cite IRC §67(b) to support their position. This section sets out those losses that are *exempt* from the 2% AGI threshold. Of the dozen exemptions, none relates directly to variable annuity losses. Based on this, the assumption is made that because IRC §67(b) does not exempt variable annuity losses from the 2% AGI threshold, that such losses are subject to the 2% AGI threshold. This argument would be more persuasive if it could be demonstrated that the exemptions listed in IRC §67(b) were intended to be a complete list. However, it appears that this is not the case. For example, gambling losses, to the extent of gambling gains, are a miscellaneous itemized deduction *not* subject to the 2% AGI threshold, but, just as with variable annuity losses, IRC §67(b) does not make reference to this deduction.

§2908. IRS PUBLICATION 529

Many tax professionals argue that variable annuity losses are deductible without regard to the 2% AGI threshold. They support their position by citing IRS Publication 529 titled *Miscellaneous Deductions*[13] and Revenue Ruling 61-201. Publication 529 sets out two exhaustive lists relating to those miscellaneous itemized deductions that are and are not subject to the 2% AGI threshold.[14] The first list contains forty-one miscellaneous itemized deductions that *are* subject to the 2% AGI threshold. Each deduction is listed and discussed fully. None of the miscellaneous itemized deductions on this list remotely deals with variable annuity losses. On a second list, seven miscellaneous itemized deductions are listed as *not* being subject to the 2% AGI threshold.[15] Included in this second list is the loss resulting from the "[u]nrecovered investment in an annuity."[16] The example provided in IRS Publication 529 of such a loss involves

---

[13] IRS Publication 529.

[14] IRS Publication 529.

[15] *Id.*

[16] *Id.*

a taxpayer who died and did not fully recover the total contributions he paid into an annuitized annuity. On these facts the decedent's estate would be entitled to a miscellaneous itemized deduction on the decedent's final income tax return for the unrecovered portion of his investment in his annuity. This deduction is taken on line 27 of Schedule A (1040) and would *not* be subject to the 2% AGI threshold.[17] It would seem logical that if a taxpayer sells an annuity for a $10,000 loss, this loss would qualify as an "unrecovered investment in an annuity" and should receive the same tax treatment as a decedent who dies before fully recovering his investment in an annuity he owned. Logic aside, many tax professionals, citing the above example, argue that the miscellaneous deduction provided for in IRS Publication 529 for the "unrecovered investment in an annuity" only applies to *deceased* taxpayers who die with annuitized annuities.

Revenue Ruling 61-201 has been interpreted by its supporters as stating that variable annuity losses are ordinary losses that may be deducted "above the line" (i.e., itemization is not required). Also pointed out by supporters of this ruling is the fact that nothing is said about taxpayers having to meet any adjusted gross income threshold. Opponents of this view point out that the 2% AGI threshold did not exist when Revenue Ruling 61-201 was issued. However, itemized deductions did exist and Revenue Ruling 61-201 did not state that variable annuity losses must be itemized. It is also important to notice that according to the IRS, a variable annuity loss is not deductible under any circumstances unless the taxpayer itemizes deductions. This rule does not apply to mutual funds, stocks or other similar investments. Those tax professionals who believe variable annuity losses are deductible without regard to the 2% AGI threshold report taking this loss deduction on Line 14 of the 1040 Form (supported with a Form 4797) or by entering a negative figure on Line 21. The determination of whether a variable annuity loss is subject to the 2% AGI threshold is important. A loss deduction that is not subject to the 2% AGI threshold will not trigger the alternative minimum tax (AMT) while one subject to the 2% AGI threshold will. Some tax practitioners make the distinction between the *sale* of a variable annuity to a third person for a loss and *surrendering* the variable annuity to the issuing company for a loss. In the first case, it is argued that the deduction would not be subject to the 2% AGI threshold.

The author believes that the issue of whether or not variable annuity losses are subject to the 2% AGI threshold will have to be decided by the courts. It is interesting to note that the only investment the IRS argues is subject to a 2% AGI threshold is the variable annuity. For taxpayers with large variable annuity losses and relatively small adjusted gross incomes this issue may be moot. However, for taxpayers with small variable annuity losses and larger adjusted gross incomes, the 2% AGI threshold could prove to be costly.

---

[17] *Id.*

Example:

Bill has a $70,000 non-qualified variable annuity loss this year. His adjusted gross income (AGI) is $150,000. If he takes a miscellaneous itemized deduction for his variable annuity loss and applies the 2% AGI threshold to the deduction, he will be entitled to a $67,000 *net* deduction.[18] If Bill's variable annuity loss was only $5,000 and his AGI was $250,000, he would receive no deduction at all for his variable annuity loss after application of the 2% AGI threshold.[19]

§2909. OTHER IMPORTANT CONSIDERATIONS

There are other issues that an annuity owner should consider if he plans to sell his annuity for a loss. The advice of a tax professional is strongly urged if such a sale is contemplated for the following reasons:

- Depending on whether the proceeds from the sale will be used to purchase another annuity, the seller may forfeit all or a large portion of his existing death benefit;

- If the variable annuity generates an unusually large miscellaneous itemized deduction, taking such a deduction may trigger an IRS audit;

- If the proceeds from the sale of the variable annuity will be used to purchase the same annuity after realizing a loss from such a sale, the repurchase may be treated by the IRS as a wash sale or sham transaction that could negate the loss deduction;

- The sale of the variable annuity may result in the imposition of surrender charges that may make such a sale less beneficial even though these surrender charges are deductible also;

- The sale of a variable annuity resulting in a large miscellaneous itemized deduction may trigger the alternative minimum tax (AMT);

- Large miscellaneous itemized deductions may be partially phased-out depending on the taxpayers's income level;

- The IRS takes the position that the loss deduction is only available for taxpayers who itemize; and

- The current variable annuity may have come about as the result of an IRC §1035 transfer and show a "phantom loss."

Each of these topics are discussed below.

§2910. LOSS OR REDUCTION IN THE DEATH BENEFIT

The sale of a variable annuity reduces to zero any death benefit once provided by the annuity. Even if a new variable annuity is purchased with the sale proceeds, the new death benefit will usually be for a lesser amount thus providing a smaller death benefit.

---

[18] $70,000 less 2% of $150,000 + $67,000.
[19] $5,000 less 2% of $250,000 = $0.

Example:

Betty purchased a variable annuity for $100,000 several years ago. The annuity provided a $100,000 death benefit. Betty decided to sell her variable annuity for $60,000 to obtain a $40,000 miscellaneous itemized deduction on her tax return. A short while later Betty purchased a new variable annuity with the $60,000 in sale proceeds. Her new death benefit would be $60,000. Had Betty decided not to buy another variable annuity, she would have lost her entire death benefit.

The loss or reduction in the value of the death benefit provided by a variable annuity must always be weighed against the benefit received from any tax deduction resulting from the sale of the annuity. An investor's age, health and number of dependents are some of the factors that should be considered before selling a variable annuity if such a sale will result in the loss or reduction of an existing death benefit. If avoiding the potential loss or reduction in the value of a death benefit is important, the annuity owner might consider adding additional funds to the purchase of a new variable annuity. For example, if an annuity originally purchased for $100,000 is sold for $60,000, the owner could add $40,000 to the $60,000 in sale proceeds to purchase a new $100,000 variable annuity with a new $100,000 death benefit. Doing so would generate a tax loss of $40,000 while preserving the $100,000 death benefit.[20] There are a few variable annuity issuers who will provide a variable annuity owner with the same death benefit he had in a prior annuity if the sale proceeds are fully reinvested in the annuity of the new issuers. For example, if $70,000 is received from the sale of a variable annuity originally costing $100,000 and the $70,000 in proceeds are reinvested in the variable annuities of certain companies, these companies will issue a variable annuity with an account value of $70,000 and a death benefit of $100,000. A reduction in a death benefit may, in many cases, be cured by purchasing term life insurance as the next example demonstrates:

Example:

Zeb, who is 56, owns a variable annuity he purchased for $100,000. It is worth $80,000 today. He wants to sell the variable annuity to realize a $20,000 deductible loss and reinvest the $80,000 into another variable annuity. He is hesitant to do this because his current death benefit is $100,000. His new annuity will provide a death benefit that will only cover his $80,000 purchase price. The death benefit in the new variable annuity ratchets up at 7% a year. In 3.3 years the death benefit in the new variable annuity will be $100,000. Zeb could buy a $20,000 term insurance policy for $150 that will provide a $20,000 death benefit to him for the next 3.3. years. When the term policy expires, his death benefit in his new variable annuity will be $100,000. By doing so Zeb obtains, without losing any death benefit, a $20,000 income tax deduction that will provide him with a cash benefit of $4,000 to $7,000 depending on his tax bracket.

---

[20] One could argue that $40,000 added to the original variable annuity would provide a $140,000 death benefit. However, if the variable annuity is not doing well and the owner wants to sell it, this suggestion will be of little value.

§2911. INCREASED AUDIT RISK

Anytime a deduction is taken that falls outside of statistical parameters set by the IRS, it can trigger an IRS audit. For example, a taxpayer with an adjusted gross income of $100,000 who takes a miscellaneous itemized deduction of $40,000 would most likely be the target of an IRS audit. As a general rule, if a deduction is proper and provable, the possibility of an audit, standing alone, should not be a reason for not taking the deduction.

§2912. WASH SALE VIOLATION

If an annuity is sold and the *same* annuity with the same sub-accounts is repurchased within thirty days, the IRS might successfully argue, by analogy, that the transaction was the equivalent of a wash sale or sham transaction thus negating any loss deduction resulting from such a sale.[21] To avoid this problem, the repurchase of a variable annuity from a different issuer might be wise or selecting different variable annuity sub-accounts in the same annuity. Waiting for more than 30 days before buying a new variable annuity might also be a solution for this potential problem.

§2913. POTENTIAL SURRENDER CHARGES

The sale of a variable annuity that generates an income tax deduction may not be advantageous after factoring in the surrender charges that may be due at the time of sale.

Example:
Jack purchased a variable annuity for $100,000. He recently sold the annuity for $90,000. Of the $10,000 loss, $5,000 was a surrender charge imposed by the variable annuity issuer. Jack's AGI was $100,000. Based on these facts, Jack could only deduct $8,000 of the $10,000 loss.[22] Because Jack is in a 25% average tax bracket this deduction will reduce Jack's tax liability to the IRS by $2,000. The $90,000 in proceeds together with the $2,000 tax benefit nets Jack $92,000 from the sale of his variable annuity. Prior to the sale, Jack's variable annuity was worth $95,000 ($100,000 less a potential $5,000 surrender charge). The premature sale of the variable annuity actually decreased the net value of the annuity to Jack by $3,000. Jack might consider waiting to sell his variable annuity until some time in the future when he will not have to pay any surrender charges.

It is also important to understand that if a second variable annuity is purchased with proceeds from the sale of a prior variable annuity, a new, and possibly longer, surrender period may be imposed on the owner.

§2914. THE ALTERNATIVE MINIMUM TAX

Taking large miscellaneous itemized deductions is one of the things that will trigger the alternative minimum tax (AMT). In light of this, the possible sale of a variable annuity to obtain a loss deduction should be weighed against the possible adjustment in income tax liability that

---

[21] IRC §1091.
[22] $10,000 less 2% of $100,000 = $8,000. See note 8 *supra.*

may result if the annuity owner is required to pay alternative minimum tax rates rather than his regular (and usually lower) income tax rates. For example, a variable annuity loss deduction of $100,000 for a taxpayer with an adjusted gross income of $100,000 will not necessarily result in the complete elimination of income taxes. The AMT could impose a stiff income tax on these facts by eliminating nearly all of the variable annuity loss deduction. There are ways to reduce or eliminate the adverse impact of the AMT where large variable annuity losses are involved. For example, instead of taking a $100,000 loss in one year, the variable annuity can be broken up into five smaller $20,000 variable annuities by making partial §1035 transfers. Over five years, each of the five new variable annuities could be surrendered to yield a $20,000 deduction for each of the five years.

> **Example:**
> Dr. Jones, who is 60, purchased a variable annuity for $160,000, recently it was worth $80,000. If the annuity is sold, the $80,000 loss could trigger the AMT and in effect, eliminate most of this deduction. Dr. Jones, following his advisor's advice, used IRC §1035 to make partial transfers of his annuity to four other annuities that had no surrender penalties. He now has four variable annuities each with a cost basis of $40,000. Each variable annuity has a value of $20,000 and a loss of $20,000. Dr. Jones could take the $20,000 loss on each variable annuity over the next four years with much less chance of triggering the AMT.

§2915. ITEMIZED DEDUCTION PHASE-OUT

Under current tax law, miscellaneous itemized deductions are reduced when married taxpayers have adjusted gross incomes above certain levels. These levels are set each year. For example, a portion of the miscellaneous itemized deduction arising from a variable annuity loss of $40,000 may be lost where married taxpayers have an AGI in excess of a specified income level.

§2916. ITEMIZATION REQUIRED

If the loss on a variable annuity is taken on Schedule A of the 1040 form, itemization is required. If the deduction is taken on line 14 or 21 on the front of the 1040 form, itemization is not required. This may be a consideration to a taxpayer contemplating the deduction of a variable annuity loss. See the discussion of itemization and Revenue Ruling 61-102 in §2908 above.

§2917. PHANTOM LOSSES

If a variable annuity appears to have a loss, it will be important to determine if the current variable annuity resulted from an IRC §1035 transfer. If so, the loss in the current variable annuity may actually be a gain.

> **Example:**
> Joe purchased a variable annuity for $100,000. When it was worth $125,000 he transferred it to a new annuity by using §1035. Later Joe sold the second variable annuity for $115,000 claiming he had a loss of $10,000. In actuality, he had a

gain of $15,000. His $100,000 original purchase price was transferred or carried over to the second variable annuity. Therefore when the second annuity was sold for $115,000, a gain of $15,000 resulted rather than the $10,000 loss Joe assumed.

§2918. DEDUCTIBILITY OF VARIABLE UNIVERSAL LIFE INSURANCE LOSSES

Many investors have purchased variable universal life (VUL) insurance policies over the past several years. VUL is a combination of an investment plus permanent life insurance. A question has arisen as to whether a loss in a VUL policy is deductible in the same manner as a variable annuity. The basic answer is no. The IRS has taken the position that a VUL is a personal insurance policy and therefore any loss on such a policy would not be deductible. However, many tax professionals have had success in transferring a VUL to a variable annuity by using IRC §1035. Such a transfer carries over the VUL basis and account value. For this reason, any loss in a VUL will be reflected in the new variable annuity. Once the transfer has been made, any loss resulting from the sale of the variable annuity in the future should be deductible.[23] Until then, gain in the variable annuity above the transferred account value up to the transferred basis is not subject to income taxes. The qualifications for deductibility of a variable annuity and the considerations discussed above should be reviewed if such a transfer is made to obtain deductibility for a VUL that has lost value. The requirement that the variable annuity be purchased with a profit motive would most likely require the variable annuity be held for some period of time. An immediate sale of the variable annuity shortly after the VUL exchange has occurred may raise questions as to whether the variable annuity was purchased with a profit motive in mind. The argument that the VUL policy was purchased with a profit motive and then exchanged for a variable annuity to obtain a profit certainly could be made. Permanent life insurance, such as whole life, could also be exchanged for a variable annuity by using §1035. The input and advice of a tax attorney or CPA should be sought when dealing with tax issues such as this.

§2919. REVIEW QUESTIONS

Explain why variable annuity losses receive better tax treatment than similar mutual fund losses.

§2920. SOURCES

See the footnotes to this chapter for sources that can be consulted regarding the tax deductibility of variable annuity losses.

§2921. CONCLUSION

Although the IRS has provided some guidance regarding the deductibility of losses resulting from the sale of *non-qualified* variable annuities, they are free to issue contradictory messages, private letter rulings or regulations in the future. Because taxpayers need to

---

[23] This type of transfer should not be attempted without the advice of tax council.

understand how to properly deduct variable annuity losses, the author believes that regulations will be issued in the near future that address this issue. If such regulations are not forthcoming, the courts or Congress may have to resolve this issue. Until this occurs, the decision to sell a non-qualified variable annuity at a loss and deduct this loss for income tax purposes should not be attempted without the advice of a tax professional.

– CHAPTER 30 –
THE SENIOR INVESTOR MYTH – SUMMARY DISCUSSION

§3001. INTRODUCTION

In the past few years state regulators have cited cases where annuities have been improperly sold to senior investors. As a result of these findings, many state regulators, using a broad brush, have taken the position that *all* annuities are bad investments for senior investors. This is a myth as it applies to variable annuities. Today's variable annuities, with their protective riders, are frequently the best possible investment a senior investor can purchase.

§3002. STATE REGULATORS AND LACK OF KNOWLEDGE

Most state regulators do not understand that there are several different types of annuities being sold today. If one type of annuity is sold to a senior investor and is found not to be a suitable investment, state regulators frequently conclude *no* annuity of any kind is a good investment for senior investors. The lack of knowledge and incorrect assumptions made by state regulators cause more harm to senior investors than the few improper annuity sales that might occur in their jurisdictions.

§3003. BENEFITS OF VARIABLE ANNUITIES

Variable annuities have several benefits that can be very important to senior investors. A partial list of these benefits include:

(1) Variable annuities can provide senior investors with a guaranteed minimum lifetime stream of income that can increase but never decrease. Mutual funds and stocks do not have this option;

(2) Variable annuities can reduce the potential taxation of a senior investor's Social Security retirement income. Mutual funds, due to forced income distributions, can increase the income taxes on a senior investor's Social Security retirement income;

(3) Variable annuities may be annuitized so as to avoid Medicaid confiscation should nursing home care be needed by a senior investor. Mutual funds and stocks do not have this option;

(4) Variable annuities provide uninsurable senior investors with the ability to obtain a death benefit to protect their loved ones. Mutual funds and stocks do not provide a similar benefit;

(5) Variable annuities are non-probate assets and can save the beneficiaries of senior investors time and money when an annuity owner dies.

§3004. CONCLUSION

Today's variable annuities may well prove to be the best investment choice facing senior investors for the reasons discussed in the next chapter.

– CHAPTER 31 –
THE SENIOR INVESTOR MYTH – DETAILED DISCUSSION

§3101. INTRODUCTION

Recently, stories have appeared in the financial press regarding lawsuits and state regulatory actions that have been initiated against financial entities for making supposedly improper annuity sales to senior investors. In each of these cases, the attorneys or state regulators involved have alleged, for various reason, that annuities make poor investments for senior investors. Included among these reasons are the following:

- Annuities, due to their surrender charges, are less liquid than other equity investments that senior investors might purchase.

- Annuities expose senior investors a heavier tax burden than other equity investments.

- Annuities are more expensive to own than similar equity investments that senior investors might purchase.

- Annuities are riskier than similar equity investments that senior investors might purchase.

These objections, and others similar to them, are not accurate when applied to variable annuities. Such objections are usually raised by people who know little about variable annuities. In many cases, these inaccurate statements can cause senior investors to avoid variable annuities and purchase investments that can actually harm them economically. This chapter examines the objections that are commonly raised regarding the purchase of variable annuities by senior investors and concludes that none of these have any merit. In fact, variable annuities, in their modern form, can be one of the best investment options available to senior investors.

§3102. VARIABLE ANNUITIES AND SENIOR INVESTORS

People who know little or nothing about variable annuities often argue that senior investors should not be allowed to purchase variable annuities. Such statements border on age discrimination and are no different than stating that African-Americans should not be able to invest in mutual funds or that women should not be able to invest in stocks. Today, people in their fifties attend college classes to expand their knowledge, people in their sixties fly privately owned airplanes, people in their seventies compete in marathons, people in their eighties travel around the world, people in their nineties get married. If age places no limits on athletic activities, travel, the desire to learn or to get married, why should age prevent a senior investor from seeking out the best possible investment for his or her particular needs? At what age should people stop investing for their future? Who has the right to determine when one is too old to invest? Should everyone over a certain age be forced to put all of their money in bank CDs? As the following material will demonstrate, today's variable annuities often prove to be excellent investments for most senior investors.

§3103. MEDIA IGNORANCE – THE PRIMARY PROBLEM

One of the major problems regarding media reports of alleged improper sales of annuities to senior investors is the media's failure to understand that there are several different types of annuities that offer different benefits and limitations. When the press reports on annuities they rarely fail to distinguish between variable annuities, immediate annuities, index annuities, fixed annuities or any other type of annuity. This failure is no different than running a newspaper story stating that because all members of the Mafia are Italian, therefore all Italians must be members of the Mafia. Each type of annuity has its own particular characteristics which may or may not make them suitable investments for senior investors. If one is not familiar with the differences among the various types of annuities, this lack of knowledge can result in inaccurate assumptions. For example, it is not unusual for a fixed or index annuity to impose a surrender charge that may not terminate at the owner's death. By contrast, the surrender charges imposed on beneficiaries who inherit a *variable* annuity terminate at the owner's death. If this distinction is not understood it may lead one to incorrectly assume that if a senior investor purchases a variable annuity he may saddle his beneficiaries with continuing surrender charges after his death. Another media shortcoming is the fact that most reports concerning variable annuities written today are rarely anything other than cut-and-paste rehashes of reports done by other reporters years ago. Few reporters today actually attempt to do their own independent research for the articles they write, so inaccurate information often reaches the public causing greater harm to senior investors than the few annuities that are improperly sold to them. This problem of sloppy reporting has not gone unnoticed. A study conducted by David Michaelson, Ph.D., in 2003 examined media coverage of variable annuities and found that the media, when reporting on variable annuities, made inaccurate statements 74% of the time. If reporters got their facts straight before writing about variable annuities, they would discover the many new benefits offered by today's new variable annuities. Once the characteristics and benefits of today's new variable annuities are understood, the objections raised about the appropriateness of seniors investing in them quickly vanish.

§3104. BUREAUCRATIC AND REGULATORY IGNORANCE – A SECONDARY PROBLEM

The knowledge most bureaucrats and state regulators have about annuities usually comes from reading inaccurate media reports made by intellectually lazy reporters who do not want facts and the truth to get in the way of a good story. In similar fashion, bureaucrats, government lawyers and state regulators supply biased and erroneous information to the press. Thus both parties feed on each others lack of knowledge about annuities. No one seems to be the least bit interested in knowing the truth. Careless accusations made about variable annuities by bureaucrats, government lawyers and state regulators do much more harm to senior investors than the few annuities that are improperly sold to these investors. State officials and regulators seem to have taken the position that *all* annuity sales to senior investors should be prohibited because a few annuities have been improperly sold to older investors.

§3105. SENIOR INVESTORS WHO OWN VARIABLE ANNUITIES – WHO ARE THEY?

The media, politicians and some state regulators would like the public to believe that all senior investors who buy variable annuities are gullible victims of some massive plot to impoverish this older population. These media members, politicians and some state regulators often stereotype senior investors as economically marginal, dull-witted patsies that cannot take care of their own finances. This is simply not the case. A recent survey conducted by the Gallup Organization found:[1]

- 62% of all annuity owners have attended college or are college graduates;

- 22% of all annuity owners have post graduate college degrees;

- 54% of retired annuity owners (and many of their spouses) were supervisors, professionals, business owners or corporate officers before retirement;

- 16% of all annuity owners have annual incomes between $75,000 and $100,000.

- 18% of all annuity owners have annual incomes in excess of $100,000;

The purchase of variable annuities by senior investors is common. The Gallup survey found:

- 52% of initial variable annuity purchases were made by investors 50 years old or older;

- 33% of first time variable annuity purchases were made by senior investors between the ages of 55 and 65 plus;

- Today over one-half of all annuities are owned by investors who are retired;

§3106. SENIOR INVESTORS – WHAT AGE QUALIFIES?

Nowhere in the media is the term senior investor defined. Senior *citizens* are usually defined as individuals sixty or older. The IRS recognizes that people can retire earlier than sixty. For example, the IRS removes withdrawal penalties imposed on most retirement accounts at age 59½. In some cases (e.g., retired workers with a 401(k), 403(b), etc.) this age 59½ penalty is reduced to age 55. AARP provides full membership in its organization at age 50. For the purpose of this book, it will be assumed that a senior is any person over 55.

§3107. VARIABLE ANNUITIES - THE PREMIER INVESTMENT FOR SENIOR INVESTORS

Most senior investors remember the three-year bear market of 2000 to 2002. Many of these investors lost large amounts by having their money invested in stocks and mutual funds.

---

[1] The Committee of Annuity Insurers, Survey of Owners of Non-Qualified Annuity Contracts (the Gallup Organization and Matthew Greenwald & Associates, 2005).

Although senior investors do not want to go through another bear market, they face a serious dilemma – invest in "safe" investments like bank CDs and forego potential stock market gains or invest in the stock market and take the risk that they could again lose a large part of their nest eggs in a future bear market.   The ideal investment for senior investors would be one that would:

- Provide senior investors with the opportunity to receive potential stock market gains;
- Protect a senior investor's principal against potential stock market losses or ensure a return of their principal in a guaranteed stream of income; and
- Guarantee senior investors that they will never outlive their retirement nest egg.

Many financial reporters and others who know little about variable annuities want the public to believe no such investment is available. As with a lot of what uninformed reporters and media members convey to the public, this is not true. Today, nearly all major issuers of variable annuities offer annuities that will protect investors against loss of their principal while allowing them to remain predominantly invested in the stock market so they can benefit from any stock market gains. Another benefit offered by many variable annuity issuers is a guarantee to refund all of an investor's investment after a stated period of time (usually five to ten years) even if the stock market has gone down. In such a case, nothing is charged for this benefit – 100% of the initial investment is returned. In addition, no matter what the markets do in the future, many of these modern variable annuities will guarantee variable annuity owners that they will receive a guaranteed stream of income for life that can increase with a rising stock market but not decrease in a declining stock market. Contrary to what reporters tell the public, these guarantees are available with variable annuities. Formal annuitization is not required to obtain these benefits. No other investment vehicle available to senior investors, including stocks, mutual funds or bonds, offers all of these benefits. It is these benefits that make today's variable annuity one of the *best* investments that senior investors can make. The following examples demonstrate this:

Example
Nate, who is 68, invested $500,000 in stocks and mutual funds eight years ago. He needed to generate at least $25,000 in income from this portfolio each year for the rest of his life starting at age 60. Nate's portfolio initially paid a 2% average dividend. Today, due to withdrawals and the bear market of 2000 to 2003, Nate's investments are only worth $300,000. If he continues to withdraw $25,000 from his portfolio, Nate could run out of money before he turns 80.[2]

Example
Nancy, who is 68, invested $500,000 in a variable annuity eight years ago. She needed to generate $25,000 in income from her annuity each year for the rest of

---

[2] $25,000 withdrawn from a $300,000 account earning 2% will last for 13.5 years.

her life starting at age 60. Today, due to withdrawals and the bear market of 2000 to 2003, Nancy's variable annuity is only worth $300,000. Regardless of what the stock market has done or will do in the future, Nancy is *guaranteed* to receive a minimum of $25,000 a year for life. If she lives to 85 she will receive at least $625,000 from her variable annuity. If she lives beyond 85, she will continue to receive $25,000 a year until her death.[3] If she dies prematurely, a death benefit will be paid to her survivors.

Of the two examples set out above, it is clear that Nancy, the senior investor who purchased the variable annuity, made the best investment choice. The following examples come to the same conclusion:

Example

Bob, who is 68, invested $500,000 in a portfolio of stocks eight years ago. Over this period the stock market was very volatile. Today his account value is $400,000. Bob liquidated his account recently and received a check for $400,000 less a selling commission. Bob has transferred his account to a new financial advisor.

Example

Dana, who is 68, invested $500,000 in mutual funds eight years ago. Over this period the stock market was very volatile. Recently, Dana sold her funds and transferred them to a new financial advisor. At the time of transfer the funds were worth $400,000.

Example

Tom, who is 68, invested $500,000 in a variable annuity eight years ago. Over this period the stock market was very volatile. Tom's variable annuity contained a rider that would protect him against a falling stock market.[4] Stocks and mutual funds offer no such protection. Tom recently surrendered his variable annuity and received a check for $500,000 even though his account was only worth $400,000. Tom transferred the $500,000 to a new financial advisor. Tom did not have to pay any commissions, costs, fees, etc., for the protection provided by his variable annuity.

Of the three examples set out above, it is clear that Tom, the senior investor who purchased the variable annuity, made the best investment choice.

§3108. VARIABLE ANNUITY SALES TO SENIOR INVESTORS - THE BOGUS ARGUMENTS

As mentioned above, state officials and regulators as well as many members of the media and others who know little about annuities (and the differences among them) advance several arguments as to why senior investors should not purchase annuities. These arguments include the following:

---

[3] If the stock market moves up, Nancy's $25,000 check can ratchet up (but never down). This can provide increased income to Nancy.

[4] An example of such a rider is the guaranteed minimum accumulation benefit (GMAB) rider.

(1)   Annuities impose surrender charges (contingent deferred sales charges) that make such annuities less liquid than similar equity investments;

(2)   Annuities impose surrender charges (contingent deferred sales charges) that senior investors may be unable to outlive;

(3)   Annuities are poor investments for senior citizens who may need income;

(4)   Annuity gains are taxed at ordinary income rates that are significantly higher for senior investors than the long-term capital gains rates they can obtain with mutual funds and stocks;

(5)   The heirs of senior citizens who own annuities do not get the benefit of a step-up in basis as do the owners of mutual funds and stocks;

(6)   Annuities generally cost more to own than comparable investments such as mutual funds;

(7)   Annuities are risky investments that are not suitable for senior investors;

(8)   Annuities impose costs and fees that senior investors may not live long enough to overcome;

(9)   Annuities are not as safe as stocks, mutual funds and other investments; and

(10)   Much of the money senior investors have is held in qualified or tax-deferred accounts (IRAs, 401(k)s, etc.) and putting this money in a annuity is inappropriate because tax-deferral is duplicated.

The problem with each of these *generalized* arguments is that when they are applied specifically to *variable* annuities they often prove to be baseless and unsupportable. Each is discussed in the following sections.

§3109. VARIABLE ANNUITY SURRENDER CHARGES AND LIQUIDITY

It is sometimes argued that if a senior investor wants to liquidate a variable annuity he or she owns, the surrender charges imposed by the annuity company make this election more costly than the liquidation of other equity investments. This rarely proves true. The truth of the matter is that the surrender charges that are incurred upon liquidation of a variable annuity will frequently impose *less* of a financial burden on senior investors than would a similar sale involving mutual funds or stocks. One point that is lost on many investors is that commissions paid to buy A-share mutual funds or stocks are an up-front, out-of-pocket cost paid by the investor and are never reduced after that point. For example, a 5% commission paid to buy an A-share mutual fund is foregone expense once the fund is purchased and, once paid, is never reduced. This is true whether the fund is held for one day or one decade. With stocks, a commission is paid at the time of purchase and again when the stocks are sold. B-share mutual funds, unlike A-share mutual funds, do not charge an up-front, out-of-pocket commission, but instead impose a surrender charge or contingent deferred sales charge (CDSC) when the fund is sold. This CDSC is usually 6% in the first year and declines 1% a year until it disappears after a fund has been held for six-years. The typical variable annuity has a commission structure that is similar to B-share mutual funds in that they require no up-front, out-of-pocket commissions, but rather impose a declining contingent deferred sales charge (CDSC) when the variable annuity is sold. This surrender charge is imposed *only if* the variable annuity has not been held for an agreed holding period. The surrender charge imposed for the sale of a variable annuity in the first year of ownership averages 6%. This figure typically declines by 1% a year until it disappears after the variable annuity is held for six or more years. Many variable annuities impose surrender charges for *complete* surrenders on the amount invested rather than the account value at liquidation although some variable annuity issuers impose their surrender charges for *complete* surrenders on the annuity's account value at liquidation. Surrender charges on partial withdrawals are usually based on the amount withdrawn from the variable annuity. Variable annuities, unlike stocks and mutual funds, typically allow investors to withdraw 10% to 15% of their account value each year without any surrender charge at all. Stocks and mutual funds do not provide this benefit. Once the commission structure of stocks, mutual funds and variable annuities is understood, it usually becomes clear that commission related costs for liquidating mutual funds and stocks are often *greater* than they are for variable annuities as the following examples demonstrate:

Example

Dan, who is 70, has $20,000 in a bank IRA that he wants to invest in equities. He is considering the following four investments:

- An A-share mutual fund charging a 5% up-front, out-of-pocket commission;
- A B-share mutual fund with a 6% contingent deferred sales charge (CDSC) or surrender charge that declines 1% a year;
- A stock portfolio imposing a 1.2% commission to buy or sell stocks;
- A variable annuity with a contingent deferred sales charge (CDSC) or surrender charge of 6% that declines 1% a year over six years. (The variable annuity allows 15% surrender charge-free withdrawals and imposes surrender charges on the total account value at sale).

Dan, who is concerned about liquidity, wants to know which of these four investments would charge the most in commissions, deferred sales charges or surrender fees if he buys the investment and later decides to roll over his IRA into similar equity investments in three years.[5] Dan assumed an 8.5% annual rate of return for three years. Dan, with the help of a financial advisor, was able to determine the total front-end charges or surrender charges for each of the four possible investments to be:

---

[5] It is assumed that the surrender will occur one day after three years resulting in a 3% surrender charge.

- A-share mutual fund $2,213[6]
- B-share mutual fund $766[7]
- Stock portfolio $841[8]
- Variable annuity $651[9]

As the above example demonstrates, the real commission cost to a senior investor for buying, liquidating and reinvesting in a variable annuity imposing a surrender charge can often be *less* than the cost of buying, liquidating and reinvesting in a mutual fund or stocks. One reason for this result is that the variable annuity does not impose fixed commissions like A-share mutual funds or stocks. Instead, variable annuities impose surrender charges that decline annually and eventually disappear. Unlike B-share mutual funds, variable annuities allow withdrawals of 10% to 15% of the premiums paid or account value without imposing a surrender penalty. B-share mutual funds do not allow similar surrender-charge free withdrawals. After just a few years, it is almost always less expensive for a senior investor to liquidate a variable annuity than mutual funds or stocks. It is also important to remember that variable annuities with short surrender periods (one to three years) are commonly available. Many variable annuities are available today that have no surrender periods and therefore no surrender charges.[10] It is important to note that the above example considered only commissions, deferred sales charges and surrender fees. No other ownership costs were considered. This was done to isolate commissions and surrender charges. The non-commission costs of owning variable annuities, mutual funds and stocks, including taxes, are discussed in Chapters 9 and 10 below. As this section will demonstrate, the non-commission costs of mutual funds are usually greater than for variable annuities.

An argument related to liquidity holds that variable annuities should be avoided by senior investors because immediate access to annuities for emergencies may be limited. Such statements are not accurate. As was pointed out above, the cost of liquidating a variable annuity is usually less than for stocks and mutual funds. In addition, most variable annuities will waive any surrender penalty for withdrawals where the owner becomes unemployed, needs to pay for nursing home care, has contracted a terminal illness or encounters similar emergencies. Other investments usually do not provide these benefits as the following two examples demonstrate:

---

[6] $20, 000 - 5% ($1,000) = $19,000 x 8.5% x 3 years = $24,269. $24,269 reinvested with a 5% commission = $1,213. $1,000 first commission + $1,213 second commission = $2,213 total commissions.

[7] $20,000 x 8.5% x 3 years = $25,546 less 3% = $766.

[8] $20,000 - 1.2% commission ($240) = $19,760 x 8.5% x 3 years = $25,239 - 1.2% commission to sell ($302) = $24,936 - 1.2% commission to repurchase ($299) = $24,636. $240 + $302 + $299 = $841.

[9] $20,000 x 8.5% x 3 years = $25,546 - 3% of 85% of $25,546 = $651. See Note 5 above.

[10] These variable annuities are often referred to as L-class variable annuities and usually have a slightly higher annual expense associated with them.

Example

Betty, who is 68, recently invested $25,000 in a variable annuity. The annuity had a 7% CDSC that declined 1% a year over seven years. Within a matter of weeks Betty learned she had a terminal illness. Although Betty's variable annuity had grown to $26,000, she had to sell it. The variable annuity issuer paid $26,000 to Betty upon notice of her illness. They imposed no surrender charges or other fees of any kind. Had Betty owned stocks or mutual funds, she would have received less because of the commissions she would have paid when these investments were purchased or because she would have had to pay a surrender charge if she owned a B-share mutual fund.[11]

Example

Jim, who is now 73, purchased a variable annuity for $70,000 when he was 69. Recently he was informed that he would need to enter a nursing home. At that time his variable annuity was worth $97,500. There was a 2% surrender charge remaining on his annuity. Jim liquidated his variable annuity and received a check for the annuity's full $97,500 value. No surrender charges were imposed because Jim's variable annuity contract waived all surrender charges for annuity owners who had to liquidate their annuity to pay for nursing home care. Although many variable annuities offer such waivers they are rarely available of with stock and mutual fund investments.

What the above examples demonstrate is that the variable annuity provides *greater* liquidity to senior investors who are confronted with unforeseen emergencies than do mutual funds and stocks.

An issue related to surrender charges is the issue of the 10% penalty imposed by the IRS when withdrawals of untaxed gain are taken from variable annuities by owners who have not reached age 59½. Individuals who do not believe senior investors should own variable annuities frequently raise this issue to support their position. The problem with this claim is threefold:

- The 10% IRS penalty applies only to people who are under 59½.[12] People in this age range are not the seniors who state officials and regulators seem to be concerned about.

- Investors under age 59½ who own variable annuities can easily avoid the 10% IRS penalty by application of IRC §72.

- Investors who purchase variable annuities and liquidate them before age 59½ are often better off financially than had they liquidated a similar equity investment even if a 10% IRS penalty is paid.

The last two points are discussed below:

---

[11] The B-share CDSC could have been as much as $1,560. Stock commissions could have been as much as $1,000.

[12] Retired workers who retired after age 55 (and remain retired) may make withdrawals from their 401(k), 403(b) and similar retirement accounts without being subject to the 10% IRS penalty. Age 59½ is the age threshold for avoiding the 10% IRS penalty on IRAs, non-qualified variable annuities, etc.

Example

Sam purchased a variable annuity at age 50 for $100,000. Today, Sam is 58 and his variable annuity is worth $200,000. At age 60, Sam planned to withdraw $8,000 from his annuity each year to supplement his retirement. Because of poor health, Sam had to retire at 58. He still needs $8,000 a year from his variable annuity but heard that the IRS imposes a 10% penalty on gains withdrawn from a variable annuity prior to the owner attaining age 59½. Sam sought the advice of a financial planner and learned that under IRC §72(q) Sam could withdraw the $8,000 he needed without penalty.[13]

The mere fact that a variable annuity may impose a surrender charge or is subject to a 10% IRS penalty or both does not automatically mean the variable annuity may not be a better investment than a similar equity investment like as a mutual fund. Tax-deferral and lower money manager fees often offset surrender charges and IRS penalties. The following example demonstrates this point:

Example:

Joe, who is 53, is considering a $20,000 investment in mutual funds or a variable annuity. He is concerned about surrender charges and the 10% IRS penalty for pre-59½ withdrawals. As the following figures indicate, Joe only needs to hold his variable annuity for six years to overcome all surrender charges and the 10% IRS tax penalty.

1. Mutual Fund Portfolio
   A. Amount to be invested $20,000
   B. Commission 5.0%
   C. Annual management fee, 12b-1 fee 1.6%
   D. Assumed rate of return 8%
   E. Annual income tax loss 1.6%
   F. Expected holding period . . . . 6 years
   G. Trading costs 0.7%
   H. Value of Portfolio after six years
      after all expenses and taxes . . . . $24,411[14]

---

[13] Surrender charges are not an issue because Sam is withdrawing less than 15% of the annuity's value. Additionally, Sam's annuity, having been owned for eight years would most likely not have any remaining surrender charge.

[14] $20,000 - 5% =$19,000 x 8% = $20,520 - 2.3% = $20,048. $20,048 - $19,000 = $1,048 gain x 20% tax (1.6% of 8%) = $838 ÷ $19,000 = 4.41263%. $19,000 x 4.41263% x 6 years = $24,619 - $208 capital gains tax ($4,619 gain x 0.30 x 0.15) = $24,411. Most of the data used in this comparison is commonly available. The annual tax loss suffered by mutual funds has been reported by several sources as being in the range of 2% of the typical fund's annual gain. See *The Great Mutual Fund Trap* by Baer and Gensler, Broadway Books, New York, 2002, p. 108 and p. 134 in *Your Money, Your Choice...Mutual Funds - Take Control Now and Build Wealth Wisely*, Professor Charles Jones, Prentice Hall, 2003. Annual trading costs for mutual funds are in the range of 1.0%. See www.Plexisgroup.com or www.personalfund.com. Variable annuity managers trade 30% less than mutual fund managers based on an average turn over for mutual funds of 118 (Morningstar) and an average turn over for variable annuities of 84 (Morningstar *Principia*). This comparison sets the trading costs for the mutual fund at 0.7% and sets the trading costs for variable annuities at 70% of 0.7% or 0.5% rounded.

2. Variable Annuity Purchase
   A.   Amount to be invested $20,000
   B.   Assumed rate of return 8%
   C.   Annual cost of variable annuity ownership 2.3%
   D.   Average income tax rate. 22%
   E.   Anticipated holding period . . . . 6 years
   F.   IRS penalty on growth if withdrawn before age 59½ 10%
   G.   7% CDSC (Declines 1% each year) 1%
   H.   Trading costs 0.5%
   I.   Value of variable annuity after six years
         after all expenses and taxes . . . . $24,430[15]

As the above example points out, a variable annuity can provide a *net* gain after liquidation that can be more than for a similar mutual fund investment even though the variable annuity owner had to pay a surrender charge and 10% IRS penalty. In reality, a variable annuity owner in Jim's situation would most likely be willing to wait a short time in order to avoid *both* the 10% IRS penalty and surrender charge. As a general rule, if a variable annuity will be held for six to seven years it will *net* more when sold than a similar mutual fund investment even if surrender charges and a 10% IRS penalty are imposed. If a holding period of less than six years is contemplated, an investor will usually be better off by investing in a mutual fund.

§3110. VARIABLE ANNUITY SURRENDER CHARGES AND DEATH

An argument frequently advanced for the proposition that annuities are inappropriate investments for senior investors is that older investors may not be able to outlive the annuity's surrender or holding period, thus passing surrender penalties on to their beneficiaries. When this objection is applied to the variable annuity, it usually proves baseless. What the public has been led to believe by the media is that variable annuity issuers continue to impose surrender charges even after the annuity owner dies. This is not true. Although some types of annuities may continue surrender penalties after an owner's death, variable annuity issuers universally waive surrender charges when an annuity owner dies. In fact, not only does the variable annuity surrender charge end at death but it is replaced by a death benefit that may provide a significant economic advantage to the beneficiaries who inherit the annuity. Competing investments such as stocks and mutual funds offer no similar benefit and frequently prove to be *more* costly for beneficiaries to liquidate when a senior variable annuity investor dies. The following example demonstrates this:

---

[15] $20,000 x 8% = $21,600 - 2.8% = $20,995 - $20,000 = $995 in gain ÷ $20,000 = 4.976%. $20,000 x 4.976% x 6 years = $26,765. Surrender penalty of $170 (0.85% of withdrawal of initial premium). Value after surrender penalty = $26,595. Income taxes of 22% on the gain of $6,765 = $1,488. 10% IRS penalty = $677 (10% of $6,765). Net value of the variable annuity after 6 years = $26,765 - $170 - $1,488 - $677 = $24,430. The 15% surrender charge-free withdrawal benefit is assumed for the variable annuity. See Note 14 on sources for data used in this comparison.

Example

Lisa, who is 88, has a $30,000 in a 401(k) she wants to invest. She is considering the following four equity investments:

- A variable annuity that has a 7% surrender charge (contingent deferred sales charge) that declines 1% a year over seven years. The annual expense ratio and trading costs for the annuity total 2.8%;[16]

- An A-share mutual fund that charges a 5% commission, the expense ratio and trading costs for the mutual fund total 2.2%;[17]

- Stocks that carry a 2.1% commission to buy or sell;

- A B-share mutual fund that has a 6% surrender charge (contingent deferred sales charge) that declines 1% a year for six years, the annual expense ratio and trading cost for the mutual fund total 3.1%.[18]

Lisa wants to know what her family would receive if she died a year from now owning any of these four investments if the market were up or down by 10% or flat at the time of her death. Lisa's financial professional created the following table for Lisa:

TABLE #1: NET VALUE AT DEATH IN ONE YEAR
(ACCOUNT UP 10%, FLAT, AND DOWN 10%)

INVESTMENT	UP 10%	FLAT	DOWN 10%
Variable Annuity	$31,660[19]	$30,000[20]	$30,000[21]
A-Share Mutual Fund	$30,660[22]	$27,873[23]	$25,085[24]
Stocks	$31,629[25]	$28,753[26]	$25,878[27]
B-Share Mutual Fund	$30,378[28]	$27,617[29]	$24,845[30]

As Table #1 demonstrates, the value of Lisa's 401(k), assuming her death one year from now, would be highest with a variable annuity regardless of whether the stock market went up, down or sideways.

---

[16] Of this 2.8%, 0.5% constitutes trading costs.

[17] Of this 2.2%, 0.7% constitutes trading costs.

[18] Of this 3.1%, 0.7% constitutes trading costs.

[19] $30,000 + 10% = $33,000 - 2.8% = $32,076. $2,076 gain taxed at 20% reduced the $32,076 value to $31,660. There are no surrender charges at death.

[20] A death benefit of $30,000 would be paid because the variable annuity's value at death would be less than $30,000 ($30,000 - 2.8%).

[21] A death benefit of $30,000 would be paid because the variable annuity's value at death would be less than $30,000 ($30,000 - 2.8%).

[22] $30,000 - 5% = $28,500 + 10% = $31,350 - 2.2% = $30,660. The step-up in basis eliminates income taxes.

[23] $30,000 - 5% = $28,500 - 2.2% = $27,873.

[24] $30,000 - 5% = $28,500 - 10% = $25,650 - 2.2% = $25,085.

[25] $30,000 - 2.1% = $29,370 + 10% = $32,307 - 2.1% = $31,629.

[26] $30,000 - 2.1% = $29,370 - 2.1% = $28,753.

[27] $30,000 - 2.1% = $29,370 - 10% = $26,433 - 2.1% = $25,878.

[28] $30,000 + 10% = $33,000 - 3.1% = $31,977 - 5% = $30,378. The step-up in basis eliminates income taxes.

[29] $30,000 - 3.1% = $29,070. - 5% = $27,617.

[30] $30,000 - 10% = $27,000 - 3.1% = $26,163 - 5% = $24,845.

§3111. INCOME NEEDS, SENIOR INVESTORS AND VARIABLE ANNUITIES

Seniors who need a reliable, guaranteed stream of income for life, will always be better off investing in a variable annuity than mutual funds or stocks if the stock market goes against them. The next three examples demonstrates this point:

Example

Steve, who is 60, retired three years ago and took a $500,000 lump sum payment from his employer in lieu of a pension. Steve invested the money with a stockbroker who created a conservative portfolio of stocks and mutual funds. The portfolio historically grew at 6%. Steve only needed 5% or $25,000 from his investments. The stock and mutual fund portfolio seemed to be the ideal investment initially but in the last 18 months the portfolio's value has dropped to $400,000. Steve was told that based on his life expectancy he could run out of money before he died.

Example

Bill, who is 60, has $500,000 on which he needs to receive a minimum income stream of 5% a year for the rest of his life. There are several variable annuities issued today that will guarantee this return and, in addition, ratchet up (but never down) Bill's investment periodically as the stock market rises allowing his $25,000 annual stream of income to increase with the stock market but not go down when the stock market is performing poorly. These increases in income are guaranteed even though no additional investment is made in the variable annuity. Such variable annuities also guarantee all income payments will last a lifetime. There is no mutual fund, stock or other investment that will give Bill the same guaranteed lifetime stream of income with the same income ratcheting benefit.

Example

Mary, who is 60 and retired, has $500,000. At age 70, Mary will receive a very large payment from a trust fund. Mary needs to supplement her current retirement income by $50,000 a year for the next ten years. She contacted a brokerage firm to see if they had any stocks or mutual funds that would *guarantee* that she could receive a $50,000 annual stream of principal and income from her $500,000 for ten years. The stockbroker Mary talked to correctly informed her that no such guarantee existed with stocks or mutual funds. Mary later talked with a financial professional who specialized in variable annuity investing. He informed Mary that there were several variable annuity companies that would accept her $500,000 investment and *guarantee* $50,000 annual payments to her for ten years regardless of what the stock market might do in the future. If the market were to go down, Mary would be guaranteed to receive her $50,000 annual payments for ten years. (These payments would be income tax free because they would be considered a return of principal). If, on the other hand, the stock market went up in the future, Mary would not only recover her full $500,000 investment in ten annual installments of $50,000, but would be entitled to any gain above her $500,000 investment less her normal costs of investing.

What the above examples demonstrate is that if a senior investor is concerned about a guaranteed stream of income for a stated period or life, the premier investment will almost always prove to be the variable annuity should the stock market go against the senior investor. If the stock market goes up, the gain in the variable annuity, mutual fund or stock portfolio will be nearly the same.

§3112. CAPITAL GAINS VS. ORDINARY INCOME

The income tax treatment for owning mutual funds, stocks or variable annuities inside a qualified retirement account (e.g., IRA, 401(k), etc.) is identical. All withdrawals from such accounts are taxed as ordinary income. Mutual funds, stocks and variable annuities receive a different tax treatment when held outside of retirement accounts (i.e., non-qualified accounts). Individuals who know little about taxation of investments claim that senior investors who withdraw gains from their *non-qualified* variable annuities pay higher taxes because such withdrawals are taxed at ordinary income tax rates while similar investments like mutual funds are taxed at 15% long-term capital gains rates. Such claims rarely prove to have any merit. The reason for this is that today's *ordinary* income tax rate for the great majority of retired senior investors is already at a 15% level as the following example demonstrates:[31]

Example
Sam Quinn and his wife are both 61 and retired. They have a combined pension income of $88,000. They want to withdraw $7,000 in gain from a large non-qualified variable annuity they own. They asked their CPA to calculate their total federal income tax liability for 2007 on their $95,000 in gross income. The CPA reduced the Quinn's $95,000 gross income by their itemized deductions and their personal exemptions, which totaled $23,475 for 2007 to obtain their taxable income of $71,525. Based on IRS tax tables for 2007, the Quinn's federal income tax liability is $10,729 which is 15% of their taxable income (the Quinn's tax liability of $10,729 is only 11.7% of their $95,000 *gross* income).

What the above example demonstrates is that for retired senior investors who are married and have gross retirement incomes of as much as $95,000, their tax liability will be 15% or less if they have normal deductions and exemptions. This is true regardless of how much of the $95,000 in gross income comes from variable annuity withdrawals (including all of it!). If a retired couple has a gross income of $95,000 and are in a 25% marginal tax bracket, their income tax liability will be $10,729 even if all of their income comes from variable annuity withdrawals.

It is important to note that similarly situated senior investors who sell stocks, receive mutual fund distributions or sell off mutual funds while in retirement will be taxed at capital gains tax rates of 15% until December 31, 2010 when these rates are scheduled to increase to 20%. In addition, it must be remembered that mutual fund investors usually pay *both* ordinary

---

[31] The current Congressional Budget Office Report puts the average individual income tax liability of all Americans at 15.6%.

and capital gains income taxes on their mutual funds each year whether the funds go up, down or remain constant. Variable annuity investors have no *annual* income tax liability because variable annuities are tax-deferred. Because of the mutual fund's annual income tax liability and the variable annuity's tax-deferral, a variable annuity investment will grow to a larger amount than a similar mutual fund investment. After paying taxes on these larger amounts, the after-tax amount received with a variable annuity can be more than that which might be produced by an equivalent mutual fund investment. The following examples demonstrate this:

Example

Ken, who is 60, is in a 25% tax bracket. He owns an A-share mutual fund that he paid $44,000 for ten years ago. The fund makes distributions that are half long-term and half short-term. Ken's average tax liability on his distributions is 20%. Ken's fund has earned an average of 10% a year over the last ten years. Ken has received an after-tax return of 8% on his fund. Today the fund is worth $94,993 (8% x $44,000 x 10 years).

Example

Lisa, who is 60, is in a 25% tax bracket. She owns a variable annuity that she paid $44,000 for ten years ago. The variable annuity grows tax-deferred. Lisa's variable annuity has earned an average of 10% over the last ten years. Today, because of tax deferral, Lisa's variable annuity is worth $114,125 (10% x $44,000 x 10 years). If Lisa's gain of $64,125 is taxed at 25%, the variable annuity will have an after-tax value of $98,094.

What the examples above show is that an investment taxed at an ordinary income tax rate of 25% that is tax-deferred can produce a larger after-tax return than an investment that is taxed each year at a combination of 15% long-term capital gains rates and ordinary income tax rates.

The following points are also important to understand:

• The mutual fund's net ending value in this example was not reduced for termination income taxes.

• The mutual fund's initial investment of $44,000 was not reduced for commissions.

• Non-tax costs, which are higher for mutual funds, were ignored.

• If was assumed that the mutual fund never had a down or flat year, which would actually increase the income tax liability of owning the mutual fund.

• Long-term capital gains rate were higher in the past than the current 15% rate.

• It was assumed that the ten years Ken did no trading in his mutual fund which could increase income taxes.

• It was assumed that Lisa would cash out of her variable annuity and pay taxes at her highest tax rate. If withdrawal were taken in retirement, Lisa's income tax liability would most likely be reduced.

If the above items were factored in, the financial advantage that Lisa has with her variable annuity would be significantly more than the $3,101 differential shown in the examples.

If senior investors own stocks, they must pay income taxes on gains every time a stock is sold at a profit. Additionally, new commissions must be paid if the sale proceeds are reinvested in new stocks. When sub-accounts within variable annuities are sold and reinvested, income taxes are not triggered due to the tax-deferral feature of variable annuities. In addition, new commissions are not incurred because variable annuities do not impose commissions or other costs when an owner trades among the variable annuity's sub-accounts. When all of these factors are considered, the overall tax liability for most senior investors will be about the same for variable annuities as with mutual funds. This is true even if *all* of a retired couples income comes from variable annuities which may put them in a 25% marginal tax bracket.

For senior investors in very low tax brackets, capital gains rates are 5% or 10% rather than 15% depending on their tax bracket. The real difference in the tax liability for senior investors receiving 5% capital gains tax treatment and those paying ordinary income taxes on variable annuity withdrawals is quite small. For example, a retired couple with a taxable ordinary income of $45,000 and $5,000 in mutual fund distributions taxed at 10% will have a total tax liability of $6,448 to the IRS in 2008. This is a total tax liability of 12.9%. The same couple with a taxable ordinary income of $45,000 and a variable annuity withdrawal of $5,000 also taxed at ordinary income rates, will have a tax liability to the IRS of $6,698 or 13.4%. The difference in tax liability between 10% capital gains rates and ordinary income tax rates at lower levels of income is usually less than 1%. It should be noted that this simple example ignores the income taxes that may have been paid on the mutual fund during ownership. Such taxes will reduce the ending value of the mutual fund. When the income taxes paid on the mutual fund during ownership are factored in, the variable annuity often proves to be the better long-term investment even for senior investors in very low tax brackets.

Another distinct advantage of variable annuity investing for senior investors is the beneficial tax treatment provided by the IRS when losses occur. Losses occurring with stocks and mutual funds do not receive this beneficial treatment. This advantage is demonstrated in the following examples:

Example
Al is 82. He invested $400,000 in stocks and mutual funds five years ago. That was the only equity investment he ever made. Al usually invested in municipal bonds and CDs. Al recently sold the stock and mutual fund portfolio and suffered a $45,000 loss. Al may only take a $3,000 capital loss deduction for this year. The remaining loss may only be deducted in $3,000 increments over the next fourteen years, assuming Al lives that long.

Example
Beth is 82. She invested $400,000 in a variable annuity several years ago. This was the only equity investment she ever made. Beth usually invested in municipal bonds and CDs. Due to ill health, Beth recently sold her variable

annuity and suffered a $45,000 loss. Beth is entitled to take the entire $45,000 loss as an income tax deduction against her *ordinary* income for the year the variable annuity was sold.[32]

What the above examples demonstrate is that the tax treatment of variable annuity losses suffered by a senior investor is significantly more advantageous than the tax treatment provided when a loss arises with stocks and mutual funds. It is interesting to note that if a senior investor buys a variable annuity with a seven year holding period, the media and many state regulators will immediately claim this is an unreasonable period of time for a senior investor to hold an investment. However, when it is pointed out that losses from investing in stocks and mutual funds could force the same senior investors to take loss deductions over a 10 to 15 year period, the media and state officials have no problem with this. The fact that any unused deduction that might remain after a senior investor dies may be lost to beneficiaries does not seem to be a concern either.

§3113. THE STEP-UP IN BASIS ISSUE

Some people believe that variable annuities are not good investments for senior investors because at death the recipients of the variable annuity must pay income taxes on any gain in the variable annuity. Those who inherit investments such as mutual funds and stocks do not have to pay income taxes on the inherited value of these investments. This supposed benefit of stocks and mutual funds is referred to as a step-up in basis. The reason stocks and mutual funds provide a step-up in basis to beneficiaries is because they do not benefit from the tax-deferral that variable annuities receive. This raises the question of which is better, a mutual fund that is taxed every year but not at death or a variable annuity that is not taxed annually but generates a tax at the owner's death? In most cases, the economic benefit of tax-deferral obtained with variable annuities is greater than the step-up in basis that mutual funds might provide. The following examples demonstrates this:

Example

Sixteen years ago, Ellen invested $100,000 in a mutual fund portfolio that grew at 10% annually. Each year taxes on her distributions reduced Ellen's rate of return by 2%.[33] The annual cost of owning the mutual fund was 1.5% and trading costs were 0.7%.[34] The commission paid by Ellen was 2½%. These expenses reduced Ellen's net rate of return to 6.064%.[35] Ellen recently died and left her mutual fund, now worth $250,088,[36] to her four young grand-children.

---

[32] The IRS takes the position that this loss must be reduced by 2% of taxpayer's adjusted gross income. Many tax professionals disagree with this position and do not reduce the deduction . At least one Private Letter Ruling and a court case supports the tax professionals.

[33] The average mutual fund loses approximately 2% of its total annual gain to income taxes according to studies conducted by Lipper, Inc., and others.

[34] The average A-share mutual fund has an annual expense ratio of 1.5% (including 12b-1 fees) and trading costs of 0.7%.

[35] $100,000 - $2,500 = $97,500 + 10% = $107,250 - 2.2% = $104,894 - $97,500 = $7,391 x 0.8 = $5,913 ÷ $97,500 = 6.064%.

[36] 6.064% x $97,500 x 16 years = $250,088.

Ellen had no other assets. The fund was sold soon thereafter for $250,088. The grandchildren avoided capital gains taxes on unrealized gains because the cost basis of the mutual fund in their hands was stepped-up to $250,088. In short, the grandchildren received the full $250,088 value of the inherited mutual fund unreduced by capital gains taxes.

Example

Sixteen years ago, Frank purchased a variable annuity for $100,000. The annuity grew at the net rate of 10% but due to the annual costs of 2.7% associated with owning the annuity, the net rate of return was reduced to 7.03%.[37] Frank recently died leaving his annuity, now worth $296,543,[38] to his four young grandchildren. Frank had no other assets. The annuity proceeds paid out to the grandchildren were subject to a total of $29,472 in *ordinary* income taxes on the annuity's growth of $196,543, thus reducing their inheritance from $296,543 to $267,071.[39] This is $16,983 more than in the first example where a stepped-up basis was obtained.

What the two examples above show is that the variable annuity's tax-deferral can often provide more economic benefit to beneficiaries than can the step-up in basis provided by mutual funds.

One of the major problems with the step-up in basis currently provided by mutual funds and stocks is that it may be eliminated or reduced dramatically in the near future. The Internal Revenue Code currently has a code section (§1022) that states that the step-up in basis currently available to mutual fund and stock owners will be repealed for the tax year 2010. Because of the soaring federal deficit, there is a good chance this repeal may be made permanent.

Another major problem with the step-up in basis rule is that mutual fund proponents never mentioned that beneficiaries who inherit non-qualified variable annuities receive a huge income tax deduction under IRC §691. This deduction for variable annuity beneficiaries can significantly reduce the supposed advantage of the step-up in basis available to beneficiaries who inherit mutual funds. Section 1913 discusses this issue in detail. The following example demonstrates how the IRD deduction works:

Example

Frank, who is 72, wants to invest $50,000 for his grandchildren. He wants to know if a mutual fund or variable annuity investment would be best. The table below shows the net amount that will pass to the grandchildren if *both* the step-up in basis and the IRC §691 IRD deduction are considered.

---

[37] $100,000 + 10% = $110,000 - 2.7% = $107,030 - $100,000 = $7,030 ÷ $100,000 = 7.03%.

[38] $100,000 x 7.03% x 16 years = $296,543.

[39] $296,543 - $100,000 = $196,543 ÷ 4 = $49,136 per grandchild. Less $5,350 for each grandchild's single standard deduction for 2007 = $43,786. It is assumed that personal exemptions are not available due to the age of the grandchildren. The tax tables for 2007 show the tax on $43,786 is $7,368 for a single person. The four grandchildren will pay a total tax of $29,472 (4 x $7,368), leaving a net inheritance of $267,071 ($296,543 - $29,472).

TABLE #2: MUTUAL FUND'S STEP-UP IN BASIS VS. VARIABLE ANNUITY'S IRC §691 INCOME IN RESPECT OF A DECEDENT DEDUCTION

DATA	MUTUAL FUND	VARIABLE ANNUITY
Initial Investment	$50,000	$50,000
Value at Death (Age 82)	$86,481[40]	$98,634[41]
Other Taxable Estate	$2,000,000	$2,000,000
Total Taxable Estate	$2,086,481	$2,098,334
Federal Estate Taxes	$38,916[42]	$44,385[43]
Estate to Grandchildren	$2,047,565	$2,054,249
Grandchildren's Income Taxes	-0-	$11,672[44]
Estate to Grandchildren	$2,047,565	$2,042,577
IRC §691 Adjustment	-0-	$5,252[45]
Net Amount to Grandchildren	$2,047,565	$2,047,829[46]

Proponents of mutual funds rarely mention the step-down in basis that negatively impacts mutual funds but not variable annuities. If a mutual fund is purchased for $100,000 and the owner dies when it is worth $80,000, the beneficiaries who receive the fund have a basis of $80,000. If the fund is sold there are no income taxes but the $20,000 loss is not available as a deduction to them. On the other hand, if a variable annuity is purchased for $100,000 and the owner dies when it is worth $80,000, the beneficiaries who receive the variable annuity receive a step-up in basis to $100,000 as a result of the annuity's death benefit. If the variable annuity is sold for $100,000, there are no income taxes and no loss of value as there is with a mutual fund.

Often the media will claim that variable annuities do not provide a step-up in basis as do mutual funds and stocks. This is not true. IRS §72(e)(4)(c)(i) provides a step-up in basis to variable annuity recipients for *lifetime* transfers of variable annuities. Owners of mutual funds and stocks may only pass a step-up in basis to their beneficiaries at *death*. In many cases the step-up in basis provided by the variable annuity will yield a greater economic benefit to donees than the step-up provided for by mutual funds and stocks. The following examples demonstrate this:

---

[40] $50,000 - 4% = $48,000 + 10% = $52,800 - 2.2% = $51,638 - $48,000 = $3,638 - 30% = $2,911 ÷ $48,000 = 6.064% x 10 years x $48,000 = $86,481.

[41] $50,000 x 10% = $55,000 - 2.7% = $53,515 - $50,000 = $3,515 ÷ $50,000 = 7.03% x 10 years x $50,000 = $98,634.

[42] 45% of $86,481 = $38,916.

[43] 45% of $98,634 = $44,385.

[44] $48,634 gain x 24% = $11,672 (The grandchildren would most likely have an average tax rate of less than 24%).

[45] The variable annuity gain of $48,634 is 49.308% of the full value of the variable annuity at death ($98,634), therefore 49.308% of the estate tax of $44,385 or $21,885 is the IRD deduction. The grandchildren's income tax would be calculated on $26,749 ($48,63 - $21,885) not $48,634. The income tax liability would be $6,420 at 24% not $11,672. This is a difference of $5,252.

[46] If there were qualified accounts the variable annuity would provide more to the grandchildren.

Example

Andy bought a mutual fund portfolio several years ago for $900,000 and it has increased in value to $1,400,000. Andy and his second wife Betty are both 70 years old. Andy has four children who are Betty's step-children. Andy also has fourteen grandchildren. He wants his $1,400,000 mutual fund portfolio to pass to his children and grandchildren. To ensure a step-up in basis for his children the grandchildren, Andy decided to leave the $1,400,000 portfolio to his children and grandchildren in his will. Andy has $2,000,000 in other assets he plans on leaving to Betty. Andy has $1,100,000 in a bank account that he also wants to leave his children and grandchildren. Assuming Andy dies in 2008, the $1,400,000 mutual fund portfolio passing to his children and grandchildren and the $1,100,000 bank account passing to them will be subject to an estate tax of $225,000, netting them $2,275,000. No income taxes will be due on the mutual fund portfolio at Andy's death due to application of the stepped-up basis rule. The remaining assets would pass to Andy's wife without any estate tax by applying the unlimited marital deduction.

Example

Bob bought a variable annuity years ago for $900,000 and it has increased in value to $1,400,000. Bob and his second wife April are 70 years old. Bob has four children who are April's step-children. Bob also has fourteen grandchildren. He wants his children and grandchildren to receive his annuity. Bob also has $2,000,000 in other assets he plans to leave to April. Bob has a bank account containing $1,100,000 that he also wants to pass to his children and grandchildren if possible. In early 2007, Bob decided to give the $1,400,000 annuity to his 18 children and grandchildren. He reported the $500,000 gain in the transferred annuity on his 2007 income tax return and paid 35% in ordinary income taxes, or $175,000, on this gain. This tax was paid from the $1,100,000 bank account. After making the gift, the children and grandchildren will receive a stepped-up basis of $1,400,000 in the annuity. The 10% IRS penalty would not apply because the annuity has no gain on which to impose the penalty because of the step-up. There will be no gift taxes on this transaction. Of the $1,400,000 gift, $432,000 is untaxed because of the split gifts made by Bob and his wife to the children and grandchildren (i.e. $24,000 x 18 = $432,000). The $968,000 excess gift is untaxed because it is more than covered by the $1,000,000 gift tax exemption amount available in 2007. Assume Bob dies in 2008. His remaining assets which are valued at $2,000,000 would pass to his wife without estate taxes by applying the unlimited marital deduction. The children and grandchildren would receive the $1,400,000 stepped-up value of the variable annuity plus the $925,000 remaining after the $1,100,000 bank account was used by Bob to pay $175,000 in income taxes. By giving the variable annuity away during life, Bob was able to pass $2,325,000 to his children and grandchildren. This is $50,000 more than Andy passed to his children and grandchildren in the previous example involving the mutual fund portfolio. The $2,325,000 transfer would not be subject to estate taxes because the *taxable* gift of $968,000 plus the $925,000 bank account balance are less than the two million dollar estate tax exemption applicable in 2008.

Another interesting fact is that with just a few *minutes* of tax planning, the owner of a variable annuity can ensure his beneficiaries will receive more from his variable annuity than if it were a mutual fund. The following examples demonstrate this:

Example

Jill, age 67, a widower, has an estate worth $3,000,000. One million dollars of her estate is a mutual fund portfolio that grew from a $250,000 initial investment. The mutual funds are intended to pass to Jill's three sons. If Jill dies in 2008 her estate will have an estate tax of $450,000. The remaining $2,550,000 will pass to her children without further taxation because Jill's mutual funds will provide a step-up in basis to them.

Example

Jack, aged 67, a widower, has an estate worth $3,000,000. One million dollars of his estate is a variable annuity of which half is his contributions and half is growth. The remainder of his estate consists of his house, car, etc. which is worth $2,000,000. If Jack dies in 2008, his estate taxes would be $450,000. Income taxes owed by his children (after any §691 deduction) could bring total taxes to $600,000 or more. Jack wants to retire but needs at least $50,000 (after taxes) each year from his annuity to supplement his other retirement income. Jack wants his entire $3,000,000 estate to pass to his three children without death or income taxes if possible. The solution for all of Jack's concerns can be resolved easily. Jack should have his children purchase (and own) a $1,000,000 life insurance policy on Jack's life. The premiums on this policy will be approximately $27,000 a year. After the policy is in place, Jack should convert his variable annuity to an immediate lifetime annuity (i.e., no guarantee other than lifetime payments). The immediate annuity will pay Jack approximately $90,000 a year for life. Jack's exclusion ratio based on a life expectancy of 15 years will be 37%. This will protect a large portion of this income from taxation for several years. The after-tax annuity payment will be $78,660. Jack can give his children $27,000 each year to pay the premiums on the life insurance they purchased. (No gift taxes would be due because of the $12,000 annual exclusion). This leaves Jack with more than the $50,000 in income he needs each year. If Jack dies tomorrow, his estate will be worth $2,000,000 and will pass to his children estate tax free due to the current $2,000,000 exemption. The immediate annuity is valued at zero because it is a lifetime annuity that ceases to have any value at death. In addition, the children will receive $1,000,000 estate and income tax free from the insurance company. (Estate taxes are avoided because the insurance is not in Jack's estate. Insurance proceeds are not subject to income taxation.) In short, a combination of annuitization and asset adjustment eliminates all estate and income taxes for Jack's children. They will receive Jack's entire $3,000,000 estate. (Any unrecovered portion of the annuity premium (if non-qualified) can be treated as an income tax deduction on *Jack's* final income tax return).

§3114. THE ANNUAL EXPENSE OF OWNING VARIABLE ANNUITIES AND MUTUAL FUNDS

The media and state bureaucrats claim variable annuities are poor investment choices for senior investors because they are more expensive to own on an annual basis that are similar investments such as mutual funds. This is not true. The typical variable annuity will have an annual ownership cost of 2.35%. A typical mutual fund will have an annual cost that exceeds 5% when all the costs of owning the fund are factored n. An excellent book that discusses the true annual cost of owning mutual funds is *The Great Mutual Fund Trap* by Gregory Arthur Baer and Gary Gensler, former U.S. Treasury officials.

Several academic studies have shown that the annual cost of owning the average mutual fund is 3.2% *before* considering annual income tax consequences. This 3.2% is a combination of money management fees, 12b-1 fees, commissions and trading costs.[47] The annual cost of owning a mutual fund can easily reach 5.7% after adding in the income tax liability imposed each year on mutual funds.[48] The annual cost of owning the average variable annuity is 2.7%.[49] This 2.7% is composed of money management fees, administrative charges, insurance costs, commissions and trading costs.[50] Variable annuities do not generate annual income taxes because they are tax-deferred. Stock that is traded in two year cycles can result in commissions and income taxes that can exceed 3.0% a year on average.[51] The following table compares the annual costs of owning a mutual fund and variable annuity:

---

[47] 1.5% money management and 12b-1 fees, 1.0% average annual commissions and 0.7% trading costs.

[48] See Table #2.

[49] 0.9% money management and 12b-1 fees, 1.3% insurance and commission costs and 0.5% trading costs.

[50] Trading costs are reported in the supplemental prospectus.

[51] A 2% annual commission to buy, sell and repurchase a stock will result in a 6% commission loss.

TABLE #3: THE VISIBLE COSTS OF *ANNUAL* OWNERSHIP - 'A' SHARE MUTUAL FUND VS. VARIABLE ANNUITY
(Assumes an A-share equity fund portfolio returning 10% annually)

Costs	Avg. M.F.	Avg. V.A.
Money Mgr. and 12b-1 Fees[52]	1.50%	0.90%
Mortality and Expense[53]	0.00%	1.40%
Annual Income Tax Loss to Mutual Fund Portfolio Value[54]	2.00%	0.00%
Trading Costs[55]	0.70%	0.50%
Annual Commissions[56]	1.00%	0.00%
Total[57]	5.20%	2.80%

As Table #2 above indicates, the annual cost of owning a average mutual fund is often greater than that of the average variable annuity.

§3115. STOCK MARKET RISK AND VARIABLE ANNUITIES

Of all the reasons advanced for the proposition that variable annuities are a poor investment choice for senior investors, the claim that variable annuities present too much potential stock market risk has nothing to support it. Variable annuities have no greater stock

---

[52] Mutual funds and variable annuities charge fees to cover the cost of paying their investment managers. Mutual funds and variable annuities also charge 12b-1 fees to help pay for marketing and advertising costs. The average mutual fund charges 1.5% to mutual fund owners to cover investment management and 12b-1 fees. The average variable annuity charges a fee of 0.90% to cover these two expenses.

[53] Mortality and expenses (M&E) fees are charged by variable annuity issuers but not mutual fund companies. This fee is designed to pay for the insurance that guarantees that beneficiaries of a variable annuity never receive less than the net investment made in the variable annuity by the owner when the owner was alive. M&E fees are also used to offset the compensation advanced by variable annuity companies to the financial professional that sells their variable annuity to investors. M&E fees average 1.4% for the typical variable annuity.

[54] Income taxes refers to the taxes paid by mutual fund owners to the IRS each year. Several sources, including Lipper, Inc., have determined this annual tax liability to be approximately 2% of a mutual fund's total annual growth. The best way to determine the annual income tax liability of owning a mutual fund is to compare the total gain of a mutual fund with its after-tax total gain. This data can be found in the prospectus. For example, if a mutual fund has a gross return of 10% but an after-tax return of 7.5%, the income tax liability will be 2.5%. Because the stock market fluctuates, this calculation should be averaged as each year's tax burden is paid. It is assumed, for the purpose of this table, that the mutual fund gain averages 10% and 2 percentage points of this 10% is lost to income taxes. This will result in a 2% reduction of an average mutual fund portfolio's value. This report uses a 2% income tax loss figure.

[55] Trading costs (i.e. commissions) are the expenses incurred by both mutual fund and variable annuity companies when they buy stock from brokerage firms. Because variable annuity companies tend to trade slightly less than mutual fund companies, their trading costs are approximately 30% less than those of mutual fund companies. The average trading cost for a mutual fund

[56] Commission figures should be *annualized*. The average A-share mutual fund commission is 4.1% and the average holding period of a mutual fund is 3.3 years. Thus, the average *annualized* commission would be 1.25%. Table #2 assumes a conservative annualized commission of 1%. If a 4% commission is charged and a fund will be held 10 years, the annualized commission would be 0.40%. If B-share funds are sold, the out-of-pocket commission for the buyer is zero but the annual expense ratio increases from 1.5% to approximately 2.4%. Because out-of-pocket commissions are not paid by variable annuity purchasers, this figure is zero.

[57] Two books that summarize the costs of owning mutual funds and variable annuities are: *The Great Mutual Fund Trap* by Baer and Gensler, Broadway Books, New York, 2002, and *Your Money, Your Choice...Mutual Funds - Take Control Now and Build Wealth Wisely*, Professor Charles Jones, Prentice Hall, 2003.

market risk than other equity investments such as mutual funds and stocks. Common sense would suggest that if three senior investors invest $100,000 in common stocks, a mutual fund and a variable annuity respectively, and the stock market drops by 20%, each investor will suffer similar losses. The truth is that, as between stocks, mutual funds and variable annuities, it is only the variable annuity that can *eliminate* stock market risk for senior investors. The following examples demonstrate this:

Example

Andy, age 68, invested $100,000 in a diversified portfolio of equity and bond mutual funds five years ago. The general stock market is 25% lower today than when Andy purchased his portfolio. Andy's current account value is $82,000.

Example

Ben, age 68, invested $100,000 in a diversified portfolio of stocks and bonds five years ago. The general stock market is 25% lower today than when Ben purchased his portfolio. Ben's current account value is $82,000.

Example

Chad, age 68, purchased a variable annuity five years ago for $100,000 and had his money invested in a diversified portfolio containing stock and bond subaccounts. The general stock market is 25% lower than it was when Chad invested his money. Chad's variable annuity had a rider that guaranteed that after five years Chad's account value would always be $100,000 regardless of market conditions. Today Chad's account value is $82,000. However, if he wanted to close out his account today he would receive $100,000. In addition, Chad would incur no commissions or other investment expenses of any kind for this protection on these facts.

If a senior investor is concerned about stock market risk he can invest in CDs, money market accounts, bonds and other low-risk, low-return investments. However, if a senior investor wants *equity* returns while eliminating stock market risk, only the variable annuity will provide him with this opportunity.

§3116. OFFSETTING VARIABLE ANNUITY COSTS AND FEES

The media and others who know little about variable annuities sometimes argue that the costs and fees associated with variable annuity ownership make variable annuities long-term, illiquid investments that senior investors are best advised to avoid because it takes so long for the tax-deferral and other benefits of the variable annuity to offset these costs and fees. As with all of the other defective arguments made about variable annuities, this one is baseless. As was pointed out earlier in this book, the costs and fees associated with variable annuity ownership are usually *less* than with mutual funds and, depending on the facts, can be less than commissions charged to own stock (See Chapters 9 and 10). Earlier, this book pointed out that variable annuities are every bit as liquid as other equity investments (See Chapters 16 and 17). The truth of the matter is that the costs and fees associated with variable annuity ownership are frequently offset *quicker* than are the costs and fees associated with similar equity investments. This is demonstrated in the next example:

Example

Sara is 70 years old and wants to invest $50,000. She is considering the following three equity investments:

- A variable annuity with a contingent deferred sales charge (CDSC) or surrender charge of 7% that declines 1% a year over seven years. Annual expenses and trading costs are 2.8%. (The variable annuity allows 15% surrender charge-free withdrawals and imposes surrender charges for complete surrenders on the total value at the time of surrender).

- An A-share mutual fund charging a 4% up-front, out-of-pocket commission. Annual expenses and trading costs are 2.2%. Income taxes will reduce the fund's gross percentage gain by 2%;

- A B-share mutual fund with a 6% contingent deferred sales charge (CDSC) or surrender charge that declines 1% a year. Surrender charges are based on the original investment. Annual expenses and trading costs are 3.0%. Income taxes will reduce the fund's gross gain by 2%;

Sara plans to hold her investment for at least ten years but had heard that variable annuities had to be held for much longer periods before their costs and fees could be overcome by tax-deferral and the other benefits of owning variable annuities. To make sure this was correct, Sara asked her financial advisor to calculate what she would receive if she bought and then liquidated each of the above investments after just five years of ownership. Sara is assuming a 10% rate of return. Sara is in a 20% average tax bracket. The net sale proceeds that Sara's financial professional calculated appear below:

- Variable Annuity $64,942[58]
- Mutual Fund (A) $64,417[59]
- Mutual Fund (B) $64,416[60]

As the above example demonstrates the myth that senior investors must hold a variable annuity for a longer period than other equity investments to overcome their supposedly higher costs and fees is not true. In many cases, variable annuities will net more to senior investors than mutual funds if they must liquidate their investments earlier than expected.

A related myth involving variable annuities and senior investors deals with the supposed long-term nature of variable annuities and the increased mortality of senior investors. There are some individuals who argue that because variable annuities are generally considered long-

---

[58] $50,000 + 10% = $55,000 - 2.8% = $53,460 - $50,000 = $3,460 gain ÷ $50,000 = 6.92%. 6.92% x 5 years x $50,000 = $69,866 less a surrender charge (85% of 2% of $69,866) or $2,091 = $68,678 less 20% tax on $18,678 ($3,736) = $64,942.

[59] $50,000 - 4% = $48,000 + 10% = $52,800 - 2.2% = $51,638.40. $51,638.40 - $48,000 = $3,638.40 - 20% tax = $2,910.72 ÷ $48,000 = 6.06%. 6.06% x 5 years x $48,000 = $64,417. (Taxes due on sale are ignored).

[60] $50,000 + 10% = $55,000 - 3.0% = $53,350 - $50,000 = $3,350 gain less 20% = $2,680 ÷ $50,000 = 5.36% x 5 years x $50,000 = $64,916 less a surrender charge of 1% or $500 = $64,416. (Taxes due on sale are ignored).

term investments, senior investors should avoid them because if a variable annuity loses value a senior investor may not live long enough to see his investment return to its original value. Like all of the other arguments that are advanced as to why senior investors should avoid variable annuities, this one is without merit. As pointed out earlier, if three senior investors respectively purchase mutual funds, stocks and a variable annuity, and the stock market drops 20%, all three investments will suffer similar losses. As the stock market begins to recover, each of these three investments will recover at about the same rate. In fact, only today's variable annuities offer senior investors a way to ensure that they can recover stock market losses *quicker* than similar investments in mutual funds or stocks as the next example demonstrates:

> **Example**
> Earl, who is 80, invested $100,000 in stocks ten years ago. Sara, who is 80, invested $100,000 in mutual funds ten years ago. Victor, who is 80, invested $100,000 in a variable annuity ten years ago. Victor's variable annuity contained a rider that guaranteed that after ten years Victor would recover his original $100,000 investment if the stock market was down in value after ten years. Recently, the stock market suffered a sharp decline. The values of the investment accounts held by Earl, Sara and Victor are currently $80,000. Earl and Sara must be concerned about whether they will live long enough to see their investments recover to their original values of $100,000. Victor, the variable annuity investor, has no such concern. He can liquidate his variable annuity today and receive back his full $100,000 original investment. There would be no commissions or other expenses charged to Victor for this protection based on these facts.

§3117. INVESTMENT SAFETY AND VARIABLE ANNUITIES

Occasionally, one will hear the objection that variable annuity companies are not as safe as mutual fund companies and brokerage firms when it comes to holding investments made by senior investors. As with all the other objections raised about variable annuities by people who know nothing about these annuities, this objection has no merit. The first thing senior investors need to understand about variable annuities is that by federal law variable annuities *must* keep all equity based assets in *separate accounts* that are not accessible to variable annuity companies or their creditors. This single requirement has prevented any investor from ever suffering a loss of principal invested in equities with any variable annuity company as a result of the company's financial problems.[61] Mutual fund companies and stockbrokerage companies do not have similar safeguards. Several times a year newspapers report that mutual fund companies have run into financial problems resulting from embezzlement, fraud or poor investment judgment. Investors who own these funds almost always suffer financial losses. In similar fashion, newspapers

---

[61] A good example of this is the bankruptcy of Conseco several years ago. Although Conseco was a major issuer of variable annuities before their bankruptcy. Conseco variable annuity owners lost money due to the bankruptcy. (Conseco has recently emerged from their bankruptcy).

frequently write articles about dishonest stockbrokers who have defrauded investors out of millions of dollars. These investors rarely recover anything close to their losses. Some people argue that mutual funds and brokerage companies are protected by SIPC (Security Investors Protection Corporation) insurance. This may be so, but such insurance does not cover losses resulting from fraud, embezzlement or poor investment judgment by a financial advisor. Another problem with SIPC insurance is that many investors are unaware of its limits even where fraud, embezzlement and poor investing judgment are absent, as the following example demonstrates:

Example

Linda, who is single, had been investing in stocks for several years. Her stock portfolio was currently worth $500,000. Linda's brokerage firm carried $1,000,000 worth of SIPC coverage on every customer account. Linda, who was 67, wanted to reduce the risk she had in her current stock portfolio. Her stockbroker told her of a fund that was less risky and historically provided a return very close to what Linda was used to receiving. Because of erratic movements in the stock market, Linda sold her mutual funds for $500,000 and held the cash proceeds in her brokerage account intending to buy the more conservative fund recommended by her broker as soon as the stock market settled down. A few weeks later, Linda's brokerage firm filed for bankruptcy. Linda was not overly worried because of the million dollar SIPC coverage she had on her $500,000 account. A short while later, Linda received a letter from SIPC explaining that cash accounts were covered by SIPC for a maximum of $100,000. Linda lost $400,000 because she was not aware of the limitations of the coverage provided by SIPC.

SIPC insurance holds only enough funds to cover a few more mutual funds or brokerage company defaults. After that, SIPC may itself go into default. As mentioned above, variable annuity separate accounts protect all variable annuity investors from losing their investment if the issuer of their annuity suffers a financial reversal. Most major variable annuity issuers have financial strength ratings of AA+ or higher. By comparison, most major national banks rarely have financial strength rating this high. Because the *guarantees* offered by variable annuity issuers, as opposed to principal, are primarily backed by the credit worthiness of the issuer, it is important to purchase variable annuities from a company that has top ratings for financial strength. Ensuring that the guarantees offered by variable annuity companies are honored is the job of state insurance regulators. All states have guarantee or default funds that usually provide coverage of up to $300,000 to investors who might lose any benefit that is *guaranteed* by a variable annuity company.[62] In addition, variable annuity issuers are subject to ongoing audits of their financial solvency by state insurance regulators. Variable annuity issuers must keep financial reserves on deposit with insurance regulators in every state in which the variable

---

[62] It is a good idea to determine what losses a state's default fund will cover.

annuity issuer does business. In short, senior investors concerned with the safety of their invested funds are usually better off with variable annuities than similar equity investments.

§3118. VARIABLE ANNUITIES AND TAX-DEFERRED NEST EGGS

Much of the money senior investors have to invest for their retirement consists of qualified funds (e.g., IRAs, 401(k)s, etc.). There are some who would argue that because variable annuities are tax-deferred investments, it makes little sense to purchase variable annuities with qualified funds because such funds are themselves tax-deferred. Although this argument is often made, it is, in most cases, totally without merit. Whenever qualified funds (e.g., IRAs, 401(k)s, etc.) are reinvested in anything they *must* be reinvested in qualified accounts offering tax-deferral. If they are not, then the full value of the qualified account is subject to income taxes and possibly IRS penalties.

There is a myth that variable annuity companies charge investors for tax-deferral. If this were true then investors who purchased variable annuities with qualified funds would be paying for something they would never use. This would be fraud. The truth is that no variable annuity company has ever charged so much as a cent for tax-deferral. In light of this, the fact that a senior investor elects to use qualified funds to purchase a variable annuity is a non-issue.

In the great majority of cases, the *best* investment for qualified funds held by senior investors often proves to be the variable annuity as the following examples demonstrate:

Example

Jane is 60 and has a $200,000 IRA. She needs a stream of income from this $200,000 of at least $10,000 a year for her lifetime. Jane's financial advisor recommended against investing in a variable annuity because Jane's IRA is already tax-deferred, as is the variable annuity. Instead, the advisor invested Jane's IRA in a portfolio of stocks and mutual funds paying an average dividend rate of 2.3%. This would allow Jane to receive $10,000 annual payments of principal and interest for 27 years or until Jane is 87. This assumes the stock market remains constant. Jane's stockbroker told her that if the market goes up, Jane's stream of income would be paid for more years or she could increase her annual payments. However, shortly after Jane invested her $200,000 in the portfolio the stock market dropped 25%. If dividend rates change or the stock market does not rebound, Jane's remaining $150,000 IRA balance may not generate the $10,000 a year she needs or may make these $10,000 payments for less than 20 years.

Example

Tom is 60 and has a $200,000 IRA. He needs a stream of income from this $200,000 of at least $10,000 a year for his lifetime. He purchased a variable annuity with his $200,000 IRA. The variable annuity guaranteed a 5% annual withdrawal right to Tom. Shortly after the purchase, the stock market dropped by 25%. Because the variable annuity *guaranteed* a $10,000 stream of income for Tom's lifetime regardless of what the stock market did, Tom can count on receiving his $10,000 payment for the rest of his life. In addition, Tom's variable annuity will ratchet up (but never down) as the stock market goes through its typical cycles. This will provide Tom with the potential for an increased income stream. Tom does not have to annuitize his account to get these advantages. It is possible that Tom could withdraw $200,000 from his variable annuity over a 20 year period and still have a large account balance that he would be free to take or pass to his beneficiaries. Tom's variable annuity also provides a death benefit.

As the above examples demonstrate the IRA investment made in the variable annuity provides lifetime income *guarantees* that a similar investment in stocks or mutual funds cannot. The fact that both a variable annuity and the IRA used to purchase the annuity are tax-deferred is immaterial in light of the fact that nothing is charged by the variable annuity issuer for the tax-deferral it provides. The critical issue for senior investors is whether a variable annuity provides some benefit or guarantee that is needed by the senior investor.

§3119. SUMMARY

The material above discussed the ten most common reasons advanced for the proposition that senior investors should not purchase variable annuities. As was determined, these ten reasons often prove to be meritless. A summary of this material is set out below:

(1)   Variable annuities are as liquid as any other equity investment that a senior investor might elect to purchase. The cost of liquidating a variable annuity will rarely be any greater than the cost of liquidating similar equity investments.

(2)   Surrender charges imposed by variable annuity issuers should pose no particular problems to senior investors. If a senior investor lives long enough, any surrender charges he may be subject to will disappear over time. If a senior investor dies prematurely, any existing surrender charges are eliminated. When surrender charges are incurred, they rarely exceed the up-front, out-of-pocket commissions charged by stocks and mutual funds.

(3)   Variable annuities are the only investments available to senior investors who desire a *guaranteed* stream of income for a stated period or for life that offers the possibility of increased payments without the possibility of the guaranteed income payment decreasing.

(4)   Most retired couples have incomes that are subject to ordinary income taxes that do not exceed 15%. For this reason the fact that some equity investments are subject to 15% long-term capital gains tax rates is immaterial and of no real benefit to most retired senior investors.

(5)   With a minimal amount of tax planning, the amount that beneficiaries will inherit from a senior investor who owns variable annuities will be greater than what might be received by beneficiaries who inherit mutual funds that provide a step-up in basis. Even without tax planning, the tax-deferred feature of variable annuities, together with their lower costs, will often produce a larger after-tax inheritance to beneficiaries than will a mutual fund portfolio benefitting from the step-up in basis.

(6)   Variable annuities have annual expenses that are generally *lower* than those of

mutual funds and still provide senior investors with benefits that mutual funds and stocks do not.

(7)   Variable annuities are not subject to any greater stock market risk than any other equity investment. In fact, many variable annuities can actually protect senior investors against such risk. Mutual funds and stocks cannot do this.

(8)   Some people claim that senior investors who own variable annuities that could lose value may not live long enough to see these variable annuities recover. The truth is that variable annuities provide guarantees that eliminate this concern while mutual funds and stocks do not.

(9)   Variable annuities offer safety to senior investors that is not available with mutual funds and stocks. Senior investors have lost money in both stocks and mutual funds as the result of fraud, theft, embezzlement or bankruptcy. No variable annuity owner has ever lost a cent due to fraud, theft, embezzlement or bankruptcy involving a variable annuity issuer. Considering financial strength ratings and other protective requirements, (e.g., separate accounts, financial reserves, state default funds, etc.), variable annuities often prove to be a safer place for senior investors to invest than either mutual funds or stocks.

(10)   Because variable annuity companies do not charge anything for the tax-deferral they provide, senior investors lose nothing by purchasing variable annuities with qualified funds (e.g., IRAs, 401(k)s, etc.) but have much to gain by doing so.

§3120. VARIABLE ANNUITIES CAN BENEFIT SENIOR INVESTORS IN MANY OTHER WAYS

In the sections that follow several benefits offered by variable annuities that are particularly attractive to senior investors are discussed. It is important to note that investments in mutual funds and stocks will rarely provide similar benefits. The following list summarizes just a few of the benefits provided by variable annuities. Each is set out below:

(1)   Variable annuities can provide a guaranteed minimum lifetime stream of income that can increase but never decrease. Mutual funds and stocks do not have this option;

(2)   Variable annuities can reduce the potential taxation of a senior investor's Social Security retirement income. Mutual funds will often increase the taxes on Social Security retirement income;

(3)   Variable annuities may be annuitized so as to avoid Medicaid confiscation should nursing home care be needed. Mutual funds and stocks do not have this option;

(4)   Variable annuities provide uninsurable senior investors with the ability to obtain permanent life insurance to protect their loved ones. Mutual funds and stocks do not provide a similar benefit;

(5)   Variable annuities allow senior investors to reap the benefit of a rising stock market without being exposed to potential stock market losses while mutual funds and stocks do not;

(6)   Up to 15% of a variable annuity's account value can be withdrawn annually by

senior investors without penalty. Mutual funds and stocks do not provide a similar benefit;

(7)   Buying and selling investments within a variable annuity is done on a cost-free basis and will not trigger an income tax. This dual benefit does not exist with mutual funds and stocks;

(8)   Variable annuities may offer creditor protection where mutual funds and stocks cannot;

(9)   Long-term investing in variable annuities will provide significantly more after-tax and after-expense income for senior investors than a similar investment in mutual funds;

(10)   Variable annuities are non-probate assets and can save the beneficiaries of senior investors time and money when an annuity owner dies.

§3121. INAPPROPRIATE VARIABLE ANNUITY SALES TO SENIOR CITIZENS

Although they can often prove to be excellent investments for senior investors, it is important to realize that variable annuities, like all investments, are not always the best investment for everyone. There are some valid reasons when senior investors might be well advised to avoid variable annuities. These situations arise when:

(1)   The variable annuity would impose a charge for a benefit not available to an investor over a certain age;

(2)   The variable annuity would impose a permanent charge for a benefit that terminates once an investor reaches a certain age;

(3)   The variable annuity provides a benefit that the investor needs but will lose at a certain age in the near future even if the charge for the benefit is dropped when the benefit is eliminated;

Example

Ken, a financial advisor, sold a variable annuity to Mrs. Smith who was 70 years old. The annuity imposed a charge for providing a death benefit. The annuity eliminated the death benefit for any investor reaching age 72 but continued charging for such benefit. On these facts, the sale of the variable annuity would be improper because the senior investor is put in a position that requires her to pay for a benefit that she will lose upon reaching age 72. If the charge for the death benefit was dropped at age 72, then the sale would be proper if this fact was clearly communicated to the senior investor *and* the variable annuity was not purchased primarily to obtain a permanent death benefit.

Example

Susan was 77 years old and wanted to purchase a variable annuity that would increase in value at 7% a year for ten years to create an annuitization base. However, the 7% would only be credited to age 80. On these facts, Susan would not get the full benefit of the variable annuity she was purchasing and should be made aware of this fact if she is still interested in buying the variable annuity.

(4) When it is obvious that withdrawals *needed* by a senior investor will result in the immediate imposition of surrender charges by the variable annuity issuer;

Example

John, who is 68, has $100,000 to invest. He needs at least $20,000 in principal and interest each year for as long as his money will last. A financial advisor recommended a variable annuity with a 7% contingent deferred sales charge (CDSC) that declined 1% a year over seven years. In the first year that John owned his variable annuity he withdrew $20,000. Even though the variable annuity allowed surrender-free withdrawals each year of 15%, this was not enough to prevent John from having to pay a $350 surrender charge because his withdrawal was 20%. [NOTE: This type of problem rarely arises because most competent financial advisors confronted with these facts would have recommended a no surrender charge variable annuity to their client or would have recommended another investment].

(5) A contractual benefit provided by the variable annuity could be lost by complying with state or federal law;

Example

Mike used a $300,000 IRA to purchase a variable annuity at age 75 that would allow him to withdraw 7% of his purchase price ($21,000) each year until he recovered 100% of his $300,000 purchase price. Even if the stock market went down, Mike was guaranteed to recover his full $100,000 back in 7% installments. If the market went up by more than 7%, on average (plus the costs of owning the variable annuity), then any excess gain in his account would be his to keep after he withdrew his $100,000. The variable annuity issuer guaranteed this withdrawal right so long as no more than 7% was withdrawn from the variable annuity in any year. Several years later when Mike was 86, his CPA informed Mike that, according to the IRS's required minimum distribution rules, he had to withdraw 7.1% from his IRA or face a large IRS penalty. Because this amount is in excess of the variable annuity's maximum withdrawal rate of 7%, Mike will lose the guarantee that he was promised when he bought his variable annuity. [NOTE: Nearly all variable annuity issuers will allow excessive withdrawals without jeopardizing the guarantees they provide if such withdrawals are made in order to comply with current state or federal tax law. This issue should be investigated before selecting a variable annuity].

(6) The variable annuity contractually requires the annuity owner to do something in the future that he does not want to do or is not in his best interest;

330

Example

Ned, who is 74, purchased a variable annuity that provided an attractive death benefit which Ned desired. Ned was not informed that at age 80 the variable annuity issuer would automatically, by contract, annuitize Ned's contract which would in effect void the death benefit. Because the variable annuity would force Ned into a situation that was not in his best interest, such a sale would be improper.

(7)   The variable annuity has an unreasonably long surrender period; and

Example

Judy, who was 70, purchased a variable annuity with a seven year surrender period. She informed the seller of her annuity that she would need her entire investment in two years to buy into an assisted care living facility. Based on these facts, the seven year surrender period was unreasonable. If Judy had other significant assets and did not need to draw on her variable annuity for assisted care, the seven year surrender period would not be deemed unreasonable. [NOTE: Most variable annuities issued today have surrender periods that rarely exceed seven years. In addition, purchasers of variable annuities are free to pick variable annuities without surrender periods or with surrender periods of as little as one or two years. In some cases, surrender periods will exceed seven years because the purchaser has elected a specific benefit that requires the longer surrender period.[63] Today, many variable annuities allow withdrawals for nursing home care to be made without having to pay a surrender fee].

(8)   The variable annuity is sold to a senior investor who, due to their age, suffers from a disease (i.e., Alzheimer's) that may prevent them from understanding what they are buying.

Example

Terry is 84 and lives in a rest home. She suffers from dementia and understands little of what goes on around her. Recently a financial advisor sold a $100,000 variable annuity to Terry. Such a transaction would be improper. [Note: The sale of *any* goods, services or financial products to a person in Terry's position would be improper.]

Just as there are some reasons why senior investors should avoid variable annuities, there are several reasons why senior investors should seriously consider them. Many of these reasons are discussed below.

§3122. VARIABLE ANNUITIES, SENIOR INVESTORS AND GUARANTEED STREAMS OF INCOME

A major advantage of variable annuity ownership by senior investors is the ability to obtain a guaranteed, lifetime stream of income while being invested in the stock market without

---

[63] Guaranteed minimum income benefit (GMIB) riders usually require a 10-year holding period.

being subject to stock market risk. Mutual funds and stocks do not offer this advantage as the examples below demonstrate:

Example

In late 1999, Rita at age 60, invested her $800,000 life savings in a portfolio of stocks and mutual funds. Rita needed to withdraw $40,000 a year to live on. Because the stock market had returned double digit returns for several years Rita believed that she could withdraw $40,000 a year and watch her nest egg grow. During the 2000-2002 bear market, Rita's account dropped by $200,000 in value to $600,000. Three annual withdrawals of $40,000 further reduced Rita's nest egg to $480,000 by 2005. Rita's stockbroker told Rita that there was no guarantee that she could continue to withdraw $40,000 a year from her portfolio for life. In fact, there was a strong likelihood that Rita would run out of money if she continued to withdraw $40,000 from her nest egg each year.[64]

Example

In late 1999, Pat at age 60, invested his $800,000 life savings in a variable annuity that provided a rider that guaranteed a $40,000 stream of income to Pat as long as he lived. (Technically, such riders are referred to as Guaranteed Minimum Withdrawal Benefit for Life riders or a GMWB-Life). During the bear market of 2000-2002, Pat's account value dropped by $200,000 to $600,000. Three annual withdrawals of $40,000 further reduced Pat's nest egg to $480,000 by 2005. Regardless of what the stock market does in the future, Pat will be guaranteed to receive $40,000 for the rest of his life. Formal annuitization is not required. Based on payments already received and future payments, Pat will be guaranteed to receive a minimum of $1,000,000 over his life expectancy (25 years x $40,000 = $1,000,000). If Pat dies prematurely, his annuity will pay out a death benefit to his survivors.

What the above examples demonstrate is that for senior investors who want the peace of mind of a guaranteed stream of income for life while being fully invested in the stock, they should consider variable annuities. Stocks and mutual funds will not provide similar income guarantees. Another all too common problem facing senior investors like Rita (in the first example) is the fact that fear may cause them to pull their money out of the equities market and buy "safer" investments such as bonds, bank CDs, etc. This market timing attempt will usually result in senior investors actually *increasing* the likelihood that they will outlive their money.

§3123. VARIABLE ANNUITIES, SENIOR INVESTORS AND TAXATION OF SOCIAL SECURITY RETIREMENT INCOME

Single taxpayers who have adjusted gross incomes of $25,000 or more and married taxpayers who have adjusted gross incomes of in excess of $44,000 are subject to having from 50% to as much as 85% of their Social Security retirement income subject to ordinary income taxes. This additional tax burden can be a major problem for retired persons who own mutual

---

[64] $40,000 annual withdrawals from a $480,000 account paying 5.5% will last 20 years.

fund portfolios. The following example demonstrates this problem:

Example

Jack is 65 years old and has pension income of $24,000 a year. He has a mutual fund portfolio worth $150,000. He and his wife receive $20,000 a year in combined Social Security retirement income. Jack and his wife do not have a need for any income above his pension and their Social Security. Although Jack and his wife do not have a need for any money, Jack's mutual fund annually distributes $15,000 in capital gains to him. This forced or involuntary mutual fund income distribution increases the annual income of Jack and his wife to $59,000. Because of this, a large part of the Social Security income paid to Jack and his wife will be subject to ordinary income taxes.

In the above example, had Jack held his mutual funds within a variable annuity, none of the Social Security retirement income he and his wife received would be subject to income taxes. The reason for this is that gains made within variable annuities are tax-deferred and do not count in determining whether Social Security retirement income will be taxed. Retired persons who find themselves in a situation like that of Jack and his wife frequently ask if shifting their mutual funds to a tax-free bond fund would solve their problem. The answer is no. The reason for this is that, unlike tax-deferred income, tax-free income must be taken into consideration when determining whether Social Security retirement income will be subject to income taxes. One of the best ways for retired persons to protect their Social Security retirement income from taxation would be to convert their mutual fund portfolio to a variable annuity. The problem with this is that commissions and income taxes due on the sale of mutual funds could be quite large. Preparing for retirement by owning variable annuities instead of mutual funds in the first place eliminates this problem.

§3124. VARIABLE ANNUITIES, SENIOR INVESTORS AND NURSING HOME EXPENSES

Mutual fund ownership may pose a serious problem if the owner of such funds, or his spouse, needs Medicaid assistance should they go into a nursing home. The reason for this is that states count the value of mutual funds in determining eligibility for nursing home coverage under Medicaid. On the other hand, most states do *not* count the value of annuities that are making payments to either or both spouses as an asset for Medicaid eligibility. A portfolio of mutual funds can result in Medicaid disqualification, as the following examples demonstrate:

Example

Mary, age 72, went into a nursing home three years ago. Mary's only asset at that time was a variable annuity worth $144,000 she purchased eight years ago. Mary had a spouse that she was concerned about. Shortly before going into the nursing home, Mary annuitized her annuity and started to receive $1,222 per month for life with payments being guaranteed for ten years. Mary had to use this income toward her nursing home care expenses of $4,000 a month. Mary recently died.

Her spouse will receive the remaining annual annuity payments of $14,664 for seven years, for a total of more than $100,000.

Example

Mark, age 72, went into a nursing home three years ago. Mark's only asset at that time was a mutual fund and stock portfolio worth $144,000 he purchased eight years ago. Mark had a spouse that he was concerned about. The cost of Mark's nursing home care was $4,000 per month. Medicaid requires that both the *income* and *principal* of mutual fund and stock portfolios be exhausted before Medicaid will pay for nursing home care. Mark made each month's nursing home payment from his mutual fund and stock portfolio. Mark recently died. Mark used his entire mutual fund and stock portfolio for his nursing home care over the three years he was in the nursing home. His spouse will receive nothing. Had Mark liquidated his fund portfolio and bought an annuity, he would have had a smaller nest egg and would have incurred transaction costs and income taxes that Mary, in the prior example, avoided because she had invested her money in a variable annuity initially. In addition, many states will not grant preferred status to immediate annuities derived from variable annuities that were not purchased at least six years prior to annuitization.

§3125. VARIABLE ANNUITIES, SENIOR INVESTORS AND THE DEATH BENEFIT

Variable annuities provide a basic death benefit that is available without having to undergo a physical exam or answer health questions. Mutual funds and stocks do not offer this benefit.

Example

Chad is 64 and in poor health. He wants to invest $300,000 that has been ear marked for his wife should he die. If Chad invests the money in a variable annuity he knows his wife will never receive less than the $300,000 he invested (plus any additional investments, less any withdrawals). If his variable annuity is worth more than $300,000 at his death, his wife gets the larger account value. Neither stocks nor mutual funds provide this benefit. The death benefit also allows Chad to be more aggressive with his investments.

Another major benefit offered by many variable annuity companies is the ability of senior investors who are uninsurable to obtain a death benefit that is guaranteed to increase over time. Neither stocks nor mutual funds provide this benefit. This benefit is demonstrated in the following example:

Example

John, who is 60, has $500,000. He wants to buy an insurance policy on his life for the benefit of his grandchildren. He recently learned that he was not insurable due to two strokes he had recently suffered. As an alternative, John invested the money in a variable annuity that included a death benefit that would increase his $500,000 investment by a compounded 7% rate of return each year regardless of what the stock market did. If John dies at age 70, his grandchildren will receive a *minimum* of $1,000,000. If the market value of John's variable annuity exceeds

$1,000,000, John's grandchildren will receive this larger figure. Neither stocks nor mutual funds provide this benefit.

Variable annuities not only provide a basic and increasing death benefit for senior investors, but they also provide a way for such investors to increase their death benefit without any additional cost. This benefit is available to senior investors because variable annuity owners, unlike mutual fund and stock owners, may take advantage of IRC §1035 which allows the tax-free exchange of one variable annuity for another. The appropriate use of this IRS Code section can result in beneficiaries receiving more from a decedent who owned a variable annuity than a mutual fund or stocks. The following example demonstrates this:

Example

Steve, a widower, purchased a variable annuity for $350,000 when he was 60. Steve is now 70 and in poor health. Steve wants his daughter to inherit his variable annuity. When his annuity increased in value to $700,000 two years ago, Steve's financial advisor suggested that Steve take advantage of IRC §1035 and transfer his variable annuity to another similar variable annuity. This could be accomplished without costs or income taxes. The benefit of the transfer would be that Steve's original death benefit of $300,000 provided by his first annuity would increase to $700,000 with the new variable annuity. This would guarantee that Steve's daughter would never receive less than $700,000 at Steve's death. Steve followed his advisor's suggestion. When Steve died, his variable annuity had decreased in value to $500,000, yet Steve's daughter received a check from the annuity company for $700,000. The fact that using IRC §1035 to increase a death benefit may impose a new surrender period on the owner of the variable annuity is a moot issue if the owner intends to pass the variable annuity to his beneficiaries at this death because surrender charges cease at the owner's death.

§3126. VARIABLE ANNUITIES, SENIOR INVESTORS AND RISK-FREE INVESTING

Many variable annuities provide risk-free investing to senior investors. Mutual funds, stocks and similar investments do not as the following example demonstrates:

Example

Dave is 65-years old and has $250,000 to invest for five years. He initially considered a portfolio of stocks, bonds and mutual funds but realized that the last time he made a similar decision in 2000 he lost 30% of his investment. Dave has elected to purchase a variable annuity with a rider that guarantees a full refund of his $250,000 in five years should the market go down again. If the stock market were to double in the next five years, Dave's investment would be worth $500,000 less his normal costs of investing.

§3127. VARIABLE ANNUITIES, SENIOR INVESTORS AND SURRENDER-CHARGE FREE WITHDRAWALS

Variable annuities allow senior investors to withdraw from 10% to 15% of their variable annuity's contract value each year without paying a surrender penalty. Withdrawals of any amount from stocks will generate a sales commission. Withdrawals from B-share mutual funds will incur a surrender charge regardless of the amount of the withdrawal. Over a six or seven year period, in an upward moving stock market, a variable annuity owner could withdraw his entire investment without paying a commission or surrender charge. If the same thing were attempted with an A-share mutual fund or stock portfolio, the investor would still lose the original commission he paid when the fund or stocks were purchased and later sold.

§3128. VARIABLE ANNUITIES, SENIOR INVESTORS AND COST-FREE INVESTING

When senior investors purchase variable annuities and decide to change investments, they can do so without paying commissions or triggering income taxes. Stocks and mutual funds do not provide both of these advantages as the following examples demonstrate:

Example

Seven years ago Judy purchased some XYZ stock for $75,000. Today it is worth $150,000. Because Judy is 66 and a recent widow she wants to sell her stock and purchase some bonds. If Judy sells her stock she will trigger a capital gains tax of over $11,000, incur a sales commission that could easily exceed $2,000 and possibly generate another commission to buy the bonds she wants.

Example

Peter purchased a mutual fund for $75,000 seven years ago. Peter buys only A-share mutual funds. Today the mutual fund is worth $150,000. Because of his age (66), Peter wants to sell the fund and buy a bond fund with another fund company. If Peter sells his current fund he will trigger a capital gains tax that, with the annual taxes he has already paid, could exceed $11,000. Additionally, he will generate another commission to purchase his new funds that could be as much as $6,000.

Example

Seven years ago Mark invested $75,000 in a variable annuity. Today the variable annuity is worth $150,000. Mark, because he is 66, has decided to reinvest his money in a different variable annuity that has several good bond funds (subaccounts) to chose from. By using IRC §1035, Mark can transfer his first variable annuity to the second variable annuity without triggering an income tax or incurring an out-of-pocket commission. Because of his age, Mark may want to elect a surrender period for his new annuity that will run for three years or less.

As the examples above demonstrate, the liquidation of stocks and mutual funds and their reinvestment can result in unwanted income taxes and commissions that are avoided when variable annuities are exchanged for other variable annuities.

§3129. VARIABLE ANNUITIES, SENIOR INVESTORS AND CREDITOR PROTECTION

By statute, several states provide strong creditor protection for owners of variable annuities. No state protects mutual funds and stocks from creditors in the same manner. Mutual fund owners are at the greatest risk of loss to creditors when they die. Mutual funds are typically probate assets which are transferred to a deceased owner's estate. Once in the estate, mutual funds become available to creditors of the deceased fund owner. The following example demonstrates how this process can put a deceased owner's mutual fund portfolio at risk.

Example

Tom was married and had two children. His largest asset was his $700,000 mutual fund portfolio. Tom was a part owner of a large software company that recently went out of business. Tom died shortly thereafter. His estate was sued by his creditors and was required to pay $700,000 to the creditors. Tom's mutual funds, because they were assets of his estate, were liquidated to pay his creditors. This reduced Tom's mutual fund portfolio to zero and left Tom's wife and two children in financial difficulty.

Variable annuities, being insurance products, are considered non-probate property. Variable annuities pass at an owner's death directly to the named beneficiary and not to the variable annuity owner's estate. In the last example, had Tom owned a $700,000 variable annuity instead of a mutual fund portfolio, his wife and children would have received the $700,000 instead of his creditors.

Proponents of mutual funds claim that they can get the same protection from creditors that variable annuity owners receive when they die by simply owning their mutual funds jointly with rights of survivorship with their spouse or another person. This is not the case. Many states require that the portion of a mutual fund jointly owned by a decedent to be paid into the decedent's estate if unpaid taxes or other debts owed to creditors are involved. In addition, placing mutual funds in joint ownership with survivorship rights can result in significant losses. This problem is demonstrated in the following example:

Example

Dave, who is 65, owned a mutual fund portfolio worth $1,000,000. It was his major asset. Dave owed $500,000 in debts and wanted to prevent his mutual funds from passing through his estate and being depleted by these debts. Dave decided to create a joint tenancy with right of survivorship in his mutual fund account. Dave's wife was named as the other joint owner of the mutual fund. Dave recently died. Under state law, Dave's portion of the mutual fund portfolio was required to be brought back into the estate to pay Dave's debts. Had Dave owned a variable annuity, his wife would not have lost half of her inheritance to creditors. In addition, the half of the mutual fund portfolio that did pass to Dave's wife has created another problem. Dave's wife may not be entitled to a full stepped-up in basis in her half interest in the mutual fund at Dave's death. This will increase her income taxes.[65]

§3130. THE BENEFIT OF TAX-DEFERRAL

Because variable annuities grow on a tax-deferred basis, the income taxes ultimately paid on a variable annuity may be less than with an equivalent mutual fund investment. One reason

---

[65] The half ownership in the funds held by Dave's wife were received by gift and therefore do not receive a step-up in basis.

for this is that income taxes are generally higher during ones' working years than in retirement. The following two cases isolate the income tax liability for a mutual fund and variable annuity investment to demonstrate the advantage of tax deferral:

Example

At age 50, Ben invested $30,000 in a mutual fund. Each year, due to Ben's large income, the federal, state and local taxes Ben had to pay reduced his average fund's rate of return from 10% to 8%. At age 65, Ben realized that he had paid $42,546 in income taxes on his fund over the past 15 years.[66] This left an after-tax fund value of $95,165 to supplement Ben's other retirement income.

Example

Mark, at age 50, invested $30,000 in a variable annuity. The variable annuity grew to $125,317 after 15 years. Mark, because he was recently retired, elected to liquidate his variable annuity and pay all the taxes due at one time on the gain of $95,317. His tax was 20% or $19,063, leaving Mark with an after-tax variable annuity value of $106,253. This is $11,089 more than Ben received in the last example on identical facts.[67]

§3131. PROBATE AVOIDANCE

Variable annuities are designed to be non-probate assets and thus avoid the delay and costs associated with the probate process. Mutual funds are generally probate assets and often generate probate costs. These costs of probate may impact the rate of return one receives on their mutual fund portfolio. The potential cost associated with the probate of mutual funds must be considered when comparing the cost of mutual funds and variable annuity ownership.

Example

Max purchased a mutual fund for $100,000. Max recently died with is mutual fund value at $100,000. Max's wife Lisa had to wait nine months before getting the mutual fund from Max's estate. Additionally, the cost of probate was 5% of the estate's value. Because of this, Lisa only received $95,000 instead of the full $100,000 value of the mutual funds. The probate costs of 5% was, in effect, a 5% additional cost of mutual fund ownership.

Example

A year ago, John purchased a variable annuity for $100,000. John recently died with his annuity valued at $100,000. John's wife Sue was his beneficiary and received a check for $100,000 from the annuity company a week after John's death. She had no time delays or probate costs to deal with because the annuity was non-probate property.

Trying to avoid probate with mutual funds by using joint ownership with rights of survivorship can be risky as the next example demonstrates:

---

[66] $30,000 x 8% x 15 years = $95,165. *The Wall Street Journal* in its May 10, 2006 issue, p. 1, Section C, has an article on taxation of mutual funds that shows just how great a burden these taxes can be.

[67] This example ignores the fact that the non-tax costs of owning the variable annuity would be less than those of the mutual funds. In addition, the mutual funds owned by Ben were not reduced for taxes on unrealized capital gains when they were sold in this example.

338

Example

Judy, who is 72, owned $800,000 in mutual funds. She was getting married and decided to put her mutual fund portfolio in joint ownership with right of survivorship with her fiancé, Paul. Judy wanted to avoid probate and estate creditors that might seek to claim assets in her estate. Shortly afterward Judy's relationship with Paul soured and the wedding was called off. Judy asked Paul to reconvey his interest in Judy's mutual fund to her. He refused and died several months later. Judy will most likely lose $400,000. Had Judy owned a variable annuity, she could have named Paul as the beneficiary of the variable annuity. This would have kept the variable annuity out of her estate and away from her creditors had she gotten married. When the marriage was called off, Judy could have dropped Paul as the annuity's beneficiary and replaced him with a sister, brother, charity, etc.[68]

§3132. OTHER BENEFITS VARIABLE ANNUITIES OFFER SENIOR INVESTORS

The benefits made available to senior investors by variable annuities are many. A brief chapter such as this cannot address all of these benefits. The following list attempts to summarize the benefits that variable annuities offer to senior investors. Many of these benefits were discussed briefly in the earlier part of this chapter, others were not.

- Non-qualified annuities grow tax-deferred, mutual funds don't.

- Mutual funds rarely provide the 15% long-term capital gains rate that they claim owners receive. On the other hand, variable annuity payments received in retirement are taxed at 15% when the recipient's tax bracket is 25%.

- Mutual funds create an income tax trap for individuals purchasing funds late in the year. Variable annuities do not present a similar problem where late year purchases are made.

- Mutual funds can make annual *taxable* distributions to fund owners even where the value of their fund has gone down because mutual funds contain "embedded gains." In some cases, the taxation on these embedded gains can run into triple digits. Variable annuities do not present a similar embedded gain problem.

- Mutual fund ownership along with the annual distributions made by such mutual funds can subject the fund owner to taxation under the alternative minimum tax (AMT) structure. The AMT always results in increased income taxes. Variable annuity ownership cannot trigger the AMT in the same way that mutual funds can.

- Variable annuities are easy to position so that at the owner's death the variable annuity will not be subject to either estate or income taxes. The same tax reduction techniques do not work nearly as well with mutual funds.

- Mutual fund ownership can result in the loss of tax exemptions. This does not

---

[68] Some states provide Pay-on-Death (POD) or Transfer-on-Death (TOD) procedures that, if elected, can provide a form of joint ownership without the drawbacks mentioned in this example.

occur where variable annuities are owned.

- Ownership of mutual funds can result in the loss of income tax deductions. Variable annuity ownership does not create the same tax loss.

- Mutual fund ownership can cause the owner to lose tax credits. This does not occur where variable annuities are owned.

- A national sales tax would penalize mutual fund owners in retirement while providing a tax windfall to variable annuity owners.

- Under the current tax climate, it is more likely that capital gains rates and capital gains holding periods will increase rather than decrease. If either capital gains rates or their holding period increase, it will raise income taxes for owners of mutual funds. Variable annuities, being tax-deferred, would be unaffected.

- Beneficiaries of variable annuities often receive a larger amount by inheriting a variable annuity than a mutual fund even though the mutual fund beneficiaries receive a step-up in basis.

- The ownership of mutual funds can restrict or eliminate one's ability to own other retirement accounts such as IRAs. Mutual fund ownership can also prevent one from converting a traditional IRA to a Roth IRA. Variable annuities present no such restrictions or limitations.

- The ownership of mutual funds can, in many cases, cause Social Security to be subject to income taxes. Variable annuity ownership does not present the same problem.

- When a variable annuity is sold at a loss, the tax treatment of that loss is more beneficial than an equal loss with a mutual fund.

- The ownership of mutual funds may require the mutual fund owner to pay estimated taxes. Variable annuity ownership does not create the same tax problem.

- Mutual funds are subject to state and local income taxes in those states that have such taxes. Variable annuities, because they are tax-deferred, are not subject to state and local income taxes.

- Variable annuities allow the owners to place payout restrictions to beneficiaries in their variable annuities. Mutual funds do not provide this benefit.

- The record keeping requirements for owning mutual funds are significantly more complex than the record keeping requirements for owning variable annuities.

- Many states offer either complete or partial protection of variable annuities from creditors. No state provides protection from creditors for mutual funds.

- Mutual funds are commonly part of a decedent's estate which makes such funds available to all creditors of the estate. Variable annuities, on the other hand, are almost always non-probate property that do not pass through a decedent's estate and therefore are not subject to the reach of creditors of a decedent's estate.

- Mutual funds, because they are almost always part of a decedent's estate, are subject to the delays and expenses of probate. Variable annuities, because they pass outside of probate directly to beneficiaries, are not subject to similar delays and costs.

- Attempting to position mutual funds so they will not pass through probate almost always results in additional taxes, costs or delays.

- Owners of variable annuities can adjust their annuities so that they are not considered assets for Medicaid qualification. Mutual funds, except for principal protected funds, cannot be adjusted in a similar manner.

- Variable annuities provide basic as well as enhanced death benefits to the beneficiaries of the variable annuity owners. Mutual funds, except for principal protected funds, do not provide any death benefit whatsoever.

- Variable annuities provide dollar-cost averaging to variable annuity owners at no expense. Mutual funds do not provide this benefit on a cost-free basis to fund owners.

- Mutual funds do not provide cost-free asset re-balancing whereas variable annuities do.

- Many variable annuities offer premium bonuses. Mutual funds offer no similar bonuses.

- Many variable annuities today provide guaranteed protection against loss of principal. Mutual funds, except for a few stable value funds, do not offer this same protection.

- Many variable annuities today provide a guaranteed rate of return on fixed accounts within variable annuities. Mutual funds do not provide the same benefit.

- Variable annuities can be used to keep a life insurance owner from having to sell a life insurance policy at a loss. Mutual funds cannot be used for this purpose.

- Withdrawals can be made from variable annuities and used to purchase things such as retirement homes, yachts, etc. without having to pay income taxes on the withdrawals.

- The risk of insolvency rests with the owner of a mutual fund. Variable annuity owners are not exposed to similar insolvency risks.

- Variable annuities allow the annuity owner to trade funds among different families on a commission-free basis. This is rarely true for owners of mutual funds.

- A variable annuity owner may exchange his variable annuity for a completely different variable annuity without triggering income taxes. A mutual fund owner cannot move his funds from one mutual fund company to another without triggering an income tax.

- Variable annuity owners receive an income tax deduction under IRC § 691 when inheriting a variable annuity. Mutual funds do not receive a similar income tax deduction.

- If the Untied States tax system is modified to include a flat tax, mutual fund owners will be at a disadvantage while variable annuity owners will reap a tax windfall.

- Variable annuities can provide their owners with a guaranteed stream of income for their entire lifetime. Mutual funds cannot provide the same benefit.

- The exclusion ratio allows a variable annuity owner to shelter large portions of variable annuity payments from income taxes. Mutual funds do not provide a similar exclusion ratio.

- Mutual funds are subject to intangibles taxes in those states where intangible taxes are levied. Variable annuities are universally exempt from intangibles taxes.

- The owner of a variable annuity who elects to dollar-cost average into mutual funds usually receives an interest rate well above the market rate on money awaiting to be invested. Mutual fund owners who seek the benefit of dollar-cost averaging do not receive similar above market rates of interest on money awaiting investment.

- Variable annuities allow owners to control precisely how much money will be withdrawn from their variable annuity and thus allow the variable annuity owner to control taxes. Mutual fund owners have no similar control. Mutual fund owners are subject to involuntary mutual fund distributions of capital gains and dividends each year whether they want such distributions or not.

- If other mutual fund owners redeem their shares and leave a fund, this has the impact of raising the potential tax burden of those mutual fund owners who remain in the fund. Variable annuities contain no similar tax disadvantage.

- Many variable annuities waive any surrender penalties when individuals suffer a severe illness, are required to go into a nursing home, lose their job, etc. Mutual funds do not provide a similar benefit where contingent deferred sales charges are imposed on mutual fund owners.

- Variable annuities, when initially purchased, allow the owner a period of time to revoke his purchase without cost. Mutual funds do not allow this benefit.

- Some mutual funds dictate when a mutual fund owner may sell his mutual funds or impose a redemption fee when funds are sold. Variable annuities can be sold at any time without restriction. Variable annuities never charge additional redemption fees if one wants to sell their variable annuity.

- There are costly tax traps associated with the buying and selling of mutual funds. Similar tax traps do not exist for variable annuities.

- Mutual funds not only require annual taxation when the mutual fund is going up in value, but also impose income taxes when the mutual fund is going down in value. Variable annuities, being tax-deferred, impose no annual income taxes regardless of whether the variable annuity is increasing or decreasing in value.

§3133. ENDING IMPROPER ANNUITY SALES – A SUGGESTION

It is critical to understand that no annuity can be sold in any jurisdiction without approval by insurance regulators. If these government officials believe that any contractual provision in any annuity could potentially be detrimental to senior investors, they have the authority to order annuity issuers to modify or eliminate those provisions or forfeit the right to sell their annuities in the jurisdiction imposing such remedial modifications. A proactive approach to prevent annuities containing certain contract provisions from being sold to senior investors would seem to be a more intelligent approach than the current reactive process of one state regulator (e.g., an insurance commissioner) approving the sale of an annuity containing potentially detrimental contract provisions and later having a second government official (e.g., an attorney general) attempt to stop the sale of these approved annuities only after senior investors have been harmed.

§3134. REVIEW QUESTIONS

- Discuss five benefits variable annuities offer senior investors that no other investment can offer.

- Discuss three situations where a senior investor should not consider buying a variable annuity.

§3135. QUESTIONS TO ASK

With all the benefits and guarantees offered by variable annuities, why should senior investors be excluded from owning these products.

§3136. SOURCES

See the footnotes to this chapter for sources that can be consulted regarding senior investors and variable annuities.

§3137. CONCLUSION

No investment is the best investment for everyone. This includes variable annuities. The important thing is to realize that any product can be improperly sold. When this occurs, it should be understood that the product is not improper but rather the sale is improper and the person making the sale is acting improperly. If a used car dealer sells a used car to a senior and it is later discovered that the car was in a serious wreck before the sale and that the seller had rolled back the odometer, should the sale of all used cars to all seniors be prohibited? Certainly not. If a dishonest hearing aid salesperson improperly sells a hearing aid to a senior for twice its normal price, should the sale of all hearing aids to all seniors be prohibited? Certainly not. If a dishonest financial advisor sells a variable annuity to an 80 year-old woman with Alzheimer's disease, should the sale of all variable annuities to all seniors be halted? Certainly not.

Most of the reasons advanced to support the proposition that annuities are not good investments for senior investors, when applied to variable annuities, prove to be baseless. The primary reason for this is that people who know nothing about variable annuities, whether reporters or state level bureaucrats, do not understand that there are several types of annuities that provide different benefits and impose different limitations. The truth of the matter is that for a great majority of senior investors, variable annuities, with their guarantees and protections, often prove to be the best possible investment for these investors. Senior investors are much smarter than media and state bureaucrats give them credit for. Many senior investors, working with their financial advisors, have secured their financial future by including variable annuities in their retirement portfolios.

– CHAPTER 32 –
THE PERFORMANCE MYTH

§3201. INTRODUCTION

For whatever illogical reason, the media and many investors believe that the performance of mutual funds, over the long-term, is better than the performance of variable annuities. This belief is nothing more than a myth.

§3202. THE COST/TAXATION EXPLANATION

Whenever someone who concludes that mutual funds perform better than variable annuities is questioned about how this better performance occurs they almost always support their conclusion by pointing out that the lower cost of the mutual fund is responsible for its superior performance. They often will add that the more favorable tax treatment of mutual funds and their lower commissions further adds to the out-performance of mutual funds over variable annuities. The problem with this two-pronged conclusion is it is based entirely on unsupportable myth.

§3203. MYTH SUPPORTING MYTH

The myth that variable annuities underperform mutual funds is a myth that has its genesis in these other myths. As often occurs when variable annuities and mutual fund are compared, one myth can arise because it is based on one or more other myths. The performance myth is one of the best examples of this occurrence.

As was pointed out in Chapters 9 and 10 above, the typical mutual fund has annual ownership costs that are nearly double those of the typical variable annuity. As was pointed out in Chapters 24 and 25 above, the *tax-deferred* ordinary income tax rate applied to variable annuities at the point of surrender can (and usually do) provide a large after-tax return than a similar mutual fund that is taxed each year and upon liquidation at a combined long-term capital gains rate and an ordinary income tax rate. As was discussed in Chapters 22 and 23 above, commissions paid or received on variable annuities are rarely greater than those of the mutual fund. Once the cost myth, capital gains/ordinary income tax myth and commission myth are corrected, it becomes obvious that the investment product that will perform the best is the variable annuity *not* the mutual fund.

§3204. THE MEDIA'S YEAR-END PERFORMANCE FIGURES – DEFECTIVE DATA

One of the reasons that the performance myth continues is that at the end of each year many newspapers and financial magazines report mutual fund and variable annuity performance figures that offer no explanation or defective explanations of what the data shows.

§3205. FALSE NET RETURNS

Performance figures published for mutual funds are nothing more than the gross rate of return (e.g., 10%) less annual expenses, administrative fees, 12b-1 fees and trading costs which total approximately 2.2%. This would appear to yield a net return of 7.8%.

The problem with these performance figures is that they yield a false net return. These figures do *not* reflect two other reductions that must occur to obtain a true net performance figure. These two reductions are commissions and annual income taxes. These two costs are not left out of performance figures out of some malevolent plot by mutual fund companies. The truth is they have absolutely no way of knowing what commission every mutual fund investor paid because of break-point and share class differences. This is also true of income taxes. Mutual fund investors will pay different income taxes depending on several factors (e.g., tax brackets, marital status, age, etc.). From Chapter 10 it was determined that the *average* annual income tax paid by owners is approximately 2% if the fund returns 10%. Chapter 10 demonstrated that the average annualized up-front, out-of-pocket commission for owning the typical mutual fund is 1.2%. If these two "forgotten" expenses are deducted from the 7.8% false net return mentioned above, the *true* net annual performance of the hypothetical fund discussed drops to 4.6% which is a far cry from the 7.8% the public is led to believe they are receiving.

§3206. VARIABLE ANNUITY PERFORMANCE FIGURES

Variable annuity issuers report annual performance based on gross returns (e.g., 10%) less annual management fees, M&E costs, 12b-1 fees, administrative fees and trading costs which total approximately 2.7% to yield a net return of 7.3%.

This 7.3% annual performance return is a true net performance figure because it does not have to be reduced by income taxes or commission. The reason for this is variable annuities grow tax-deferred and the commission advanced to the financial professional is *included* in the annual management fees that are already deducted from the variable annuity's gross return to yield the annuity's net return.

§3207. QUESTIONS TO ASK

When a net-to-net analysis is conducted the performance of the typical variable annuity will be greater than a typical mutual fund. Shouldn't clients be made aware of this?

§3208. REVIEW QUESTIONS

- Discuss why the performance of a typical variable annuity will be greater than for an equivalent mutual fund.
- Why do newspapers, at the end of the year, show that mutual funds perform better than variable annuities?

§3209. CONCLUSION

Annual commissions and income taxes can reduce *published* performance figures for mutual funds by approximately 3%. Because of these two costs, it is the variable annuity that typically outperforms an equivalent mutual fund.

– CHAPTER 33 –
THE RISK MYTH

§3301. INTRODUCTION

Many investors believe that the risk associated with variable annuities is no different than other equity investments like mutual funds, stocks, etc. This is not true. Today's variable annuities provide riders that offer guarantees and protections against risk that are not available when investors purchase mutual funds and stocks.

§3302. VARIABLE ANNUITY RIDERS

Modern variable annuities offer several riders that provide guarantees and protect investors against risk. Although there are several protective riders available, this chapter will discuss the three most commonly purchased variable annuity riders. These three riders are discussed below.

§3303. GUARANTEED MINIMUM ACCUMULATION BENEFIT (GMAB)

With the GMAB rider, a variable annuity purchaser is guaranteed a return of his investment even if it is down in value at the end of an agreed holding period. This period typically ranges from five to ten years. If the annuity has increased in value by the end of the agreed holding period, the purchaser is entitled to keep all such gains less the normal costs of investing in the variable annuity. In short, the GMAB is similar to a money-back guarantee.

Example

Margaret has $350,000 to invest for the next ten years. She is looking for an investment that will allow her to be in the equities markets but she requires the following:

- Her entire $350,000 investment must go to work for her without reduction for up-front costs or expenses.

- Her investment must be held predominately in equities.

- She can receive professional financial advice on her investing for the next ten years without cost.

- The investment should not have an annual cost that would be out of line with a typical equity investment of $350,000.

- When Margaret withdraws her money from this investment, she is able to keep all of her gain, less her investment costs.

- To protect against risk Margaret wants to know that if her account value ten years from now is less than the $350,000 she originally invested, Margaret wants the financial institution involved to return all of her $350,000 investment without making any charges whatsoever.

The *only* investment available today that will give Margaret what she wants with complete protection against risk is a variable annuity with a Guaranteed Minimum Accumulation Benefit (GMAB) rider.

§3304. THE GUARANTEED MINIMUM INCOME BENEFIT (GMIB)

The GMIB annuity allows an individual to invest an amount of money in a variable annuity for a set period of time (usually ten years). Over this period of time, the account value is guaranteed to grow at a set rate (usually 5% to 7%). At the end of the holding period, if the stock market has gone down, the annuity owner is entitled to receive lifetime payments (usually guaranteed for twenty years) based on the value produced by the 5% - 7% guaranteed growth rate. These payments can be as much as $12,000 per $100,000 invested depending on the age of the investor. These lifetime payments will usually return the original amount invested in eight to ten years and thereafter continue to pay a stream of income to the annuity owner for life. In order to obtain the lifetime payments, the annuity owner must formally annuitize his annuity. On the other hand, if the stock market goes up, the annuity investor is entitled to keep all such gains, subject only to the normal investment costs of owning the variable annuity. In this latter case, the entire account value can be taken by the annuity owner.

Example
Sam is 59 and is exactly ten years away from full retirement. Sam wants to invest a $500,000 IRA in an investment that will give him the following benefits.

- Sam wants his investments held predominately in the equity markets.

- If the account goes up dramatically over the course of the next ten years, Sam wants to be able to take his account balance and do whatever he pleases with it.

- To protect against risk, Sam wants to know that if the stock market goes down significantly over the next ten years, Sam wants a guarantee that in ten years he will receive a check for $62,500 a year for the rest of his life, guaranteed for a minimum of twenty years (should the stock market spike any time during this ten year investment period, Sam wants his lifetime payments based on the higher spiking value of the market rather than the ending market value).

The only investment available today that will give Sam what he wants with the risk protection he needs is a variable annuity with a Guaranteed Withdrawal Income Benefit (GMIB) rider.

§3305. THE GUARANTEED MINIMUM WITHDRAWAL BENEFIT FOR LIFE (GMWB-LIFE)

The GMWB-Life annuity allows an individual to invest an amount of money and be guaranteed a stated income stream for life or a stated period of time (e.g., 20 years), whichever is *longer*. The income stream is a percentage of the amount invested. This percentage of income ranges between 5% to 7% of the amount invested depending on the age of the annuity purchaser. If withdrawals are not made immediately, most GMWB-Life annuities will increase the base on which income is withdrawn by some annual amount that usually is in the range of 5% to 7%. After withdrawals are taken, the base that determines the annual income stream will increase if the stock market increases but does not go down if the stock market does. Once an income check has ratcheted up due to a strong market, it cannot go down regardless of what the stock market does in the future. Annuitization is never required and the variable annuity account value always belongs to the annuity owner.

Example

Sara is 65-years old and a recent widow. She has $700,000 to last her for the rest of her life. She would like an equity based investment that will guarantee her a minimum of $35,000 a year in income with a chance for that income to increase (but not decrease) should the markets move up. Sara wants to know that her stream of income will last for her entire lifetime, even if she should live to well over one hundred. In addition, Sara would like to know that if she dies prematurely, any remaining account value will be paid out to her beneficiaries. Sara does not want to annuitize her investments under any circumstances and wants the option to take her account balance at any time.

The only investment available today that will give Sara what she wants with the risk protection she needs is a variable annuity with a Guaranteed Minimum Withdrawal Benefit-Lifetime (GMWB-Life) rider.

§3306. QUESTIONS TO ASK

Should clients of competent financial professionals be informed of the many guarantees offered by variable annuities?

§3307. REVIEW QUESTIONS

Discuss the three major living benefits that are available with variable annuities today.

§3308. CONCLUSION

The riders available from variable annuity issuers offer guarantees and protections that are not available with any other equity investments. For investors who are risk adverse but want a chance to receive equity type returns, today's variable annuities are the most attractive investment choice currently available.

Because investors have the protections against risk provided by variable annuity riders they can be a little more aggressive in their investing. Over time, this should produce better results than keeping money in cash-like equivalents. Chapter 33 discusses this topic.

– CHAPTER 34 –
THE AGGRESSIVE INVESTING ADVANTAGE

§3401. INTRODUCTION

One of the most important considerations in making investment recommendations to clients is the evaluation of market risk. Suitability is the financial principle that requires an investment advisor to weigh the potential market gain against potential market risk for a specific investment recommendation based on several factors – the most important of which is a client's risk tolerance. For example, an investment in an aggressive mutual fund might be suitable for a wealthy thirty-year-old entrepreneur, but not for a 65-year-old widow with limited assets. Similarly, if a client is considering two double A- rated bonds and one has a 6% yield and the other has a 7% yield, then the 7% bond would be the more suitable investment because it will provide more income to the client with no greater market risk than the 6% bond.

[NOTE: The term aggressive is not used in this chapter to mean speculative or risky. The term is used only to demonstrate that, if investment risk is reduced or eliminated, one can move from a stock/bond allocation of 60%/40% to an allocation of 70%/30% or 80%/20%].

When the element of market risk is reduced or eliminated, the investment selection process must also be altered to ensure that clients maximize their potential investment gain consistent with the decreased level of market risk. As a general proposition, as market risk is reduced, the typical investor can, and should, consider a more aggressive investment posture. The following sections discuss hypothetical case that studies examine the issue of suitability in four situations where risk has been reduced or eliminated by using variable annuity guarantees:

§3402. CASE STUDY #1

Mrs. Smith, a 67-year-old widow, has never been to Las Vegas. She has decided to spend a long weekend there and has come to you, her financial advisor, for some advice. Mrs. Smith wants to know how much money she should take out of her retirement nest-egg to gamble with while in Las Vegas. In working with Mrs. Smith you are aware of the fact that her entire life savings consists of $600,000. This nest-egg must last Mrs. Smith for the rest of her life. Currently, the income generated from this $600,000, when added to her small pension and Social Security income is slightly more than she needs to cover her current expenses.

Most financial professionals faced with these facts would explain to Mrs. Smith that the likelihood of her winning any money in Las Vegas is remote and that any money she does gamble with will most likely be lost. A competent financial planner would recommend that Mrs. Smith not use any of her nest-egg for gambling. If she insisted on gambling, the best advice would be for Mrs. Smith to limit her gambling stake to a very small amount (e.g., $100). If this amount is lost, Mrs. Smith will be able to say that she had gambled in Las Vegas but, at the same time, will not significantly reduce her $600,000 nest-egg.

351

Now, lets add some information that eliminates Mrs. Smith's risk of losing her money by assuming Mrs. Smith has won a contest in which she is allowed to visit Las Vegas and gamble as much money as she wants in any of the city's casinos for a single day. At the end of her 24-hour gambling spree, Mrs. Smith will be entitled to keep any money she wins. However, if Mrs. Smith loses any money, the casino will refund all of her losses. Mrs. Smith now asks for your advice as her financial planner as to how much of her $600,000 retirement nest-egg she should use for gambling while in Las Vegas. A competent financial professional would recommend that Mrs. Smith gamble with her entire $600,000 nest-egg.[1] The most likely outcome would be that Mrs. Smith will lose most, if not all, of her money. However, if this happens, she will receive a full refund of all of her losses. Should Mrs. Smith win anything, then she will not only have her $600,000 nest-egg, but will be able to keep all of her winnings. In short, Mrs. Smith has been placed in a win-win situation and therefore should alter her gambling decision to match the elimination of risk that the casino contest provides her. This case study demonstrates that what may have been unsuitable under one set of facts quickly becomes suitable under another set when the element of risk is eliminated.

§3403. CASE STUDY #2

Mrs. Johnson, who is 60 years old, recently retired from a medical clinic after working there as a receptionist for ten years. Although there was no formal pension plan at the clinic, the doctors for whom Mrs. Johnson worked agreed to put $100,000 into an investment account of Mrs. Johnson's choosing from which she could withdraw principal or interest or both from the account during her retirement. Mrs. Johnson calculated that she would need $7,000 from this account each year to supplement her Social Security and other retirement income. She needs this $7,000 stream of income to last for at least 14 years until she turns 74. At age 74, Mrs. Johnson will receive a large structured settlement installment from an automobile accident she was involved in a few years ago. An income stream of less than $7,000 a year over this 14 year period of time would have a detrimental impact on Mrs. Johnson's retirement. Mrs. Johnson has come to you seeking financial advice as to how she should invest the $100,000 her employers are providing for her retirement. A knowledgeable financial advisor would recommend that Mrs. Johnson put the $100,000 into investments that would have little or no possibility of loss should the stock market move down in the future. Investments such as government or corporate bonds, fixed annuities or immediate annuities or money market accounts would be suitable investments for Mrs. Johnson on these facts. If the investment account grew at the rate of 2% a year, Mrs. Johnson would be able to withdraw $7,000 a year without exhausting her account for just short of 17 years.[2] As with the prior case study, let's add some information that will eliminate any market

---

[1] It is assumed that such a contest is legitimate.

[2] $7,000/year x 2% x 16.99 years = $100,000.

risk for Mrs. Johnson by assuming that the doctors she worked for have promised Mrs. Johnson that she could withdraw $7,000 each year for 14.3 years from the $100,000 investment account they gave her regardless of whether the account went up or down in value. If the account were to go down in value, the doctors would add money to the account to ensure it would generate $7,000 a year for 14.3 years. On the other hand, if the account were to go up in value and had excess funds in it after 14.3 years of $7,000 annual withdrawals, Mrs. Johnson would be entitled to keep all such excess investment gains. Based on these additional facts, Mrs. Johnson once again seeks your services as a financial professional and wants to know how she should invest the $100,000 account offered by the doctors. Any competent financial planner would recommend that Mrs. Johnson invest the $100,000 in a more aggressive manner. If the aggressive investments result in her account increasing in value over the next 14.3 years, Mrs. Johnson will be in a position where she would be able to withdraw the $7,000 a year that she needs over that period and would still have excess money in the account after withdrawing the original $100,000 investment. Should the stock market go against Mrs. Johnson, she will still receive the $7,000 annual stream of income she needs for the next 14.3 years. Either way, Mrs. Johnson is guaranteed to receive the $7,000 she needs for the next 14.3 years. By eliminating market risk, the determination of what constitutes a suitable investment for Mrs. Johnson's $100,000 retirement account changes dramatically.

§3404. CASE STUDY #3

Mr. Brown recently retired. He had a retirement nest-egg containing $700,000. He needed to earn at least 5% on this retirement account to supplement his other retirement income. Payments must start immediately. Mr. Brown's risk tolerance is zero. Most financial professionals helping Mr. Brown would most likely suggest long-term, fixed income investments such as U.S. Treasuries if a 5% rate of return could be obtained. Other no-risk investments such as CDs, immediate annuities, etc., could be considered if they paid 5%. Depending on the investment selected, Mr. Brown would have to be told that a 5% rate of return might be obtainable today, but could not be guaranteed in the future. Let's add a few additional facts to Mr. Brown's scenario. Mr. Brown has a wealthy relative who has told Mr. Brown that he can invest his $700,000 however he wants because the rich relative has set up a funded trust that will guarantee the following to Mr. Brown:

- Mr. Brown will always receive a 5% rate of return on his $700,000 which will provide the $35,000 he needs each year;
- The 5% payments will last for Mr. Brown's life or 20 years, whichever period is *longer*;
- If the invested funds do not return 5%, the trust fund will make up the difference;
- If Mr. Brown's investments do well and produce more than 5% in any year,

Mr. Brown will be entitled to the larger income check. This check will not go down in the future even if Mr. Brown's retirement investment account goes down; and

- The retirement investment account will always belong to Mr. Brown, and he is entitled to take this account value whenever he wants.

Based on this additional data, Mr. Brown would want to consider a more aggressive investment position. A good mix of bonds and equities would be appropriate. In the long run, such an allocation will most likely produce increased income in the future. If Mr. Brown is wrong, his trust fund will provide him with the $35,000 minimum annual income he needs during retirement.

§3405. CASE STUDY #4

Mr. Green, who is 59, was recently informed that he is one of the beneficiaries of his deceased uncle's estate. The executor notified Mr. Green that he would be receiving a check for $250,000 within the next few weeks. Mr. Green has come to your office seeking financial advice as to where he should invest this money. In his discussions with you, Mr. Green has made you aware of the fact that in order for him to have the kind of retirement that he wants, he needs to count on his $250,000 inheritance generating $30,000 a year in income for him when he retires ten years from now. You realize that at a 6% rate of return it would take a principal amount of $500,000 to generate $30,000 in annual net income.[3] This means that Mr. Green's $250,000 inheritance must double in value in ten years and then consistently return 6% in order to provide the $30,000 Mr. Green needs for retirement. You also realize that for $250,000 to double in ten years, Mr. Green will have to earn a 7.2% annual net rate of return.[4] If the $250,000 investment goes down in value, both principal and interest will need to be withdrawn to generate the $30,000 needed by Mr. Green. For example, if the $250,000 inheritance drops in value to $200,000 in ten years it will yield $30,000 for less than nine years at a 6% rate of return.[5] This falls short of the lifetime stream of income Mr. Green needs. The smallest account value that will yield $30,000 a year for Mr. Green's 25-year life expectancy, using both principal and interest (at 6%), is $406,511.[6] The best advice for Mr. Green would be to invest the $250,000 conservatively and hope that between growth of the investment and future interest rates the investment will double in value and be able to generate the $30,000 annual payments required by Mr. Green. As was done with the three earlier case studies, lets add some information that will eliminate Mr. Green's risk by assuming that in addition to the $250,000 inheritance Mr. Green will receive, there is also a trust that was established for him by his uncle. The trust provides that, at the end of ten years, if

---

[3] $500,000 x 6% = $30,000.

[4] $250,000 x 7.18% x 10 years = $500,000.

[5] $30,000/year x 8.77 years x 6% = $200,000.

[6] $30,000 x 25 years x 6% = $406,511.

Mr. Green's $250,000 inheritance has gone up in value, he is free to keep it to generate income during his retirement or return whatever is left of the original $250,000 inheritance (whether up or down in value) and take in its place a check for $30,000 a year for the rest of his life. The trust guarantees to make at least twenty annual payments either to Mr. Green or his beneficiaries. Based on this new information, Mr. Green has contacted you for your advice on how to invest his $250,000 inheritance. A well-trained financial advisor would recommend the $250,000 inheritance be aggressively invested. At the end of ten years, such aggressive investing may very well increase Mr. Green's investment to a point that it might easily generate the $30,000 a year he needs and still provide him with a large nest-egg. However, if the stock market goes against Mr. Green and he loses a large part of his inheritance, he can return whatever is left of it to the estate (even if nothing) and immediately start receiving a check for $30,000 a year for the rest of his life. The additional information eliminates Mr. Green's market risk. Based on this elimination of risk, the suitability of investments recommended to Mr. Green would also have to be significantly changed.

§3406. GUARANTEED ANNUITIES

Until just a few years ago, every major investment vehicle, including stocks, mutual funds and variable annuities presented potential upside stock market returns as well as potential downside market risk for investors. However, beginning about eight years ago, variable annuity issuers began offering annuities that provided riders that, under certain circumstances, can eliminate market risk for investors seeking to protect their principal or obtain a guaranteed lifetime stream of income. These riders are most commonly referred to as living benefit riders. For simplicity, variable annuities offering these living benefit riders will be referred to in this article as guaranteed annuities to differentiate them from variable annuities that do not provide these riders. Because guaranteed annuities eliminate market risk for investors, financial advisors must reassess the issue of suitability when helping clients select sub-accounts within these new annuities. The four major guaranteed annuities are the:

- Guaranteed Minimum Accumulation Benefit (GMAB) Annuity
- Guaranteed Minimum Withdrawal Benefit Period Certain (GMWB-PC) Annuity
- Guaranteed Minimum Withdrawal Benefit for Life (GMWB-Life) Annuity
- Guaranteed Minimum Income Benefit (GMIB) Annuity

Each of these four guaranteed annuities is discussed below:

• **Guaranteed Minimum Accumulation Benefit (GMAB) Annuity** - With the GMAB rider, a variable annuity purchaser is guaranteed a return of his investment even if it is down in value at the end of an agreed holding period. This period typically ranges from five to ten years. If the annuity has increased in value by the end of the agreed holding period, the purchaser is entitled to keep all such gains less the normal costs of investing in the variable annuity. In short, the GMAB is similar to a money-back guarantee. The purchase of a GMAB variable annuity has a risk structure similar to Case Study #1 discussed above involving Mrs. Smith and the casino contest.

• **Guaranteed Minimum Withdrawal Benefit Period Certain (GMWB-PC) Annuity** - The GMWB-PC annuity allows a purchaser to invest money in a variable annuity and withdraw the full amount invested at a stated rate until the purchaser has withdrawn his full investment. The typical withdrawal rate for GMWB annuities ranges, depending on age, from 5% to 7%. With a GMWB-PC rider, if the stock market goes down over time, the owner will still receive back 100% of his investment over a stated period of time.[7] For example, withdrawals of 7% a year on any investment amount will last for approximately 14.3 years. If the stock market goes up, the annuity owner will not only recover his entire investment, but will also be entitled to any additional gain in the annuity less the normal investment expenses of owning the variable annuity. The purchase of a GMWB-PC variable annuity has a risk structure similar to Case Study #2 discussed above involving Mrs. Johnson and the retirement assistance she received from the medical clinic she worked for.

• **Guaranteed Minimum Withdrawal Benefit for Life (GMWB-Life) Annuity** - The GMWB-Life annuity allows an individual to invest an amount of money and be guaranteed a stated income stream for life or a stated period of time (e.g., 20 years), whichever is *longer*. The income stream is a percentage of the amount invested. This percentage of income ranges between 5% to 7% of the amount invested depending on the age of the annuity purchaser. If withdrawals are not made immediately, most GMWB-Life annuities will increase the base on which income is withdrawn by some annual amount that usually is in the range of 5% to 7%. After withdrawals are taken, the base that determines the annual income stream will increase if the stock market increases but does not go down if the stock market does. Once an income check has ratcheted up due to a strong market, it cannot go down regardless of what the stock market does in the future. Annuitization is never required and the variable annuity account value always belongs to the annuity owner. The purchase of a GMWB-Life variable annuity has a risk structure similar to Case Study #3 discussed above involving Mr. Brown and his need for a guaranteed lifetime stream of income.

• **Guaranteed Minimum Income Benefit (GMIB) Annuity** - The GMIB annuity allows an individual to invest an amount of money in a variable annuity for a set period of time (usually ten years). Over this period of time, the account value is guaranteed to grow at a set rate (usually 5% to 7%). At the end of the holding period, if the stock market has gone down,

---

[7] Based on 5% to 7% withdrawal rates, all principal invested is returned in 14 to 20 years.

the annuity owner is entitled to receive lifetime payments (usually guaranteed for twenty years) based on the value produced by the 5% - 7% guaranteed growth rate. These payments usually average $12,000 per $100,000 invested depending on the age of the investor.[8] These lifetime payments will usually return the original amount invested in eight to ten years and thereafter continue to pay a stream of income to the annuity owner for life. In order to obtain the lifetime payments, the annuity owner must formally annuitize his annuity. On the other hand, if the stock market goes up, the annuity investor is entitled to keep all such gains, subject only to the normal investment costs of owning the variable annuity. In this latter case, the entire account value can be taken by the annuity owner. The purchase of a GMIB variable annuity has a risk structure similar to Case Study #4 discussed above involving Mr. Green and his $250,000 inheritance and trust fund.

§3407. TRADITIONAL SUITABILITY ISSUES

Until recently, nearly all litigation or compliance issues regarding suitability of variable annuity sub-account selection has dealt with investment recommendations that have been *more* aggressive than they should have been in light of a client's risk tolerance. Many cases heard before NASD arbitration panels today involve financial advisors who, in the late 1990's, put most or all of their clients' assets in aggressive investments only to watch the stock market decline dramatically in the bear market of 2000-2002. Many investors who purchased non-guaranteed variable annuities during this bear market and lost money sued their financial advisors for placing them in unsuitable sub-accounts within these variable annuities. Some (but certainly not all) of these cases had merit. One reported case involved a financial advisor who invested a widow's entire nest-egg in recently created technology companies that had never shown a profit.

Advisors have come to understand that making an investment recommendation that exceeds a client's risk tolerance can result in a claim being filed against them for making an unsuitable investment recommendation. However, when recommending guaranteed annuities, the advisor must be just as vigilant not to make sub-account investment recommendations that are *too conservative* if a client's market risk has been eliminated by the guaranteed annuity. Claims based on lack of suitability resulting from an overly conservative investment selection are becoming common.[9]

Whether recommending a guaranteed or a non-guaranteed variable annuity to a client, a financial advisor has two *general* suitability obligations that must be met. They are:

- The financial advisor must become thoroughly familiar with the key terms, features, limitations, costs, penalties and benefits of the variable annuity being

---

[8] This assumes such annuity is purchased at age 59. Ages above or below 59 will raise or lower lifetime payments.

[9] *Williams v. Security National Bank of Sioux City, Iowa*, 358 F.Supp.2d 782 (2005), *In Re Estate of Scharlach*, 809 A.2d 376 (Pa.Sup. Ct. 2002) and *Atwood v. Atwood*, 25 P.3d 936 (Okla. 2001).

recommended; and

- The financial advisor must fully explain the major terms, features, limitations, costs, penalties and benefits of the variable annuity to his client.

For example, recommending a variable annuity to a 58-year-old knowing that he would be making immediate withdrawals that would subject the client to a 10% IRS early withdraw penalty would *not* be suitable regardless of whether the annuity was guaranteed or not.

§3408. QUESTIONS TO ASK

If variable annuities with living benefits can protect clients from a bear market, shouldn't they consider being more aggressive in their investing? Won't this more aggressive investing help clients in the future?

§3409. REVIEW QUESTIONS

Discuss why clients who purchase variable annuities with living benefits can be more aggressive in their investing and of what benefit such investing might provide.

§3410. CONCLUSION

If a client purchases a variable annuity and retains all of the market risk, then basic suitability rules must be followed when sub-accounts are selected for the client. However, if a guaranteed annuity is purchased by a client and the annuity contract shifts the market risk to the issuing company, then financial advisors must take into consideration this altered market risk when selecting variable annuity sub-accounts for their clients.

– CHAPTER 35 –
THE MANDATORY ANNUITIZATION MYTH

§3501. INTRODUCTION

Many investors believe that any variable annuity they purchase will only allow them to get their investments back in the form of payments made over a longer period or possibly for their entire lifetime. This is a myth.

§3502. ANNUITIZATION

Annuitization occurs when one investor gives an amount of money to an insurance company in exchange for a stream of payments that could last for life or at least for several years. This type of annuitization is common with *immediate* annuities but not variable annuities. Annuitization of a variable annuity is possible but is *always* optional, *never* mandatory. As with any other investment, the account value of a variable annuity always belongs to the annuity owner and can be taken at any time (subject to any surrender fees). In some cases it might be smart to annuitize a variable annuity in order to obtain its full benefit, but such annuitization is *never* a requirement.

> **Example**
>
> In 1998, at age 58, Bill purchased a variable annuity for $500,000 with a Guaranteed Minimum Income Benefit (GMIB) rider that would give him the election of a lump sum payment at anytime or a payment of $60,000 a year fro life with payments guaranteed for at least 20 years starting in 2008. In 2008, if the variable annuity is worth a million dollars or more Bill may decide to take the variable annuity's value in a lump sum. If the variable annuity account value is only $320,000, he may *opt* for the lifetime payments that will total $1,200,00. This *choice* belongs to Bill. Annuitization is not mandatory.

§3503. GUARANTEED INCOME WITHOUT ANNUITIZATION

Today, variable annuity issuers offer guaranteed income for life without the requirement that one annuitize.

> **Example**
>
> Dora, a 60 year-old recent widow, inherited $500,000. She needed $25,000 a year in guaranteed income for life. Her advisor recommended a variable annuity that would guarantee Dora the $25,000 she needed while providing Dora full access to her account value at anytime. He also let Dora know that if her account value grew her annual income check could grow, but could never be less than the largest income check she received in the past.[1]

§3504. REVIEW QUESTIONS

What should a financial professional say to a client who believes that if he buys a variable annuity he can only get his money back in a series of lifetime payments?

---

[1] The rider Dora had was a Guaranteed Minimum Withdrawal Benefit for life (GMWB-Life) rider.

§3505. CONCLUSION

Annuitization of a variable annuity is *never* mandatory but is optional with the variable annuity owner. If annuitization provides a larger economic benefit, the variable annuity *may* elect to annuitize. Today, there are variable annuities that provide guaranteed income without the requirement of annuitization.

– CHAPTER 36 –
THE INVESTMENT SELECTION MYTH

§3601. INTRODUCTION

Some investors believe that variable annuities do not provide as good a selection of investments as do mutual funds. This is a myth.

§3602. INVESTMENT SELECTION

Most major variable annuities issued today have as many as fifty or sixty sub-accounts to select from. These sub-accounts usually provide more than one option that will cover nearly every investment area. Most major variable annuity issuers provide small-cap, mid-cap and large-cap sub-accounts together with international sub-accounts. Variable annuities offer sector sub-accounts as well as managed portfolios. Several variable annuities offer safe-havens such as money market or fixed sub-accounts. Although mutual funds often provide similar investment choices, many mutual funds do not offer a wide array of investment choices. Many mutual fund families have only a handful of investment choices. Some mutual funds offer only one investment option. When mutual fund investment options are sparse, investors may be forced to move their money thus incurring potential taxes and new commissions for reinvestment. Whenever a variable annuity or mutual fund is recommended, it would be wise to make sure that they provide a large selection of investment choices.

§3603. REVIEW QUESTIONS

What should a financial professional tell a client who is reluctant to buy a variable annuity because he has heard that variable annuities don't have a good selection of investments as mutual funds do?

§3604. CONCLUSION

The investment choices provided by variable annuity issuers today can often exceed those choices found with mutual funds.

– CHAPTER 37 –
THE DEATH BENEFIT MYTH

§3701. INTRODUCTION

Many investors believe that over time, most investments, including variable annuities, go up in value and therefore the death benefit provided by variable annuities is worthless.

For example, from 2001 to 2003, $2.8 billion was paid out in variable annuity death benefits by variable annuity issuers. This figure was in excess of the underlying account values. (NAVA).

§3702. THE BASIC DEATH BENEFIT

Variable annuities, with few exceptions, provide a basic death benefit. The basic death benefit pays to a deceased variable annuity owner's beneficiaries the greater of the variable annuity's account value or the original investment (less additions and withdrawals). The basic death benefit offered by variable annuity issuers is, unlike other types of life insurance, not subject to health questions, a physical exam, etc. This can be important for uninsurable individuals.

Example

John is a conservative investor. He has $500,000 in bank CDs. The money is earmarked for retirement. He has a 40-year-old wife and twins in college. John has just learned he has a form of cancer that has reduced his life expectancy to five years. John would be well advised to purchase a variable annuity for four reasons:

- Knowing that he cannot leave his wife and children with less than a $500,000 death benefit, John can be more aggressive with his investment choices.

- If the variable annuity, for example, doubles in value, John's wife will have $1,000,000. If the variable annuity goes down in value, John's wife will still have $500,000 as a death benefit when John dies. Mutual funds don't provide this benefit.

- John can purchase an increasing death benefit that could provide his family with a minimum death benefit well in excess of $500,000.

- Many variable annuities offer a death benefit that increases by a set amount each year. For example, a death benefit that increases at 5% a year would provide John's wife with an account value of $638,141 in five years even if the variable annuity's account value goes down.

A mutual fund investment would not have helped John in his situation.

§3703. THE RATCHETING DEATH BENEFIT

Today many variable annuities, for a small additional fee, offer a ratcheting death benefit. These variable annuities will increase the basic death benefit from 5% to 7% a year until the death of the variable annuity owner.

Example

Betty, at age 60, purchased a variable annuity for $500,000 that had a 7% ratcheting death benefit. She was not insurable and could not buy regular life insurance. At age 80 Betty died. Her beneficiaries received a ratcheting death benefit of $1,934,842 ($500,000 x 7% x 20 years) when she died even though Betty's variable annuity was worth only $1,117,421. Had the variable annuity been worth more than the $1,934,842 death benefit, Betty's beneficiaries would have received the higher account value. It is also interesting to note that at anytime prior to her death Betty can take her account value. Other investments do not offer such a benefit.

§3704. INCREASING THE DEATH BENEFIT WITH IRS §1035

Long-term variable annuity investors who plan to leave their variable annuities to beneficiaries have discovered a no-cost way to greatly increasing their death benefit.

Example

Fred purchased a variable annuity in 1992 for $350,000. His intent was to leave it to his grandchildren at his death. In mid-1999 the seven year surrender charge period expired. His variable annuity was worth $1,000,000. Fred did a IRC §1035 transfer to a new variable annuity and in late 2002 he died. At his death, his variable annuity was worth $650,000. His grandchildren received a check for $1,000,000 form the annuity issuer. Had Fred bought mutual funds instead, his grandchildren would have received $650,000.

§3705. REVIEW QUESTIONS

Explain how §1035 can be used to increase a variable annuity owner's death benefit.

§3706. SOURCES

See §1907 above on the earnings enhancement benefit.

§3707. CONCLUSION

Anyone who believes the death benefit provided by variable annuities is not of value is buying into a myth. There are many ways the various death benefits offered by variable annuity issuers can be of significant benefit to variable annuity purchasers.

INDEX